Vico's Uncanny Humanism

VICO'S
UNCANNY HUMANISM

Reading the *New Science*
between Modern and Postmodern

SANDRA RUDNICK LUFT

Cornell University Press

ITHACA AND LONDON

First published 2003 by Cornell University Press

Printed in the United States of America

Library of Congress Cataloging-in-Publication Data

Luft, Sandra Rudnick, 1934–
  Vico's uncanny humanism : reading the New science between modern and postmodern / Sandra Rudnick Luft.
      p. cm.
Includes bibliographical references and index.
    ISBN 0-8014-4108-0 (alk. paper)
    1. Vico, Giambattista, 1668–1744. Principi di una scienza nuova.   2. Humanism.
3. Hermeneutics.   4. Poetry.   I. Title.
    B3581.P73L84 2003
    195—dc21

                                                            2003003532

Cornell University Press strives to use environmentally responsible suppliers and materials to the fullest extent possible in the publishing of its books. Such materials include vegetable-based, low-VOC inks and acid-free papers that are recycled, totally chlorine-free, or partly composed of nonwood fibers. For further information, visit our website at www.cornellpress .cornell.edu.

Cloth printing   10 9 8 7 6 5 4 3 2 1

For Rachel and Joshua
And for Rufus, who knows why . . .

Once the limit of the nature/culture opposition makes itself felt, one might want to question systematically and rigorously the history of these concepts. This is a first action. Such a systematic and historic questioning would be neither a philological nor a philosophical action in the classic sense of these words. To concern oneself with the founding concepts of the entire history of philosophy, to deconstitute them, is not to undertake the work of the philologist or of the classic historian of philosophy. Despite appearances, it is probably the most daring way of making the beginnings of a step outside of philosophy. The step "outside philosophy" is much more difficult to conceive than is generally imagined by those who think they made it long ago with cavalier ease, and who in general are swallowed up in metaphysics in the entire body of discourse which they claim to have disengaged from it.

—Jacques Derrida, "Structure, Sign, and Play
in the Discourse of the Human Sciences"

Being subject as humanity has not always been the sole possibility belonging to the essence of historical man, which is always beginning in a primal way, nor will it always be. A fleeting cloud shadow over a concealed land, such is the darkening which that truth as the certainty of subjectivity . . . lays over a disclosing event [Ereignis] that it remains denied to subjectivity itself to experience.

—Martin Heidegger, "The Age of the World Picture"

We find that the principle of these origins both of languages and of letters lies in the fact that the first gentile peoples, by a demonstrated necessity of nature, were poets who spoke in poetic characters. This discovery, which is the master key of this Science, has cost us the persistent research of almost all our literary life, because with our civilized natures we [moderns] cannot at all imagine and can understand only by great toil the poetic nature of these first men.

—Giambattista Vico, *The New Science*

Human existence is uncanny.

—Friedrich Nietzsche, *Thus Spoke Zarathustra*

Contents

Preface

INTERPRETATIONS OF GIAMBATTISTA VICO'S *New Science* are for the most part efforts to place the work in the history of ideas, either as the fruition of various intellectual traditions of the past, or as the origin or precursor of a multitude of later intellectual developments. Against this relentlessly linear or genetic approach, I turn to an alternate, "alchemical" interpretive strategy in which the reader, attuned to "fundamental transformations" of issues and problems in intellectual history, is sensitive to "the confrontational, dislocative tendencies" in Vico's text that "make room" for less traditional interpretations.[1]

The term "alchemical" suggests readings that ignore the search for historical and eidetic influences or relationships and engage texts interactively, hermeneutically, fragmentarily, as one holds conversations with strangers only to discover shared insights. Ironically, though Vico presented himself as a relentlessly genetic reader, he was a most alchemical one. Distinguishing himself from Descartes, who considered his own work a radical break with the past, Vico provided a genealogy of his sources. He claimed he brought together the truths of an ancient philosophic tradition with the certainties of an equally hoary philological one, and cited four authors—Plato, Tacitus, Bacon, Grotius—who enabled him to arrive "at a clear conception of what

---

[1] Nancy S. Struever, "Rhetoric and Philosophy in Vichian Inquiry," *New Vico Studies* 3 (1985): 131–45, 138. Struever puts forward this characterization of an "alchemical" interpretative strategy in her review of Michael Mooney's *Vico in the Tradition of Rhetoric.* Attributing the strategy to Eugenio Garin, Struever distinguishes it from the genetic or "incremental" approach of Paul Oskar Kristeller and Mooney. See also Hayden White's review of *Vico in the Tradition of Rhetoric* in *Eighteenth Century Studies* 22, no. 2 (winter 1988–89): 219–22. Similarly critical of Mooney's "genetic" approach, White contrasts it with that of Struever, who reads Vico "backward," from contemporary views more open to "tensions *between* rhetoric and philosophy that existed . . . *within* rhetoric."

[he] had been vaguely seeking."[2] The difficulty in understanding the importance to Vico of his four authors is that they do not resemble one another. Moreover, if they resemble Vico, it is in a sense not readily apparent to his readers, who have only his own idiosyncratic claim to go on.

There is, I believe, no *substantive* relation between Vico and his four authors: they were important to him because he identified them as such. "Every writer," says Jorge Luis Borges, "creates his own precursors. His work modifies our conception of the past, as it will modify the future."[3] In struggling to formulate a science "new" to his intellectual tradition, Vico created his own precursors. He recognized something in the texts of his authors which, at the time he read them, he thought close to his own ideas, and which enabled him to clarify "what he had been vaguely seeking"—and he did so with a sense of "recognition" his own readers cannot have.

Vico identified his four authors in the *Autobiography* in 1725, the year after he had completed the first version of the *New Science,* the *Scienza nuova in forma negativa,* and before the two positive versions of 1730 and 1744. Yet, in the quotation I include at the beginning of this book, he describes a twenty-year struggle to grasp the "poetic"—that is, creative—nature of the first men of the human race, the discovery he calls the "master key" of the *New Science.* He characterized that struggle as an effort to get beyond traditional readings of ancient myths, to understand the strangeness of the historical origins they depict, which modern readers cannot grasp. Vico believed his discovery transformative, not only of the philosophical and philological scholarship of his age, but of the anthropological assumptions of his entire intellectual tradition. The final version of the *New Science* is the working out of the consequences of his insight, consequences of which even he may not have been fully aware. As he wrote, his insight deepened, alchemically transforming the familiar conceits he received from his intellectual tradition into a view of human existence, of human activity, knowledge, language, far more radical than, and radically incompatible with, the views of Plato, Tacitus, Bacon, and Grotius he had set out to unify.

If the effort to find *substantive* relations between Vico and his four authors is futile, so too is the practice of finding them between Vico and those who

---

[2] Giambattista Vico, *The Autobiography of Giambattista Vico,* trans. Max Harold Fisch and Thomas Goddard Bergin (Ithaca: Great Seal Books, 1944), 138–39, 155–56. Vico writes as if all share the same intellectual concerns, saying though Plato contemplates man in the "nobility" of "intellectual wisdom" and Tacitus on the level of utility and "practical wisdom," Bacon combines both, and Grotius is the catalyst who grasps the secret—a system of universal law—that brings philosophy and philology together.

[3] Jorge Luis Borges, "Kafka and his Precursors," *Labyrinths,* eds. Donald A. Yates and James E. Irby (New York: New Directions, 1964), 199–201. Though Borges first considered Kafka "as singular as the phoenix of rhetorical praise," he says he came to "recognize [Kafka's] voice, or his practices," in such diverse texts as those of Zen writers, Han Yu, Kierkegaard, Robert Browning, Leon Bloy, and Lord Dunsany. "If I am not mistaken," he adds, "the heterogeneous pieces . . . resemble Kafka; if I am not mistaken, not all of them resemble each other. This second fact is the more significant."

preceded him or those he is said to influence.[4] Borges's claim that every writer creates his own precursors cleanses the historical position of "precursor" of connotations of priority. Chronology recedes in significance before the process of reading itself. Borges's sensitivity to the idiosyncratic "voices and practices" in Kafka's texts alerts him to Kafka's own "voice, or his practices," in diverse texts, but, Borges insists, "if Kafka had never written a line, we would not perceive this quality; in other words, it would not exist." In the same way, my own awareness of "fundamental transformations" in our contemporary intellectual tradition has alerted me to heterodox voices and practices in the *New Science*. Reading the last edition of that work through my readings of contemporary "precursors" alerts me to a strangeness that more traditional readings cannot hear.

Genetic relationships, eidetic or historical, between Vico and other writers are imposed by the theoretical templates through which Vico is read. Taken as a whole, Vico's readers resolutely place him within two of the dominant and most familiar intellectual traditions of the West. The first is the tradition of philosophic humanism originating with the Greeks. Founded on metaphysical assumptions grounding the possibility of knowledge, philosophic humanism encompasses, I claim, all later views that retain those assumptions, including the natural and social sciences and more delimited conceptions of knowledge, such as pragmatism or historicism. The diversity of epistemic positions masks the ubiquity of those foundational metaphysical assumptions that, from Plato on, ground the possibility of knowledge at all: that reality was intelligible, and that it was inherently knowable to humans insofar as they possessed a rational subjective substance or essence in some sense "like" intelligible reality. Belief in that ontological "likeness," homology, or *homoiousis* constituted the pervasive idealism of Western thought.

The second tradition through which Vico is read is the theological. Even secular interpretations that do not emphasize the role of providence in the *New Science* reveal the influence of medieval Christian theology in their understandings of such notions as Vico's conception of language, of human creativity, or of *verum et factum convertuntur,* the claim Vico makes in an early work of the convertibility of the true and the made which, taken as an epistemological principle, insures knowledge of a thing by its maker. Despite their apparent differences, humanist and theological interpretations of Vico are merely variations of one theme, grounded, as they are, on the same metaphysical assumptions. Although Christianity originated in a biblical tradition alien to humanism and its epistemic goals, it derived its ontology from the idealism of Neoplatonism. In imposing on a scriptural religion a con-

---

[4] Those who attempt to read Vico alchemically are few; I take Hayden White and Nancy S. Struever to do so, and include Norman O. Brown, Edward Said, John O'Neill, Ernesto Grassi, James Joyce, and Samuel Beckett. This is a partial list, to be sure, but even a comprehensive one would comprise a small and decidedly idiosyncratic flock.

ception of God and humans as subjective, even spiritual, beings, Neoplatonism transformed it into an onto-theological variant of philosophic humanism. Only in this way did a Christianized West retain the assumptions that made secular knowledge possible.

All interpretations of Vico, even those that do not consider his philosophy epistemological, or even idealist, still read him from a modernist perspective that takes for granted the conception of human nature conditioned by the subjectivism inherent to the West.[5] For them, humans are, if not at the beginning of their genetic development, then certainly at their maturity, subjective beings and subjects of knowledge or action. This anthropology is so familiar it is not recognized as culturally determined. In order to denaturalize this subjectivist anthropology I intend to read Vico alchemically, in relation to two very different sets of texts: postmodern writings, and writings that interpret scripture from the rabbinic hermeneutic perspective.

So alien are postmodern writings and rabbinic hermeneutic texts to the literature on Vico that they help to expose the relentlessly idealist lens through which Vico is read. Though they differ as much from one another as from Vico's writings, they share with him, I argue, voices and practices alien to humanism's subjectivism and epistemic goals, the very struggle to get beyond a dualist anthropology. The note common to all is the identification of language as an alternate source of order, meaning, and value. Since none of these writings trust in an inherently orderly world or in an inherent human subjectivity, all find in language an originary power capable of constituting order and meaning in the human world.

Postmodern writings, primarily those of Nietzsche and Heidegger, expose the ubiquity and gratuitousness of humanist assumptions. I do not argue a historical or eidetic relation between Vico as precursor and these writings. In Borges's enriched understanding of the term, in which "every writer *creates* his own precursors," Nietzsche and Heidegger become the "precursors" through which I read Vico.[6] In different ways, Nietzsche and Heidegger take themselves beyond the comforts of familiar beliefs and, like Vico, raise the question of the origins of the human world in more radical senses than had their philosophical and theological traditions. Reading Vico in the context

---

[5] Some interpretations of Vico do not overtly accept idealist assumptions: materialism, for example, which, nevertheless, retains belief in the possibility of knowledge. Interpretations that emphasize the role of language in social existence relate Vico to a rhetorical humanism seemingly distinct from the idealism of philosophy or theology. I discuss the extent to which they too are influenced by subjectivist assumptions in chapter 1.

[6] See also my articles "Derrida, Vico, Genesis and the Originary Power of Language," *The Eighteenth Century: Theory and Interpretation* 34, no. 1 (spring 1993): 65–84, and "The Secularization of Origins in Vico and Nietzsche," *The Personalist Forum* 10, no. 2 (fall 1994): 133–48, and two articles that focus on Heidegger: "Situating Vico Between Modern and Postmodern," *Historical Reflections/Reflexions Historiques* 22, no. 3 (fall 1996): 587–617, and "Embodying the Eye of Humanism: Giambattista Vico and the Eye of *Ingenium*," *Sites of Vision: The Discursive Construction of Sight in the History of Philosophy*, ed. David Michael Levin (Cambridge: MIT Press, 1997), 167–96.

of their efforts, one hears more strongly the "strangeness" of the existential situation of Vico's "first men of the human race," their radical need for an originary power to make a human world not found in nature, the artfulness of a language Vico believes the only means of doing so.

Heidegger provides the most pointed critique of humanism. In response to a question by Jean Beaufret—"How can we restore meaning to the word 'humanism'?"—Heidegger lays bare an original complicity between humanism and the metaphysical determination of human essence. Humanism became *metaphysical,* he insists, when, in the Latin mistranslation of *zoon logon echon* as *animal rationale,* it determined the essence of *humanitas* as soul, spirit, mind, and, ultimately, Cartesian subject.[7] Even before that fateful mistranslation, Plato had identified the ontological ground of knowledge as a substantive "likeness," a *homoiousis* or homology between human subjectivity and intelligible Being. In the context of metaphysics's privileging of the pursuit of knowledge, all other forms of mediation with the world—doing (*praxis*), making (*poiesis*), the interpretive mediation of language—were devalued.

Heidegger's critique brings out the demonic implications of humanism which culminate in the modern "age of the world picture." Humanism, "that philosophical interpretation of man which explains and evaluates whatever is, in its entirety, from the standpoint of man and in relation to man," is for Heidegger the source of the nihilism Nietzsche identifies as the *telos* of the entire tradition. "In the planetary imperialism of technologically organized man . . . subjectivism . . . attains its acme, from which point it will descend to the level of organized uniformity and there firmly establish itself."[8] Yet, immediately after this apocalyptic pronouncement and his acknowledgment that "man cannot, of himself, abandon this destining of his modern essence or abolish it by fiat," Heidegger raises the possibility of an alternate way of being-in-the-world. I have prefaced this book with a quotation in which he suggests that being subject is not the sole possibility belonging to historical man, and hints at other ways of being-in-the-world.

Recognizing the need "of restoring to the word 'humanism' a historical sense that is older than its oldest meaning," Heidegger urges us to "experience the essence of man more primordially . . . [as] ek-sistence."[9] Like Zarathustra before him, he calls man "the strange, the uncanny <*das Unheimliche*>," who "surpasses the limits of the familiar."[10] It is my thesis that

[7] Martin Heidegger, "Letter on Humanism," *Basic Writings,* ed. David Farrell Krell (New York: HarperCollins Publishers, 1993), 217–65, 226–7.

[8] Heidegger, "The Age of the World Picture," *The Question Concerning Technology and Other Essays,* trans. William Lovitt (New York: Harper & Row Publishers, 1977), 115–54, 133–4, 152.

[9] Heidegger, "Letter on Humanism," 247–8.

[10] Martin Heidegger, *An Introduction to Metaphysics,* trans. Ralph Manheim (New Haven: Yale University Press, 1987) 149–51; Friedrich Nietzsche, "Thus Spoke Zarathustra," *The Portable Nietzsche,* ed. and trans. Walter Kaufmann (New York: Penguin, 1976) 132.

Vico too experienced the essence of man more primordially than did his contemporaries. As did postmodern writers he came to understand the metaphysical assumptions of humanism as the conceits of scholars, and his insight into the nature of the first men enabled him to go beyond those conceits to a poetic humanism more radically alien, more *uncanny*, than the tradition can imagine or understand.

Even so, I am mindful of voices and practices equally strong in the *New Science* that distinguish Vico's "new" humanism from other aspects of postmodern writings. In rejecting the assumptions of human subjectivity and subjectism that ground anthropocentrism, postmodernists such as Nietzsche and Heidegger, unable to imagine a human-centered perspective that does not presume that metaphysical ground, turn resolutely anti-humanist.[11] Vico's alien poetic humanism is, however, a philosophy of human agency. Not only are his first men, abandoned by God in an abyssal world, the source of human existence, they are so by virtue of their "divine-like" creativity. But where traditional humanism identifies the source of agency, whether human or divine, as conscious and intentional, the creativity Vico attributes to his first men derives from the potency of a subjectively unconditioned originary language.

That language is *itself* ontologically creative is not a notion Vico could find in his philosophical or theological traditions, given their assumptions of an orderly world and of the rational subjectivity of God and humans.[12] Heidegger believes the tradition forgets Being; I argue that what it forgets is the ungrounded originary power of language. Only in the texts of a Hebraic tradition too alien to be understood by humanism or onto-theology does one find voices and practices attributing an ontological power to language—a power constituting the very "divinity" of a Creator-God. Only in the Hebrew scripture, or, rather, in the understanding of scripture from a rabbinic perspective, is the divine agent not Being, Architect, Spirit, or Subject, but Poet—that is, Creator. Heidegger never realizes this; in his writings he goes back to the pre-Socratics to recover a view of language as unconditioned event. As one scholar says, "What Heidegger calls the forgetting of Being is simply the forgetting of Writing. . . . When Heidegger, then, thinks he is thinking Greek (ur-Greek), he is thinking Hebrew."[13]

The poetic language Vico attributes to his first men and considers divine because it is creative of the human world is a secularization of the linguistic agency of the Poet-God of the Hebrews. Vico accounts for the origins of the

[11] Heidegger thought even Nietzsche's will to power too anthropocentric, and listened instead to the call of Being.

[12] Though rhetorical texts may assert the ontological power of language, the significance of the claim is muted by the subjectivist readings of those texts by modernist writers.

[13] Geoffrey H. Hartman, *Saving the Text: Literature, Derrida, Philosophy* (Baltimore: The Johns Hopkins University Press, 1981), xix. A substantial literature brings out the affinities between postmodern and Hebraic thought, which I discuss in chapter 2.

human world with that originary language—*it is the heart of his uncanny poetic humanism.* What links Vico to the tradition in which God is not Being, Spirit, Architect, or Subject, but Creator or Poet, is not historical influence but a thematic affinity between the relationship of making to knowing realized in the *New Science* and in rabbinic texts. The latter, newly appreciated in the context of postmodern interpretations of language, is the second set of texts through which I read Vico. I argue that in the religious tradition that first claimed that the true is made, that making is a linguistic event, meaning emerged through the creative power of language—a power lost to a subjectivist tradition which, from Philo on, identified divine language with the cognitive intentionality of God's mind. In tracing the *verum-factum* principle back to medieval onto-theology—admittedly the source of the epistemological version of *verum-factum* in *On the Most Ancient Wisdom of the Italians*—Vico scholars miss the radical shift in meaning the principle undergoes with the poetic insights of the *New Science.*

The *New Science* is too fragmentary, too heterodox, to be pressed into the procrustean bed of any one totalizing interpretation. In bringing together under one cover the intimations I hear in the *New Science,* not only of postmodern writers who come after it, but also of the alien Hebraic-rabbinic tradition that preceded it, I marvel at the protean richness of Vico's last work. What all these texts share is the notion of humans as embodied, finite, temporal beings who exist in a world governed by material necessity, and who are dependent on the constitutive power of language to fabricate their human existence. I present them, and Vico's *New Science,* as diverse expressions of *poiesis,* the interpretive sense-making of beings-in-the-world that takes place in language, a hermeneutic process *ontologically* creative of a real, though artifactual, human world.[14]

If an interpretation of Vico's new science as *poiesis* is literary, speculative, and idiosyncratic, it is no more so than historical or philosophical studies whose scholarly or explanatory force derives from the very methodological assumptions Vico's poetic science brings into question. Such an interpretation responds to the urgent cultural and existential issues raised by postmodern critiques of the humanist tradition which claims Vico as its own. Assertions of the nihilism inherent in humanism and in the privileged role it attributes to epistemology have brought about a crisis of belief in that tradition itself. The death of humanism, and with it a loss of faith in immanent sources of meaning and value in the world, seems implicit in the death of the subject.

[14] The term "ontological" is inappropriate outside the context of Greek metaphysics. I use it in a nontechnical sense, as Heidegger does, to emphasize a conception of humans whose sense-making is not epistemic, nor even subjective, but the interpretive activity, linguistic and practical, of beings-in-the-world.

Vico is certainly a humanist in the sense that he never loses his belief that meaning is made by humans for the sake of a humane social existence. I believe, however, that he transcends the subject-centered humanism characteristic of his philosophical and theological tradition, whose belief in the primacy of human subjectivity leads, Nietzsche and Heidegger claim, to the nihilism of an epistemic mentality. Vico's skepticism about the tradition's comforting foundational beliefs and the possibility of knowledge they assert forces him to a new understanding of being-in-the-world, one more resolutely "humanist," despite its abyssal sensibility, than most postmodern critiques. What slowly emerges in Vico's last work is an uncanny poetic humanism affirming both the role of humans in the making of the social world, and the value of communal existence, affirmations not central to post-modern concerns. But Vico's humanism affirms human creativity and communal existence outside the assumptions of traditional humanism and modernism, without the problematic belief that agency is the privilege of subjectivity.[15]

I begin this interpretation of the *New Science* as a secularization of the linguistic creativity of the poet-God of the Hebrews by presenting, in the Introduction, an exemplary version of the traditional secularization argument. In the relation Jürgen Habermas draws between Vico's and Marx's conception of the human subject of history and the God of medieval theology, one can still see the image of the Platonic and Neoplatonic Divine Architect, a subjective, spiritual substance or being who acts consciously and intentionally. In chapter 1 I discuss the range of interpretations of Vico, secular and secularizing, which illustrate the ubiquity of the belief that for Vico humans become, at the end of their historical development, subjective beings—even, for some, subjects of knowledge; that the genetic process productive of that subjective human existence begins with Vico's first men, whose nascent subjectivity lies buried in their beastly bodies. The belief in an inherently subjective human nature grounds almost all epistemological interpretations of *verum-factum*. I make that case with discussions of the literature on Vico. I do so at greater length than readers not immersed in that literature may need or value, and such readers may prefer to skim those sections. For those with a greater interest, I have put more extensive discussions on a website. They may be found at *http://online.sfsu.edu/~srluft*.

Chapter 2 presents an alternate conception of *verum-factum* as an ontological principle identifying humans as makers, beings-in-the-world who create their human world, even their own "subjective" humanity, with an ontologically constructive language. The divine model of that creative agency is the poet-God of the rabbinic tradition, whose radically originary language

---

[15] When measured against such humanist views of social existence as liberalism or Marxism, Vico's new humanism is, however, conservative. Vico had too tragic a vision of the human condition to believe it could be ameliorated by intentional social action.

is newly appreciated by readers from a postmodern perspective. In chapter 3, I retell the story Vico tells in the *New Science,* bringing out the strange "dislocative tendencies" that the reading of rabbinic and postmodern texts enables me to hear.

Since space does not permit inclusion of a bibliography, the website also includes an annotated bibliography.

My effort to understand the strange, poetic nature of the *New Science* has taken twenty years, the span of time it took Giambattista Vico to understand the strange, poetic nature of the first men of the human race. It is with pleasure and gratitude that I acknowledge the support and encouragement I received from colleagues, friends, and family over the years.

I first read Vico as a graduate student at Brandeis University, in a seminar taught by Professor Frank Manuel. Though I am not sure he would approve of my thesis, I know the excitement I always feel in reading Vico I derived from him, who was, at that time, one of the few scholars to have written on Vico in English, and who is himself a reader always attuned to the "dislocative tendencies" within texts. Like most American scholars writing on Vico in the last fifty years, I am indebted to Giorgio Tagliacozzo, who almost single-handedly nurtured Vico scholarship in this country. I can still hear him urging me to complete the manuscript, and I deeply regret that he did not live to see the fruit of his encouragement. I am grateful to Professor William J. Bouwsma, who early on took an interest in my work. I am particularly indebted to Professor Hayden V. White, whose writings on Vico and on philosophy of history have influenced me greatly, whose personal support has been unwavering, and whose critical comments on the manuscript were extremely perceptive and helpful. I am also grateful for the sensitivity and perceptiveness of the two scholars who read the manuscript for Cornell University Press, and whose critical comments were very valuable, Professors Hans Kellner and G. Douglas Atkins.

I owe a great debt to the friends and colleagues who read the manuscript over the last several years, and whose thoughtful critical comments were invariably helpful, however much I resisted them: Professors Robert R. Alford, Suzanne Duvall Jacobitti, Edmund E. Jacobitti, David W. Price, Patrick H. Hutton, Marvin Nathan, Susan Kupfer. I am especially grateful to my daughter Rachel, who gave me a very perceptive reading at a time when she was completing work on her doctoral dissertation. Over the years Joseph Luft has been very supportive. Jamie Davidson was a great help in preparing the manuscript, as was Jeff Gburek with translations. I am very appreciative of the support I received from Cornell University Press, from Karen Laun, Karen Bosc, and particularly from Bernhard Kendler.

My husband, Rufus P. Browning, has been a constant source of intellectual and emotional support, comfort, love, and comic relief, even when I was at my most trying. Only he knows how much I owe him, and in how many ways. During the years my narrative was taking shape, my two children, Rachel Etta Luft and Joshua Morris Luft, grew into loving, thoughtful, caring, wonderful human beings. I dedicate this book to them, and to Rufus, with gratitude and love for the joy they give me.

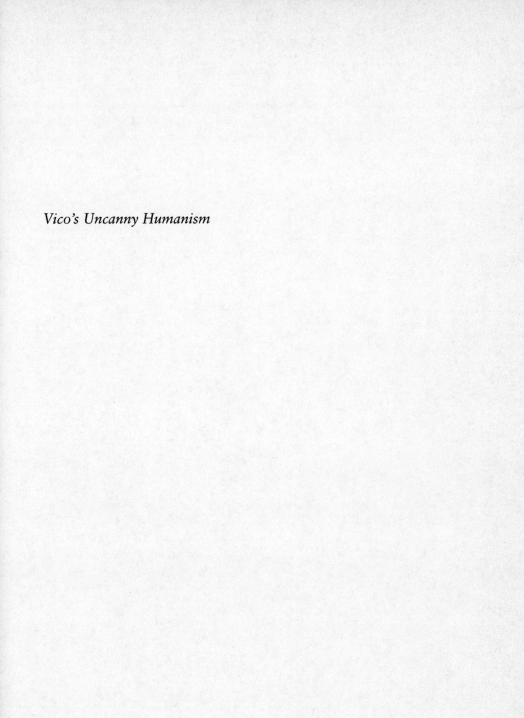

Vico's Uncanny Humanism

Introduction

EARLY IN THE *New Science* Vico gives "the basis for refuting all opinions hitherto held about the principles of humanity." Chief among them are the axioms that "because of the indefinite nature of the human mind, wherever it is lost in ignorance man makes himself the measure of all things" and "whenever men can form no idea of distant and unknown things, they judge them by what is familiar and at hand." These inadequacies account for the conceits of nations—the belief that each nation is the most ancient and the source of all human comforts—and of scholars, "who will have it that what they know is as old as the world." Vico presents the *New Science* as the outcome of a twenty-year struggle against those conceits as he tries to understand the "origins of both languages and letters." That effort culminates in the discovery he calls "the master key of this Science," "that the first gentile peoples, by a demonstrated necessity of nature, were poets who spoke in poetic characters." The discovery required "the persistent research of almost all our literary life, because with our civilized natures we [moderns] cannot at all imagine and can understand only by great toil the poetic nature of these first men."[1]

Vico's twenty-year struggle "to descend from these human and refined natures of ours to those quite wild and savage natures" took him from the familiar—the understanding of human nature, human activity, and knowledge derived from the humanist tradition—to the strange. Despite differences in historical manifestations of humanism and Neoplatonism, all reinforced for him the familiar beliefs foundational to the West: a dualistic ontology identifying human nature with a corporeal body and a subjective essence

[1] Giambattista Vico, *The New Science of Giambattista Vico,* trans. Thomas Goddard Bergin and Max Harold Fisch (Ithaca: Cornell University Press, 1988), 120–27, 34. References to the *New Science* are to paragraphs, not pages.

(whether soul, spirit, consciousness, thinking substance) and the belief that the goal of human life is the attainment of knowledge. The epistemic and normative significance of human activity—even the extent to which activity is human at all—is always a function of its relation to subjectivity.[2] What is strange—the "distant and unknown things" of which the human mind "can form no idea"—is the abyssal condition of the first gentile peoples, wholly embodied beasts rather than humans, living in their own filth, wandering solitary in primeval forests, mute and incapable of thought, who, "by a demonstrated necessity of nature were poets." The existential distance Vico travels to grasp the significance of his master key that the first men were "poets," which, he says, is Greek for "creators," can be traced in his writings. They begin with early works on familiar pedagogic and metaphysical concerns, continue through more historical writings on jurisprudence as his understanding of the nature and extent of human making deepens, and culminate in the *New Science,* written, then rewritten twice—the strangest of all narratives produced in the modern age.

Vico tries to convey to his contemporaries what is "new" and unfamiliar" about his new science. It is *scienza,* he insists—that is, a knowledge of causes—but unlike the new science of his day his new science does not study causes in the natural world. Nor is it "new" in the Cartesian sense, grounding certainty on subjective doubt cut off from social and historical existence. He distinguishes it from all traditional philosophy, which "contemplates reason, whence comes knowledge of the true," because philosophers have "failed by half in not giving certainty to their reasonings by appeal to the authority of the philologians." But the new science is not philology either, which "observes that of which human choice is author, whence comes consciousness of the certain," because philologians have "failed by half in not taking care to give their authority the sanction of truth by appeal to the reasoning of philosophers."[3] Nor does the mere unity of philosophy and philology constitute the newness of Vico's science, a newness too strange to be understood even by those drawn to it. Most who are so attracted hold the traditional view that, insofar as the new science is philosophy, it derives universal truths from the certains of history. They retain an epistemic conception of science, one as "old as the world"—at least as old as the philosophic world that first determined what constituted "knowledge" in an "epistemic" sense. For the Greeks *episteme* was a correspondence between ideas held by subjective beings and intelligible being, possible only insofar as a substantive likeness or *homoiousis* existed between knower and knowable. It was the need to insure the possibility of knowledge that led Plato to attribute to humans an immortal soul.[4] Though the conception of knowledge changed in the humanist tradition, what did not change was the metaphysical belief insuring the possibility of knowledge, that humans are subjective beings.

Vico's new poetic science challenges all claims to knowledge in an epistemic sense. As central to Vico's new science as the master key that the first gentile peoples were "poets," creators, are his insights into the genetic nature of the human world: that "the nature of institutions is nothing but their coming into being (*nascimento*) at certain times and in certain guises," and that "things do not settle or endure out of their natural state."[5] Vico came to believe that, in their originary state, the "first men" were embodied beings without a subjective essence, and, thus, wholly incapable of knowledge in the traditional sense. The sense-making of which they were capable was divination, an interpretive linguistic activity, the reading of the "language" they found in the sky, which they took to be the language of God. Since Vico's genetic axioms apply to *all* human institutions, *all* forms of human knowing, including the one practiced in the *New Science,* had to derive from that poetic wisdom.

Thus the new science as a unity of philosophy and philology cannot be merely a synthesis of the two, since both traditions are grounded on the familiar conceit Vico's insight enables him to get beyond—the belief in the essentially subjective nature of humans which insures *homoiousis* with the knowable. As the epigraph from Derrida suggests, once one questions the assumptions of philosophy and philology, one "steps outside" them, however unintentionally. In taking its beginnings from corporeal, poetic men, in identifying the very humanity of first men as a *factum* made by poetic skills of the body, Vico's new science becomes, in effect, *poiesis*—a "science" of the causes of the human world, certainly, but causes now understood to be *poetic*. What is new about Vico's new science is that it is the first to "know" that the causes it "knows," the causes of all human institutions, *including its own way of knowing,* are acts of originary human making, and that originary making takes place in language. This reflexive "knowing" is not knowledge in an epistemic sense, but hermeneutic understanding.

The *New Science* has never been understood as a "poetic science"; that is, as a hermeneutic sense-making about the originary linguistic sense-making of the human world. Ironically, the more Vico came to understand the strangeness of poetic first men and their poetic way of knowing, the stranger his own writings became to his modernist contemporaries. He accounts the 1725 edition "as fallen on barren ground," writing to a friend, "I avoid all public places, so as not to meet the persons to whom I have sent it; and if I

---

[4] For Plato, the soul was rational, but historically rationality has not been as necessary for knowledge claims as the assumption of subjectivity. Pragmatists, for example, give up the former but not the latter.

[5] Ibid., 134, 147.

cannot avoid them, I greet them without stopping; for when I pause they give me not the faintest sign that they have received it, and thus they confirm my belief that it has gone forth into a desert."[6] Even more ironic—though Vico is read and appreciated perhaps more today than at any time since his own age, his current readers, for the most part modernists, are as likely as his contemporaries to succumb to the tendency of the human mind to make itself the "measure of all things," to judge the "distant and unknown" by the "familiar and at hand." Vico did not realize that readers who had not struggled twenty years to grasp the poetic nature of first men would reduce his account of the strangeness of poetic being to that familiar humanist understanding of human nature from which he had freed himself.

The purpose of this book is to recover the strangeness of a conception of human existence that cannot be understood within the context of humanism and modernism; to denaturalize "familiar" assumptions and to draw out the poetic nature of the *New Science*. In doing so I deny that Vico's new science is epistemology, in the "epistemic" sense in which philosophy defines knowledge, since it does not assume the metaphysical belief in human subjectivity that, unacknowledged, grounds even modern conceptions of knowing. Indeed, I deny that the *New Science* is a work, however idiosyncratic or quirky, of traditional humanism. What related Vico's early writings to philosophic humanism was the epistemological significance of *verum et factum convertuntur* in *Ancient Wisdom*. In that work, the claim of the convertibility of the true and the made was understood as the claim that an intellectual knowing of made conceptual truths was possible for their maker. The mark of Vico's new uncanny poetic humanism is the *ontological* or onto-genetic implications of that principle as realized in the *New Science*: the claim that *verum* is the *made*, a *factum*; that *facta* are, at one and the same time, the true words, deeds, *concrete things* of the human world; that the "knower" of true words, deeds, things is their maker, *whose "knowing" is the hermeneutic understanding of himself as maker*. In Vico's alien humanism humans are not essentially subjects of knowledge but "poets," creators, "divine" because, like God, they make a real human world with language.

The Cartesian Vico

The humanist tradition culminates in modern anthropology's reification of human subjectivity as the human subject. Vico's readers are for the most part modernists who do not question that humans are subjects of knowledge and action. This is the case not only for Cartesians, but also for those who value Vico's work. A not untypical example credits Vico as the first to ex-

<hr>

[6] Giambattista Vico, *The Autobiography of Giambattista Vico*, trans. Max Harold Fisch and Thomas Goddard Bergin (Ithaca: Great Seal Books, 1944), 14, quoted in a letter to Father Bernardo Maria Giacco.

press the anthropology of the subject. Despite what obviously divides Vico and Descartes, Tom Rockmore argues, "From an epistemological perspective . . . the difference between them, which Vico saw as absolute, is in fact merely relative. . . . Both defend the versions of the basic view which Vico expressed in his famous claim, *verum et factum convertuntur.*" Vico's status as a modernist is even stronger than that of Descartes or Kant, Rockmore continues. Descartes considered human knowledge of the natural world limited because God, not humans, had made it. It was Kant who "render[ed] the conditions of experience and knowledge of objects . . . dependent on subjectivity," but neither Descartes nor Kant "proposed more than an epistemological concept of subjectivity. Vico's enormous merit, which paved the way for the widespread anthropological turn in modern philosophy later followed by others, including Marx, is to have made the transition from an epistemological principle to a view of human being as the real historical and epistemological subject."[7] Rockmore's interpretation minimizes even the widely held view of Vico's philosophy as an alternate to the Cartesian. Insofar as both legitimate knowledge and do so with *verum-factum,* insofar as for both the "made" is an object of cognition produced by human subjectivity, both are modernists, Vico even more than Descartes in grasping the anthropological nature of the subject. Ironically, Rockmore's interpretation places Vico in the context of Descartes's epistemological transformation of philosophy, thus taking for granted his position within the Cartesianism he struggled to reject.[8]

Alternately, though Jürgen Habermas shares Rockmore's estimate of the significance of *verum-factum* in leading to the modern conception of the subject, he faults Vico for not drawing out the implications of that position. Habermas's interpretation is particularly relevant because he understands the modern conception of the subject as a secularization of the theological notion of God as knower/maker of the world. While I too present a secularization thesis, I disagree with Habermas as to the nature of the God Vico secularizes. Indeed, I argue that the difference between the "divine" power that both the modernist conception of the subject and Vico's poetic view of humans as creators attribute to humans is due to the differences in creative potency of two distinct gods. Habermas provides a good account of the traditional conception of God the moderns secularize. The development of ideas that culminates in Marx's material and critical philosophy of history begins,

[7] Tom Rockmore, "A Note on Vico and Antifoundationalism," *New Vico Studies* 7 (1989): 18–27, 21–23.
[8] Similarly, Jääko Hintikka, arguing the difference between Vico and Descartes is one of degree rather than kind, considers Vico "bolder or perhaps less critical" ("Practical *vs.* Theoretical Reason—An Ambiguous Legacy," *Practical Reason,* ed. Stephan Körner (New Haven: Yale University Press, 1974), 83–102, 88.). For J. G. Merquior, Vico "had to be anti-Cartesian only in order to become, in a deeper sense, the Descartes of historical science" (J. G. Merquior, "Defense of Vico against Some of His Admirers," *Vico and Marx: Affinities and Contrasts,* ed. Giorgio Tagliacozzo (Atlantic Highlands: Humanities Press, 1983), 401–26, 426).

he says, "in a certain way . . . with Vico's famous explication of the *topos verum et factum convertuntur*." His interpretation of that *topos,* which he considers an epistemological principle identifying historical knowledge with the "made," focuses on the analogy Vico draws between the "*intellectus originarius* [who] creates the world by thinking it" and historical reason. Where theology makes God the subject of history, Vico places man, who would "think [history] as his own creation . . . [and] comprehend his spirit as the product of history." Measured against the *telos* of the realization of a critical philosophy of history, Vico's effort is inadequate, Habermas believes. The analogy between God and man cannot hold. Since Vico says of the divine subject of history "to know and to do is the same thing," the human subject of history must not only create but also know what it creates. Vico, however, neither invests man with omnipotence, nor makes him provident: for him "men make their history, yet . . . not . . . with will and consciousness." Vico's retrospective epistemology cannot construe future states "according to laws of progress": history is for him a cyclic recurrence of periods of progression and regression. The prospective stance so important to critical thought, including the "justification of prediction in the critique of knowledge," escapes him. For Habermas, the development of philosophy of history through Kant and Hegel to Marx culminates in Marx's overcoming of Vico's failure. Marx identifies labor as the material form that moves history, an "active appropriation . . . [by] revolutionary praxis that is only initiated and guided by theory." With Marx, philosophy of history becomes both "retrospective and prospective . . . transform[ing] contemplation into critique," an accomplishment "reconcil[ing] Vico, who is preserved [sublated] in Hegel, with Kant." Marx, like Kant, makes Vico's "maxims of knowledge"—the unity of knowing and making—the basis of a prospective philosophy of history, and man the subject of history.[9]

Habermas's reading is no more than a mildly revisionist version of dominant secular interpretations of Vico. Since the nineteenth century, Vico has been understood as precursor of various forms of idealism—Kantian, Hegelian, historicist—flourishing in that century. Comfortable with a history of ideas tracing a continuous intellectual process from *arche* to *telos* Habermas merely relocates the idealist tradition within a grander dialectical process with a different *telos.* In the process, idealism—and Vico—become precursor of a materialist and critical philosophy of history.[10] Yet whether Marx's philosophy of history is the end of a process begun with Vico's prin-

---

[9] Jürgen Habermas, *Theory and Practice,* trans. John Viertel (Boston: Beacon Press, 1973), 242–50. The passage from the *New Science* Habermas explicates is 349.

[10] Though the history of institutions Vico traces is also a history of ideas, since "the order of ideas must follow the order of institutions," in Habermas's more idealist view it is ideas that have causal efficacy. Moreover, though the process ends in a materialist rather than idealist philosophy, Habermas conceives that end idealistically. History comes to fulfillment in historical consciousness—the self-understanding of man as subject of history.

ciple—whether, indeed, that end is materialism or idealism—is the least interesting question that Habermas raises. More telling is the theoretical and normative context within which Habermas identifies, then finds inadequate, the aspects of Vico he considers significant. Many of his assumptions, such as the priority of knowledge, or even of thought or subjectivity, in human making, constitute foundational beliefs of modernism. That Vico too held them at the beginning of his professional life is apparent from early writings, but by the time he grasps the implications of his master key, he recognizes them as more insidious, because more pervasive, versions of the conceit of scholars. Though Vico claims the study of history yields "science," his readers do not recognize that his science has become "poetic." To deem Vico's *verum-factum* inadequate because he fails to grasp Marx's critical notion of knowledge or the notion of man as subject begs the question of whether he shares the modern project at all. Indeed, as Habermas and Rockmore both acknowledge, "modernism" in the sense of the identification of humans as subjects of knowledge and historical *praxis* is not achieved until the nineteenth century. If any interpretation of Vico is anachronistic, it is one that assumes Vico's role, intentionally or not, in a philosophy not formulated until long after his death.

The unquestioned belief that *verum et factum convertuntur* is an epistemological principle is a major source of misconceptions about Vico, making him complicit in the very nihilistic character of modernism he was the first, and sharpest before Nietzsche, to identify and condemn. What should make Vichians most uncomfortable about the assumption of his modernism is that it reduces the *New Science* to the "familiar" effort to legitimate some form of knowledge, in however quirky a way it is assumed it does so. What if, however, Vico's master key makes epistemological interpretations of the relation between knowing and making, and a subjectist anthropology, impossible? What if the first men were poets *precisely because they were not subjective beings or knowers*? If that were the case, since the nature of things is "nothing but their coming into being at certain times and in certain guises," and since "things do not settle or endure out of their natural state," in all later stages of development, despite whatever artifactual human condition poetic beings make for themselves, they remain *poetic* beings.[11] Rockmore is right to credit Vico with going beyond epistemology to anthropology, but his anthropology was not that of *subjects* but of *makers*, ontological beings-in-the-world, and no one took *that* way until Nietzsche too rejected the anthropology of the subject and identified humans as artists. Nothing within the philosophic tradition in general, much less modernist beliefs in particular, is adequate to an understanding of the strange way of being of the "human" who is neither knower nor subject but *poietes*.

---

[11] Vico, *New Science*, 134, 147.

Theological Models of Human Creativity

Habermas's interpretation is particularly relevant because he focuses on the theological origins of *verum-factum* and the conception of humans as divine creators of history. Tellingly, he uses the phrase *intellectus originarius* rather than Creator-God, thereby identifying the theological paradigm of the modern conception of the subject as a God whose creativity is a function of intellect. It is understandable that in their effort to legitimize the new form of human activity made possible by their science, a demiurgic activity yielding mastery over nature, the moderns attribute to themselves the divine predicate of the unity of knowing and making, and that they understand that unity on the model of an *intellectus originarius.* But the belief that thought or knowledge informs all activity—whether human or divine—was not initially a theological notion but an assumption of Greek philosophy. The God of Western Christendom Habermas invokes in his narrative is in effect a hellenized deity modeled on the Divine Architect of the *Timaeus* and transmitted to the West by Neoplatonism. In that onto-theological tradition a divine making conditioned by divine knowing is a mimetic reproduction of rational forms or ideas existing *a priori* in the *nous,* or mind of a spirit God. Though that God's making and knowing are chronologically identical, his making is *logically* conditioned by his knowing. Only on that assumption can the made be intelligible to a subjective knower as conceptual epistemic truths.

The Neoplatonic conception of God is a "familiar" one for a philosophic tradition that believes that subjectivity conditions all activity, whether human or divine. It provided medieval Christian theologians with the conception of a Creator-God enabling them to retain belief in the intelligibility of the world, now understood as created and temporal. When modernists secularized the scholastic version of *verum-factum,* they did so to legitimate the enriched conception of human activity implicit in their new science. In the context of that science, *praxis* became *techne,* a productive activity giving humans mastery over nature, and *imago Dei,* the traditional conception of humans, became *homo faber.* Though Vico differed from his contemporaries in denying that constructed truths yielded demiurgic control over nature, he too held a Neoplatonic conception of God in *Ancient Wisdom* and drew on the scholastic conception of *verum-factum* to justify knowledge of constructed mathematical truths. Most interpreters of Vico take for granted the essential continuity of his thought and attribute to the *New Science* the principle formulated in *Ancient Wisdom*—epistemological, but enriched by a historical understanding of the products of human making.

My interpretation of the *New Science* as a poetic ontology offers a different version of secularization, arguing that the God whose creative activity Vico attributes to his first men is radically different from the *intellectus originarius* of *Ancient Wisdom.* The need for a "stranger," less conceited understanding of originary activity came from Vico's hard-won insight into the nature of the first men. By the last edition of the *New Science,* his under-standing of the gentile peoples as wholly embodied beings had taken him be-yond the subjectivist anthropology grounding the epistemological version of *verum-factum,* and he could not attribute to his poets the making of the Neo-platonic God. Vico says as much, claiming their creativity "was infinitely dif-ferent from that of God . . . [because] they, in their robust ignorance, did it by virtue of a wholly corporeal imagination . . . for which they were called 'poets,' which is Greek for 'creators.'" Readers for whom making—divine or human—is always subjectively conditioned have not understood that the notion of a creative process "infinitely different from that of God"—one, that is, derived from "corporeal imagination"—also has a theological model. That model is the creativity of a God who is not a spirit but is, rather, wholly one with a creative language inseparable from his acts, and from the con-crete things created by his words and acts. In attributing an originary lan-guage to his first men—a language concrete and metaphoric because it is derived from the bodily skills of perception, memory, and imagination—Vico claims their poetic word is inseparable from "deed" and "thing," and likens it to the Hebrew *davar.*[12]

The anthropological significance of interpreting Vico's conception of the poetic creativity of the first men as a secularization of the linguistic creativ-ity of a poet-God rather than of an *intellectus originarius* is profound. In the context of his genetic axioms that "the nature of things is nothing but their coming into being at certain times and in certain guises" and that "things do not settle or endure out of their natural state," his insight into the creative nature of the gentiles is also a statement about the creativity of the men de-scended from them. Vico's readers have not realized the import of the fact that he presents not one but three distinct conceptions of "creativity" in the *New Science*—that of a God who creates by "knowing"; that of the poets, who, with a "corporeal imagination," an originary language inseparable from deeds and things, create a world of nations "with a reality greater that points, lines, surfaces and figures are"; and *that of the men of what Vico calls "the third age."* Though by the third age humans have made themselves subjective beings, they can never become Cartesian subjects or knowers. On-tologically, they are never other than creators, their creativity that of beings-in-the-world.

Vico may not have realized that the divine model of a creativity derived from "corporeal imagination"—that is, a creativity unconditioned by sub-jectivity and identified with language, in which the creative "word" is in-separable from "deed" and "thing"—was that of the God of Genesis. In the spiritualizing of the biblical tradition, the West had lost the understanding

---

[12] Ibid., 376, 401.

of a Creator-God who was poet rather than intellect or spirit, who brought a real, material world into existence with language unconditioned by knowledge or subjectivity. For such a poetic ontology, "knowledge" as conceptual or subjective truths corresponding to an intelligible historical process is not possible, since the metaphysical assumption of that *episteme,* a subjective anthropology insuring a *homoiousis* or homology between object and knower, does not exist. The Judaic tradition itself does not claim an epistemology; for it, the language of God, whether constituting the finite, temporal world or the Torah, can only be interpreted, and interpretation is an endless process. If the paradigm of divine creativity Vico attributes to his poets is an ontological *poiesis,* the "trues" convertible with the made are not epistemic "truths," but the concretely made true *things* (*cose*) of the human world themselves, and "knowledge" is the reflexive hermeneutic understanding that the "knower" is himself or herself their maker. I intend to recover the "forgotten" *poiesis* of that alien God who is not knower but poet by drawing on contemporary texts that find affinities between postmodern views of language and of humans as embodied beings in-the-world, and the rabbinic tradition. I find these thematic affinities, which constitute an *ontological hermeneutic,* in Vico's uncanny poetic humanism as well.

Despite the wide range of interpretations of Vico, most, I argue in the following chapter, presume the familiar humanist and modernist conceits that activity (whether divine or human) is conditioned by subjectivity, that in the third age Vico's poets become subjective human beings, that the principle of the unity of knowing and making insures those beings epistemic recovery of the conceptual truths of their historical world. So tenacious is the hold of these conceits in reading Vico that efforts appealing to perspectives alien to them or *post* modern are dismissed as anachronistic. Those efforts are as important today, however, as was an earlier challenge to dominant nineteenth and twentieth century interpretations by Pietro Piovani. Piovani attacked "the presumed coincidences" Croce had drawn between the "historicisms" of Vico and Hegel. While Hegel emphasized the culmination of history, its *perficere,* Vico's concern, Piovani claims, was with beginnings characterized by *ingenium,* an inventive force in which man shows "the creative capacity of his thought in the raw concreteness of the *facere.*"[13] Rejecting Croce's view of Vico "as a column . . . of idealistic and neo-idealistic thought" Piovani calls Vico "a true anti-Cartesian" while Hegel is "not really an enemy of Descartes, but continues his work." Vico and Hegel "are not traveling down the same street, but two divergent highways," a "hypothesis" Piovani advances "with . . . confidence today" because "in the context of contemporary philosophy . . . [one can] distinguish between one historicism and an-

---

[13] Pietro Piovani, "Vico without Hegel," *Giambattista Vico: An International Symposium,* ed. Giorgio Tagliacozzo and Hayden V. White (Baltimore: Johns Hopkins University Press, 1969), 103–23, 117.

other . . . [and when] one begins clearly to discern the multiplicity of the forms of historicism, and to combat the monopolistic claims of one form . . . doubt concerning the essential affinity that might bind Vico to Hegel acquires particular value."[14]

Writing in the context of the philosophies of his day, Piovani identified Vico with Wilhelm Dilthey's form of historicism rather than Hegel's. He did not perceive the idealism inherent in *all* historicisms, indeed, in the Western epistemic project itself; did not perceive that, insofar as epistemology rests on the assumption of *homoiousis* between human subjectivity and object of knowledge, insofar as epistemology presumes that subjective anthropology, it is always, *inescapably,* idealist. That presumption is so ubiquitous in interpretations of Vico that though most commentators agree with Piovani's critique of Vico's purported idealism, insofar as they find in Vico's philosophy an epistemological intent, they too are idealists missing the more radically *poetic* sense in which his new science is a "science of the beginnings of things." The situation of contemporary philosophy today is such, however, that a doubt concerning Vico's idealism even more radical than the one occasioned by distinctions among historicisms is possible. That doubt is raised by postmodernism's challenge to the privileged role of subjectivity for humanism, its challenge to modernity's anthropology of the subject and identification of philosophy with epistemology, and by postmodernism's responses to those assumptions—a more "primordial" and "ontological" formulation of humans as "beings-in-the-world," and the attribution to humans of an originary language. At a time when it is possible to "discern the multiplicity of forms" of being-human and to combat the "monopolistic claims of one form," it is appropriate to doubt interpretations that take for granted the subjectivity and subjectism of Vico's conception of humans in the *New Science.*

The issue raised by the title of this book is, thus, not *whether* Vico's writings are "modern" or "postmodern" but, rather, the need to draw on the alien perspective of the latter to bracket the uncritical assumptions of the former. In this sense the terms go beyond chronology, beyond the view of historical periods as fixed by linear causal relationships, to make the determination of the meaning of "modern" and "postmodern" the very issue to be raised. Without the authority of chronology, the terms are conceptual or aesthetic sites that cut across historical periods, metaphors for different sensibilities. In providing an alternate perspective from which to read Vico's texts, postmodernism does not impose an alien view onto his writings but, rather, corrects the co-option of those writings within modernist—that is, familiar—assumptions. Just as Piovani's rejection of interpretations of Vico as "the nineteenth century in germ" led to richer, more diverse readings of him, so too rejection of interpretations based on humanist and modernist as-

[14] Ibid., 106, 114–15, 110–11.

sumptions allows for more original, more complex—more tragic—readings than possible within those assumptions.

Chapter 1, "The Familiar: *Verum-Factum* as an Epistemological Principle," traces the pervasiveness of the subjectivist assumptions of an idealist humanism and modernism in the contemporary literature on Vico. Though the commentators I discuss overtly reject idealist interpretations of Vico, all assume that by what Vico calls the "third age of men" humans attain a fully human—that is, subjective—nature, and most identify Vico's achievement as the formulation of an epistemological principle legitimizing knowledge of history. That Vico conceives of humans and human activity not as subjectivist, but as poetic in *every* historical age, thus rendering humanism's epistemic project illusory, has not been understood. Even theological interpretations that attempt to emphasize making rather than knowing by relating Vico's *verum-factum* to a biblical conception of divine creativity fail because of their inability to conceive of God in other than Neoplatonic terms, and of humans as other than subjective beings. I argue that, though Vico is preoccupied with the same issue of origins in the *New Science* as in *Ancient Wisdom,* by the later work his poetic insights into the impoverished nature of first men make traditional humanist and theological views of causal agency impossible. *Verum-factum,* which in *Ancient Wisdom* had been an epistemological claim legitimating a delimited form of knowledge, becomes in the *New Science* an ontological principle. For Vico, humans are creators by nature, and the products of their making the true things of their human world.

In chapter 2, "*Verum-Factum* and the Poetic Ontology of the Hebrews," I turn to contemporary texts that develop alternate versions of the secularization thesis or alternate images of the God who first possessed the predicate of the unity of knowing and making. Though both versions find relationships between the Hebraic conception of omnipotent divine making and radical human making, they differ as to what constitutes "radical making," a function of the difference between modern and postmodern readings of Hebraic texts. In the first part of chapter 2, "Hans Blumenberg and *Verum-Factum* as Principle of the Originary," I discuss the version of *verum-factum* Blumenberg claims the moderns appropriated. Blumenberg attempts to "legitimize" the age's epistemic claims by interpreting Descartes's *cogito* as a radical secularization of the constructive power of the Hebrew God. Though his effort is inadequate—his conception of that power is not radical enough—he brings out two implications of *verum-factum* that, I claim, contribute to Vico's skepticism of its epistemological value and his turn to *poiesis*—that the "knowledge" insured by *verum-factum* is never other than "self-knowledge," and that art is more primary than truth. In the second part of chapter 2, "The Originary as Language," I characterize the originary power of the Hebraic God with writings from a postmodern Judaic perspective. The writers I discuss, José Faur, Susan A. Handelman, and Jacques Derrida, identify the originary creativity of the biblical God not with the divine mind but with an ontologically potent language. Indeed, for the writings on which I draw, the "divinity" of the Hebrew God, who is not substantively a subjective spirit, is itself a function of his originary language. Those who construct order and meaning with such a language, gods or men, are "divine" poets, their constructs true, though artifactual, things.

Chapter 3, "The Strange: "*Verum-Factum* and the Secularization of Poetic Ontology," is a reinterpretation of the *New Science* that takes Vico's claim that his principle of the origins of the human world cannot be understood within the familiar conceits of civilized beings, in its most radical and subversive sense. That principle, Vico's "master-key" that the first gentile peoples were poets who spoke in poetic characters, is usually interpreted as a rejection of rationalist and ahistorical conceptions of human nature and knowledge, leaving in place such familiar conceits as humanism's identification of humans as inherently subjective beings and, ultimately, subjects of knowledge. Where, I ask, would an interpretation that takes Vico's readers beyond these familiar assumptions lead? What would constitute a truly *poetic* understanding of the *New Science*?

Chapter 3 takes up that question by distinguishing the third edition of the *New Science* from Vico's earlier exploration of the nature of origins in *Ancient Wisdom*. Though a genetic relation exists between the two works, the earlier search for the origins of knowledge and human existence takes place in the context of traditional Neoplatonic metaphysical and theological assumptions about the nature of God, of humans, and of creative activity. When Vico again takes up the question of origins in the *New Science,* it has become radically existential, deepened by his insights into the abyssal poverty of the first men of the human race.[15] One section, which discusses Vico's response to that existential question in the *New Science,* insists, against all interpretations that moderate Vico's claim, that his "first men" are not human but *wholly corporeal beasts*. That claim is too strange to be understood, however, and Vico's commentators "familiarize" his *bestioni* with analogies to children, or primitives, or the "fallen" of the Christian tradition. Though I am mindful of the differences between Vico's conception of the origins of human existence and those of Nietzsche and Heidegger, my readings of the more radically existential senses in which these later writers raise the question of the setting up of historical worlds free me from imposing those traditional conceits on Vico, who himself warned his readers against doing so.

Vico calls his first men "poets," creators, emphasizing that they *make* their human world, their very human existence, and do so with language and the

---

[15] The *verum-factum* principle is stated only indirectly in the *New Science,* but is referred to in 331, 349–50.

social practices and physical labor arising from and informed by language. Chapter 3 continues by attempting to capture the ontologically originary nature of a language that, Vico insists, derives wholly from bodily skills.[16] Unable to attribute the language of the first men to an inherent subjectivity and believing in its ontological potency, Vico claims that poetic words, metaphors formed from random sense perceptions, are inseparable from the "things" named by those metaphors and the deeds occasioned by them. I argue that the corporeality of poetic language can never be captured within a subjectivist metaphysical tradition, and pick up on Vico's own suggestion of an affinity between the unity of word, thing, deed, and *davar,* the creative word in scripture. I draw on the Hebraic understanding of *davar* as "dynamic happenings," and suggest affinities between this understanding and Heidegger's notion of originary poetic language. Though Heidegger finds his conception of language in German poetry, it is in Genesis that one finds the "alien" ideas that the real is not eternal and given but "artifactual," that making takes place in an ontologically potent language—ideas that, in different ways, echo in Nietzsche's, Heidegger's, and Vico's claims that the human world is brought into existence in works of art.

Once I have argued for the corporeal, prehuman nature of the *bestioni* and the ontologically originary power of their imaginative language, I retell the story Vico tells in the *New Science* of the making of the human world from its genetic origin. Vico himself characterizes that process in its most radical terms, saying it is the making not only of the human body, but also of the human soul—that is, of human subjectivity—from the bodies of the *giganti.* The "subjectivity" constructed in this process is artifactual. Though reified as "consciousness" or "mind" by men of the third age, it is functional rather than substantive, and always inseparable from the concrete linguistic and social practices of humans in-the-world. I argue, moreover, that beings who construct their subjective existence by the third age *retain their genetic nature as makers rather than as knowers,* and continue to construct in the third age. With their abstract conceptual languages they construct sciences and theoretical systems, and with their pedagogic practices they create both rationalist scholars who believe themselves subjects of knowledge, and humanist scholars capable of understanding that humans themselves are the creators of their human world. These creators of the third age manifest their genetic relation to the first men, and the poetic nature of their science, performatively, by creating their own ironic narratives of the creation of the human world, like the *New Science.*

Vico's commentators have not appreciated that, ontologically, men of the third age are not Cartesian subjects or knowers but creators, creating human institutions and meaning. Vico himself claims his readers experience "a di-

---

[16] This claim does not reduce language to physical processes, however, since for Vico language emerges only in imaginative responses of bodily skills to external stimuli.

vine pleasure" in reading the "proofs" of his science, "since in God knowledge and creation are one and the same thing."[17] Perhaps it would be easier for his readers to grasp the sense in which Vico attributes to them a "divine pleasure," if they could understand the affinity between their linguistic creativity, the creativity of their poetic ancestors, the fathers of the human world, and that of a Creator-God who creates with an originary language at one and the same time word, deed, thing.

[17] Vico, *New Science*, 349.

I   *The Familiar*
Verum-Factum *as an*
Epistemological Principle

> The function of philosophy . . . is no longer to be the theory of the world or
> . . . Ideas, no longer to administer a treasure imparted to man along with his
> existence, but rather to imitate the Creation. . . . The zero point of the dis-
> appearance of order and the point of departure of the construction of order
> are identical; the minimum of ontological predisposition is at the same time
> the maximum of constructive potentiality.
> —Hans Blumenberg, *The Legitimacy of the Modern Age*

Verum-Factum and the Emergence of *Homo Faber* in the Modern Age

The "philosophy" to which Hans Blumenberg refers was the new philosophy of the moderns, and the change of function he chronicles was imposed
by the epochal crisis with which the age began, the critique Nominalism
mounted against the "maximum of ontological predisposition" affirmed
by scholastic theology. It was loss of belief in the rational order and intelligibility of divine creativity that forced the moderns to assert a "maximum of
constructive potentiality." Belief in an ontological maximum and the corresponding unwillingness to acknowledge a need for constructive potency had
characterized the Western intellectual tradition from its foundation in Greek
metaphysics. Hellenic philosophy constituted itself on the postulate of a pre-
given rational, orderly cosmos whose eternal and unchangeable nature insured its correspondence to human rationality. That very correspondence
was itself assurance of the benign purposefulness of the cosmos. In the face
of that comforting teleology, the Greeks devalued human activity, which
they, indeed, never formulated as ontologically constructive. It was only
when the "maximum causality" of the arbitrary God of Nominalism challenged that ontological maximum that human constructive ability became

necessary. In a fundamental sense the modern age began only when humans took upon themselves the originary power that had been the prerogative solely of that deity.

The Greeks—with the significant exception of the Sophists—never faced that crisis. For them the privileged form of activity was contemplation of pregiven formal order. The contemplative life was not strictly speaking a *human* life since it was possible only "in so far as something divine [reason] is present in [man]." The rational soul contained, however, a practical intellect concerned with doing (*praxis*) and a productive intellect concerned with fabrication (*poiesis*), activities that took place in a contingent world of change. Aristotle's conception of fabrication, dominant in the West until the modern age, was based on an analogy between art and nature. Though *poiesis* was concerned with art, it was, as Blumenberg suggests, delimited by the degree of formal order Aristotle attributed to the real. Aristotle defined art, the paradigm of which was architecture, as "a state of capacity to make, involving a true course of reasoning." Reasoning was essential because, both in nature and art, making was action for the sake of an end, and purposeful action was always intelligent.[1] "Intelligence" existed in nature in the form of final cause, in art in the form of the thing to be made preexisting in the artist's soul. Art originated in the thinking of the maker, and Aristotle dwelt on the intimate relation between thought and making: "That which proceeds from the starting point and the form is thinking, and that which proceeds from the final step of the thinking is making." In the sense that all making presupposed prior existence of a form determining the *telos* of activity, no real difference existed between nature or art. "It is impossible that anything should be produced if there were nothing existing before. . . . [S]ome part of the result will pre-exist of necessity."[2] The only real difference was that "in the products of art . . . we make the material . . . whereas in the products of nature the matter is there."[3] Thus, the most significant aspect of Aristotle's conception of *poiesis* was not that the artifactual was inferior to nature because it imitated or completed it, but that all making, natural or human, was purposeful. Since purposeful activity either reproduced prior formal order or realized a *telos,* it was always conditioned by intelligence; *poiesis* was never originary—that is, unconditioned.[4]

Though Plato did not articulate formal distinctions among contemplation, *praxis,* and *poiesis,* he created the paradigmatic image of making as a mimetic process conditioned by intelligence, the Divine Architect of the

---

[1] Aristotle, *The Basic Works of Aristotle,* ed. Richard McKeon (New York: Random House, 1941), "Nicomachean Ethics," 1177b 26–28; 1140a 1–11. See "Physics," 199a, 10–11, b 27–31.

[2] Aristotle, "Metaphysics" VII, 7, 1032b, 15; 30–33; 1032b 13–1034a 8; "Physics," 194a 27.

[3] Aristotle, "Physics" II, 2, 194b 6–8. See "Metaphysics" VII, 6, 1032a 13–25.

[4] For a history of the idea of nature as craftsman, see Friedrich Solmsen, "Nature as Craftsman in Greek Thought," *Journal of the History of Ideas* 24 (1963): 473–96.

Timaeus. While the existence of unchanging and intelligible Being—"that which always is and has no becoming"—was necessary, the "always becoming and never is" needed explanation.[5] Plato provided that explanation with the productive act of a divine "Artificer" he called "creator," "father," "maker." Productive activity was not ontologically significant, however, since it merely reproduced intelligible Being. Divine making was an intellectual skill of the Artificer, who was a craftsman creating with measure and number, an architect following a blueprint constituted by the necessary truths of mathematics. Plato conceptualized the relation between being and becoming in logical terms, as, for example, the "participation" of copy in exemplar. Production was ultimately a logical rather than ontological problem; it was the relation between two sorts of existences, rather than the process by which the lesser came about, which needed explanation.

Even if philosophy had taken seriously the active role of the Timaean Artificer in the production of moving images of rational forms, its conception of productive process would have differed radically from the only ontologically originary act formulated in the ancient world, that depicted in Genesis. That event was a maximum of constructive potentiality unconditioned by preexistent matter or, because the Creator-God was willful rather than rational, intelligible purpose. The contingency of both creative act and created reality in Hebrew scripture was inconceivable for metaphysics, given the assumptions by which matter was necessarily ordered by Ideas in the *Timaeus.*[6] The alternative to that mimetic process was not an originary process unconditioned by formal order or intention: it was no making at all.[7] Philosophy's view that "it is impossible that anything should be produced if there were nothing existing before" was a fundamental bias toward the prior ontological existence of formal order, the "proper way" for a thing or act to be. Rejection of or indifference to that assumption was not possible *within* metaphysics, since it was the cornerstone *of* metaphysics. Originary—that is, unconditioned—activity was truly inconceivable for the Greeks.

Remarkably, the syncretic process in which Greek metaphysics transmuted a scriptural religion into Christian onto-theology reduced even the originary event of Genesis to a mimetic and purposeful process. In the Middle Ages the *topos* of God as *Deus Artifex*—an image modeled on the *demiurgos* of the *Timaeus*—was "revive[d] in the Christian sense" by Origin, because, Ernst Robert Curtius explains, of "the influx of analogous concepts from the

---

[5] Plato, *Timaeus,* trans. Benjamin Jowett (New York: Bobbs-Merrill Library of Liberal Arts, 1949), 7.

[6] Though there are no accounts in Greek metaphysics of an originary cosmological event, there are passages in Plato that attribute creative activity to humans, a function of madness or divine frenzy. In general, creativity is devalued in the Dialogues.

[7] This point is made by Hannah Arendt, who finds an affinity between contemplation and fabrication for the Greeks. In both, the materialization of ideas constituted a loss of perfection. Hence the desire to renounce "work," to behold eternal ideas. Hannah Arendt, *The Human Condition* (New York: Doubleday, 1959), 276.

Bible." Curtius's unquestioned assumption of the "analogous" relation between biblical and Timaean images of God illustrates the problem raised by syncretism, however, since it begs the very question at issue. Curtius gives three sources of the image of *Deus Artifex:* ancient myths accounting for the creation of the world through "the handiwork of a God . . . as weaver . . . needleworker . . . potter . . . smith" (which Curtius, quoting Robert Eisler, describes as "lowly handicraft, with the toil of physical demiurgy"); the "sublimation" of that artisan-God in the "world-creator of the *Timaeus";* and the "potter, weaver, and smith of the Hebrew scripture."[8] Yet Curtius does not explore the differences in conceptions of making obscured by the general category "craftsmanship," nor question whether the different conceptions he cites are indeed analogous—a blind spot inherent in the very syncretism that reduced the Hebrew God to Timaean Architect.

In general the Middle Ages lacked theoretical awareness of material practice. "The category of production," one commentator says, "seems to have fallen into oblivion" since Aristotle identified "productive knowledge with art and thus had suggested that it was not a genuine type of *knowledge.*"[9] As for the idea of a radically originary activity, it would become conceivable again only when the world itself became a "minimum of ontological predisposition," an abyss to be ordered by a "maximum of constructive potentiality." That was the ontological situation of the writers of Genesis and of Nominalists, and, Blumenberg argues, the situation in which the moderns found themselves. They responded to their need for constructive potency by appropriating a predicate previously attributed only to God and formulated in the principle *verum et factum convertuntur,* the claim of the unity of making and knowing. With it the moderns asserted their "divine" power to make and to know what they made, even in an abyssal world. While the moderns found authority for their claim to Godlikeness in the biblical image of man as *imago Dei,* their version was actually a subversion of the biblical analogy. The traditional interpretation, which identified man as *imago Dei* because of his rationality, enabled him to know a world divinely created. The modern analogy, based on the predicate of creativity that traditionally belonged *only* to God, made man knower of a world he himself created.

Equally consequential to the age's self-understanding was its conception of the God whose creativity it appropriated. Though the moderns believed that creative power belonged to the God of Genesis, their conception of it derived from the metaphysical tradition, in which divine creativity was a function of God's knowledge. Only in the last edition of the *New Science* was the originary *poiesis* of the biblical God attributed to humans, though, since

---

[8] Ernst Robert Curtius, *European Literature and the Latin Middle Ages,* trans. Willard R. Trask (New York: Bollingen, 1967), 544–46. Eisler's quote is from *Weltanmantel und Himmelszelt* (1910), 235.

[9] Nicholas Lobkowicz, *Theory and Practice: History of a Concept from Aristotle to Marx* (Notre Dame: University of Notre Dame Press, 1967), 81.

Vico's readers do not distinguish between the two conceptions of divine process, the radical nature of his interpretation has not been understood. In the rest of this section I survey representative interpretations of the *verum-factum* principle formulated by the moderns, in which, for all, making is a function of knowing. In the next section I present sustained analyses of a range of interpretations of the *verum-factum* formulated by Vico, to argue that none grasps its ontologically constructive nature, nor the radical creativity of the God who first possessed the unity of knowing and making that Vico attributes to humans.

In Habermas's account, the secularization of *verum-factum* culminates in the modernist assertion of historical and political subjecthood. Amos Funkenstein dates the beginning of that secularization process in the rise of modern science in the seventeenth century. "Never before or after were science, philosophy, and theology seen as almost one and the same occupation," Funkenstein claims, calling that occupation a "secular theology" whose laymen included Galileo, Descartes, Leibniz, Newton, Hobbes, and Vico.[10] For Funkenstein, medieval controversies concerning the predicates of God converged in a new ideal of scientific knowledge as *ergetic* or pragmatic. The predicate of the unity of divine knowing and making became the claim that human knowing was constructive in Galileo's and Descartes's adoption of a new method of knowing common to mathematics and mechanics, the "reconstruction of reality" through experiment: "only the doable—at least in principle—is also understandable: *verum et factum convertuntur.*"[11]

For the moderns the constructive making of the human subject was demiurgic, since it yielded power over nature. Bacon, Paolo Rossi comments, insisted that "the artificial does not differ from the natural in forme or essence, but only in the efficient." Art was merely "man added to nature," a sentiment echoed by Sir Thomas Browne: "nature is not at variance with art . . . they being both in the service of his providence. . . . [A]ll things are artificiall, for Nature is the art of God."[12] The belief that nature and art were alike because they were "artificiall" found expression in a formative

[10] Amos Funkenstein, *Theology and the Scientific Imagination from the Middle Ages to the Seventeenth Century* (Princeton: Princeton University Press, 1986), 3. Funkenstein traces the completion of the process to Kant, who explicates the conception of knowledge by construction "without theological baggage" (116). See my review-essay "'Secular Theology' in the Modern Age," *Journal of the American Academy of Religion* 56, no. 4, 741–50.

[11] Funkenstein, *Theology and the Scientific Imagination,* 178–79. Geometry had been the paradigm of constructed knowledge since the Greeks, but mathematical reasoning did not become a model for reasoning about the physical world until the notion of mathematics as an "inventory of ideal relations" gave way to the idea of mathematics as a formal language of relationships.

[12] Paolo Rossi, *Philosophy, Technology and the Arts in the Early Modern Era,* trans. Salvator Attanasio (New York: Harper & Row, 1970), 137–45. The references to Bacon are *The Works of Francis Bacon,* ed. R. L. Ellis, J. Spedding, D. D. Heath (London: 1857–74), III, 531 ("*Temporis partus masculus*"); III, 592 ("*Cogitata et visa*"), I, 496–97, 624 ("*De augmentis*").

metaphor of the age, the world as "machine." For Rossi "the assumption of the model *machine* for the explanation and comprehension of the physical world, and the image of God as artificer, engineer, clockmaker" flowed from "[t]he criterion of knowledge as *making*," and "applied to man as much as it did to God. The human intellect . . . can have access only to those truths which have been structured by men: the truth of physics, of geometry, and of mathematics." Hobbes adds to those truths by extending the mechanistic model of mathematical and physical knowledge to human behavior. Like geometry, in which knowledge is demonstrable, so "politics and ethics, namely the knowledge of the just and unjust . . . can be demonstrated *a priori:* in fact its principles are known to us because we ourselves create the causes of justice, that is, laws and conventions," a passage, Rossi says, "rightly . . . compared to a page in Vico in which he proclaims the celebrated principle of *verum factum.*"[13]

Rossi attributes the mechanistic character of the practice justified by the constructive theory of knowledge to Bacon, Descartes, Gassendi, Mersenne, Kepler, Boyle, Vico.[14] For all, making becomes a causal process structured by the relation of means to ends, a process characterizing not only the making made possible by a science of nature—now characterized as *techne*—but also "doing" in the human world. The conceptualization of all activity as productive, the grounding of production on theory, the identification of theory with technique, reduces political "doing," *praxis,* to *techne* as well. But *praxis* anchored on a technical conception of knowledge cannot retain the character it had for the ancients. In the *polis praxis* flowered into *phronesis,* but, Habermas argues, activity based on theory is wholly instrumental. Lost is the normative import of doing, and with it the valuing of life in the *polis* as the highest form of human existence. The instrumental goals of political and social activity take priority over the ethical, a process Habermas traces from Machiavelli and More to Hobbes, who grounds political and social philosophy on the conception of the world as machine. In contrast to *episteme* "[t]heory is measured by its capacity for artificially reproducing natural processes. . . . [I]t is designed for 'application' in its very structure. . . . [W]e *know* an object insofar as we can *make* it." Drawing on the analogy between nature and machine, Hobbes reformulates the normative conception of Natural Law, and lays out a "physics of sociation."[15] With the reduction of reason to technical rationality and of society to technical control, "a new peril

---

[13] Rossi, *Philosophy, Technology and the Arts,* 143–45. Rossi refers to several passages in *Ancient Wisdom.* The Hobbes quote is from *De homine* X, 5; *De cive* XVII, 4; and *De corpore* XXV, 1.

[14] Paolo Rossi, "Hermeticism, Rationality and the Scientific Revolution," *Reason, Experiment and Mysticism in the Scientific Revolution,* ed. M. L. Righini Bonelli and William Shea (New York: Science History Publications, 1975), 254.

[15] Jürgen Habermas, *Theory and Practice,* trans. Josh Viertel (Boston: Beacon Press, 1973), 60–61, 51, 70.

has entered the world," the "self-alienation of man . . . the danger of the creator losing himself in his work."[16]

The danger of "self-alienation," of "self-produced objectivity," concerns Hannah Arendt as well, though she finds the tendency to subsume *praxis* to *poiesis,* the corruption of public life to a process structured teleologically by fabrication, already in Plato and Aristotle. Their frustration with the imperfections of *praxis,* the affinity they see between contemplation and fabrication in the priority and permanence of form, the conditioned, teleological activity of the craftsman, make *poiesis* the more desirable model of human activity for them. Arendt deplores that tendency, which leads to the modern identification of man as *homo faber* rather than *animal rationale,* man as maker rather than as man of speech (*lexis*) and deed (*praxis*). She identifies that process with the emergence of *verum-factum* in Galileo's and Descartes's "discovery of the Archimedean point," their securing of the ground of certain knowledge in human subjectivity.[17] The shift from knowledge of objective qualities to subjective ground of knowledge is made through mathematics, which is no longer a "science" of Being, but "of the structure of the human mind." The telescope symbolizes the fact that man knows only what he makes himself: "Instead of objective qualities . . . we find instruments, and instead of nature or the universe—in the words of Heisenberg—man encounters only himself."[18] The making of instruments symbolizes *homo faber,* the making of the human world his ultimate achievement; the natural process of "making" "serves as well or even better as the principle for doing in the realm of human affairs."[19]

If *verum-factum* was one means by which humans asserted a maximum of constructive potentiality in the face of a "zero point," it represented as much a loss as gain. With the transformation of *animal rationale* into *homo faber* the classical ideal of activity in the *polis* as the highest form of human life was lost; the valuing of human existence as a communal social process lived in the eventful world of words and deeds. The earliest voice to warn of that danger—and, ironically, to use *verum-factum* as recourse against it—was Vico's. Before the historical implications of the modern conception of knowing and making, against which Habermas and Arendt warn, became apparent, Vico understood the danger that conception posed. "[F]rom the viewpoint of the humanistic rhetorical tradition," Habermas says, Vico "presented the new philosophy inaugurated by Galileo, Descartes, and Hobbes with a reckoning of profits and losses." Lost was "prudence" and a "her-

---

[16] Jürgen Habermas, *Knowledge and Human Interests,* trans. Jeremy J. Shapiro (Boston: Beacon Press, 1972), 349 n. 14. Habermas quotes Helmut Schelsky, *Einsamkeit und Freiheit* (Hamburg, 1963), 299.

[17] Arendt, *The Human Condition,* 24, 257. See also 272.

[18] Ibid., 237. The observation predates Heisenberg. It is Nicholas of Cusa who identifies human knowledge with self-referentiality. See my discussion of Cusa, chap. 2.

[19] Ibid., 273. Like Habermas, Arendt finds in Hobbes the sharpest articulation of that development.

meneutic power in the theoretical penetration of situations which were to be mastered practically." Understanding that the "founding of practical philosophy as a science . . . appears misguided," Vico retained the distinction between *phronesis* and *episteme*,[20] and used the *topos verum et factum convertuntur* to justify the historical making of the human world through words and deeds. For Arendt too Vico was the "first to comment on and criticize the absence of common sense in Descartes" and the moderns. Realizing that, in accordance with *verum-factum,* nature could not be known by humans, and responding to the same need for certainty that led Descartes to use *verum-factum* to justify knowledge of nature, Vico turned to the study of history: "The modern discovery of history and historical consciousness owed one of its greatest impulses [not] to a new enthusiasm for the greatness of man, his doing and sufferings . . . but to the despair of human reason, which seemed adequate only when confronted with man-made objects."[21]

Though acknowledging the differences in Vico's use of *verum-factum,* neither Habermas nor Arendt grasps the most original feature of Vico's principle. Funkenstein is subtler in delineating Vico's use of *verum-factum* to mediate between natural law and the mechanistic-egoistic conceptions of human nature and activity dominant in the period. Though Vico agrees with mechanistic theorists such as Hobbes and Spinoza in denying the natural social instinct assumed by natural law theorists, and believes society is artificial, he does not, Funkenstein insists, agree that social artifacts are mere conventions. For Vico natural law is "founded neither on social instincts nor on a computation of enlightened interests. It is rather the very immanent, regular, 'ideal' process through which civilization emerges time and again as man's acquired collective 'second nature.'" Though Vico radicalizes the antithesis between nature and convention, making human nature itself an artifact, he more significantly reinterprets "nature to stand for the very processes through which man acquires a second, social nature," processes accomplished by the "mediatory function of imagination. Rather than the product of mechanistic-deterministic forces, history was the result of man's spontaneous creativity."[22] The insight Vico calls his "master key"—that the first humans were poets, their constructive activity imaginative—enables him to mediate "between the reality of man's original, brutal nature, and the ideal eternal law, between Hobbes and Grotius," thus resisting the mechanistic model of human construction. "He refused to accept the paradigmatic role of mechanics *precisely because* he endorsed . . . *verum et factum convertun-*

[20] Habermas, *Theory and Practice,* 44–46. See also 73–75.
[21] Arendt, *The Human Condition,* 371 n. 43. See also 373 n. 62 and 272.
[22] Amos Funkenstein, "Natural Science and Social Theory: Hobbes, Spinoza, and Vico," *Giambattista Vico's Science of Humanity,* ed. Giorgio Tagliacozzo and Donald Phillip Verene (Baltimore: Johns Hopkins University Press, 1976), 187–212, 203–4; and *Theology and the Scientific Imagination,* 279–89, 281. The chapter on Vico in *Theology and the Scientific Imagination* reproduces the article in *Science of Humanity.*

tur." Since that principle renders the natural world unknowable, human making can yield only philological or "contextual" knowledge of the socio-historical world.[23]

That Vico's formulation of an *ergetic* conception of knowledge is an effort he shares with his age does not lessen Funkenstein's sense of his accomplishment. Vico's understanding of the imaginative nature of human creativity, his use of imagination to mediate between mechanistic-egoistic and natural law political theories, is for Funkenstein the culmination of modernity's effort to transform humans into agents of historical existence. Vico most fully "appropriates" the "divine" unity of knowing and making on behalf of humans. The most unappreciated thinker of his age most completely voices its underlying preoccupations, but with an irony only he himself would have recognized.

Epistemological Interpretations of Vico's *Verum-Factum*

Most interpreters of Vico appreciate the differences between the technical character of *verum-factum* in the study of nature and Vico's use of the principle to justify the study of the human world. Despite this, and regardless of the degree to which the role of imagination is stressed in Vico, most interpretations consider his *verum-factum* an epistemological principle. Vico, after all, calls his philosophy "science." For him, as for Aristotle, science is *scire per caussas,* and his new science derives the philosophic truths of the causes of the human world from the study of historical certains. Commentators disagree, however, as to the sense in which these "truths" constitute "knowledge"—the strong sense of the sciences of nature, the historicist sense of the human sciences, even a historical "knowing" based on imagination and *fantasia.* Whatever the position, epistemological interpretations of Vico's *verum-factum,* like the technical version from which they are distinguished, are merely variations of traditional themes. All are grounded on humanism's identification of the essence of *humanitas* with subjectivity, the assumption culminating in the modern anthropology of the subject. Only that assumption insures the possibility of knowledge, whether epistemic or pragmatic. It enforces the idealism inherent in the tradition, an idealism far more pervasive than the Hegelian or Crocean versions so easy to disown today.

That idealism is exemplified even in Piovani's critique, which, though fatal to an overt identification of Vico and Hegel, follows Croce in understanding Vico's project as the recovery of knowledge of the historical world, and never questions Vico's place in the epistemic project of modernity itself. Most Vichians still do not; certainly most do not question that for Vico genetic development culminates in the third age in subjective beings capable of

---

[23] Funkenstein, *Theology and the Scientific Imagination,* 328 (emphasis added), 285.

knowing what they make.[24] The familiarity of modernist anthropology makes it difficult to appreciate the strangeness of a new science in which causes are poetic, making linguistic and originary language emergent from the bodily skills of beings *by nature* creators rather than knowers.

Verum-factum provides a good litmus test for exposing the pervasiveness of the belief that knowledge is possible and humans subjective beings and subjects of knowledge—beliefs that cannot be held outside idealist metaphysics. The Neoplatonic tradition that transmitted the principle expressed in *Ancient Wisdom* to scholastic and Renaissance thinkers also transmitted that subjectivist anthropology to Cartesian and nineteenth century idealist philosophy. In the broad sense in which I use the term "idealism," even Habermas's analogy between Marx's "materialist" conception of man as the critical, prospective-thinking subject of history and the *intellectus originarius* who creates the world with thought is idealist.[25] The issue to be raised, however, is whether *verum-factum as realized* in the *New Science* is that same Neoplatonic principle; whether there are other versions of the principle to which Vico's has greater affinity (and it is the claim of *affinity*, not *historical influence*, I make here). Belief in the eidetic continuity between *Ancient Wisdom* and the *New Science* reduces all interpretations of the principle implicit in the later work to the procrustean bed of the epistemological-idealist formulation in the earlier, and accounts for the difficulty in understanding the *aporias* in that last work.

As Vico slowly begins to grasp the implications of his master key—his insight into the embodied nature of humans and the poetic nature of their making—his understanding of *verum-factum* changes. Without a grounding in an idealist anthropology the *verum-factum* principle can no longer be an epistemological claim of the making and knowing of subjective truths. The making Vico understands as a subjectively unconditioned, concrete, linguistic fabrication of true things—what Piovani calls the "raw concreteness of the *facere*"—becomes ontological. Productive of true things of the human world and of the men of the third age, it cannot produce the *substantive* human subjectivity that belief in the possibility of epistemic knowledge takes as given. A principle attributing the ontological creativity of a Creator-God to humans but denying them epistemic knowledge of their creations is, however, too strange for modernists to understand. In this section I show the pervasiveness of the assumption of essential human subjectivity in Vico scholarship and its influence on interpretations of *verum-factum,* and argue that all such interpretations are idealist.[26] Only Vico's insight into the em-

[24] Even pragmatic conceptions of theory presume that anthropological or ontological ground of justification. Only overtly materialist views reject it, though not consistently.

[25] Nor does Marx's "materialism" escape this idealist assumption. For him, not only is human activity conditioned by rational goals; it also is distinguished from animal behavior because it is purposeful and intentional.

[26] The views I discuss illustrate the range of interpretations of Vico. Most are overtly episte-

bodied, poetic nature of first men enables him to go beyond the idealism of humanism.

If, moreover, what Habermas calls the *topos verum et factum convertuntur* secularizes a divine predicate, then an ontological interpretation of Vico's conception of the "divine" unity of poetic making and knowing points to a different deity who originally possessed that predicate than the *intellectus originarius* who creates by thinking. If the epistemological version of *verum-factum* so clearly present in *Ancient Wisdom* secularizes the Timaean-Neo-platonic conception of God whose activity, human or divine, is purposive and conditioned by formal order or intention, the ontological creativity of his poets secularizes the potency of a very different God, a strange poet God who creates not with mind but with originary language, bringing forth a real, though artifactual, world.

Verum-Factum *as the Secularization of a Divine Predicate.* In discussing the ancient sources of *verum-factum* Rodolfo Mondolfo finds several "anticipations" of the belief in the "generative aspects of thought" among the Greeks, though not until Philo does he find a *"principio gnoseologico,"* "the principle demonstrating the omniscience of God as creator and maker of all thing . . . [and] making as the source and condition of knowing."[27] Mondolfo interprets this to mean that, for Philo, the various forms of divine making are a function of the "omniscience of God." Mondolfo finds the Philonic formulation in the Renaissance, particularly in Ficino, who admired Philo, read him through Platonic and Neoplatonic lenses, and was the first Renaissance writer to assert the intimate relation between making and knowing.[28] His understanding of Philo's "gnoseological principle" was itself

mological, and all presuppose the subjectivist anthropology that is the metaphysical ground of epistemological interpretations. I draw here on Andrea Battistini's distinction among three "poles of attraction": Italian-Neapolitan, dominated by philological, historical, and scholarly concerns; German, characterized by two currents that emphasize *verum-factum*—a rhetorical-juridical approach depicting Vico as the culmination of Latin-Renaissance humanism, and the hermeneutic, making Vico founder of the *Geisteswissenschaften;* and Anglo-American, dominated by philosophic, primarily epistemological, concerns.

[27] Rodolfo Mondolfo, *Il "Verum-Factum" Prima di Vico* (Naples: Guida Editori, 1969), 10–13 (my translation). Mondolfo's reference to Philo is *Quod Deua sit immutabilis* 6, no. 30, in *Les oeuvres de Philon d'Alexandrie*, vols. 7–8, *a cura di Moses* (Paris, 1963): 76. See also Mondolfo, *La comprensione del soggetto umano nell'antichita classica* (Florence: La Nuova Italia, 1967), 594–600; and *Momenti del pensiero greco e cristiano* (Naples: Morano, 1964), 37–58.

[28] In notes 1 and 2 on 23 and 24 Mondolfo refers to Ficino's discussion *De cristiana religione*, cap. XXII in *Opera Omnia, t. I, Parisiis*, 1641, 25, and *Theologia platonica de immortalitate animorum, libro IV, cap. I, in Opera Omnia*, cit., t. I, 120. Alternately, Eugenio Garin rejects the link between Vico and the Italian Renaissance made by Francesco De Sanctis, Gentile, Nicolini, as well as Mondolfo and Croce. Garin says Ficino's brand of Neoplatonism is one in which "physics are Pythagorean . . . metaphysics Platonic" reconciled with Catholicism (101), while Vico distinguishes his "new science" from Galileo's precisely because his Baconian sense of the concreteness of experience goes beyond Galileo's Pythagorean ontology. Vico uses *verum-factum* to break the link between physics and mathematics in Neoplatonism. Garin claims Vico uses the *topos "verum-factum,"* a commonplace in the period, polemically, against dogmatists and Pythagorean idealists (110), and believes Vico's discovery of the primitive and

Neoplatonic, treating God's universal creation as source and proof of God's omniscience and identifying human making with the conceptual activities of mathematical construction and physical experiments.[29] Leonardo, Cardano, and Galileo picked up the principle, and, if Vico took it from Cardano, Mondolfo suggests, the inspiration he drew from Italian philosophers for his own gnoseological principle can be taken back "with great exactness" to Philo.

Croce too suggests as "probable" source of Vico's theory of knowledge "the philosophers of the Renaissance," particularly Ficino, and cites their distinction between the "divine art" of the geometrician and human art in the physical sciences. While the soul of the geometer encased in the body touches "dust when he describes figures upon the earth," his mind creates like nature, "which is divine art . . . produc[ing] its creations from within, by living reasons." Thus the "human soul, situated in the body," cannot grasp the substance of things, while the mind, which "creates the fact, is in a sense itself the fact, just as . . . the knowledge of a triangle, that it has three angles equal to two right angles, is practically identical with the truth." Here, Croce says, "in the definition of divine knowledge and of the procedure of human knowledge in the case of mathematics, as opposed to that of physical science, is implicit the principle that true knowledge consists in the identity of thought with its object." Yet, unlike Mondolfo, Croce denies the influence of Renaissance philosophers as well as Christian scholastics on Vico, emphasizing instead his originality.[30]

Regardless of whether Neoplatonism influenced Vico historically—and on this Mondolfo and Croce disagree—the affinities both find between Vico and Neoplatonism are based on the subjectivist conception of making and the idealist conception of knowing they attribute to him. Croce characterizes these conceptions most succinctly as "the principle that true knowledge consists in the identification of thought with its object," the metaphysical assertion that knowledge rests on the substantive *homoiousis* of thought and object. Though Mondolfo claims to find that principle in a theological archetype, Philo himself took his conception of a God whose making is tied to "*onniscienza*" from Plato's Timaean Architect and imposed it on the biblical Creator-God, an event of Hellenistic syncretism that transformed a scriptural religion into onto-theology. The Neoplatonic conception of God emerging from that syncretism retained the presumption that causation is a function of knowledge. It is God's *knowing* of a thing's essence (*ens*)—the idea internal to God—which is its cause. Only in the context of the subjectivist meta-

poetical nature of ancient conceptions rejects Ficino's and Pico's belief in a "primordial revelation of the true" (111). Those who relate Vico to Neoplatonism do not realize, Garin adds, how profound was Vico's understanding of the conceit of scholars, a sentiment I share (Eugenio Garin, "Vico and the Heritage of Renaissance Thought," *Vico: Past and Present*, ed. Giorgio Tagliacozzo (Atlantic Highlands: Humanities Press, 1981), vol. 1, 99–116.

[29] Mondalfo, *Il "Verum-Factum" Prima di Vico*, 25.

[30] Benedetto Croce, *The Philosophy of Giambattista Vico*, trans. R. G. Collingwood (New York: The MacMillan Co., 1913), 287–88.

physics transmitted by Neoplatonism, whether in theological or secular form, could Cardano and Ficino characterize the making of the geometer as a "mental" creation of the intelligible object, or claim the mind that "creates the fact is . . . itself the fact," or could Croce appeal to "the principle that true knowledge consists in the identity of thought with the object."

Though he traces *verum-factum* to Philo, Mondolfo himself does not overtly argue a secularization thesis. For his part, Croce takes great pains to deny a relation between Vico's principle and scholastic theology, though, ironically, his idealist interpretation of *verum-factum* is but a variant of the scholastic version he rejects. Even more ironic, in defending the originality of Vico's *verum-factum* against the suggestion "of certain Catholic editors" that it derives from scholastic versions, Croce brings out the more voluntarist element of the principle stressed by two secularization theorists, Karl Löwith and John Milbank. This emphasis opens the way for a secularization thesis different from the Neoplatonic or scholastic, though all who emphasize causation undercut that emphasis by retaining a subjective conception of God and man.[31] Though the theological arguments of Croce, Löwith, and Milbank are dense and arcane, a detailed discussion of them is necessary at this point to sharpen the contrast between traditional secularization arguments and the one I attribute to Vico.

Croce presents his version of Vico's *verum-factum* to counter efforts to derive it from Thomas's doctrine that "truth and reality are convertible" (*ens et verum convertuntur*). For Thomas nothing can be known except what exists, and nothing can exist but what is good. Therefore, existence, truth, and goodness are convertible: "*Et ideo sicut bonum convertitur cum ente, ita et verum.*" Moreover, things are good insofar as they correspond to the idea in their creator's mind, since a thing "partakes of the truth of its nature insofar as it imitates the knowledge of God, like an artefact insofar as it agrees with the art." For Thomas "the condition of making a thing is to know it." But, Croce asks, what does the principle that knowing is prior to making have in common with Vico's idea "that the condition of knowing a truth is to create it," that truth "is convertible with the created"? Croce draws on the "learned and subtle Spanish Thomist Jaime Balmes" to show Vico's criterion of knowledge "is not only different from but inconsistent with Thomism." Balmes had attacked Vico's criterion as "unique from the scholastic position": whereas the scholastic position is that God "creates because he understands," Vico claims "God understands because he creates." Balmes argues that Vico's position—that "intelligence is only possible through causality"—actually involves skepticism. Thus, "God could never know himself, because He is not His own cause." For Balmes knowledge is not a

---

[31] I do not discuss Catholic interpretations of the principle, only theological interpretations that sharpen the distinction between two conceptions of divine creativity; one a function of originary language, the other of subjectivity.

function of causality but identity: the Word of God was conceived not by God's omnipotence but "by cognition of divine essence." Croce makes clever use of Balmes's argument, which is based on the scholastic view that knowledge is of the *rei* itself, against Nominalism's voluntarist version of the causal argument. Croce acknowledges that Vico studied Nominalism and has "points of affinity" with Scotus, who refuted the Thomist doctrine *adaequatio intellectus et rei* [the adequacy of the intellect to reality]. For Scotus, objects do not have reality in God; God knows objects He wills, and they exist because He wills them. Nominalism asserts the priority of creating to knowing against scholasticism's view that God's knowing of the reality of a thing precedes His creating. For Croce, however, *neither* version is equivalent to Vico's, since "the question for Vico is . . . the convertibility or identity of knowing and creating."[32]

Croce bases his claim of Vico's originality on Vico's grasp of convertibility and use of that idea. Before Vico, he says, it was a "Christian commonplace . . . that God only can fully know because he alone is their creator," and Francisco Sánchez used it in a skeptical sense as a warning against "presumptuous claims of human knowledge." Sánchez did not realize, Croce says, "his hand was resting upon a treasure." For Vico, however, skepticism becomes the real meaning of the principle that science is knowledge of causes—"*per caussas scire*"—and he uses it to counter Descartes's identification of knowledge with self-evident truths.[33] Vico delimits knowing to mathematics, the only thing humans have made, thus expressing a second original claim, that mathematics is a constructed science and, because arbitrary, "unfit to rule over and transform the rest of knowledge," as Descartes believed.[34] Though this "first phase" of Vico's theory of knowledge is ultimately "an achievement of despair and impotence," it leads to Vico's third original claim, his "vindication of . . . intuition, empirical knowledge . . . probability, and authority . . . which intellectualism ignored or denied," and to the second phase of Vico's theory of knowledge, his justification of knowledge of the historical world.[35]

In explicating this second phase Croce rejects any affinity between Vico and Nominalism's voluntarist version of the causal theory of knowledge, resting Vico's epistemology on the criterion of identity. That criterion enables him to distinguish Vico's view of the philosophic knowledge of philological certainty from Cartesian certainty, "in which the object, however internal it is said to be, remains extrinsic to the subject." Certainty for Vico "was truly

---

[32] Croce, *Philosophy of Giambattista Vico*, 279–85. Croce's response to "certain Catholic editors" is reproduced as Appendix III in Collingwood's translation. The reference to St. Thomas is *Summa Theologica*, part I, question xvi, art. 3.

[33] Ibid., 5.

[34] Vico's grasp of the arbitrary nature of mathematics is one reason Croce rejects any relation between his *verum-factum* and the Neoplatonists, who assumed the objective reality of mathematics in a Pythagorean sense (297).

[35] Croce, *Philosophy of Giambattista Vico*, 4–19.

internal certainty, reached by an internal process." Vico was reconstructing the history of man, which was a product of man himself. "Is not the mind of man, the creator of history, identical with the mind which is at work in thinking it and knowing it?" Croce concludes, "The truth of the constructive principles of history then comes not from the validity of the clear and distinct idea, but from the indissoluble connexion of the subject and object of knowledge." This assertion of internal identity between subject and object does not break with but confirms Vico's first phase of knowledge, since the creative cause of the fictions of geometry was also internal to the creator: "Like God, *ad Dei instar* [man, God's image,] from no material substrate and, as it were, out of nothing . . . creates the point, the line, and the surface. . . . Thus mathematics overcomes the failing of human knowledge, that its objects are always external to itself, and that the mind which endeavors to know them has not created them. . . . Mathematics . . . creates . . . in itself its own elements, and thus forms a perfect copy of the divine knowledge."[36] Since both phases of Vico's theory of knowledge rest on the internal identity of subject and object, Croce believes the metaphysics of the *New Science* and *Ancient Wisdom* are the same.

The second phase of Vico's theory of knowledge is not, however, merely an extension of the first, which lacked "an effective relation between the conception of God who creates the world and, as creating it, knows it," and man. In the second phase "Man creates the human world . . . by transforming himself into the facts of society: *by thinking it he re-creates his own creations . . . reconstructs the whole ideally. . . .* Here is a real world; and of this world man is truly the God." The purely metaphoric analogy between human and divine based on the convertibility of knowing and making becomes "strict" and "qualitative" in the *New Science*. No difference exists between the making and knowing of God and man except that for the latter, knowledge is "quantitatively more restricted." Croce finds an indication of Vico's "gradually dawning consciousness that he had now for the first time . . . discovered a true and proper knowledge, not a mere fiction of knowledge," from the "much greater conviction, warmth, and enthusiasm with which he now uses the epithet 'divine': quite a different thing from the chilly, if not absolutely ironical, *ad Dei instar* of the *De antiquissima*. The proofs of the New Science . . . 'are divine in their nature, and should give thee, Reader, a divine joy: since in God knowledge and creation are one.'"[37]

Though Croce's argument for the originality of Vico's *verum-factum* is that, against scholasticism and Nominalism, Vico grasped the real nature of God's constructive activity as the convertibility of knowing and making, Croce's understanding of that convertibility rests on his rejection of Nominalism's causal argument that God knows what He wills for the identity of

[36] Ibid., 22–23, 11.
[37] Ibid., 22–30. Emphasis added.

the subject and object of knowledge. The principle of identity is, in turn, a function of the subjectivist assumption at the heart of Croce's theory of knowledge; that, because it is mind that makes history, the object made can be known by mind "ideally." Only that anthropological assumption insures the *homoiousis* Croce believes the necessary condition of knowledge. He does not recognize that his epistemology—based as it is on the identity between mind and object of knowledge—is in effect but a secular variant of scholasticism's conception that God makes what he knows, that both positions assume knowledge is possible because making is *conditioned* by mind. Croce thus places Vico in the context of that idealism to which the Greek belief in the necessity of a *homoiousis* between object of knowledge and subjective knower led, even to the point of identifying Vico with the modernist turn in philosophy: "It is true that with the new [historical] form of his theory of knowledge Vico himself joined the ranks of modern subjectivism, initiated by Descartes. In a sense, indeed, he had already done so in his activist doctrine of truth as the reconstruction of the created. In this quite general sense Vico might himself be called a Cartesian."[38]

Croce initiated the period of secular epistemological interpretations of *verum-factum* still dominant in contemporary Vico studies, not realizing what the Nominalists had realized, that if causation is equivalent with knowing, knowledge *in an epistemic sense* is impossible. That conclusion is even more apparent in the secularization argument Karl Löwith gives in response to Croce, and in John Milbank's more recent secularization argument. Their efforts to strengthen the voluntarism elided by scholastic and Crocean idealism are undermined because they retain the subjectivist God of Neoplatonic onto-theology.[39] Löwith agrees with Croce that Vico differs from the scholastics, for whom knowing was not convertible with but prior to making, but believes Vico takes *verum-factum* from scholasticism and uses it in a new and unorthodox, but still theological, sense.[40] The coincidence of knowing and making that Croce considers distinctive of Vico's principle is

[38] Ibid., 26.

[39] I limit the following discussion to secularization arguments focusing on God's voluntarist nature. For a bibliography of contemporary theological discussions of Vico, see Mark Lilla, *G. B. Vico: The Making of an Anti-Modern* (Cambridge: Harvard University Press, 1993), 243–45.

[40] Löwith rejects Croce's "absolutely un-Vician conclusion that man is the god of history, creating his world . . . and . . . spontaneously knowing what he has made," since it renders providence "as superfluous and disturbing" as chance and fate. For Löwith Vico's providence is closer to Hegel's cunning of reason. Yet Löwith also acknowledges that Vico's providence "almost coincides with the social laws of the historic development itself. It works directly and exclusively by secondary causes . . . becom[ing] as natural, secular and historical as if it did not exist at all" (*"Verum et factum convertuntur: le premesse teologiche del principio di Vico e le loro consequenze secolari,"* *Omaggio a Vico* [Naples: A. Morano, 1968], 85–87; and *Meaning in History* [Chicago: University of Chicago Press, 1949], 115–36, 123–26). Fred R. Dallmayr observes that Löwith stops just "short of embracing a naturalist or positivist interpretation" of providence (Fred R. Dallmayr, "'Natural History' and Social Evolution, Reflections on Vico's *Corsi e Ricorsi,*" *Social Research* 43, no. 4 (winter 1976): 857–73, 859.

possible, Löwith insists, only in the context of the doctrine of creation *ex nihilo*. Not even the Greeks had the doctrine, and, without the Christian premise that the divine word creates, that knowing and making are indivisible in God, "Vico's principle would be deprived of a metaphysical foundation, namely an onto-theology."[41]

The earliest formulation of that onto-theological premise, Löwith believes, was the prologue of the Gospel of John, in which the principle of all things is the divine *logos* or word. In the creative word knowing and willing coincide. Löwith asks what the relation of Vico's principle is to the theological, the sense in which Vico calls the relation between human making and knowing "*quasi-divino*," and responds that Vico, following Christian tradition but differing from scholasticism, "does not place the emphasis on knowing which conditions making but on the ability to make as the condition of true knowing." Retaining the "Christian-theological" emphasis on creation, Vico distinguishes divine creativity from human making in the *Prima Risposta*, drawing on scholasticism's doctrine of the convertibility of the Good with Being and the True to distinguish creation *ad intra* from *ad extra*. Divine truth, uncreated and eternal, is begotten (*ab aeterno ad intra*). The model of that process is the *logos* generated by the Father. Human truth, on the other hand, created in time, converts with the made (*in tempore ad extra facit*). The only human making that "proceeds on the model of the Divine science" is mathematics, since the truths of mathematical axioms are "eternal."[42]

Löwith claims that Vico's distinction between divine eternal truth, which is begotten, and human truth, which is made in time, provides an onto-theological foundation for the convergence of knowing and making. What is not sufficiently appreciated, however, is that Löwith's intent is to distinguish Vico's *verum-factum* from the scholastic version in order to elevate making to knowing. Unlike Croce, however, Löwith does not identify Vico's version with Nominalist voluntarism, but with the biblical source of voluntarism, creation *ex nihilo*. He thus recovers that aspect of the scriptural tradition not retained by Neoplatonism. Unfortunately, Löwith himself conflates the biblical emphasis on creativity with the Johannine conception of the generation of the *logos*, the divine word (*verbum*). This undermines his effort to relate *verum-factum* to creation *ex nihilo*, since it was the Johannine formulation that interjected pagan subjectivism and spiritualism into the biblical conception of creation as a linguistic process.

Similarly, John Milbank argues against secular epistemological interpretations of *verum-factum* and theological interpretations based on scholasti-

[41] Löwith, "*Verum et factum convertuntur*," 80. Translations of Löwith are by me and Jeff Gburek.
[42] Ibid., 77 n. 5, 78–80. Vico likens the divine word to the ancient Italian saying "*dictum factum*," though acknowledging that ancient wisdom lacked belief in the creation of the world. The reference to *Prima Risposta* in the English text is Giambattista Vico, "Vico's First Response," *On the Most Ancient Wisdom of the Italians: Unearthed from the Origins of the Latin Language*, trans. L. M. Palmer (Ithaca: Cornell University Press, 1988), 118–35, 122.

cism's valuing of knowing over making, to recover a more activist conception of the principle. Like Löwith he goes back to creation *ex nihilo* and, like Löwith, undermines that move by identifying the biblical notion with the generative theology of John in which Christianity recast that model. He believes Vico elevates making to the significance of knowing with *verum-factum* by drawing on trinitarian theology while minimizing the implicit emanationism of that theology with the "metaphysics" of creation *ex nihilo*. In abandoning "the Platonic paradigm of truth," the priority of knowing to making, Vico's *verum-factum,* Milbank claims, constitutes a "radical break with most preceding philosophy."[43]

Milbank credits Löwith as one of the few commentators "to take the trinitarian dimension of Vico's work seriously," though he believes that Löwith "spoilt" his account "by his mistaken contention that God's knowledge is only a maker's knowledge *ad extra;* while *verum* retains its priority within God." Milbank focuses on the distinction between creation *ad extra* and *ad intra*—that is, between the creativity of an "artisan God" whose artifacts are external to himself, and the onto-theological trinitarian conception of creation as mystical emanation of God's spiritual substance. Vico, Milbank says, believed *verum-factum* first emerged as a criterion of truth in an ancient pagan theology in which the world was eternal, and, in that context, God's making was always from the outside, *ad extra,* and God an artisan. But Vico says "our theology denies" that belief, adding, "[I]f . . . we today are to receive this principle, it must be accommodated to Christian notions." For Milbank these Christian notions include the creation of the world and the Trinity. Vico, he claims, turns to a God who creates *ex nihilo* because he realizes that "[o]nly in the biblically based religions does the principle that intelligibility is coterminous with being emerge, and . . . it was Philo who [in the context of a biblically based religion] first put forward the arguments for divine omniscience and omnipotence"—that is, for the convergence of knowing and making in God. But Milbank insists that in the *Prima Risposta* II, Vico "wishes to reject" an artisan God molding pre-existent matter because a "cause" must contain the elements of the things it produces. By appealing to trinitarian theology Vico can argue that creation in time "does not exhaust divine activity or . . . truth." The doctrine of the generation of the second person of the Trinity allows him to retain *verum-factum* within the Godhead: *"verum creatum convertatur cum facto, verum increatum cum genito* [Temporal truth is made, eternal truth is generated]."[44]

Insofar as eternal truth converts not with the made but the begotten, Milbank argues, the Son or *logos* or *verbum* is "the supreme locus of *verum-fac-*

---

[43] John Milbank, *The Religious Dimension in the Thought of Giambattista Vico* (Lewiston: Edwin Mellon Press, 1991), pt. 1, 90. That "Platonic paradigm" governs not only scholastic theology but also, Milbank claims, theologically based interpretations of Vico and idealist interpretations attributing to Vico a secular view of man as God of history. All err in valuing knowing over making.

[44] Ibid., 131, 82–85. See also 117.

tum." Creation *ex nihilo* is, in effect, *"creation ex Deo."* Identification of the locus of *verum-factum* with the divine word enables Milbank to emphasize the linguistic as well as activist character of the principle. He points out that Vico uses the concrete image of reading to characterize convergence. As the true is convertible with the made, so too is *"intelligere"* equivalent to "perfect reading." Vico is drawing on the scholastic argument *verbum mentis,* the "word of the intellect," in which God *"reads* 'all the elements of things'," and "God's words, in which consist his understanding, are identified with the entire sum of infinite realities. . . . Thus God's fate, providence, or determination of how things *are to be* is identified with *factum,* or how things *actually are* in their outcome."[45]

Milbank observes that only with Heidegger does the question of being express itself in the paradigm of making. He believes Vico anticipates Heidegger in seeing that one could not go beyond that paradigm, though unlike Heidegger Vico "postulates an absolute making as the locus of all being."[46] Vico thus "raise[s] . . . *factum* (creation) to the status of a transcendental." "[B]y asserting the transcendality of *factum* or *verbum,"* Vico inverts "the traditional picture that . . . knowing was the cause of making. . . . [Now] making is the cause of knowing." Vico's position is basically Thomist, differing only in making creation or *factum* or *verbum* the central term rather than *esse* or *unum.*[47] In claiming that Vico's *factum* has the status of a transcendental Milbank can argue that Vico subverts the Platonic paradigm in scholastic thought by drawing out the implications of creation *ex nihilo* in the context of the trinitarian notion of creation *ad intra.* In addition, he can claim that Vico invests the priority of making with the linguistic character of divine creation, thus linking language and thought in a way the Platonic paradigm did not.

Milbank's projection of the doctrine of transcendentals onto the notion of creation *ex nihilo* is revelatory of the way spiritualist onto-theological assumptions compromise the radical implications of the biblical view that language *itself* is originary.[48] The argument for the transcendentality of *factum*

---

[45] Ibid., 117–48, in particular 120. Milbank uses this argument to emphasize the linguistic nature of God's creativity, but acknowledges that it could be an assertion of the priority of the externally made in divine understanding. His trinitarian conception of creation leads him to reject this conclusion.

[46] Ibid., 129. Neither Milbank nor Heidegger conceives of making outside the context of being, however, which, I argue, is the case for creation *ex nihilo* and Vico's conception of the originary event.

[47] Ibid., 129–31, 126. Aquinas develops a metaphysic of *esse,* Leibniz, of *unum* (129).

[48] That process is apparent in an earlier discussion of Vico's use of transcendentals by Max H. Fisch, though Fisch's source is Aristotle, who elevated the categories of *ens, unum, verum, bonum* above all others. Though the Greeks did not include *factum,* Fisch points out that in the *Timaeus* "craftsmanship is a standing paradigm both of creation and of knowledge." Though Plato rejected the possibility of a science of the physical world, he believed in a "probable account" if the world had been made by a craftsman "after a perfect model given in the . . . forms." Aristotle went further, at times treating physics as a productive science. For him "[n]atural

enables him to reject Löwith's characterization of God's knowledge as maker's knowledge *ad extra*. With external making God becomes "dependent on . . . [his own] creation . . . his knowledge constantly altered by the vagaries of things and the free-will of human beings." God's knowledge would no longer be "perfect *scientia*. . . . This is why Vico rejects the ancient Italian 'artisan' God."[49] Ultimately, however, Milbank's reason for rejecting an "artisan" God is that it "would not allow Vico to remain within the orthodox criteria, as he clearly desires to do," begging the very question of whether Vico desires "to remain within orthodox criteria"—that is, trinitarian theology.[50]

I sympathize with the efforts of Löwith, Milbank, and Max Fisch to elevate making in Vico, and with their understanding that the privileging of making takes place in the context of a biblical theme—creation *ex nihilo*—lacking to the Greeks. I also share Milbank's desire to emphasize the linguistic nature of making, and his belief that Vico's understanding of making has affinities with Heidegger (though he makes the additional historical claim that Vico anticipates Heidegger). I argue, however, that if the biblical model of creativity is subsumed by Johannine and trinitarian theology or by the metaphysics of transcendentals, it loses its radical character as an originary linguistic event unconditioned by spiritual or subjective intent or *a priori* order. Milbank's and Fisch's easy reduction of the Vulgate's characterization of the world as *factum* to the metaphysics of transcendentals exhibits the tradition's blind spot found in Curtius—that of eliding the differences between biblical and Aristotelian notions of craftsmanship (though Löwith's identification of Vico's position with creation *ad extra* rather than

---

things . . . have the same kind of truth that works of craftsmanship have—which, an impetuous reader might think," Fisch adds, "is as much as to say that for physics, as for the crafts, the true is the made." Fisch makes an analogy between craftsmanship as the Greek paradigm of creating and knowing, and biblical making. While "[t]here was no formal doctrine of transcendentals in which *factum* . . . was . . . made convertible with *verum* . . . there were hints from which such a doctrine might have been developed. In the Vulgate, God says, 'Let *x* be made' (*fiat*), and *x* is made so (*factum est ita*), and God sees that *x* is good (*bonum*). The Maker intends, He makes true, and He inspects and passes what He has made." Fisch believes Vico develops those hints in *verum-factum*. In *Ancient Wisdom* Vico draws on the scholastic view that being (*ens*) is convertible with *unum, verum, bonum,* but "since all but God that in any way is, is made . . . *verum-factum.*" And, Vico adds, "[I]t is only as *factum* that it is *verum,* only as made that it is true or intelligible—and intelligible only to its maker" (Max H. Fisch, "Vico and Pragmatism," *Giambattista Vico: An International Symposium,* ed. Giorgio Tagliacozzo and Hayden V. White (Baltimore: Johns Hopkins University Press, 1969), 401–24, 403–7). Fisch, Milbank says, "fails to note the full novelty of insisting on *factum*" as a transcendental.

[49] Milbank, *The Religious Dimension,* pt. 1, 120–21. See Elio Gianturco's discussion relating Francisco Suarez's formulation of *verum-factum* to Vico's distinction between creation *ad intra* and *ad extra* and the convertibility of *unum, verum, bonum,* "Suarez and Vico: A Note on the Origin of the Vichian Formula," *Harvard Theological Review* 27, no. 3 (July 1934): 207–10).

[50] Milbank, *The Religious Dimension,* 131. Milbank acknowledges that Vico may have referred to trinitarian theology in *Ancient Wisdom* only "to safeguard himself against charges of heterodoxy for tying God so closely to a world outside himself," but rejects that suggestion.

ad intra shows his surer sense of its radical nature). If creation as a spiritual emanation takes precedence over an external making, if creation *ex nihilo* is reduced to creation *ex Deo*—an "excessive effect of an infinite inner cre-ation"—the primacy of making all desire is lost.

The point at issue in the difference between creation *ex nihilo* and creation *ad intra* is expressed most sharply in Croce's defense of Vico's *verum-factum* against both Balmes and Nominalism. Balmes charges that the Vichian (and Nominalist) position that "intelligence is only possible through causality" actually leads to skepticism, and insists knowledge is a function not of causality but identity, an essential relation between knower and knowable. Thus the word of God was conceived by God's rational knowledge of His ra-tional essence.[51] Though Croce defends Vico's *verum-factum* as a "unique" assertion of convergence, he too identifies convergence with identity. Against Descartes, Croce argues, for whom the object of knowledge is external to the subject, Vico claims certainty is "truly internal certainty, reached by an in-ternal process." The human mind can have certain knowledge of history be-cause it is the creator of history.

Croce does not realize that the principle of identity with which he justifies Vico's "unique" assertion of convergence is the same principle founding the primacy of knowing for scholasticism. The idealist identification of knowing and making, which presumes that both are subjective events, diminishes the unconditioned nature of "causality" as surely as does Johannine, trinitarian, and scholastic theology. Idealism makes that assumption, moreover, for the same purpose as onto-theology. Balmes was right that the priority of causal-ity leads to skepticism; it did for Nominalism and, I argue, it does for Vico, who comes to doubt the possibility of even a delimited "maker's" knowledge and turns, in the last edition of the *New Science,* to a hermeneutic of poetic language. Scholasticism turned away from the danger of skepticism and em-braced a metaphysical principle insuring the possibility of knowledge, even of a created world—a subjective *homoiousis* between knower and knowable. Nineteenth century idealism is even more directly bound to that principle. The epistemology Croce attributes to Vico, to idealism, and to himself is but a variant of all epistemic positions within the tradition.

As for Milbank, he remains so squarely within the Platonic paradigm he struggles to transcend that even his arguments against interpreting Vico's God as an artisan creating *ad extra* derive from it. For him such creativity is the demeaning activity of a craftsman. That creation *ad extra* was an act of a God at one and the same time an artisan creating with his hands and a poet creating with language, that language was *itself* originary and unrelated to *verbum mentis,* never occurs to him. He is surely right that Vico considered making to be linguistic, but the conception of language he attributes to Vico is nothing but the subjectivized, idealized language of philosophy, rather

---

[51] Croce, *The Philosophy of Giambattista Vico,* 282–83.

than the originary language of Genesis.[52] Moreover, his interpretation is undermined by another bias prevalent in the Vico literature, belief in an eidetic continuity between *Ancient Wisdom* and the *New Science*. Most commentators do not appreciate the extent to which the twenty-year struggle to grasp the nature of the first men profoundly transformed Vico's conception of human nature and productivity. When Vico makes an analogy between the making of poets and of God in the *New Science,* the God he invokes is no longer the Neoplatonic or trinitarian God of *Ancient Wisdom*. If there is a model for Vico's divine, poetic creators, it is the poet-God of Hebrew scripture, an "artisan" whose artifacts are, at one and the same time, both linguistic and concrete.

Nineteenth- and Twentieth-Century Humanist Interpretations of Verum-Factum. Though Croce's Hegelian interpretation of Vico has been discredited, it is only one version of idealist interpretations characteristic of Vichian scholarship. Insofar as idealism is identified with the assumption of a *homoiousis* of thought and object, and with the subjectivist anthropology insuring that homogeneity, it characterizes all epistemological interpretations. The equation of human nature with a "thinking" substantively different from or transcendent of linguistic and social practices in-the-world is so "natural" and familiar not even Descartes doubted it; even epistemological skeptics who delimit knowledge in some way—as, for example, to maker's knowledge—assume it. Thus interpretations of Vico's *verum-factum* take for granted the subjective nature of men of the third age and equate the convergence of knowing and making with the recovery of some form of historical knowledge by a knower/subject, retaining, thereby, Croce's idealist concep-

---

[52] The tendency to identify the biblical paradigm of creation with the syncretic version spiritualized by Platonic, Neoplatonic, Philonic, and Johannine influences is most apparent in Milbank's claim that the doctrine of the *logos* was a modification of the "traditional" understanding of divine omniscience in "Judaic, Islamic and Christian thought," which he characterizes as "God's modeling Creation upon his eternal, innate ideas." When innate ideas became identified with the second person of the Trinity, they were no longer "absolutely primordial *as* ideas . . . [but only] . . . in so far as . . . generated or spoken by the Father. . . . The *Logos* as containing the ideas is later spoken of . . . as *Ars.*" (Milbank, *The Religious Dimension,* pt. 1, 121–23). When *Logos* becomes *Ars,* the generation of the word becomes entirely "creation *ad intra* . . . and . . . the finite universe represents a mysterious superabundance or exstatic 'excess' of this activity." Thus creation *ex nihilo* adds nothing: it is an "excessive effect of an infinite inner creation." This is, in effect, the position of theologians such as Aquinas, for whom the Word is the Word of intellect. Milbank's argument rests on faulty genealogy, however, because the position he claims "traditional," that of creation modeled on the priority of innate ideas, *is not Judaic at all,* but the Platonic metaphysical paradigm projected onto Judaic thought in Philo's rewriting of Genesis. Believing it is "relatively easy to combine Hebraic monotheism with the Platonic paradigm," he does not appreciate the radical difference between Judaism and pagan thought. Arising outside Greek metaphysics, Judaism did not conceive of God as spiritual Being in the ontological sense, as subjective substance or essence, nor creation as the mimetic reproduction of innate ideas, nor "knowledge" as the identity of the ideas of a knower/maker and created artifacts. In embracing the absoluteness of causality and the linguistic nature of creation, Judaism never presumed that "knowledge" in the Greek sense was possible, nor did it need the theology of John or of *verbum mentis* to counter metaphysics.

tion of knowledge as an identity of thought and object. This is the case whether thought is considered rational and analytic, or *Verstehen,* or imaginative recollection. Even interpreters who turn from overtly epistemic views to the rhetorical or hermeneutic nature of Vico's new science take for granted the subjective nature of men of the third age.[53] Thus they miss the radical character of Vico's insight into the poetic nature of first men and the genetic relation between men of the first and third ages, the relation constituting the latter as makers rather than knowers. They miss the sense in which "knowing" becomes for Vico an interpretive activity, an immanent *making* by means of social and linguistic practices in-the-world. They miss, that is, the sense in which Vico goes beyond the subjectivist humanism of the West to an uncanny poetic humanism.[54]

While Croce considers Vico the first to grasp the "total immanence of mind in nature," for him immanence translates into nature subjectivized. He admits that Vico, in "terror of pantheism," ultimately "curtailed and repressed" immanence and retained a transcendent providence, but does not doubt that Vico's "love of idealism" was matched by an aversion to materialism. The theory of metaphysical points, the attribute of which was *conatus,* is for Croce "a symbol of the necessity of interpreting nature in idealistic language. We find here and there a theologian Vico, an agnostic Vico . . . but look where we will among his works, we shall never find a materialistic Vico."[55] The "total immanence of mind" that escaped Vico was ultimately achieved, Croce believes: "Almost all the leading doctrines of nineteenth century idealism . . . may be regarded as refluxes of Vician doctrine. . . . [H]e is neither more nor less than the nineteenth century in germ."[56] Croce traces those "refluxes" "in the speculative moment beginning with Kant and Hegel and culminating in the doctrine of the identity of truth and reality, thought and existence," in German philosophy of history. In rejecting "transcendence" and understanding nature as product of mind, philosophy was able to go beyond Vico, to grasp the "concept of progress," and to make "the

---

[53] The rhetorical perspective and the hermeneutic (such as Hans-Georg Gadamer's) attempt to escape from onto-theology. Their implicit critique of subjectivism rarely becomes explicit, however.

[54] Twentieth century writers whom Milbank identifies as holding epistemological interpretations of *verum-factum* include Croce, Berlin, Verene, Gadamer, Betti, Aronovitch, Otto, Viechtbauer, Fellmann, and Pompa (Milbank, *Religious Dimension,* pt. 2, 181–204).

[55] Croce, *The Philosophy of Giambattista Vico,* 139–42. Croce is right to focus on metaphysical points as the most important concept of Vico's cosmology, but wrong in the conclusions he draws from it. He recognizes that the function of metaphysical points is to reconcile mind and matter, making Vico's cosmology and conception of matter dynamic rather than mechanistic, but since he thinks of materialism only as mechanistic, he assumes that a dynamic view of matter is idealist, the immanence of the thought of God. He does not get far enough beyond dualism to see that the "attribute of *conatus*" functions just as much to make matter *itself* dynamic as to infuse it with mind.

[56] Croce gives as examples the aesthetics of Kant, Schelling, and Hegel, the views of language of Herder and Humbolt, and the conception of imagination in romanticism (*Philosophy of Giambattista Vico,* 241–43).

demigod Man into a God."[57] Though for Croce it is Hegel, and for Habermas, Marx, who first succeeds in making man God, both agree on the criteria of that theoretical moment—the convergence of practice and knowledge characterizing both God and the human subject, the freedom of historical action that convergence brings, and the progressive course of history that it insures. And for both Croce and Habermas the conception of man as subject of history secularizes the divinity of a spirit-God.

Idealist interpretations of Vico continued after Croce in the writings of those who consider him precursor of Hamann, Herder, Dilthey, and the *Geisteswissenschaften* of nineteenth century historicism.[58] For Vico and Dilthey, one commentator says, "man in his acting and creating endows cultur[al] objects with his own subjectivity," and concludes, the "'inner-outer' distinction in epistemology . . . allow[ing] Dilthey to reserve the inner domain for the human studies . . . [was] among the ends of Vico's labors."[59] Those who assert such affinities engage in the alchemical or heterogeneous readings Borges describes, as I do with a different set of texts—Vico can be precursor to Dilthey only for readers of Dilthey. What these readers do not do, however, is achieve the "knowing" they claim Vico and Dilthey believe possible, in which "spirit" of creator and interpreter meet. Ironically, even Anglo-American writers who reject Croce's interpretation and attempt to free Vico from idealism—writers as diverse as Sir Isaiah Berlin, Donald Phillip Verene, Leon Pompa, Gino Bedani, Michael Mooney—retain the conceits that bind them to it; that, despite the bestial origins of first men, sense-making presumes a nascent human subjectivity, or that, at least by the third age, humans have developed into subjective beings. Thus, however those writers redefine historical "knowing," it remains "epistemic," based as it is on an identity with the object of knowledge. Even where epistemological goals are explicitly rejected, a subjective *homoiousis* between men of the present and of the past that enables understanding is taken for granted.

These generalizations hold true for Berlin and Verene, despite their efforts

[57] Croce, *Philosophy of Giambattista Vico*, 238, 241.

[58] See R. G. Collingwood, *The Idea of History* (New York: Oxford University Press, 1956), 63–71; Joseph Levine, "Collingwood and Vico," *Vico: Past and Present*, ed. Giorgio Tagliacozzo (Atlantic Highlands: Humanities Press, 1981), vol. 2, 72–84; H. P. Rickman, "Vico and Dilthey's Methodology of the Human Studies," *Giambattista Vico: An International Symposium*, ed. Giorgio Tagliacozzo and Hayden V. White (Baltimore: Johns Hopkins University Press, 1969), 447–56; H. A. Hodges, "Vico and Dilthey," *Giambattista Vico: An International Symposium*, 439–45; Robert Welsh Jordan, "Vico and Husserl: History and Historical Science" *Giambattista Vico's Science of Humanity*, ed. Giorgio Tagliacozzo and Donald Phillip Verene (Baltimore: Johns Hopkins University Press, 1976), 251–61; Enzo Paci, "Vico and Cassirer," *Giambattista Vico: An International Symposium*, 457–73, 461; Donald Phillip Verene, "Vico's Influence on Cassirer," *New Vico Studies*, vol. 3, 1985, 105–11. See also Verene, "Vico's Science of Imaginative Universals and the Philosophy of Symbolic Forms," *Giambattista Vico's Science of Humanity*, 295–317, 311–17; and "Vico's Philosophical Originality," *Vico: Past and Present*, vol. 1, 127–43.

[59] Howard N. Tuttle, "The Epistemological Status of the Cultural World in Vico and Dilthey," *Giambattista Vico's Science of Humanity*, 241–50, 246–48.

to transcend Crocean idealism by substituting imaginative for cognitive activity. Berlin's idealism is explicit in his claims that Vico makes an absolute distinction between inner and outer life, that Vico's great achievement is to add a new form of knowledge to traditional forms—that of self-knowledge, an understanding of the inner life *from the inside*.[60] "This is the doctrine, above others, on which Vico's claim to immortality must rest. For upon it rests that crucial distinction between *Geisteswissenschaft* and *Naturwissenschaft*."[61] Berlin differs from Croce in believing that knowledge as a unity of making and knowing was not new with Vico or nineteenth century German philosophy, but closely related to the ancient distinction between "macro" and "micro" worlds in panpsychism and pantheism, a Platonic and Neoplatonic tradition stretching from Plato's *Symposium* to the Renaissance, stemming "from the ancient . . . doctrine . . . that in the beginning, subject and object, man and nature, sensation and thought, were one."[62] Thus for Berlin the object of knowledge for Vico is not the *certum* embedded in a social context but its inner nature, as subjective and non-material as the mind that converts it to *verum*. This is Vico's dualism, cut differently from Descartes but "no less sharply dualistic."[63] But even this dualism is compromised by Berlin's idealism: he understands *certum* so completely as the product of subjective activity that its materiality and temporality—the "raw concreteness of the *facere*"—are lost.[64] Berlin never appreciates the *corporeal* nature of poetic making; for him, making is always a "perpetual intentional activity" of mind. For this reason he is more interested in the historian's *remaking* than in originary poetic making—so much so he takes it as paradigm of all human making.

Though pantheism or panpsychism could account for recovery of an originary inner life, Berlin believes "historical knowledge does not . . . require such transcendentalist assumptions." Rather, the ability to "mentally live through the creations of others" was for Vico a function of *fantasia*, of "rule-guided imagination." Berlin acknowledges that Vico "nowhere . . . explains the way in which men understand other men," but claims "his interpreters" do, elaborating that understanding as what Dilthey and others call *Verstehen*.[65] *Fantasia*, imaginative understanding, is Berlin's functional equivalent of "transcendentalism," explaining how *verum-factum* insures scientific

[60] Sir Isaiah Berlin, *Vico and Herder: Two Studies in the History of Ideas* (New York: Vintage Books, 1977), 141, 21–22.

[61] Ibid., 67.

[62] Ibid., 14–15, 22, 35. Berlin even goes so far in relating Vico to the most mystical currents of Neoplatonism that he identifies Vico's conception of humans as "divine spark[s]"—so much for the "beastly" origins of humans that Vico struggled so hard to understand (69).

[63] Sir Isaiah Berlin, "A Note on Vico's Concept of Knowledge," *Giambattista Vico: An International Symposium*, 371–77, 372. See also *Vico and Herder*, 121.

[64] Rather than as a concrete institution in the material world Berlin identifies *certum* with its *logical* status—that is, as a "particular" reducible to Platonic universals. See *Vico and Herder*, 111.

[65] *Vico and Herder*, 26–30, 107. See "A Note on Vico's Concept of Knowledge," 375–76.

knowledge. Science is knowledge of *verum*, the *a priori* laws of history *fantasia* recovers from the modes of its development in the microcosm.[66]

Berlin's notion of *fantasia* rests on the subjectivity he takes for granted, insuring a *homoiousis* between humans and the "inner" of the object. One reason Berlin cannot get beyond Platonic idealism is that he does not appreciate the ontological power of linguistic construction. He quotes approvingly Vico's statement "languages create minds (*ingenium*), not minds language"— Vico's "socio-linguistic approach"—but does not grasp its radical nature.[67] In describing how men make themselves with "*fantasia,* which creates myths and rites in which primitive conceptions of the world are acted out," he fears that Vico "comes perilously close to implying—if he does not actually state—that our historical consciousness, *even in our sophisticated, self-conscious, civilized condition,* may be no more than the vision which belongs to the particular stage that we have reached: *itself a kind of myth, the myth of the civilized;* in other words, the view that all history is mythological . . . *something which human imagination creates as a pattern demanded by the needs of practice,* by men's needs to domesticate themselves in the world." But he pulls back from this insight, saying, "This . . . would destroy . . . all distinction between history as a rational discipline and mythical thinking. But Vico, unlike some modern irrationalist thinkers, does not make this move."[68]

Verene shares Berlin's emphasis on imagination, which, he acknowledges, continues the theme of imagination in German idealism, but believes he does so as an *Aufhebung.*[69] The theme developed within the tension between the philosophies of *Geist* and of *Leben,* and Verene believes that Vico offers a way out of the disjunct between them. Vico's philosophy is neither: it begins with "imagination, with *fantasia,* as an original and *independent power of mind.* . . . [I]mages [*universali fantastici*] . . . are themselves manifestations of an original power of spirit which gives fundamental form to mind and

[66] Berlin acknowledges that Vico's belief that knowledge is limited to what men make seems to preclude knowledge of *a priori* laws, and tries hard to explain that conundrum, but, ultimately, sacrifices Vico's claim that humans can know history to maintain belief in a providential *storia ideale eterna.* Given the latter, we do not know the human world "because we have made it. We do, in some sense, make our own cultures, but not the laws which . . . we . . . obey; these are the work of God. . . . [I]t is difficult to see . . . how [*verum*] can be grasped . . . by men. Yet Vico knows it: and knows that he knows it" (*Vico and Herder,* 113–14). Vico does not resolve "[t]he tension between theism and his humanistic historicism," Berlin admits, but Berlin does—for him the former cancels out the latter. For Berlin's interpretation of the role of providence in the *New Science,* see "Vico and the Ideal of the Enlightenment," *Social Research* 43, no. 3 (autumn 1976): 640–53, 653. For my critique of his argument, see Luft, "A Genetic Interpretation of Divine Providence in Vico's *New Science,*" *Journal of the History of Philosophy* 20, no. 2 (April 1982): 151–69.

[67] *Vico and Herder,* 101. The reference is to *De Nostri.*

[68] Ibid., 112. Emphasis added. His "modern irrationalist thinkers" are N. O. Brown, Joyce, Schelling, Nietzsche.

[69] Donald Phillip Verene, *Vico's Science of Imagination* (Ithaca: Cornell University Press, 1981), 10–11.

life."[70] The *universale fantastico,* a "concrete universal" formed by a poetic trope, creates a position "outside Western philosophy," placing image over concept, mythic divination over fact.

Verene transcends Berlin's more overt idealism by relating imaginative activity to the bodily responses of the first men, to the point that "mentality" is "on the border between animals and humans."[71] He vividly describes that border—the perceptual flux that bombards *grossi bestioni,* a sheer immediacy made up of particular sensations existing only in the moment. And, unlike Berlin, he grasps the significance of Vico's insight that language enables the *bestioni* to cross that border. By "fixing" and naming phenomena, the *universale fantastico* creates an identity in the flux, making possible "the operations of the mind." Verene is so successful in capturing the *eventfulness* of metaphoric language, its ontological power, that I draw on his account in chapter 3 in my interpretation of the non-subjectivist nature of that language. But he is not content merely to attribute to Vico a "theory of poetic mind." Though he condemns the epistemological nature of philosophy, his condemnation is limited to its *conceptual* foundation. For him, the *universale fantastico* is not only a "theory of poetic mind" but also, as the imagistic basis of "recollective *fantasia,*" a means of recovering original poetic *fantasia* through memory, the form of knowledge possible in the third age.

Recollective *fantasia* is "the basis of philosophical thought rather than reflection and speculation," its epistemic nature secured by its correspondence to original *fantasia.*[72] "Recollective *fantasia* contains in itself elements that reflect in a one-to-one fashion the elements in the memory structure of original or mythic *fantasia.* It is the result of basing reflective thought on the image."[73] The relation between the *universale fantastico* and recollective *fantasia* is Verene's version of the principle of identity grounding the possibility of knowledge for idealism. Though insisting on Vico's originality, his understanding of that "originality" does no more than substitute an imaginative for a cognitive *homoiousis.* His interpretation of recollective *fantasia* necessarily assumes *homoiousis,* though *homoiousis* in turn assumes the subjectivity of subject and object of knowledge. Only that assumption enables *verum-factum* to retain its *epistemic* function in recovering and remaking original making.[74] For Verene *verum-factum* asserts that metaphysical in-

---

[70] Ibid., 30–33. Emphasis added.

[71] Ibid., 71, 80–81.

[72] Ibid., 102. See 155 n. 72, in which Verene distinguishes his theory of recollection from Pompa's emphasis on reflection. Verene acknowledges the similarity of their views, but distinguishes them because for Pompa reflection is cognitive and does not originate in the image.

[73] As the form that the original collective activity of poetic imagination takes is the imaginative universal, the first of which is Jove, so the form of recollective activity based on memory is a recollective imaginative universal, the master universal of which is the *storia ideale eterna,* the form of history in the *New Science* (99–108).

[74] In arguing for that epistemic function, Verene refers to Fisch's identification of Vico's *verum-factum* principle with the medieval metaphysical principle of transcendentals, in which

telligibility, "the true in metaphysics, is itself something made. This making involves the recovery of the original forms of human wisdom, of the ancient apprehension of the real."[75] For him, as for Berlin, the made convertible with the true is not the original ontological *factum,* but a "truth" *re*made by philosopher-historians.[76] Verene's consciousness of the radical nature of the move he attributes to Vico, a move beyond a cognitively based epistemic tradition, obscures for him the fact that it does not take Vico out of the subjectivism and idealism that make epistemology possible. Verene's devaluation of original making is even stronger in a later article, in which he goes beyond denying that original poetic making converts with the true, to deny that making takes place *at all,* offering instead "the sense in which, in Vico's view, history and the true are not made."[77] Verene's inability to capture what is truly alien in Vico's philosophy, to escape the influence of German idealism, reveals the dilemma of Vico scholarship in general, caught as it is in the subjectivist anthropology and epistemological preoccupations of the moderns. Verene sets his sights too narrowly—against the cognitive character of epistemology, rather than against epistemology itself.[78]

---

verum means the "intelligible" of the object. As such, it is the "principle of metaphysical knowledge itself which issues from the *sensus communis* as present in an ancient mentality, from the *archai* or first human understandings upon which any subsequent reasoning about the nature of things is based" (*Vico's Science of Imagination,* 45–46). Verene says he follows Grassi in identifying those *archai* as "original forms of speech."

[75] Ibid., 51.

[76] Verene acknowledges the relation of this remaking to an *original* making of *universale fantastico,* the "mind's activity as giving form to experience," a "way of making intelligibility" (71). But this original "way" is not convertible with the true until remade in historical narratives.

[77] Donald Phillip Verene, "Imaginative Universals and Narrative Truth," *New Vico Studies,* vol. 6 (1988): 1–19, 3, 6. "The science of the civil world," Verene insists, "not only imitates the divine in its act of converting the true and the made, but the principles of humanity are not made but must in some sense be *found* because they express what a human is, and humans are made by God" (9–10). Verene supports this later position with a puzzling argument based on Fisch's distinction between *scienza,* knowledge of the true, and *coscienza,* knowledge of the certain (Fisch, "Vico and Pragmatism," 412), concluding that "Vico's conception of the true is the made is not a free-floating principle through which humans make their history," but a science that requires *coscienza* "of divine making that grounds the principle of human making or science" (17). This is a theological mystification of Verene's earlier secular epistemological interpretation of *verum-factum,* reducing the principle to a *mimetic remaking* of divine truth and turning *coscienza* into a spiritualized "witnessing." Even more, Verene cannot derive support from Fisch to identify *factum* solely with narrative making and deny that the historical world is made. Though Fisch does say the new science is not a making but "a *re*-making, a *re*-construction," he insists "the new science takes place in the world of sciences, which is part of the world of nations, and so the remaking not only represents but continues and is part of the *first* making, and *partakes of its reality*" (emphasis added). Moreover, for Vico in *Ancient Wisdom,* Fisch adds, "God made realities, and man, in his most Godlike making made only fictions [whereas i]n the *New Science* man in his most Godlike making makes realities." Thus "science itself is true or intelligible only as made along with the making of the world of nations, and the history of science is therefore the science of it" ("Vico and Pragmatism," 413).

[78] Though he acknowledges he has been "especially affected" by Kant's *Critique of Judgement,* Hegel's *Phenomenology of Spirit,* and Cassirer's *Philosophy of Symbolic Forms,* Verene believes he "allow[s] Vico's ideas to speak for themselves" (Verene, *Vico's Science of Imagination,* 9). He does not realize the extent to which the idealism of his three authors permeates his

In chapter 3 I return to Verene's interpretation to argue that he gives us a conception of radical linguistic *making* that his own idealist conceits prevent him from appreciating as such. Vico's philosophy is not epistemology as *recollective fantasia* but an ontological hermeneutic, in which his first men are poets—creators—who make the human social world, the form of the human body. Indeed, eventually they make human subjectivity itself with their constructed abstract language and the social practices and institutions that language enables—an artifactual subjectivity that the conceits of the moderns reify as "mind." In Vico's ontological hermeneutic the made is never an object of knowledge in any epistemic sense; the "recovery of poetic wisdom" Verene calls recollective *fantasia* is not a knowing as remaking but *itself an originary making.* The poetic makers of the third age do not, of course, make as do the poets of the first, who believe in the reality of what they make. But, like the making of the first age, the making of the third is linguistic, taking place in the abstract languages that poets and heroes themselves had made by the end of the heroic age. The making of philosopher-historians, enabled by the pedagogic practices that strengthen their skills of perception, memory, and imagination in the third age, takes place in narratives such as the *New Science.* Narrative making is ironic, of course, suffused with the hermeneutic self-understanding that it is man's nature to be a maker, that linguistically made realities are always fictive, though no less true for being so.

The inability to get beyond the humanist metaphysical assumptions that render all epistemologies idealist characterizes even those who believe that Vico's conception of scientific knowing fits the "hard" criteria of natural science or analytic philosophy. When Ernan McMullin asks, "In what sense *was* [the *New Science*] a science?" he insists "the intention of the work . . . [is] to discover the 'universal and eternal principles' of all nations." Because Vico makes that claim "in the strongest sense possible," McMullin dismisses those who "challenge" it on behalf of rhetoric and poetry.[79] Acknowledging that Vico identifies his first men as poets, he insists what made imaginative universals poetry, "was not just . . . feeling and imagination . . . nor the leaps of metaphor," but "an 'eternal property' of poetry that its material should 'be the credible impossibility': the poet by his art makes the impossible appear 'credible'. . . . The contrast between science and poetry is here quite sharp. The first men were poets, not scientists. . . . [Vico's science, on the other hand] will be reflective, analytic, methodologically self-conscious; in other

---

work and grounds his notion of recollective imagination. Grassi, whom Verene credits with pointing him toward the concreteness of rhetorical language, is more successful in achieving concreteness. Drawing more on Heidegger's existential ontology and Marx's emphasis on labor than the tradition of *Geist,* he does not begin with mind but embodied being, and, thus, material necessity, social practice, physical labor.

[79] Ernan McMullin, "Vico's Theory of Science," *Social Research* 43, no. 3 (autumn 1976): 450–80, 451, 453, 457. He refers specifically to Angus Fletcher's "What Vico Suggests to the Aesthetician of our Time."

The Familiar | 45

words . . . typical of the rational products of the age of men."⁸⁰ The contrast
between science and poetry is not as sharp as McMullin believes, however,
since he does not take into account the genetic relation between poetic and
"rational" men. The same problem mars other writings identifying Vico's
new science with the "typical rational products of the age of men," the most
extensive of which is Leon Pompa's. Even more fatal to the epistemic claims
of scientistic interpretations is that, though McMullin, Pompa, and others
sharply distinguish their interpretations from the idealism of Hegel, Croce,
Berlin, and Verene, they share the same subjectivist assumptions that make
epistemology and methodology inherently idealist.

Claiming that Vico's new science is adequate to the epistemological and
methodological criteria of the social sciences, Pompa derives the measure of
its adequacy from analytic philosophy. In doing so, Hayden White observes,
Pompa reduces the *New Science* to a univocal, self-consistent, systematic science, in which Vico becomes "a proponent of a Cartesian *esprit de géome-
trie,* a precursor of modern, positivistic social science, and . . . a secret—even
if unknowing—rationalist and social scientist before the fact."⁸¹ I agree, but
what particularly interests me are the idealist assumptions *implicit* in the interpretation Pompa puts forward against *overtly* idealist positions, primarily the assumption of human subjectivity. That assumption enables Pompa
to solve the *aporia* he sees at the heart of Vico's project, Vico's appeal "to
some point of identity between man as historical agent and man as historian
as a ground for the possibility of historical knowledge." Pompa claims that
appeal is problematic since "the historical agent is the maker of events and
institutions . . . [the] *res gestae* . . . whereas the historian is the maker of the
history of those events and institutions." Thus, the "principles of [the *res gestae*] can be recovered from the mind of the historian . . . but not from the
minds of the agents who made it."⁸²

Pompa's solution to this *aporia,* that of the relation between the agents of
the ontological making of history and the subjects of epistemological *re*-
making, presumes the traditional philosophic belief that what insures knowledge is a subjective *homoiousis* between knower and known. Ironically,
despite the vigor with which Pompa rejects idealist interpretations of Vico,
he does not perceive the idealism inherent in that epistemological assumption. For him "the historian can reconstruct the changing ways in which men
have seen their world in the past only if he can know what they were *really*
thinking about." He does not consider that identifying what historian and

⁸⁰ McMullin, "Vico's Theory of Science," 454–55. The phrase "credible impossibility" appears in the *New Science,* 383.
⁸¹ Hayden V. White, "Vico: A Study of the *New Science,*" *History and Theory* 15, no. 2
(1976): 186–201, 188.
⁸² Leon Pompa, *Vico: A Study of the 'New Science'* (London: Cambridge University Press,
1975), 158–62; and *Vico: Selected Writings,* ed. and trans. Leon Pompa (Cambridge: Cambridge University Press, 1982), 25–26. See also his "Human Nature and the Concept of a Human Science," *Social Research* 43, no. 3 (autumn 1976): 434–44.

agents have in common as *thought,* that identifying not only knowing but also making as the activity of mind, is idealist, since he identifies "idealism" with the Crocean/Hegelian belief in a transcendent causal agency identical with Objective Reason or *a priori* historical laws.[83]

Since for Pompa the metaphysical ground enabling the scientific historian to know the mind of historical agents is not only subjective or mental, but also conceptual, historical study is "reflective": "[R]*eflection* is therefore the crux of Vico's later theory of knowledge. . . . [B]y self-conscious reflection upon our own ways of seeing our world and our own attitudes to it, we can . . . see . . . how . . . rational thought . . . is a genetic modification of other modes of thought based upon certain natural propensities."[84] Pompa responds to criticism that this interpretation ignores the role of imagination in Vico by referring to Vico's claim "we cannot at all imagine" those wild and savage natures but "can understand" them "with great effort," and privileges the epistemological significance of understanding over imagination. Insofar as the historian *understands* what it is to imagine, he can understand what it means that first men imagine the sky as Jove even if he cannot enter into or recollectively recover that act himself.[85]

Even more important than Pompa's rejection of the epistemic significance of imagination is his denial of its ontological power to make a real world convertible with the true. Quoting Vico—"It is impossible that bodies be minds, yet it was believed that the thundering sky was Jove"—he asks, how could "poetic man . . . imagine and believe in a false world," how could poetic man produce "a world-view . . . entirely false and . . . described by Vico as 'impossible'?"[86] Imagination may constitute the content of a belief but not its referent, which must be the objective reality known by the scientific historian.[87] Only by knowing "the frequent occurrence of floods, thunder and lightning" can the historian know the role imagination played in the con-

[83] Leon Pompa, "Vico and the Presuppositions of Historical Knowledge," *Science of Humanity,* ed. Giorgio Tagliacozzo and Donald Phillip Verene (Baltimore: Johns Hopkins University Press, 1976), 125–40, 135. Pompa's idealism is manifest in two later essays. In one he rejects Hume's empirical claim that "ontological primacy belongs to our experiences," because "social relationships presuppose ideas and . . . changes in the institutional frameworks . . . presuppose changes in human conceptual schemes" (Leon Pompa, "Vico and Hegel: A Critical Assessment of Their Accounts of the Role of Ideas in History," *Vico: Past and Present,* ed. Giorgio Tagliacozzo (Atlantic Highlands: Humanities Press, 1981), vol. 2, 35–46, 35–36). Similarly, he argues that Vico was more successful in "understanding . . . the ways in which ideas change" than Marx because of two "idealist" elements missing in Marx but present in Vico—a *homoiousis* between historian and agent, inherent in the notion of the "modifications of the human mind," and a "coherent and continuous account of the development of those same modifications" between agent and historian (Pompa, "Ontological and Historiographical Construction in Vico and Marx," *Vico and Marx: Affinities and Contrasts,* ed. Giorgio Tagliacozzo (Atlantic Highlands: Humanities Press, 1983), 62–77, 77, and n. 24).

[84] Pompa, *Vico,* 166–68; "Imagination in Vico," *Vico: Past and Present,* vol. 1, 162–70, 169–70; "Vico and the Presuppositions of Historical Knowledge," 136–37.

[85] Pompa, "Imagination in Vico," 164–65, 169. The reference to Vico is 338.

[86] Ibid., 168–69. Pompa's example from the *New Science* is 383.

[87] Ibid., 162 n. 1.

struction of Jove, Pompa argues, thus emptying poetic activity of the *onto-logical* significance Vico attributes to it—the claim that the human world is artifactual and made by imagination.[88]

Pompa's belief that the scientific historian can bring the "certain truths" of an objective world to bear on the poetic is, however, precisely what *verum-factum* denies. His distinction between real and false worlds is no more than the belief he shares with metaphysics that the real is ontologically given, un-changeable, intelligible, that the nonessential—the products of *poiesis* no less than dreams and the delusions of madmen—is "false." Even Berlin shares that belief. Yet the "objective reality" to which poetic making is a re-sponse is not an intelligible cosmos but an abyss that must be ordered by the existential choices of embodied beings. Those choices, which satisfy "needs and utilities," are limited only by natural necessity. The imaginative univer-sal "Jove" fits that criterion, since it occasions the social institutions of reli-gion, marriage, and burial that enable *grossi bestioni* to survive, albeit in a "human" manner not envisioned by them. The artifactual social world thus produced is not *false,* but *the only real world* in which humans can live, its truth the *poetic* truth that only fear aroused by a Jove-like being and limit-ing beastly passions makes human life possible. The proper material of po-etry may be the "credible impossibility"—the beliefs, for example, that "bodies should be minds" or the thundering sky Jove—but without those beliefs there can be no "real" human world.[89]

Though Pompa's rejection of the epistemic capability of imagination puts him at odds with Berlin and Verene, the three have more in common than any acknowledges. For all, making is an epistemological process rather than the ontological construction of a real social world of concrete social institu-tions. Indeed, in different ways all qualify the sense in which Vico's new sci-ence is constructive at all.[90] Berlin's sharp distinction between history as "mythic thinking" and "rational discipline," McMullin's and Pompa's be-tween poetic sense-making and scientific rationality, cannot be made: if "the nature of institutions is nothing but their coming into being at certain times

[88] Pompa, "Vico and the Presuppositions of Historical Knowledge," 132–35. Vico "pre-supposes the historian's right to introduce certain truths," from "his own conceptual scheme" because he wants to tell us "not only how poetic man conceived his world . . . but also *what his world really was*" (emphasis added). See note 117 for Struever's more poetic "re-situation" of "reference" for Vico.

[89] Vico, *New Science,* 383.

[90] For his part, Pompa claims Vico conflates a creative theory of knowledge with a causal theory of truth; that is, with "'knowing the causes of' and 'knowing by virtue of causing'" (*Vico,* 81). Pompa measures the validity of the latter by the former and finds Vico's constructive new science inadequate. But this is simply not to understand, or to understand and reject, the onto-logical nature of *poetic* science. And indeed, at the end of his book Pompa drops the other shoe, concluding "in the *Scienza Nuova* for the first time Vico finds the purely conventional aspect of mathematics a limitation . . . [and suggests] this limitation be transcended by an appeal to some knowledge derived from 'within the modifications of our own human mind.' It is at pre-cisely this point . . . the theory of knowledge of the *Scienza Nuova* departs from the purely con-ventional theory of the *De Antiquissima*" (157 n. 2).

and in certain guises," "knowing," too, must be genetic.[91] Since the poetic origin of knowledge is the practice of "divination," the interpretation of the language of God the poets read in the sky, the sense-making genetically derived from it can only be a hermeneutic interpretation of linguistic and social practices by "divining" philosopher-historians. The subjective men of the third age—made so in an onto-genetic poetic process—*remain* makers rather than knowers, just as human making and knowing *remain* activities taking place in linguistic and social practices. It is because poetic making is *ontological*—the making of real true *things*—that Vico can call the knowing convertible with it "divine."[92]

The assumption that imaginative or scientific historians can know historical agents depends on a subjective (for some even conceptual) *homoiousis* between them. That assumption is fundamental, though not always stated explicitly, in *all* epistemological interpretations of *verum-factum*.[93] The idealism of epistemological interpretations of *verum-factum* brings to the fore the problematic anthropology on which it rests, the anthropology that accounts for modernity's misunderstanding of the ancient Hellenistic principle of making. The historical and theoretical developments that preceded that misunderstanding began with Nominalism's skepticism concerning the possibility of knowledge, and the age's search for a ground of certain knowledge. While Vico's critique of Descartes's response to that crisis came out of his traditional humanist reaction to the dangers in identifying knowledge with abstract rationality, it was also fueled by his radically new understanding of the anthropological implications of that epistemology—the identification of man as an essentially subjective being, a subject cut off from social existence. Even in his early writings, when Vico himself was concerned with insuring the attainment of knowledge, he insisted against Descartes that philosophy cannot determine the nature of knowledge independent of the onto-genetic condition of humans. In the context of Vico's insight into the embodied and poetic nature of first men and the linguistic construction of the human world,

---

[91] Vico, *New Science*, 147.

[92] Pompa notes Vico's frequent comparison between the human knowing made possible by his science, and God's knowledge, but distinguishes between them, since God "is the ultimate cause of actual natural phenomena," while the historian produces mere accounts of creative activity" (*Vico*, 168–69). If, however, Pompa had understood ontological making *poetically*, as a concrete, linguistic process rather than a subjective, conceptual one, he would have appreciated the analogy. Both God and poets create real worlds with language, differing only in that God creates the matter of his created world, while poets create the human world out of existing matter.

[93] With the exception of naturalistic ones. While naturalists too are committed to the possibility of knowledge in which ideas in some sense correspond to an objectively given world, they do not justify that epistemology on the basis of a subjective *homoiousis*. Naturalistic interpretations cannot account for a poetic science, however, since they reduce language to material processes. Vico enriched and transformed the naturalism he inherited from Epicurus, not with an insight into the *material* world, about which men could know nothing, but with an *anthropological* insight into the poetic nature of beings. For a naturalistic interpretation, see Gino Bedani, *Vico Revisited: Orthodoxy, Naturalism and Science in the Scienza Nuova* (Oxford: Berg, 1989), chap. 18, 255–74.

it is anachronistic to reduce the *verum-factum* principle implicit in the *New Science* to the epistemological preoccupations of a post-Cartesian tradition.[94] Vico responded to the Cartesian turn in philosophy not by formulating an alternate epistemology, but by returning to what had been forgotten in Descartes's radical doubt, the ontological condition of embodied beings and the social nature of their world.

Modernist Interpretations of Vico and the Rhetorical Tradition

In reacting against the idealist and epistemic interpretations of philosophy, some Vico scholars identify Vico's writings with the rhetorical tradition.[95] Certainly Vico's professional interests as professor of rhetoric and the pedagogical and jurisprudential concerns of his early and middle writings grew out of his lifelong engagement with theories of rhetoric, with its holistic conception of human nature and understanding of the significance of language in social existence. Acutely aware of philosophy's tendency to "forget" the material, social, and linguistic conditions of human existence, he consciously situated the *New Science* in the presumed antithesis between philosophy and philology, insisting knowledge begins with the study of things "of which human choice is author, . . . language, and deeds of people, . . . their customs and laws." His science would give "certainty to the[] reasonings [of philosophers] by appeal to the authority of the philologians," and authority "the sanction of truth by appeal to the reasoning of the philosophers."[96] Yet Vico characterized his major work not only as *scienza,* in yielding knowledge of causes, but also as *nuova,* in identifying causal knowledge with knowledge of *facta,* the *certa* of history. In turning to rhetorical interpretations of Vico I ask, is the "newness" of Vico's new, causal science of the made accounted for wholly by the familiar conceits of the rhetorical tradition?

[94] Or to its subjectivism. As Nikhil Bhattacharya points out, Pompa and McMullin err in "viewing Vico's philosophy of science from the historical perspectives that have grown out of Descartes," and Bhattacharya questions "what justification there is for believing a statement about human history. . . . is asking for the grounds within our consciousness for accepting or rejecting a belief, which is what Descartes taught us to ask. . . . Vico's theory of science . . . is not based, like Descartes', on an examination of the contents of our consciousness" (Nikhil Bhattacharya, "Knowledge '*Per Caussas*': Vico's Theory of Natural Science," *Vico: Past and Present,* ed. Giorgio Tagliacozzo (Atlantic Highlands: Humanities Press, 1981), vol. 1, 182–97, 184 n. 8.
[95] See 69 n. 80 in Michael Mooney's *Vico in the Tradition of Rhetoric* (New Jersey: Princeton University Press, 1985) for a good bibliography. Since Mooney's book was published John D. Schaeffer's *Sensus Communis: Vico, Rhetoric, and the Limits of Relativism* (Durham: Duke University Press, 1990) has appeared. Mooney does not include Ernesto Grassi's works, grounded as much in rhetoric as philosophy. See especially Grassi, *Heidegger and the Question of Renaissance Humanism: Four Studies* (Binghamton: Center for Medieval and Early Renaissance Studies, 1983); *Rhetoric as Philosophy: The Humanist Tradition* (University Park: Pennsylvania State University Press, 1980); *Vico and Humanism: Essays on Vico, Heidegger, and Rhetoric,* Emory Vico Studies, vol. 3 (New York: Peter Lang, 1990).
[96] Vico, *New Science,* 138–40.

In *Vico in the Tradition of Rhetoric,* Michael Mooney makes a strong case both for Vico's relation to the rhetorical tradition, and for his originality. Deriding Croce's idealist epistemological interpretation of Vico and the "disproportionate" importance he gives to *verum-factum,* Mooney considers the principle mere "corollary to [Vico's] early rhetorical and pedagogical writings."[97] Mooney finds in Vico a strong sense of the poetic, "effective" nature of language, of its constitutive power, and the holistic nature of humans and the social world it produces: if there is a "deepest truth" in the *New Science,* it is "that language, mind and society are but three modes of a common reality."[98] In effect "mind" is for Vico "ingenuity," a faculty of insight "proper to know[ledge]" yet distinguished from intellect by "bring[ing] together and relat[ing] . . . things which . . . seem to have no connection." Ingenuity accounts for the first *universale fantastico,* Jove, a metaphoric image, the logic of which derives from rhetorical theories of the *topos.* The "rise of mind reveals itself as a process of naming . . . a poetic construction,"[99] an understanding Mooney claims Vico draws wholly from Aristotle's conception of metaphor, from Cicero's of *sententia,* and from Quintilian.

Mooney's discussion supports the view that it is in the rhetorical tradition (and, I argue, the rabbinic) that a holistic conception of human nature and of social and historical existence emerges in the West. While philosophy transcends anthropological dualism only by reducing the sum of human characteristics to an idealist or a materialist substance, leaving unquestioned the assumptions grounding a metaphysics of substance, rhetoric conceives the difference between natural and human worlds *functionally,* the human a function of the linguistic and social practices producing it. Even so, I do not believe that the rhetorical tradition can account for what is new and original in Vico's new science, the radically ontological sense in which Vico claims that his first men—who are not human, but embodied beasts—are "poets."[100] While Mooney is right that *verum-factum* is not an epistemological principle, it is more than mere "corollary of [Vico's] early rhetorical and pedagogic writings." Though the rhetorical tradition may be free of the assumption of ontological dualism, contemporary writers such as Mooney

---

[97] Mooney, *Vico in the Tradition of Rhetoric,* 153 n. 116.

[98] Ibid., ix.

[99] Ibid., 230–31. For his argument Mooney draws on the tropological pattern of history described by Hayden White, for whom "the development of consciousness from metaphorical identification to metonymic reduction to synechdochic construction to ironic statement is strictly analogous to transformations in social structure. . . . Vico's dialectic . . . is not that of the syllogism . . . but of 'the exchange between language on the one side and the reality it seeks to contain on the other'" (Hayden White, "The Tropics of History, The Deep Structure of the *New Science,*" *Giambattista Vico's Science of Humanity,* ed. Giorgio Tagliacozzo and Donald Phillip Verene [Baltimore: Johns Hopkins University Press, 1976], 77).

[100] Not even the Epicurean view of origins to which Vico was drawn in his youth and which, I believe, remained important to him throughout his life could account for a holistic, poetic conception of human nature. Epicurus's view was essentially a metaphysical materialism within which language was a literal labeling of perceptual objects.

who interpret Vico in terms of rhetorical notions are still modern thinkers who retain the familiar assumption that humans, even at the first stage of human development, are subjective beings. Thus these writers do not capture the more radical sense in which Vico raises the question of origins, or the ontologically originary nature of his new science of *poiesis*.

Mooney himself asks in what sense Vico claimed that his thought was new, given that he "was so literate, so read, so drunk with tradition," and responds that Vico was more comprehensive in pulling together traditional insights, more novel in breaking the "'conceit' of nations and scholars" with his understanding that "Mind does not precede language, but arises with it." Yet Mooney's emphasis on the comprehensiveness of Vico's new science hampers Mooney's ability to appreciate its originality. In emphasizing Vico's ties to the rhetorical tradition, for example, Mooney says, "Almost alone among Vico's concepts that of ingenuity appears in his work with utter consistency, maintaining its essential meaning throughout the sundry applications it receives." Thus the poetic insight that Vico said cost him the labor of twenty years Mooney attributes to a "blaze of ingenuity" in which he "*recalled* the logic of discourse he had been maintaining for years in his lectures and pedagogical orations . . . *recalled* Cicero's view that metaphors and tropes are necessary to life . . . since, as Aristotle had held . . . *there are more things in the world than there are words* . . . *remembered* the line from Aristotle's . . . *Poetics* . . . that poetic statements . . . have the nature of universals. . . . Not philosophy or human wisdom, but *poetic* wisdom," Mooney concludes, "was the wisdom of the ancients."[101]

Mooney finds the first occurrence of this "blazing insight" into the tropological nature of language in an early work of Vico's, the *Institutiones oratoriae*. Yet what was it about that insight that blazed more brightly after "the labors of a good twenty years" than in 1711? Mooney never really identifies that difference, but Vico himself tells us. He claims the labors leading to the later insight were arduous because "[we had] to descend from these human and refined natures of ours to those quite wild and savage natures, which we cannot at all imagine and can comprehend only with great effort."[102] What Vico realizes in that twenty-year struggle is that language is tropological *not only* because "There are more things in the world than there are words" (Aristotle) or because "Language . . . is part of the indigence of our race. . . . [T]ropes and figures . . . aris[e] from the poverty of our language" (Cicero),[103] but also because the fathers of the race *were not human but beasts without language or social existence*. Vico's blazing insight was not only linguistic, but also *anthropological;* the first language was poetic because the first "men" were embodied beasts, and the language of which they were ca-

---

[101] Mooney, *Vico in the Tradition of Rhetoric,* 255, 258–62, 150, 207–8. Emphasis added.
[102] Vico, *New Science,* 338.
[103] Mooney, *Vico in the Tradition of Rhetoric,* 79.

pable, and their *ingenium,* were derived from skills of the body. The beasts were poets, "creators," because with their bodily skills they brought together perceptions that did not belong together, forming tropes that created an artifactual human reality, their very human nature. The tropological structure of their ingenious language was far more originary than conceived by rhetoric, at least by Aristotle and Cicero, because it *had to be ontological;* it had to bring into existence a reality that did not exist. Aristotle was in fact *wrong:* there are not *more* things in the world than there are words, *there are no things until there are words.* Cicero too was wrong: the language that creates a human world is *not impoverished, but fecund.*

Because Mooney reduces Vico's "blazing insight" to a compilation of ideas from others, he does not grasp the radical originality of Vico's conception of *ontological* creativity. He asks, "What can it mean . . . to reason with a mind . . . immersed in the senses?" and answers, "It means to reason as a rhetor must reason when speaking *inter rudes,* arguing among the simple who cannot take in a complicated argument."[104] Since he believes that Vico's poetic conception of *ingenium* is the same as he held in 1711, he considers the difference between humans and Vico's first men no greater than the difference between the rhetor or sage and the "simple." As "crude, dim, violent, bodily" as the *bestioni* are, they are not really "strange and unfamiliar": they respond, after all, to oratory. They are as human as *rudes* or *stulti,* as the "fools" of Machiavelli, Bovillus, and Bodin,[105] or as the "fallen souls of Augustine," whose humanity, though diminished by postlapsarian wandering, exists buried in their bestial bodies. Similarly, in 1710 Vico had understood *ingenium* as "the faculty by which we grasp similarities," a notion that goes back to Horace, and draws on that understanding in the *New Science.* Thus, "When the thunder sounded in the heavens . . . [t]he *recognition* in the sky of their bodily actions led to a transfer of these images and thereby to the creation of Jove . . . [a] *transfer of meaning . . . through the 'ingenious' discovery of relationships heretofore unnoticed . . .* and so made the *rudes see the truth that bound them together.*"[106] Yet, if Vico is drawing more on Lucretius than on scripture, if he is describing a more radically originary event than merely a diminution, then recovery, of an essential human condition—if he assumes, that is, an *original bestial existence*—then rhetoric's act of "seeing similarities" is not strange enough to convey Vico's sense of poetic ingenuity. The creation of Jove is a more consequential event, a violent projection of totally *dissimilar* perceptions—the first sound of thunder and flash of lightning, the shaking and grumbling of bestial bodies, the experience of fear—onto a blank expanse of sky. That the violence of the storm was heard as an "*argument,*" that the event of thunder enabled the beasts to "*see the truth that*

---

104 Ibid., 226–27.
105 Ibid., 126.
106 Ibid., 210–14, 222, 229. Emphasis added.

bound them together," that their response was a *"recognition"* of what nature *argued* attributes far more humanity to the beasts—and more inherent meaning to violent and disjunctive natural occurrences—than does Vico.[107]

A similar domestication of Vico's poetic insight effects John Schaeffer's otherwise excellent *Sensus Communis: Vico, Rhetoric, and the Limits of Relativism.* Influenced by both Mooney and Grassi, Schaeffer differs in identifying *"sensus communis* as the concept that concretely relates Vico's thinking to the rhetorical tradition," and in interpreting it "as an essentially oral concept."[108] Schaeffer importantly stresses the intimate relation between language and *sensus communis,* not only in the ages of gods and heroes but also of men, saying, "[E]ven the abstract language of law and philosophy derived from metaphors that reflect the primal, community-founding judgments of the first men." For Schaeffer the whole of human development emerges from the productive force of an oral, practical, communal language inseparable from *sensus communis,* a relation that constitutes the ethical consensus of each age and provides the nexus for Vico's synthesis of philosophy and rhetoric. Not only are the rationalist and formalist ethical theories of traditional philosophy irrelevant to those practical needs, but Schaeffer also believes that Vico's insight into the practical, oral, social nature of ethics inherent in *sensus communis* can moderate the relativism of such contemporary views as Gadamerean hermeneutic and Derridean deconstruction.[109]

Yet, despite Schaeffer's perceptive reading of Vico, he, like Mooney, ultimately reduces the poetic insights of the *New Science* that Vico claims took twenty years to grasp to the rhetorical ones of *Study Methods* and *Institutiones oratoriae.*[110] For him the oral, topical metaphors of the *New Science*

---

[107] Critical of Mooney's placement of Vico in the "good" tradition of Plato, Aristotle, Cicero, and Renaissance civic humanism—a "patent but thin humanistic idealogy"—Struever stresses Vico's relation to the "bad," stretching from the sophists through Quintilian to Valla and Machiavelli (and ultimately Nietzsche) (Nancy S. Struever, "Rhetoric and Philosophy in Vichian Inquiry," *New Vico Studies,* vol. 3 [1985]: 131–45, 133). "Vico does not simply add pieces of Aristotle," but *"denies* Aristotelian poetics . . . [and] theory of language," just as he does not continue the tradition of Renaissance civic humanism but *replaces* it (138). "[W]ithout being too Derridian or DeManian," she says, "it is necessary to recognize the strongly focused, subversive, indeed, self-subversive aspects of rhetorically controlled inquiry." Such inquiry has a pessimistic and skeptical edge: Vico's "etiology of social action" is a "tissue of unintended results, deceptions and self-deceptions, and discursive interstices, [which] subverts the premise of voluntarism" or faith in "simple moral therapies" (136, 138–39). See also Hayden White's critical review of *Vico in the Tradition of Rhetoric* in *Eighteenth Century Studies* 22, no. 2 (winter 1988–89): 219–22.

[108] Schaeffer, *Sensus Communis,* 5, 7. See also John Schaeffer, "The Use and Misuse of Giambattista Vico: Rhetoric, Orality, and Theories of Discourse," *The New Historicism,* ed. H. Aram Veeser (New York: Routledge, 1989), 89–101.

[109] In particularly interesting chapters Schaeffer examines the relevance of Vico's view of language and *sensus communis* to Hans-Georg Gadamer's hermeneutic and Jacques Derrida's deconstruction. See also Schaeffer, *"Sensus Communis* in Vico and Gadamer," *New Vico Studies* (1987): 117–30. Schaeffer believes the communal nature of *sensus communis* avoids the ethical relativism resulting from both Derrida and Gadamer.

[110] See John Schaeffer, "The Use and Misuse of Giambattista Vico," 97.

are rhetorical arguments, *enthymemes,* syllogisms whose major premises are probable, and whose connections (*ligamens*), rest on the perception of *similarities.*[111] His interpretation is further weakened by the modernist "conceit" that shows up as he goes beyond his emphasis on the ethical nature of Vico's conception of *sensus communis* to insist on its epistemological function. He believes that Vico's response to Descartes explicates an epistemology *implicit* in rhetoric, the key to which is *sensus communis,* an "affective, pre-reflective and somatic quality of language . . . mak[ing] eloquence possible. With *sensus communis* as an epistemological base, Vico explores the critical and hermeneutic possibilities latent in the rhetorical tradition."[112] Believing that ethics must be grounded in philosophy or theory, that philosophy is primarily epistemology, Schaeffer does not realize that both Vico and he have gone *beyond* the belief that ethics *must* have an epistemological base. The "affective, pre-reflective and somatic" qualities of *sensus communis* that he characterizes as "epistemological" are exactly the qualities of rhetorical and poetic language that forced Plato to turn away from it, to ground knowledge on method and to posit a subjective human soul to insure a *homoiousis* between thought and intelligible reality. Schaeffer's insistence that rhetoric be epistemic obscures those differences between philosophy and rhetoric that make the latter more desirable for him (and Vico). What is most important in the rhetorical tradition for both is the notion of a practical, orally based ethics arising out of communal existence. That practical ethics *does not need* to be epistemological, and philosophers who try to ground it on a theoretical base (such as Aristotle and Gadamer) are not successful in doing so. The "conceit" that ethics must be grounded on epistemology obscures Vico's achievement, which is not that he transforms *sensus communis* into an epistemological principle, but that he rejects Descartes's epistemological turn in philosophy for a new, *poetic* science.[113]

Though Mooney and Schaeffer themselves do not avoid the conceits of

---

[111] Schaeffer, *Sensus Communis,* 91–92, 87. Struever says that in drawing more on *Study Methods* than on the *New Science,* Schaeffer makes Vico's philosophy of history too optimistic, failing "to see the pessimism which enables Vico's poetic insights." Nancy S. Struever, review of *Sensus Communis: Vico, Rhetoric, and the Limits of Relativism, New Vico Studies,* vol. 9 (1991): 68–76, 71–76.

[112] Schaeffer, *Sensus Communis,* 151. Schaeffer uses the epistemological nature of *sensus communis* to resolve an *aporia* in contemporary philosophy—the doubt raised by such writers as Richard Bernstein, Richard Rorty, Bernard Williams, and Alasdair MacIntyre about the ethical relevance of philosophy. Believing each struggles toward some version of *sensus communis,* he puts forward Vico's conception as a rhetorically based "epistemological principle that relates ethics and hermeneutics to the world of concrete social practice . . . that challenges modern relativism and for which modern ethicists call" (160).

[113] Schaeffer himself understands the radical nature of the *New Science* very well. He knows that for Vico social existence is not possible without an awesome, terrifying, originary event, though he does not identify that event as *poetic* but *religious.* (See "The Use and Misuse of Giambattista Vico," 98–99.) But though the originary event that for Vico awakens awe and fear *produces* the divine image and social practices of the age of gods, it is not *itself* religious in the sense that it is an experience of God or one that establishes a relation between man and god. It is *poetic,* creating the *image* of a divine being and the institutions that constitute the social practice of religion.

scholars, the turn from epistemic philosophy to rhetoric brings us closer to a poetic understanding of Vico's master key. Ernesto Grassi, who also approaches Vico from the concerns of rhetoric, has a firmer grasp of the originary nature of *poiesis*. So does White. Acknowledging the *apparent* idealism of some of Vico's views, White goes beyond those "superficial similarities" to Vico's "true originality," a hermeneutic "principle of interpretation . . . deriv[ing] from the perception, original with Vico in the form that he gave to it, that speech itself provides the key for interpreting cultural phenomena and the categories by which the evolutionary stages of a given culture can be characterized."[114] Though at times White seems to attribute agency to consciousness, he identifies consciousness with the poetic logic of sensory topics.[115] His focus on the tropological character of poetic language is not in itself novel, but the relation he draws between it and the development of human history and consciousness is. For him, "What *is* original is [Vico's] use of the tropological analysis of figurative language for the construction of a model by which both the stages in the evolution of consciousness can be defined and the transitions from one to another of them can be accounted for in terms of the 'modifications of the human mind.'" There is "a strict analogy between the dynamics of metaphorical transformations in language and the transformations of both consciousness and society. . . . [T]he theory of metaphorical transformation serves as the model for a theory of the autotransformation of human consciousness in history . . . [and] a model by which to describe the structural characteristics of ancient societies. . . . [T]he mode of social organization of a given stage of cultural development is analogous to the . . . four master tropes."[116]

White's conception of "linguistic transformation" as ontologically constitutive of the human world is as close a formulation of Vico's philosophy of *poiesis* as is found in the Vichian literature.[117] Though White refers to "the dialectic of the exchange between language on one side and the reality it seeks to contain on the other," by "reality" he means not an objective order, but the random sensations of the *giganti* that metaphor forms into the gods and social institutions of the first age, images and practices that are themselves transformed by successive tropes in successive stages of society. The conception of *poiesis* I develop here differs from White's more formal structural

[114] Hayden White, "The Tropics of History," 65–85, 70.

[115] Ibid., 70–71. Metaphor creates the image of Jove; metonymy and synechdoche also characterize pre-rational minds, while irony is a trope of the third age.

[116] Ibid., 76–78, 72. See also 84. The transition between the age of gods and heroes is from metaphor to metonymy; from aristocracy to democracy is from metonymy to synechdoche; and from democracy to decadence is from synechdoche to irony.

[117] In her oral remarks on Mooney's book at the American Society for Eighteenth Century Studies conference in 1987 Struever also emphasized the poetic. Making is "*poiesis,* linguistic making, poetry," she says, and suggests *poiesis* is ontological; "Vico completely resituates the problem of reference; reference is not to an objective, rationally ordered external physical reality, but to an ignorant social one; an adequate representation of the subtleties of ignorance becomes the scientific goal." Creative language is durable: "[L]anguage is an archive we inhabit. . . . We live in language; it lives in us."

view in that I identify poetic language hermeneutically, as violent, eventful, transformative happenings taking place in linguistic and social practices and physical labor in-the-world. Accordingly, while for White historical development is mandated by the structural nature of the relation among tropes, my hermeneutic view of language assumes a non-reductive naturalism in which linguistic "events," limited only by natural necessity, are existential responses to emergent human needs and utilities. Further, White seems to hold a more benign conception of Vico's philosophy, while I stress the abyssal, tragic sensibility of his last work, which accounts for the affinity I find between it and postmodern views.[118]

Even so, White is more successful in capturing the poetic, hermeneutic nature of Vico's new science than other rhetorical interpretations. And, because he does so in the context of the linguistic turn in contemporary thought his interpretation brings out the differences between Vico's poetic hermeneutic and the idealist hermeneutic of German philosophy. Hans-Georg Gadamer, on the other hand, who examines Vico from the perspective of Vico's influence on Dilthey and the hermeneutic turn in German thought, questions neither the epistemic nature of Vico's philosophy nor its idealism.[119] Despite this, Gadamer's critique of the idealism of historicism applies to all epistemological interpretations of Vico's philosophy. In addition, the position he formulates to go beyond it—a hermeneutic of history analogous to a hermeneutic of art—is valuable in understanding the issues involved in Vico's own move from an epistemological to an ontological *verum-factum*, and from an epistemic to a hermeneutic "knowing."

---

[118] In an early article White rejected a relation between Vico and Nietzsche and the radical wing of the human sciences, citing Vico's belief in the philological sciences and a science of reality. But White did not take into account the genetic relation between the makers of the first age and the knowers of the third, which makes any "science of reality" a mature form of poetic "divination." The convertibility of truth with the ontologically made identifies "truth" as *factum* as well. The realization that science *and* reality are *both* human creations, that the relation between them is a hermeneutic circle that never takes us beyond our own making, is as much the radical core of Vico's thought as Nietzsche's. Even Vico's belief that civilized life is better than a bestial one does not constitute an "unbridgeable divide" between them. For Vico the abyss is always below the surface, and the fall into it no less inevitable for the fact that humane learning and prudential social practices are the only means of keeping us from it. Vico is closer to Nietzsche's sense of eternal recurrence than White credits, though there is no joy in that vision but, rather, a profound sense of the finite and ultimately tragic quality of human existence (Hayden V. White, "Vico and the Radical Wing of Structuralist/Poststructuralist Thought Today," *New Vico Studies*, vol.1 [1983]: 63–68). In later writings White moderates that early estimate.

[119] One problem is Gadamer's focus on Vico's early work, particularly *Study Methods,* thus missing the hermeneutic import of the *New Science.* Like Gadamer, Emilio Betti places Vico in the German hermeneutic tradition, but Betti means by hermeneutic an epistemology and methodology of historical understanding, put forward in philological proofs (Emilio Betti, "The Principles of New Science in G. B. Vico and The Theory of Historical Interpretation," *New Vico Studies*, vol. 6 [1988]: 31–50). Hilliard Aronovitch, "Vico and *Verstehen*" (*Vico: Past and Present,* ed. Giorgio Tagliacozzo [Atlantic Highlands: Humanities Press, 1981], vol. 1, 216–26), also attributes hermeneutic to Vico, by which he means a morphological understanding of rule-governing phenomena. In effect, none of the hermeneutic interpreters of Vico grasp the *poetic* dimension of Vico's linguistic hermeneutic.

Gadamer himself believes that Vico did not make that move. Vico's response to Descartes is "based on old truths," he asserts, a recovery of the Roman conception of *sensus communis* and defense of rhetoric that kept alive a humanistic conception of truth after the emergence of modern science. In "constructing a new . . . epistemological basis between historical experience and the idealistic heritage of the historical school," Dilthey repeats Vico's argument "and writes, 'The first condition of the possibility of a science of history is that I myself am a historical being, that the person studying history is the person making history'. What makes historical knowledge possible is the homogeneity of subject and object." Vico provides Dilthey the basis of a historical epistemology concerned with "reconstructing what the author [of the text] really had in mind." But, Gadamer argues, since historical texts are inexhaustible, "Vico's famous definition" must be disqualified.[120]

Gadamer's assessment of Vico's *verum-factum*—damning to the hermeneutic significance of Vico's work if accurate—is, however, wrong. Like Schaeffer and Mooney he focuses solely on Vico's early writings, missing the poetic insights of the last. He does not realize Vico transcends a subjectivist epistemology, and does so, as Gadamer himself does, through an analogy between a hermeneutic of the historical world and a hermeneutic of the ontological being of the artwork. Regardless, Gadamer's discussion is enlightening in explicating the difference between the subject-object dualism grounding the possibility of epistemology, and the ontological nature of hermeneutic understanding. Gadamer traces the former to the "Greek" solution to the problem of knowledge, the age-old metaphysical question of the "belongingness" of thought to the real, "the transcendental relation between being and truth." The traditional response to that question grounded knowledge *ontologically* "as an element of being itself and not primarily as an activity of the subject. That knowledge is incorporated in being is the presupposition of all classical and medieval thought. What is, is of its nature 'true.' . . . [T]hought does not start from the concept of a subject. . . . On the contrary, Plato defines the being of the 'soul' as participating in true being. . . . [B]oth [self-conscious speech and world] belong originally to each other." That position was undermined by Nominalism, forcing the moderns to secure a ground of certainty in the subject. Though the object of knowledge became the "historical world . . . constituted and formed by the human mind," the traditional epistemological problem, the sense in which "the interpreter *belongs* to his text," persisted. Though Vico tries to solve that problem, Gadamer questions whether it is possible to avoid "the implicit consequences of idealistic metaphysics . . . if one starts from the methodological bases of Vico's principle," assuming, as he does, that Vico's princi-

---

[120] Hans-Georg Gadamer, *Truth and Method*, trans. Joel Weinsheimer and Donald G. Marshall (New York: Crossroad, 1992), 19–23; 219, 222, 373, 572. Indeed, Vico's relation to the hermeneutic tradition is not only minimal and indirect, but also negative, since the foundation it provides is idealist.

ple is "the postulate of speculative idealism . . . the identity between consciousness and object."[121]

"The epistemological question must be asked here in a fundamentally different way," Gadamer believes, since "history does not belong to us; we belong to it. Long before we understand ourselves through the process of self-examination, we understand ourselves in a self-evident way in the family, society, and state in which we live. The focus of subjectivity is a distorting mirror. The self-awareness of the individual is only a flickering in the closed circuits of historical life." It is Heidegger who, drawing not from Dilthey or Husserl but Nietzsche, moves beyond Cartesian subjectivism and historicism to a "hermeneutic of facticity." Heidegger aims not at a methodology of the human sciences but at a revival of the "long forgotten Greek argument about being," which transforms the problem of historical consciousness. On Heidegger's existential analytic of *Dasein* Gadamer formulates a phenomenological hermeneutic in which historical knowledge "ultimately has the same mode of being as *Dasein*. . . . [Against] a 'homogeneity' between the knower and the known . . . the coordination of all knowing activity with what is known . . . draws its significance from the *particular nature* of the mode of being that is common to them . . . [that is,] *historicity*. . . . Historicity . . . is the condition of our being able to re-present the past . . . because belonging to traditions belongs . . . originally and essentially to the historical finitude of *Dasein*."[122]

In effect Gadamer returns with Heidegger to the Greek and medieval view of the ontological belonging of thought to being, though unlike Heidegger he makes belonging the ground of a hermeneutic of historical understanding. He believes he avoids idealism because the "homogeneity" he assumes between knower and known is not spirit, but the historicity of the being of art.[123] Art "has the character of a work, of an *ergon* and not only of *energeia*." Art is not a product of activity, but an ontological "event, which goes beyond the subjectivity both of the creator and of the spectator," an "*event of being that occurs in presentation*." Because art (and analogously, history and the historical text) is not an object of knowledge but an ontological event, understanding is a part of the event in which meaning occurs.[124]

Gadamer's embrace of the ontological belongingness of hermeneutic un-

---

[121] Ibid., 458–59; 276. See also 254–76.

[122] Ibid., 276. See also 254–76; 261–62.

[123] Gadamer rejects the aesthetic consciousness of German idealism and romanticism and approaches art and history through the experience of play (xxiii; see also xxi–xxxvi, 137, 59–60, 65–70). Like art, play is not an object for a subject but "has its true being in the fact that it becomes an experience that changes the person who experiences it" (102).

[124] Gadamer, *Truth and Method*, 110; 118 n. 218; 116. See also 137–44. Historical understanding is an insight into the historicity, the finitude, of experience, the medium of which is language. Because historical understanding is always interpretive, it never reproduces an original event but is itself a re-creation of meaning—a happening—in the present.

derstanding to art and to history as "events of being" repeats similar gestures in Vico, Nietzsche, and Heidegger, though he is less successful in freeing hermeneutic from subjectivity, retaining, as he does, the methodology of phenomenology. In different ways—and without using the language of "ontology," as Heidegger does—Vico and Nietzsche achieve a hermeneutic in which meaning arises out of the "coming to presentation of being" taking place in art and history.[125] Gadamer misses Vico's ontological turn. Even when he acknowledges a relation between *verum-factum* and historical and artistic making, he asks, "Is Vico's oft repeated formula correct? Does it not transpose an experience of the human artistic spirit to the historical world, where, in the face of the course of events, one can no longer speak of 'making'—i.e., of planning and carrying out?"[126] He does not realize that by the *New Science* Vico too had gone beyond the conceit that making is "planning and carrying out," to the poetic insight that meaning emerges out of unintended linguistic and social practices and physical labor in-the-world. Even in the third age, when humans become subjective beings, subjectivity can never be other than a *factum* of the abstract languages and practices constructed by the end of the heroic age. In the context of Vico's genetic understanding that things do not settle out of their *natural* state, the men of the third age can never be other than makers. The hermeneutic of philosopher-historians produces the eventful making of art—the making, that is, of historical narratives. But the hermeneutic understanding that belongs ontologically to the narrative making of philosopher-historians does not yield the historical understanding sought by Gadamer, who is still too close to German historicism. What "comes to presentation of being" in the narratives of philosopher-historians is the hermeneutic understanding that they are genetic descendants of originary makers and, like them, *makers* of their *narrative trues*. Hermeneutic for Vico, as for Nietzsche, is never other than self-referential.

Both Gadamer and Croce misread Vico's *verum-factum* as German idealism's claim of a homogeneity between subject and object, though Croce values and Gadamer derides that unity. Croce also believes that Vico contributes to that achievement by going beyond the scholastic version of the principle favoring the primacy of divine knowing to elevate causality. In a critique of what Jääkko Hintikka calls "maker's knowledge," J. L. Mackie argues the impossibility of human knowing ever "converting" with making. Hintikka

---

[125] Even if Gadamer had gone beyond the epistemological nature of Vico's early *verum-factum* to grasp the ontological nature of the principle implicit in the *New Science,* he would not have appreciated Vico's hermeneutic significance. For Vico, as for Nietzsche, art is the activity of the artist, while Gadamer—who, like Heidegger, believes agency always entails subjectivity and intentionality—strives to free art from agency.

[126] Gadamer, *Truth and Method,* 230–31. See Milbank's discussion of this passage (*Religious Dimension,* pt. 2, 183).

had used the principle to support the view that theory and practice are so inextricably related they cannot be separated. However, Hintikka also believes that practical knowledge, as the "cause of what it understands," is always intentional. He draws for examples on Maimonides and Bacon, for whom "the producer produces in accordance with his knowledge," an Aristotelian argument that only a maker can know what he produces "because only he can know its purpose." Mackie argues against Hintikka that insofar as practical knowledge is *intentional,* it always in some sense assumes knowing. Since what is intended is known by the maker (at least in the trivial sense that knowledge is a prerequisite of intentionality), "making depends on the knowing, not the knowing on the making." Making "does not in itself give the maker any knowledge of what he has made."

Mackie's argument undermines not only Hintikka's interpretation but *all* interpretations of *verum-factum* as well, *insofar as they rest on the traditional belief that making is an intentional — that is, subjective — activity.* The only example Mackie gives of a making unconditioned by subjectivity and productive of that which is known by the maker is the case of God who, he says, quoting Maimonides, by "*enact[ing]* the laws of nature, brings them into existence by *fiat.*" He agrees with Maimonides, however, that *only* God makes by *fiat.*[127]

Mackie is right that none of the versions of maker's knowledge, including those attributed to Vico, successfully attributes to humans that convertibility of knowing and making that characterizes divine *fiat*—nor could they, insofar as the conception of productive activity retains the belief Mackie attributes to it, that making is always in some sense intentional; that is, conditioned by subjectivity. It is not incidental that the one theological conception Mackie claims attributes knowing to making, that of a God who creates by *fiat*—an act which is linguistic, though Mackie does not mention it—he finds in Maimonides, who had in his own Judaic background such a conception. Yet all interpretations of maker's knowledge deriving the model of the unity of knowing and making from theology assume an intellectual God whose actions are rational and purposeful, the conception of action derived from the Greeks. Habermas's secularized version of Vico's *verum-*

---

[127] J. L. Mackie, "Comment," *Practical Reason,* ed. Stephan Körner (New Haven: Yale University Press, 1974), 103–12, 103–6. See also Jääkko Hintikka, "Practical *vs.* Theoretical Reason—An Ambiguous Legacy," *Practical Reason,* ed. Stephan Körner (New Haven: Yale University Press, 1974), 83–102, 84–85; Horst Steinke, "Hintikka and Vico: An Update on Contemporary Logic," *New Vico Studies,* vol. 3 (1985): 147–55; and Milbank, *Religious Dimension,* pt. 1, 87–89. Even in the case of making by *fiat,* Maimonides assumes God's making is conceptual. Agreeing with Mackie, Andrew Harrison puts forward a more promising conception of the relation between making and knowing, a process of "free design," as in action painting. Rather than a purposive, linear, means-ends process, it is only in "acting and reacting to the material world, the world in which one may make and design, that one formulates and comes to know what one's goals are" (Andrew Harrison, *Making and Thinking: A Study of Intelligent Activities* [Brighton, Sussex, U.K.: The Harvester Press Limited, 1978], 154; see also 144).

factum is typical. Even efforts to elevate causality that go back to the biblical God—Löwith's and Milbank's, for example—fail to do so because they understand that deity as a spiritual being whose acts are subjectively conditioned.

If there is a knowing that is wholly convergent with making, it would have to be a "knowing" and a "making" radically different from the conceptions that follow from traditional assumptions. Belief that that "other" can be found in the biblical text is promising, but, as Vico realized, one cannot understand the strange from the perspective of traditional conceits. In the following chapter I present two very different formulations of the unity of the knowing and making of the biblical God. If the onto-theological precursors through whom Hans Blumenberg reads scripture characterize God as spirit and divine creativity as intentional, thus undermining the unity of his activity, contemporary postmodern readings by Judaic scholars suggest alternate precursors, for whom making is linguistic rather than mental, and "knowing" is the interpretive reading of that originary language.

2 Verum-Factum *and the Poetic Ontology of the Hebrews*

Hans Blumenberg and *Verum-Factum* as Principle of the Originary

> Man comprehends himself only by way of what he is not. It is not only his situation that is potentially metaphorical; his constitution itself already is. . . . So the most daring metaphor, which tried to embrace the greatest tension, may have accomplished the most for man's self-conception: trying to think the god absolutely away from himself, as the totally other, he inexorably began the most difficult rhetorical act, namely, the act of comparing himself to this god.
>
> —Hans Blumenberg, "An Anthropological Approach to the Contemporary Significance of Rhetoric"

THROUGHOUT ITS HISTORY *verum-factum* has been taken as a gnoseological principle providing a criterion for a delimited conception of knowledge, thereby blunting skeptical challenges to the possibility of epistemic knowledge. For moderns such as Bacon, Galileo, Boyle, Descartes, and Gassendi, it salvaged *ergetic* knowledge, mathematical and experimental, of the natural world. For others, however, the principle deepened rather than alleviated skepticism. For Cusa, Sánchez, Mersenne, and Locke, it effectively denied knowledge of nature without providing an alternative, though Cusa, at least, attributed to humans the construction of mathematics.[1] Vico is credited with

---

[1] See Antonio Pèrez-Ramos, *Francis Bacon's Idea of Science and the Maker's Knowledge Tradition* (Oxford: Clarendon Press, 1988), 58, 179–86; José Faur, "Francisco Sánchez's Theory of Cognition and Vico's *verum/factum*," *New Vico Studies*, vol. 5 (1987): 131–46; and review of "*That Nothing Is Known (Quod nihil scitur),*" by Francisco Sánchez. *New Vico Studies*, vol. 8 (1990): 104–6; Jääkko Hintikka, "Practical *vs.* Theoretical Reason—An Ambiguous Legacy," *Practical Reason*, ed. Stephan Körner (New Haven: Yale University Press, 1974), 83–

responding to and overcoming that skepticism by turning the very inability of the principle to ground a knowledge of nature into the basis of a new form of knowledge. Developing a notion found in Hobbes and Grotius that humans were makers of their political and historical institutions, Vico, it is argued, used *verum-factum* to justify knowledge of history. Certainly, when Vico used that *topos* in his early writings, it was as an epistemological principle. However, none who have understood it in that sense, neither moderns nor contemporary scholars of modernity, nor Vico himself in *Ancient Wisdom,* identify or question the metaphysical assumptions that insure the possibility of knowledge, whether epistemic or *ergetic,* for the tradition. Those assumptions include the existence of a *homoiousis* between humans and intelligible object, given *or* made, and of a subjective human essence grounding that *homoiousis.* Yet, it is exactly that latter assumption that Vico's master key reveals as a conceit. His "insight" into the embodied and poetic nature of the first men made that assumption—the anthropological ground of modern versions of *verum-factum*—indefensible. Though Vico's insight strengthened skepticism by rendering the tradition's pursuit of epistemic knowledge futile, it enabled him, ultimately, to achieve a nontraditional poetic alternative to that skepticism.

The argument that *verum-factum,* as realized in the *New Science,* is not an epistemic but ontological principle of poetic making is supported by the claim that, as such, it secularizes a theological account of originary creation. That secularization argument rests, in turn, on a conception of divine *poiesis* that, insofar as it is linguistic and concrete, presumes neither divine nor human subjectivity. Understandably, traditional secularization interpretations of Vico derive his conception of divine creativity from the scholastics on whom he drew in *Ancient Wisdom.* As the onto-theological product of a syncretic process, scholastic theology, however, owed as much to Greek metaphysics as to scripture. By producing a hybrid conception of God who was both omnipotent creator and Timaean Architect, syncretism initiated that tension within Christianity between the Hellenic desire to satisfy "theoretical curiosity," and the biblical tradition's indifference to and skepticism toward natural knowledge. Croce locates that tension in the antithesis between the scholastic God, whose knowing is prior to his making, and the Nominalist, for whom causality is primary, and rejects both as models for Vico's *verum-factum,* which asserts the convergence of knowing and creating. When the moderns likened the mastery over nature their knowledge gave them to the divine unity of knowing and making, their divine model, as Habermas's secularization thesis attests, was an *intellectus originarius* closer

---

102, 85–86. Hintikka says, "[I]n many respects pessimistic conclusions from [*verum-factum*] should have been as close at hand in Bacon's time as the optimistic ones. . . . It is a sobering thought that the leading idea of the intellectual background of modern applied science and scientific technology can be traced back to skeptical and theological principles calculated to extol the superiority of the Divine practical reason over the human one."

to scholastic theology.[2] In their effort to strengthen the causal potency of the God whose unity of knowing and making Vico secularizes, Löwith and Milbank attempt to move beyond the "Platonic paradigm" to the biblical conception of creation *ex nihilo.* Both elevate God's causal potency by identifying it with language. Yet neither is successful in achieving a conception of convergence *even for divine knowing and making,* since ultimately each conceives the biblical deity as a spiritual being whose creative activity is subjective and purposeful. By identifying language with Johannine and trinitarian mystical conceptions of *verbum,* both compromise originary potency, though Löwith remains truer to his insight by retaining the notion that divine creation is also *ad extra.* Vico was as influenced by the dualist and subjectivist tradition that transmitted the intellectual model of divine and human activity to the West as were his contemporaries, though his early interest in Epicurus testifies to his serious questioning of its assumptions. Not until his master key took him beyond subjectivist conceits to an embodied and poetic anthropology, however, could he conceive of a knowing convertible with a making as originary as the unconditioned linguistic creativity of the biblical God. In effect, he recovered the ancient paradigm of a creative process that was ontological rather than epistemological, in which the "true" was *thing* rather than *idea* or goal in the mind of a knower, and "knowing" never more than the "divination" of language.

That ancient paradigm is still too strange to understand for most contemporary thinkers, caught as much by the conceit of divine and human subjectivity as were Vico's contemporaries. Nothing illustrates the retroactive influence of later "precursor-texts" on the reading of scripture more than the differences between Judaic and onto-theological readings. And nothing illustrates the force of Hans Blumenberg's claim that "man comprehends himself" by what he is not—by a divine "totally other"—more than the differences between the anthropology he derives from his onto-theological reading of Genesis, and one derived from Judaic readings. Though he insists on the inadequacy of traditional cosmological assumptions to counter acosmic skepticism, though he turns to the biblically based *verum-factum* principle for a paradigm of absolute creative potency, Blumenberg, no more than Löwith or Milbank, is able to conceive of divine creativity other than as subjective activity.

That inability is vividly illustrated as I turn, in this chapter, from the analogy between divine and human agency Blumenberg draws in *Legitimacy of the Modern Age,* to the analogy made possible by Judaic and postmodern insights into the constructive power of language. In contrasting these differ-

[2] Where you find emphases on causality or power over intellectual grounds among the moderns, as in such political theorists as Machiavelli or Hobbes, causation is still conditioned by subjective intention. While the mathematical sciences presumed, as Galileo claimed, a God who created by number, experimental science was compatible with the view that a world created by an arbitrary, omnipotent deity was knowable *a posteriori.*

ent conceptions of divine and human creativity, I argue that the skeptical implications Blumenberg tries to exorcise from the *verum-factum* principle— the self-referentiality of any knowing convergent with making, and the absoluteness of art or creativity necessitated by insight into the illusory nature of truth—are inherent, not only in the Judaic paradigm of the principle, but in the poetic humanism Vico's own primordial thinking finds in it.

Descartes and the Legitimation of Constructed Knowledge

If "[t]he zero point of the disappearance of order and the point of departure of the construction of order are identical," then, Blumenberg asserts, "the minimum of ontological predisposition is at the same time the maximum of constructive potentiality."[3] And, if the West's traditional assumption of a "maximum of ontological predisposition" made possession of a constructive potential unnecessary (even, indeed, inconceivable), any threat to that plenitude made constructive potential not only desirable but essential. Arguing that the modern age was forced to the "self-assertion" of a maximum of constructive power for the radical beginnings of its theoretical formulations, Blumenberg describes the movement of ideas that led to that existential act—the recurring dialectical alternations or "reoccupations" of two antithetic worldviews; a cosmic vision of an ordered and intelligible world aimed at making humans comfortable; and an acosmic challenge to that effort. The heart of the antithesis between these worldviews was a problem "unsolved by the ancient world," the "origin of what is bad [*des Übels*]." The Greeks themselves identified "badness" with matter and necessity, and the myth of the demiurge in the *Timaeus* reflected philosophy's optimistic belief that matter could be brought to order by reason. That first version of cosmic order was challenged in the Hellenistic period, as Gnosticism and Epicureanism emphasized the worldly evil, pain, and suffering metaphysics never successfully explained. Gnosticism itself was overcome, first, by Augustine's resolution of the problem of "badness," his belief that the world was wholly good, and man responsible for the bad; second, by scholasticism's effort to retain a place for reason, albeit within a theological context. The price scholasticism paid for its "trust in inherent purposes" was its "flight into transcendence," its acceptance of the "senselessness of self-assertion."[4] Its "reoccupation" of the historical position initially held by metaphysics was itself challenged by Nominalism, which "reoccupied" the position vacated by Gnosticism. Nominalism drew out the doctrinal contradictions in scholasticism's struggle to retain the ancient belief in a purpose-

---

[3] Hans Blumenberg, *The Legitimacy of the Modern Age,* trans. Robert M. Wallace (Cambridge: MIT Press, 1983), 220. Portions of this chapter were published as "The Legitimacy of Hans Blumenberg's Conception of Originary Activity," *Annals of Scholarship* 5, no. 1 (fall 1987): 1–36.

[4] Blumenberg, *Legitimacy of the Modern Age,* 127, 132–36. See also 309–23.

ful, benign world in the face of the biblical insistence on divine omnipotence, distinguishing between *potentia absoluta,* God's absolute power, and *potentia ordinata,* his ordained power, and claiming that the latter did not exhaust the former. God became *Deus absconditus,* a hidden God. As the "cosmos" became a "performance of reified omnipotence," what was lost was the comfort of an anthropocentric teleology.

Blumenberg's view of history as the functional rather than substantive recurrence of ideas leads him to explore the function of the modern age's claim to an absolute beginning. The age was not a "monologue, beginning at point zero, of the absolute subject," but a "system of efforts to answer in a new context questions . . . posed to man in the Middle Ages." Nominalism's insistence on a "transcendent absolute" was a claim so extreme it elicited an extreme "uncovering of the immanent absolute." By radicalizing Nominalism's *potentia absoluta* into a *genius malignus,* Descartes sharpens a doubt resolvable only by the *cogito,* the minimum that can serve as a foundation of knowledge. That act of "self-assertion," an "anthropological minimum under the condition of a theological maximum," accomplished in the name of the human subject, constitutes the age's uniqueness. Confronted with a reality transcending the "*economy* of classificatory concepts," the age is forced to accept those concepts as the "activity (*actio*) of the knowing subject." The products of human construction are the hypotheses that constitute the theories of modern science, the model of which is astronomy, "with its resignation vis-à-vis the provision of causal explanations . . . and . . . conception of itself as a mere 'art,' the business of which was . . . to render the unknown and inaccessible mechanism of the . . . heavens sufficiently calculable to meet . . . human needs." This transformation of knowledge transforms, in turn, the age's conception of human activity. Theory becomes "technique," a means to ends chosen in other ways. Behavior need not merely adapt itself to nature: if "reality proves . . . inconsiderate of man," it must "be altered and produced in accordance with human purposes. . . . [M]an . . . reserv[es] the right to interfere in nature, to subjugate it as the substrate of demiurgic production."[5] Grasping the import of the demiurgic mastery of nature for the idea of progress, Kant proclaims the world "unfinished."

Ultimately, Blumenberg argues, the truths owned by modernity do not belong to it because it achieves an absolute beginning in reason, but because it *claims to do so.* Though the very extremity of the claim of self-assertion suggests the naivete and hubris of reason, Blumenberg turns it into the existential cry of humans abandoned to themselves in an indifferent universe. Self-assertion is "an existential program, according to which man posits his existence in a historical situation and indicates to himself how he is going to deal with the reality surrounding him and what use he will make of the possibilities that are open to him." Blumenberg identifies that program with a

---

[5] Ibid., 379, 178, 153, 197, 200, 164, 209. See also 181–229.

principle he finds in Philo Judaeus, that "the legitimate ownership of ideas can be derived only from their authentic production," the convertibility of *verum* and *factum*.[6] Philo introduces a theme new to philosophy, the biblical preoccupation with absolute beginnings, which offers an alternate source of legitimate knowledge in the face of challenges to the metaphysical pursuit of knowledge. He gives that theme philosophic form by applying "the identity of *verum* and *factum* [truth and fact], to the *solus scire potest qui fecit* [only he can know who makes (the object)]," thus expressing the idea of the "Author's 'ownership' of the truth of His work." Insofar as truth is created by divine omnipotence, "[l]egitimate knowledge can only derive from God, the origin and source of all skills and sciences, and should not try to found itself on unmediated, as it were, unauthorized inspection of the cosmos." The inadequacy of philosophy forces reason to become submissive before "God's sovereign right to the secret of His creation, which is communicated by Him alone on the condition of knowing and acknowledging His authorship."

Dependence on an authorial source transforms the nature of the knowledge available to humans. Philo describes the spiritual journey from theoretic curiosity (in the form of astronomical speculation) to self-knowledge, "which in turn leads through the self's discovery of its ignorance to recognition . . . of the world as God's work." Though reformulation of the end of knowledge as knowledge of one's created and contingent nature does not preclude knowledge of the world, the latter becomes part of a sequential order in which "contemplation of the world is conditional on prior self-knowledge and knowledge of God." Augustine severs this relation: in the face of God's ownership of his truths, he denies the legitimacy of theoretic curiosity, which turns outward, claiming that the soul attains self-knowledge only by returning to its origin in God through inner experience. The antithesis between self-knowledge and curiosity that begins with Augustine persists until Kant, who makes the former an object of theoretic study.[7]

For Blumenberg, the tension between the desire to satisfy theoretic curiosity and the withdrawal to self-knowledge is a secondary theme in the history of epochal change. His disdain for the latter fuels his support of modernity's desperate effort to salvage some form of theory against the repudiation implicit in the original *verum-factum*. He finds the ironic means to do so by attributing to the age its own version of the principle, an anthropological reoccupation of the position filled by a theological "maximum."[8] That recourse can succeed, however, only if it itself is free of all dependence on the teleology of metaphysics. The version of "originary" ac-

---

[6] Ibid., 138, 72.

[7] Ibid., 284–85, 287, 313, 289.

[8] Blumenberg is not rejecting the claim that the age secularizes theological ideas, but the "*eidetic*" historiography on which the secularization thesis rests. He considers the relation of modern to theological views functional rather than substantive.

tivity Blumenberg attributes to *verum-factum,* one productive of theory, is not radical enough. Blumenberg believes that it meets acosmic critiques because it does not claim a *homoiousis* between knowledge and reality, but even the notion that *techne* is grounded on constructed theories rather than epistemic truths retains a "remnant of teleology," the unquestioned, "familiar" belief that "constructive potentiality" is a function of human subjectivity. That belief is as indefensible in the wake of acosmic critiques as the age's claim to an absolute beginning in reason.

Blumenberg himself attempts to avoid any "presumption of order" in the *verum-factum* he attributes to Descartes by insisting that the truth unique to the age is not the *cogito* itself, but the freedom with which the *cogito* is asserted. Descartes's anxiety that God might be a *genius malignus* who deceives leads him to emphasize the "primacy of freedom . . . over the certainty of the *Cogito.* . . . [a] minimum of freedom in the act of withholding assent. . . . [M]an is not free in that he has grounds for his action but rather in that he can dispense with grounds." Descartes "transformed the late medieval crisis of certainty into an experiment with certainty,"[9] a transformation not appreciated by his critics, who take his "pretended spontaneity" at its word and believe his claim to make "men independent through the power of *ratio.*" Blumenberg includes Heidegger among those critics, citing his claim that Descartes's "experiment," his "interpretation of man as *subjectum . . .* creates the metaphysical precondition of the anthropology to come."[10] He does not, however, do justice to Heidegger's critique, which hits directly at the "remnant of order" to which Descartes, the age (and Blumenberg) cling. "The rise of the anthropologies" is Descartes's "greatest triumph" because, Heidegger charges, Descartes not only transforms humans into subjects, but also, by reducing human nature to mind, begins the process of transforming philosophy *itself* into anthropology. Heidegger's critique is aimed at the assumption that grounds not only modernist anthropology, but which, he believes, also renders the entire tradition from Plato to Nietzsche anthropocentric and humanist, the primacy of the activity of spirit, soul, mind over being-in-the-world. And, indeed, despite Blumenberg's insistence on the radical nature of epochal change, his interpretation of both cosmic and acosmic positions reinforces Heidegger's charge of the hegemony of that subjectivism, since his version of Western history is no more than a series of variations on that theme.[11] Turning the *cogito* into a pragmatic, even existential, act does

---

[9] Blumenberg, *Legitimacy of the Modern Age,* 185–87.

[10] Ibid., 615 n.9. The reference to Heidegger is "The Age of the World Picture," *The Question Concerning Technology and Other Essays,* trans. William Lovitt (New York: Harper Torchbooks, 1977), 115–54, 139–40.

[11] Though Gnosticism and Nominalism called into question the metaphysical view of cosmic intelligibility and the adequacy of knowledge, they shared with metaphysics the belief in and valuing of subjective, even spiritual, activity over being-in-the-world. They even pursued some form of "knowledge," though Blumenberg discredits those pursuits because the "knowledge" desired was not "adequate" to nature.

not acknowledge this "remnant of teleology," but presupposes it. With his dualistic anthropology, Blumenberg has loaded the dice. The age may identify order as a construct of originary activity, but it reduces originary activity to the activity of abstract thought; it may abandon its desire for epistemic knowledge, but never the subjectivism that grounds its epistemological pretensions.[12]

The issue between Blumenberg and more radical positions is, ultimately, not an epistemological one over the nature or possibility of knowledge, but an anthropological one over the nature of being-human. He does not do sufficient justice to postmodern acosmic critiques that go beyond epistemology to deconstruct both subjectivity and the subject. Heidegger says the *cogito* forgets the being of self-understanding: Blumenberg's existential revision of it forgets the being of originary activity. Blumenberg even ignores alternate versions of *verum-factum* within the modern age. He never mentions Vico's name in *Legitimacy,* for example, explaining that omission elsewhere by saying Vico's view of history "does not take part in Descartes's fiction of the zero-point. That fiction conflicts with Vico's fundamental assumption that history is the temporal form of experience and consequently cannot set up its new beginnings without regard for what has been and for what has been handed down. In this unity of a history of experience that is common to all mankind the decisions were made very early on."[13] He is right that Vico does not accept Descartes's fiction of the zero point, but not because Vico's view of history precludes the idea of beginnings. More profoundly than anyone in the age, Vico knows that history begins in originary activity. What he denies is that beginnings are constituted by abstract thought. He goes beyond skepticism of the *adaequatio* of science to deny that thought can provide "inventively" for human "needs and utilities," and achieves a conception of making that rejects all "remnants of teleology."

Blumenberg's retention of the "remnant" of subjectivity is apparent in his sustained attack on two alternate efforts to attribute creativity to humans, those of Nicholas of Cusa and of Nietzsche, each of whom makes explicit an implication in *verum-factum* subversive of the attempt to legitimize theoretic curiosity. Both identify human creativity as in some sense divine; Cusa, indeed, for whom the original owner of *verum-factum* is the omnipotent God of the Hebrews, so radicalizes the notion of man as *imago Dei* that the substantive difference between original and image, infinite and finite, disappears, while Nietzsche's announcement of the death of God makes room for

[12] A number of reviews comment on Blumenberg's bias. See William J. Bouwsma, *Journal of Modern History* 56, no. 4 (December 1984): 698–701; Martin Jay, *History and Theory* 24, no. 2 (1985): 183–96.

[13] Hans Blumenberg, *Work on Myth,* trans. Robert M. Wallace (Cambridge: MIT Press, 1985), 377. Vico would consider Blumenberg's appropriation of *verum-factum* on behalf of Descartes a "conceit of scholars." Though Blumenberg mentions Vico's identification of the origin of myth with imagination, poetry, *ingenium,* he does not see imaginative making as an application of *verum-factum.*

human originary power. "If there were a God," Zarathustra cries, "how could I bear not to be him." Though both—Cusa at the dawn of the modern age, Nietzsche at its waning—identify divinity with the convergence of knowing and making, neither draws out the analogy with God in the aggrandizing manner of the moderns—not Cusa, for whom human creativity is never more than an *imitatio* of the divine, nor Nietzsche, who denies human subjecthood. Both, however, draw out the implications of *verum-factum* inherent in its biblical formulation, implications so subversive of self-empowerment that Blumenberg discusses them with disdain and horror. For Cusa, as for Philo and Augustine, the relation between originating activity and knowledge is a closed hermeneutic circle, and knowledge is always of the self as its source; for Nietzsche, the inability to satisfy intellectual curiosity leads to an affirmation of the artifactual nature of reality, the absoluteness of art.

The Limits of Constructed Knowledge

Cusa and the Closed Circle of Self-Knowledge.   Blumenberg presents his critique of Cusa's *verum-factum* by contrasting it with the activism of Giordano Bruno. Both are "threshold figures," "witnesses" of an epochal turn marked by a radical transformation of human self-understanding and a heightened sense of the nature and import of human activity. Both contribute to those developments in the context of the late medieval preoccupation with the notion of infinity, either as attribute of a world created by an omnipotent God, or as attribute of a world inseparable from God. Where Bruno, however, is certain, with "his triumphant backward glance, of having crossed [the epochal threshold]," Cusa is concerned "for the endangered continuance of his [medieval] system." Recognizing the force of Nominalism and the vulnerability of scholasticism, Cusa tries to make the latter more responsive to the former by providing scholasticism with "human compensation for the . . . intensification of metaphysical transcendence,"[14] though the radical implications of his anthropology are held in check by the theological framework of his thought.

The theological issues around which Cusa rethinks traditional anthropology concern the relationship of creator to created and the nature of the creative process appropriate to an infinite deity. Cusa is influenced by Nominalism's insistence that creative activity be adequate to its Author. Yet, in the context of his Neoplatonism creation is no longer "the sovereign decree of arbitrarily chosen content . . . the epitome of transcendence, but . . . a likeness of the absolute; it unfolds in time and space the original unity, the *complicatio . . .* the *explicatio quietus.*"[15] In the face of this likeness Cusa replaces

---

[14] Blumenberg, *Legitimacy of the Modern Age,* 469, 175.
[15] Ibid., 508–9. The reference is to *De docta ignorantia* II 2.

a passive anthropology with "an active existential determination of man, realized in terms not of his circumstances in the world but of self-realization." Created in the image of God, man is *quasi alius deus,* like another God, and, as such, is a creator: "performance of the divine likeness . . . imitates not the world, but the origin of the world."[16]

As the predicate distinguishing Creator-God from creatures, creativity had not been attributed to humans before Cusa. Nominalism challenged that limitation on human power as a limitation of God's ability to create a being with the power to create. Cusa identifies the locus of human originating potency with intellect, expressed most significantly in epistemology. The impossibility of attaining knowledge in a world that is a "performance of reified omnipotence" occasions embrace of a new conception of knowledge in which cognition is not receptive but projective. Man as *"humanus deus"* is himself "a 'unity'"—that is, "an infinity realized in a human manner."[17] As divine creativity had been the unfolding of this infinity out of God's own nature, so too is human creativity an unfolding of man's. "Conjectures . . . issue from our mind as the real world issued from God's infinite reason. . . . [M]an's mind participates—so far as possible—in the fertility of creative nature and produces from itself . . . intellectually existing things in approximation to concretely existing things."[18] Mathematics is the paradigm of this cognitive creativity. Appealing to the axiom "the author of a thing could alone be the possessor of its complete truth," traditionally "applicable only to God," Cusa gives it a radically new application. Humans can know mathematics because they create it: "our spirit, which creates the mathematical world, has in itself more of the truth and reality of what it can create than exists outside it."[19] For Cusa, Godlikeness becomes a relation of *accomplishment* rather than *substance.*

A question arises as to whether man can be a creator since, though he is an *imitatio* of God only insofar as he is creative, to be creative is precisely not to be an imitator. Cusa seems to respond in the affirmative, believing man could resolutely "turn his gaze to the scope of what was not pregiven in the factual world but could perhaps be realized by his own power," but, Blumenberg claims, he pulls back from the radical implications of his anthropology. Because he is an *imago,* "man, who is creative in the unfolding of his essential unity, produces only the universe of possibilities that is already laid

---

[16] Ibid., 516, 530.

[17] Ibid., 533.

[18] Ibid., 526. Blumenberg refers to book 3, chap. 1 of *coniecturis.*

[19] Ibid., 357. Blumenberg quotes Nicholas of Cusa, *De beryllo* c. 32. Mathematics is the "specific instrumen[t] of human knowledge of nature precisely" because it and nature are not commensurate. That fact forces man to face his human pretensions. Plato's claim that knowledge of mathematics was knowledge of the essence of things was such a "pretension." He erred in not distinguishing between ideas "given to us . . . and those that we ourselves produce and consequently fully understand."

out in him and therefore creates nothing new in the process."[20] For this reason human creativity and true knowledge are ultimately identical. Cusa
"breaches the principle of imitation in describing man's productive relation
to the world only . . . to use the concept of *imitatio* all the more emphati-
cally." Human creativity, never more than an *imitatio* of divine, does not constitute self-empowerment: man is "like another God because his God is
great," but *only* because *He* is so.[21]

Blumenberg reserves his harshest criticism for Cusa's belief that human
knowledge of the created is never other than self-referential, a form of self-
knowledge: "'the more [the soul] stretches out to other things so as to know
them, the deeper it penetrates into itself so as to know itself.' Self-referentiality [is] the basic form of all cognitive acts, even those directed outward."[22] Blumenberg's disdain for Cusa's "ineffectual" use of *verum-factum*
is palpable. For Cusa "the guide for the investigation of human spontaneity
is not the tools of self-assertion but rather the invention of a game as a reality closed in itself, a 'world' that unfolds itself with its own elements according to set rules . . . [a game] the soul practices with itself so as to assure
itself of its power [and] self-movement." Blumenberg considers as an especially characteristic simile "[t]he world map the cosmographer produces . . .
while . . . [the cosmographer] works up, orders, and brings to a common
scale the data and information brought to him from outside, nevertheless in
fact he remains at home, shuts the door, and turns his gaze inwards to the
world ground that lies in himself, which alone provides him with the principle of the unity of all the facts brought to him from outside."[23]

Ultimately Blumenberg's hostility toward the self-contained nature of the
knowledge Cusa legitimizes with *verum-factum* exposes his own unwillingness to accept the implications of acosmic critiques. He rejects the limitation
verum-factum imposes on epistemological pretensions, though he describes

---

[20] Ibid., 530–34. Cusa, Blumenberg says, believes, ultimately, in a Platonic "adequacy" between man and world as object of knowledge (529). Blumenberg describes the one occasion
when Cusa suggests that man creates things that differ from God's. In the *Idiota* Cusa refers to
human artifacts, which differ from nature, and has a craftsman say, "I . . . make spoons . . . and
dishes and pots. . . . In this activity I do not imitate the form of any naturally given object, since
the[ir] forms . . . arise by virtue of human skill alone. Consequently my art is more perfect than
one that imitates the forms of objects, and thus is more similar to infinite art" (*Idiota de menta*,
c. 2). Though Blumenberg is right to consider this passage radical in making human technicity
creative, even in it creation remains an intellectual act. The artifact does not emerge in the
process of material making; rather, "[t]he spoon has no original other than the idea in our
mind."
[21] Ibid., 527, 530, 535. For Blumenberg, Bruno is the more radical thinker. With his belief
that creativity is immanent in historical process, which itself takes on the infinity characteristic
of divinity, he takes possession of the truth of human "self-empowerment," thus crossing the
epochal threshold. He did not, however, have an anthropology, since he did not understand man
as subject.
[22] Ibid., 526. See also 533.
[23] Ibid., 535–36. Blumenberg refers to *Compendium* 8, 6; *De ludo globe* 2; *De coniecturis*
I, 13.

it eloquently with reference to Cusa: "the diagram of circle and center represents the inclusiveness of the relation between creative origin and projected world, the way in which the reality that arises from man refers back to him. 'Human being itself alone is the goal of the creative process. . . . Man does not go beyond himself when he is creative: rather, in the unfolding of his power, he comes to himself.'"[24] Blumenberg rejects the reflexivity of maker's "knowledge" because he does not really comprehend the radically acosmic nature of beginnings, the implication that a "knowledge" dependent on an authorial source is *itself transformed*: it can *never* be other than knowledge of the self's dependence on its source. Blumenberg disdains that circularity on behalf of his own and modernity's goal of ownership of theoretic knowledge. He can do so, however, only by retaining the "remnant" derived from classical and Neoplatonic metaphysics, that construction is a function of subjectivity.

Blumenberg also misses the more radical significance of his own turn from a substantive to a functional analysis of the relations among historical periods. He eschews the historiographic assumption that epochs are related to one another *substantively* by virtue of eidetic continuity for one in which prior historical positions vacated by the inadequacy of their ideas are reoccupied by *functionally* equivalent ideas, and he credits Cusa with moving beyond a *substantive* understanding of the relationship between *imago Dei* and its original for the more radical *functional* relation of accomplishment or performance. He does not seem to realize, however, that Cusa's interpretation of the functional sense in which human creativity is an image of the divine—that is, as *cognitive* creativity—is possible precisely because Cusa presupposes a *substantive* likeness between humans and God. Only because his God is neither biblical nor Nominalist but the spiritual deity of Neoplatonism can Cusa legitimately attribute to humans cognitive creativity. Blumenberg cannot, since his legitimation of modernity's truths depends on rejection of such metaphysical beliefs as the subjectivity of man or God. Moreover, appeal to a biblical God would not have enabled him to characterize that creativity as cognitive in any case.

Nietzsche and the Absoluteness of Art. Blumenberg's failure to give up every remnant of order is nowhere more apparent than in his rejection of the "absoluteness of art" he attributes to Nietzsche. He accuses Nietzsche of drawing out the implications of the acosmic insistence on the unintelligibility of the world and the inadequacy of reason. For Nietzsche, self-assertion is "only the first stage of [human] self-enhancement and self-surpassing," a stage compromised by the remnant of teleological order to which it clings. As a way of "centering . . . the world's meaning on man" science itself is no more than an "equivalent to . . . providence," an attempt to ask "nature for information regarding man's destiny and fullness of power." Nietzsche's cri-

---

[24] Ibid., 533. The quotation is from *coniecturis*.

tique goes beyond science and the progress view of history, the constructs of modernity's self-assertion which are merely new limitations on man's will and creativity, to reject the very will to knowledge, "the assumption that if not reality itself, then at least the truth about it must be . . . beneficial to man." Belief in the "human relevance of truth" is modernity's theoretic version of teleology.[25]

Where modernity's version of creativity is dependent on "reality as [man] finds it or believes he finds it," Nietzsche imputes "the least possible binding force to reality." Creativity is possible only insofar as nature's "pregiveness . . . is reduced to a minimum—to the most external, mechanistic contingency." The doctrine of eternal recurrence enables Nietzsche to accomplish that reduction, abandoning humans to a contingent world in which their own creativity is the only source of order. "The cycles of the world process were not to repeat the model of a prescriptive lawfulness in nature, as in the Stoic cosmology": rather, they "raise the sum total of the consequences of human action to the role of the ineluctable lawfulness of the world and thus . . . charge man with absolute responsibility for the world." Where modern man's relation to the world is mediated by theory, the *Übermensch* relates to the world with a "praxis that changes it." The embrace of so radical a cosmology is made possible by Nietzsche's rejection of the last remnant of teleology to which modernity clung, the belief in the primacy of self-preservation. Self-preservation is an attitude based on a sense of "endangered" reality, while man's relation to nature cannot be a function of "reality" at all, since "[t]here is neither order nor disorder in nature."[26] Life does not seek to preserve itself, but to "*discharge* its strength—life itself is *will to power.*"[27] Humans take possession of creativity not on behalf of self-assertion, which is nothing more than a response to the "indifference of reality" to man, but of will to power, which expresses man's indifference to reality. As self-assertion reflects disappointment in the loss of cosmic illusion, will to power celebrates "man's triumphant awakening" to and acceptance of his own creative power in the face of loss of cosmic and theoretic illusion. Art, not knowledge, is the unfettered expression of human creativity, the activity in which the teleological mentality represented by science and historical consciousness is transcended. "Not in knowing but in creating lies our health! . . . If the universe has no concern for us, then we want the right to scorn it."[28]

The presence of Nietzsche and Heidegger is felt throughout *Legitimacy*—

---

[25] Ibid., 139–40.

[26] Ibid., 141, 143. Blumenberg refers to Nietzsche, "*Die Teleologie seit Kant,*" *Musarion ed.*, vol. 1, 410.

[27] Ibid., 143. The quotation from Nietzsche is "Beyond Good and Evil," part 1, section 13, *Basic Writings*, trans. Walter Kaufmann (New York: Random House, 1992), 211; *Musarion ed.*, vol. 15, 20–21.

[28] Ibid., 142. The quotation from Nietzsche is "*Vorarbeiten zu einer Schrift über den Philosophen von 1872/5,*" *Musarion ed.*, vol. 6, 35.

the work is in large measure an effort at exorcism. Blumenberg never engages them at the point of their most telling criticism, however.[29] In going beyond a critique of reason's ability to grasp the essence of things to question the very appropriateness of abstract thought as a medium of interaction between humans and the world, Nietzsche and Heidegger replace the epistemological subject with an ontology of beings in-the-world, whose linguistic and social practices constitute the human world. Though Blumenberg eloquently argues that the "zero point of the dissolution of order and the point of departure of the construction of order are identical," he never brings the age to that "minimum of ontological predisposition," never faces the necessity of a radically alien way of being-human. In his cosmic overestimation of the adequacy of cognition to meet the crisis he vividly describes, he never considers the more disturbing question raised by acosmic critiques: What if the age had responded to the challenge posed by Nominalism without its "remnant of teleology," its trust in the ability of abstract thought to establish order?

Because Blumenberg never asks that question, he never grasps the master key it took Vico twenty years to understand, an insight into the poverty of the human condition so extreme that even subjective existence must be constructed, that radical beginnings can take place only in an originary language. And, he never achieves a truly radical understanding of the convergence of knowing and making in *verum-factum*—a convergence characterizing both human and divine activity—though it is closer to the one he disparages as Nietzsche's response to acosmic challenges, the "absoluteness of art." Heidegger too, despite his own critique of Nietzsche, affirmed the absolutism of art, albeit in the context of an effort to transcend Nietzsche's anthropocentrism. For both, art is the only response to the realization that neither knowledge nor order derives from mind. Awareness of the radical contingency of the world forces art to accept its own radical creativity, to accept the artifactuality of the "real," the fictiveness of truth, the finitude of the world it makes. Art has no need of the illusions of an unfinished world or of infinite progress to justify its own unconditioned acts.

If the age had given up its subjective remnant of teleology, if it had appropriated, on behalf of anthropology, the notion of the world as a work of art created by an ontologically constructive language, it would have identified humans as artists—poets—rather than as subjects, as creators of their own artifactual reality, their own fictive truths. Such a yea-saying was not the response of the moderns to their epochal crisis, but one that defined the

[29] The reductiveness of Blumenberg's reading of the history of Western thought, its grounding in subjectivism and subjectism, is nowhere more apparent than in his discussion of Nietzsche. Nietzsche's rejection of the truths of modernity is presented as a critique *internal* to the tradition, a stage in the anthropological response to theological absolutism begun with modernity. The confrontational nature of Nietzsche's relation to modernity—indeed, to humanism—is blunted thereby. Blumenberg's "epochal changes" reveal more continuity than he acknowledges, comprising mere variations on traditional themes, while Nietzsche's critique of cosmic order is more radical and disjunctive than Gnosticism's or Nominalism's.

break between modern and postmodern, and Nietzsche could more appropriately be called its herald than the last voice of the modern age. Before Nietzsche, at the beginning of the epoch, Vico too grasped the master key of that poetic anthropology. Rejection of the ontological dichotomy between real and artifactual was not, however, new with Nietzsche or Vico. That the real is made, that originary activity is linguistic and poetic, is the message of the Hebrew Bible. In the following part I characterize more fully the nature of biblical creativity, as read from the perspective of contemporary occupants of the acosmic position, postmodern writers, then turn to a discussion of Vico's *poiesis*.

The Originary as Language

> [I]t would be the ultimate error if one wished to explain the sentence about man's ek-sistent essence as if it were the secularized transference to human beings of a thought that Christian theology expresses about God (*Deus est suum esse* [God is His Being]).
> —Martin Heidegger, "Letter on Humanism"

> Consciously or not the idea that man has of his poetic power corresponds to the idea he has about the creation of the world, and to the solution he gives to the problem of the radical origin of things.
> —Georges Canguilhem, quoted in Derrida's "Force and Signification"

Scripture and Its Precursors: The Onto-theological Reading of Genesis

Blumenberg's misunderstanding of the radically alien message of the Hebrew Bible is a function of the syncretic process that from the Hellenistic period transmitted to thinkers a biblical literature conditioned by metaphysical assumptions. His passing reference, when discussing Greek cosmic assumptions, to the "different but equally orderly" nature of the biblical worldview, shows no appreciation for an "order" that renders satisfaction of theoretic curiosity illusory, or for the originary potency of language that brings order into existence *ex nihilo*. If human self-understanding is ultimately an act of comparison with God, then it is contingent on the understanding of that original. Though the biblical text announcing man's creation in God's image authorized the modern age's analogy between man and God, the God to whom the moderns likened man was not the Creator-God of Genesis, whose originary activity would not have enabled them to possess *theoretic* truths. Their desire to do so led them into that "ultimate error" against which Heidegger warns, of likening themselves to a God of Being, whose Being was identified with rational subjectivity. Only a likeness to such a God enabled them to ground a science of nature on their own subjective reason. Heidegger's warning applies retroactively, against the onto-theological tradition effectively begun with the spiritualizing of the divine nature in the Hellenistic period and given modern formulation in Descartes's identification of humans as subjects. Alternately, Derrida quotes Georges Canguilhem, whose self-understanding evokes a radically alien Judaic God who is not a God of Being but of originary power. Like Canguilhem, Derrida realizes what escapes Blumenberg and the moderns, that originary power is linguistic, not conceptual, that the God who owns that power is one who absents himself, whose silence enables humans to take possession of their own originary language.

For a tradition that conceived of the Creator as a spiritual being, the increased appreciation of the originary power of human language since Nietzsche makes it easier to figure that Creator as a poet-God. What would human self-understanding be if the God to whom it likened itself was not a Christianized version of the Divine Architect of the *Timaeus,* but a poet? I suggest an answer to that question here by drawing on several contemporary discussions that distinguish the Judaic worldview from the metaphysical tradition to which it has been subsumed. The most radical of those discussions is Derrida's, who calls himself Reb Derissa. In the writings of Derrida and Judaic scholars God is not Being but poet, reality not logocentric but linguistic, and human self-understanding not of the self as subject, an anthropological *imago* of a Divine Subject, but as creator, with a poetic language, of human meaning.[30]

The "ultimate error" against which Heidegger warns, of a human self-understanding based on an analogy with the God of Being, transmitting belief in a subjective human essence to the moderns, was itself the result of the assimilation of the biblical passage "And God said, Let us make man in our image, after our likeness," to the classical definition of man as *animal rationale.*[31] Man was *imago Dei,* it was believed, because he was created as a rational being akin to the divine, a likeness lost in the Fall. That theological misreading compounded an earlier philosophic error. As Heidegger charges,

---

[30] Though I focus only on Jewish postmodern writings relevant to my particular themes, there is a growing literature on the affinities between Judaism and postmodernism. In particular, see Steven Kepnes, *Interpreting Judaism in a Postmodern Age* (New York: New York University Press, 1996) and *Reasoning After Revelation: Dialogues in Postmodern Jewish Philosophy,* ed. Steven Kepnes, Peter Ochs, and Robert Gibbs (Boulder, Colo.: Westview Press, 1998). In the latter work the editors acknowledge that, in their search "for more adequate paradigms [of Judaism, they] derive support from the work of Continental, academic postmodernists and literary theorists . . . hermeneutics, pragmatism, and semiotics" (1–2), in which the "modern, autonomous self . . . becomes subject to the play of speech, text, and interpretation. . . . The self no longer recognizes itself in itself but through manifold, refracted linguistic forms" (24). See in particular 123–30, Edith Wyschogrod's claim: "postmodern thinking is, in fact, in no small measure the result of turning both to recent Jewish experience and to traditional Jewish modes of interpretation. . . . [P]ostmodernism is, in important respects, a creation of Jewish history and hermeneutics rather than a cluster of adopted strategies" (128).

[31] Genesis 1:26–7. See also Genesis 5:1–3; 9:17.

animal rationale was itself a Roman mis-translation of *zoon logon echon,* "a metaphysical interpretation of it." Heidegger questions "whether the essence of man primordially and most decisively lies in the dimension of *animalitas* at all . . . even when *anima* [soul] is posited as *animus sive mens* [spirit or mind], and this in turn is later posited as subject, person or spirit [*Geist*]. Such positing is the manner of metaphysics."[32] For Heidegger the Roman mistranslation fixed the ek-sistence of man as subjective essence, bringing to the fore the humanist, anthropocentric perspective of metaphysics.

But Heidegger himself seems unaware that the analogy was faulty not only because of the subjectivizing of *animal rationale* and subsequent misinterpretation of *imago Dei,* but also because the analogy assumed a spiritual conception of the Creator-God. The section on the "image of God" in the *Encyclopedia of Religion and Ethics* exemplifies that error: "'God is a Spirit,' said Jesus to the women of Samaria at Jacob's well. . . . This great idea is the basal conception on which the interpretation of man as made in God's image . . . must proceed. For if God is a Spirit, then man, reflecting Him, must be a spirit too. . . . [H]uman nature has more in it than . . . sensuous experiences, animal proclivities, and fleshly inclinations." The encyclopedist supports Jesus's utterance with the creation narrative, which says man became "the image of his Maker" when "the breath of life [was] 'breathed into his nostrils' by God Himself."[33] Remarkably, the writer is unaware that the identification of God as Spirit, which he takes as central to the scriptural notion of God and the spiritual conception of man, derives from mystifying metaphysical beliefs alien to the Israelite text. He does not consider the possibility that the God of the Hebrew scriptures, whom some Jewish biblical scholars even consider corporeal, may not be "Spirit" at all.[34] What does emerge from his reading is the significance that a spiritual interpretation of God and man has for a Christianized West, transmitting, as it does, the as-

[32] Martin Heidegger, "Letter on Humanism," *Basic Writings,* ed. David Farrell Krell (San Francisco: Harper, 1993), 213–65, 226–27.

[33] William L. Davidson, "Image of God," *Encyclopedia of Religion and Ethics,* ed. James Hastings, vol. 7 (New York: Scribner, 1951), 160–64, 160–61. E. C. Selwyn quotes from *Expositor,* 8th ser., v. (1913): 169. Man's spiritual nature includes immortality, Davidson concludes, since "[t]his is a logical deduction from the possession by man of the Divine image: spirit cannot die." How far this was understood by the Jews, he acknowledges, "is subject to dispute."

[34] See for example *The Interpreter's Dictionary of the Bible: An Illustrated Encyclopedia,* ed. George Arthur Buttrick (New York: Abington Press, 1962), vol. 2, 682–85. The latest translation of Genesis gives the second verse, which is usually translated "And the Spirit of God moved upon the face of the waters," as "and a wind from God sweeping over the water," because *ruah* can mean wind, spirit, breath. It supports the choice of "wind" with reference to the most ancient versions of the Bible, and argues that wind is one of the series of material elements created together, including "heaven, earth, light, darkness, water, day, night." It claims that the translation "spirit," which it traces to Philo, is problematic since it represents the creation of a spiritual being who serves no function and undermines the monotheism of the biblical text (*Tanakh, The Holy Scripture; The New JPS Translation According to the Traditional Hebrew Text* [Philadelphia: The Jewish Publication Society of America, 1985], 3; *Notes on the New Translation of the Torah,* ed. Harry Orlinsky [Philadelphia: The Jewish Publication Society of America, 1970], 49–57).

sumption of a *homoiousis* between humans and ultimate reality. That assumption was foundational for later philosophers concerned with justifying knowledge of God—the scholastics, for example, and modern humanist philosophers justifying knowledge of the human world. Human subjectivity plays the same epistemic role for the encyclopedist, who takes it as given that since the "rational creature is thus far stamped with the stamp of the Creator . . . God cannot be unknown, much less unknowable, if man bears in him the Divine image. . . . [B]oth natural theology and Divine revelation become possible, and indeed . . . inevitable."

The spiritualizing of the images of God and man in Genesis is symbolized—if not actually effected—by identification of the Hebrew *davar* with the Greek *logos,* most systematically by Philo, and most consequentially in the Gospel of John. Both terms meant "word," though the meanings of each differed so greatly that the one that came to the fore necessarily elided the other. Though *logos* also meant "to speak," it derived from the root "*leg,*" "to gather" in the sense of "put in order, arrange." Thus it also meant reckoning and thinking.[35] For the Greeks, one commentator says, "[t]he deepest level of meaning in the term 'word' [*logos*] is thus nothing which has to do with the function of speaking . . . [but] ordered and reasonable content. The term was generally used 'only with regard to the principal functions of the reasonable man.'"[36] *Davar* also came from the verb "to speak," (*dibber*), but for the Hebrews, the meanings associated with *davar* were "word," "deed," "thing," the latter two associations not distinguishable from, but the very meaning of, "word" itself. As such there was no distinction between language and thought or language and the world of action and concrete things created by it.[37] *Davar* was the very power of God, an active, effective force, a dynamic event at one and the same time linguistic, meaningful, concrete, temporal. God's word was *the very reality* of the world, a reality "in compacted or concentrated form, which [the ancient Israelites] name[d] and thus charge[d] with their specific characteristics. As such words were . . . quite palpable, concrete . . . veritable concentrations of power that could act, move, create, destroy, prosper ('bless') and harrow ('curse')." Nor was a world so created material, in the metaphysical, substantive sense, but a con-

---

[35] Thorleif Boman, *Hebrew Thought Compared with Greek* (New York: W. W. Norton and Company, 1960), 67. The English spelling of the Hebrew for "word" varies considerably; for example, *dabhar, dabar, davar.* I use *davar* except when quoting others.

[36] Ibid. Boman quotes Franz Passow, *Handwörterbuch der griechischen Sprache* (Leipzig: W. Vogel, 1847).

[37] The Hebrews had no word for thing separate from the word for speech and deed. *Davar,* while material, was not so as separate object, but "efficacious fact," a dynamic reality. For this discussion of Hebrew I draw on Boman; Claude Tresmontant, *A Study of Hebrew Thought,* trans. Michael Francis Gibson (New York: Desclee Co., 1960); Hans Jonas, *The Phenomenon of Life: Toward a Philosophical Biology* (New York: Dell Publishing Co., 1966), and *Philosophical Essays: From Ancient Creed to Technological Man* (Englewood Cliffs: Prentice Hall, 1974); H. Wheeler Robinson, *The Christian Doctrine of Man* (Edinburgh: T & T Clark Press, 1946).

crete reality, meaningful because it was created with language.[38] Tresmontant calls such a world a "poetic materialism," but von Rad is closer to the mark in saying it was "surely far more abyssal than the one which shelters under our term 'Nature.'"[39]

Correspondingly, the Hebrew word for "be," *hayah*, meant as much "becoming" as "be." It was not an objective "datum at rest in itself. . . . The 'being' of things and of the world . . . was . . . something living, active, and effective. . . . [T]he effective expresses itself in activity, and so existence is identical with effectiveness: it is not at rest but is dynamic."[40] Even the *hayah* of God, Boman says, "is its *effect*." This alien holistic, dynamic, linguistic sense of reality was lost when *davar* was translated as *logos*—lost so completely that even awareness that an alien view of reality had been lost was no longer possible. The process through which *logos* came to supplant *davar* and onto-theology came to suppress a linguistic, dynamic conception of God and creative activity can be traced in the increasingly mystified use of the term in Philo, Paul, and John. Thus Blumenberg's reference to Philo to characterize the biblical theme of absolute beginnings "new to philosophy" is especially problematic. The scriptural God was an absolute, transcendent deity whose creative activity was willful, free, and unconditioned, a creativity unparalleled in Greek philosophy. Though Philo himself retained the Israelite's belief in God's transcendency and ineffability, his reinterpretation of the creation narrative and use of *logos*, with the meanings it had and would come to have in Neoplatonism and Christianity, introduced the notion of an ontological homogeneity between Creator and the created world that compromised the radical distinction between them, enabling later theologians to legitimize knowledge both of God and of his creation. Eventually it provided thinkers the basis for assuming the likeness between a subjective knower/maker and the made.

For his reinterpretation of Genesis Philo drew on the *Timaeus*, arguably the most important source for the notion of creation for Neoplatonism and Christianity. Though there was no conception of creative activity in that work, there was a productive process, that of a craftsman, a Divine Architect who formed matter in accordance with an intelligible pattern. On the analogy of an animal Plato insisted the intelligible could not be formed out

[38] Isaac Rabinowitz, "'Word' and Literature in Ancient Israel," *New Literary History* 4 (1972–73): 133. See also Susan A. Handelman, *Slayers of Moses: The Emergence of Rabbinic Interpretation in Modern Literary Theory* (Albany: State University of New York Press, 1982), 32. Handelman says, "*Reality* is a far more appropriate word to use than *thing*, for it does not evoke the same connotations as do substance and being."

[39] Tresmontant, *A Study of Hebrew Thought*, 47; Gerhard von Rad, *The Problem of the Hexateuch and Other Essays*, trans. Rev. E. W. Trueman Dicken, D. D. (Edinburgh: Oliver and Boyd, 1966), 152. For a work distinguishing the onto-theological conception of God in Christianity from the biblical, see Brian D. Ingraffia, *Postmodern Theory and Biblical Theology: Vanquishing God's Shadow* (Cambridge: Cambridge University Press, 1995). Since Ingraffia's intent is to "save" the biblical conception of God for Christianity, he does not discuss Judaism.

[40] Boman, *Hebrew Thought*, 45–48.

of matter alone. The productive process required that a "world-soul," which the *demiurgos* made by mixing matter and Ideas, be infused through it. Knowledge of the Ideas realized in the ensouled material world would lead the human soul—itself, like the Ideas, unchanging, eternal, rational—to an intuition of the highest Form of Being, the Good. The *homoiousis* of rational soul, world soul, *eidos,* and the Good provided later Hellenistic religious movements such as Neoplatonism and Christianity with an ontological ground justifying both Gnostic and epistemic conceptions of knowledge of God and the world. For Plotinus and Neoplatonism Plato's Good became the One or Absolute, a self-sufficient Being, and the creative process a substantive emanation of it, a necessary objectification or hypostatization that undermined the craftsman model of creation.[41] Christianity too eventually distinguished itself from Judaism by claiming the instantiation of God in the created world.

When Philo reinterpreted the creative process in Genesis in the context of the *Timaeus,* it was not to replace but, rather, to *save* the idea of cosmic intelligibility from threats posed by Hellenistic challenges. He did so by providing philosophy with an alternate version of cosmic order, making the omnipotence and creativity of the biblical God its source, thus rebuking those "who, having the world in admiration rather than the Maker . . . pronounce it to be without beginning and everlasting, while with impious falsehood they postulate in God a vast inactivity; whereas we ought . . . to be astonished at His powers as Maker and Father." He claimed to find in Genesis two separate creations, the first the willful creation of an intelligible world that provided an incorporeal pattern for the creation of a second, material world: "For God, being God, assumed . . . no object of perception would be faultless which was not made in the likeness of an original discerned only by the intellect."[42] Creation of the "incorporeal world . . . firmly settled in the Divine Reason" is followed by material creation grounded on the *logos.* "The Mind of all things has brought the universe into existence," since "Divine Reason . . . is the helmsman and Governor of the universe."[43]

Philo's revision of the creative process played a formative role in the development of the Christian notion of the instantiation of God in the world by undermining the biblical emphasis on divine transcendence and suggest-

---

[41] It also rendered problematic Greek philosophic dualism, since pluralism and materiality emerged from spiritual unity. The substantive relation between the One and an emanated world inherent in pantheism was explicit for mysticism, which conceived of human souls as sparks of divinity. Jewish Neoplatonism struggled to maintain a distinction between God and world.

[42] Philo, "On the Account of the World's Creation Given by Moses" (*De opificio mundi*), *Philo,* trans. F. H. Colson and G. H. Whitaker (London: William Heinemann, 1929), vol. 1, ii, 9; 1, iv, 15.

[43] Philo, "On the Migration of Abraham" (*De migratione Abrahami*), *Philo,* vol. 4, xxxv, 245; "On the Cherubim" (*De cherubim*), *Philo: Complete Works,* trans. C. D. Yonge (London: Henry G. Bohn, 1854), vol. 1, xi, 184. See also "On the Account of the World's Creation" (1, ii, 11).

ing a greater intimacy—even some degree of *homoiousis*—between God and the world. He identified *davar* with *logos,* and *logos* with the Platonic Ideas as a substantive part of God's essence—as eternal thoughts or ideas in the divine mind—then with a created incorporeal real being distinct from God's essence and immanent in the world, the means by which the material world was ordered by divine Ideas.[44] For one commentator, "Such an attempt to bridge the gap between a highly sublimated idea of God and the world of the senses, by . . . convert[ing] an absolute opposition into one of degrees, was original in Philo and was to be repeated time and again in the history of metaphysics."[45] It introduced into the biblical tradition a hierarchical relation between God and the world that was substantive and spiritual. Whether Philo's own cosmology was pantheistic or mystical, it was certainly onto-theological, and a God whose relation to humans had been personal, ethical, linguistic, historical, and eventful had become Spirit. In turning the God of the Whirlwind into a God of Being, Philo turned a scriptural religion into a variant of the subjectivism Heidegger considers the definitive character of metaphysical humanism.[46]

Philo's spiritualized ontology led to a corresponding spiritualization of anthropology. The King James version of Genesis 2:7 reads, "And the Lord God formed man *of* the dust of the ground, and breathed into his nostrils the breath of life; and man became a living soul." The Jewish text, which uses the phrase "living being" rather than "living soul," does not assert the presence of a soul in the Greek sense—an unchanging, immortal, substantively incorporeal being—or characterize man dualistically as body and soul. The soul (*nefesh*) identifies man as a "living creature," in no way distinguishable "from the animal world." What did so was "the special 'inbreathing' of Yahweh in man's case," but even in that case breath is not metaphor for spirit but is quite literally "air," the principle of life for the Israelites. When extin-

---

[44] The term was Stoic, but the *logos* of the Stoics was immanent in the material world. Philo drew not only on Stoic *Logoi* (forces or powers) but also on Platonic Forms. For this discussion of Philo I draw primarily on Harry Austryn Wolfson, *Philo: Foundations of Religious Philosophy in Judaism, Christianity, and Islam* (Cambridge: Harvard University Press, 1947), 289–94 (see also 325–32); and *The Philosophy of the Church Fathers* (Cambridge: Harvard University Press, 1970), vol. 1, chaps. 13, 14, 15. Wolfson says despite the fact that Philo called Ideas eternal, he also considered them created. Eternal meant everlasting, not ungenerated. Since Ideas were objects of God's thinking, Philo introduced a notion not in Plato, that of mind (akin to Aristotle's *nous*). He also dropped the notion of universal intellectual soul, considering souls individual.

[45] Julius Guttmann, *Philosophies of Judaism: The History of Jewish Philosophy from Biblical Times to Franz Rosenzweig,* trans. David W. Silverman (New York: Holt, Rinehart, and Winston, 1964), 26. The extent to which Philo's *logos* actually introduced *divine substance* into the created world is disputed by Philo scholars. Though Wolfson denies it, Erwin Goodenough, who finds in Philo a fully realized mysticism, says the Form that infuses matter is the "lowest point in God's single emanation" (Wolfson, *Philo,* 280–87; Erwin Goodenough, *By Light, Light: The Mystic Gospel of Hellenistic Judaism* [Amsterdam: Philo Press, 1969], 243).

[46] For this reason Philo is often called "the first theologian" (Guttmann, *Philosophies of Judaism,* 29).

guished, "breath-soul" again becomes dust; the Hebrew bible has no explicit concept of immortality.[47]

Since man is a "concrete, sensible being entire," references to the soul do not refer to distinctive, "higher," or more noble activities. Bodily functions are attributed to the soul and psychological and psychic ones to the body; consciousness to the liver, for example, compassion, pity, distress to the bowels, and so on.[48] Though understanding and intellectual activities involve the whole man, their seat is the heart.[49] Since understanding is not an inner faculty, the distinction between speculative thought and action cannot be made: knowledge is *effective,* an *acknowledgment* of the heart as well as concrete action in the world.[50] If "[t]he Hebrew idea of personality is that of an animated body, not (like the Greek) that of an incarnated soul," Philo's anthropology was certainly Greek and Hellenistic.[51]

Though Philo understood the soul as created, which Plato did not, he identified the rational part, which was immaterial and distinct from the body, as a copy of the Idea of soul in the mind of God. God breathed into Adam "not air in motion, but a certain impression and character of divine power, which

[47] See Robinson, *The Christian Doctrine of Man,* 69–70, 14. Similarly the "Spirit" of God, *ruah,* could be translated as "wind." For this discussion of biblical anthropology I draw on Robinson, 1–27, 69–70, 151–56; Tresmontant, *Hebrew Thought,* 83–149; Rachel Elior, "Soul," *Contemporary Jewish Religious Thought: Original Essays on Critical Concepts, Movements, and Beliefs,* eds. Arthur A. Cohen and Paul Mendes-Flohr (New York: Charles Scribner's Sons, 1987), 887–96; *Interpreter's Dictionary of the Bible,* sections on "Soul," vol. 4, 428–29, and "Heart," vol. 2, 549–50. Tresmontant warns, "By applying to the Hebrew *Nephesch,* which the Septuagint translates by *psuche,* the characteristics of the Platonic psyche (conceived in the terms of a dualism of orphic origin), we let the real meaning of *Nephesch* escape us and . . . are left with innumerable pseudo-problems" (94).

[48] "Nothing is more contrary to the biblical conception of knowledge and understanding," Tresmontant says, "than a separation of thought and action" (127). Failure to understand the holistic nature of the Judaic conception of "soul" leads to many misconceptions. Richard Kearney, for example, places "Hebraic imagination" in the subjectivist tradition of the Greeks, missing Judaism's paradigmatic conception of originary linguistic creativity (Richard Kearney, *Wake of Imagination: Toward a Postmodern Culture* [Minneapolis: University of Minnesota Press, 1988]). For Judaic interpretations of "imagination," see R. C. Dentan, for whom the "power of forming mental images" is "a concept entirely unfamiliar to the ancient Hebrews, who were not given to fantasy and who conceived of mental activity primarily in terms of preparation for action" (*Interpreter's Dictionary of the Bible,* vol. 2, 653). More pointedly, Geoffrey H. Hartman says the notion of productive imagination in Judaism is not a visual but "verbal imagery," of which we understand "too little," and refers to the "text dependency of the Jewish imagination" ("Imagination," *Contemporary Jewish Religious Thought,* 460.) Kearney himself attributes the notion of linguistic creativity to Derrida without appreciating Derrida's debt to biblical and rabbinic sources (*Wake of Imagination,* 290).

[49] See "Soul," *Interpreter's Dictionary of the Bible,* vol. 4, 429, and "Heart," vol. 2, 549–50.

[50] Tresmontant, *Hebrew Thought,* 119–30. See also *Interpreter's Dictionary of the Bible,* "Mind," vol. 3, 383. Albrecht Dihle says, "Faith, in the Biblical view, is not primarily seen as knowledge or the cognitive effort leading to such knowledge. . . . It appears . . . as the way to *acknowledge* the will of God and . . . act accordingly" (Albrecht Dihle, *The Theory of Will in Classical Antiquity* [Berkeley: University of California Press, 1982], 75; emphasis added).

[51] Robinson, *The Christian Doctrine of Man,* 27.

divine power Moses calls by an appropriate name image."[52] Not only was that image immortal, but Philo often referred to mind, a "branch of the soul," as *itself* divine, calling it a "fragment of that divine and blessed soul from which it cannot be separated," or saying, "[T]he soul is of ether, a divine fragment"—that is, "a genuine coinage of that divine and invisible breath."[53] Whether or not Philo explicitly identified the soul as divine, thus contributing to the later emergence of mystical Judaism in the Kabbalah, his anthropology transformed and Platonized the dominant understanding of the biblical analogy between man and God. For Philo the human mind was "shaped after the archetypal idea, the sublime Logos."[54] Though Philo's speculative anthropology did not have much influence on Judaism, the notion that man was an *imago* of God, that God was *logos,* became, in mystified form, foundational for Christianity.

Though Philo's Platonized interpretation of *imago Dei* was patently anachronistic, scholars dispute the original meaning of the biblical metaphor. It can be interpreted as an analogy between the human body and the divine form, since the word for image, *selem,* can refer to physical likeness.[55] Other interpretations suggest that God is bodiless and base the analogy on qualitative or functional similarities rather than physical similarities, an interpretation supported by the Hebrew word for likeness, *děmut.* Since the biblical passage goes on to say God gave man dominion over the earth, the most common *functional* interpretation identifies Godlikeness with power of dominion. In denying that the analogy between man and God was based on substantive participation, David Tobin Asselin claims "man is God's image because God breathed His own breath of life into man's nostrils: therefore, he shares God's vital, productive, dynamic mode of existence."[56] The likeness between *nefesh* [breath-soul] and God is not "found in the spiritual sphere . . . with the faculties of man's soul as its fundament. For it seems impossible that the Israelite understood *selem* of anything so purely spiritual as

---

[52] Philo, *Quod Deterius Potiori Insidiari Soleat,* 23, 83, quoted in Wolfson, *Philo,* vol. 1, 394. See also 238. Wolfson himself considers "breath" in scripture incorporeal.

[53] Wolfson, *Philo,* vol. 1, 390–95. Wolfson gives as references, 90; *Quod Deus Sit Immutabilis,* 10, 46; *Legum Allegoria* III, 55, 161/*De Somniis* I, 6, 34; cf. Diogenes, VII, 143/cf. 156; *De Plantatione,* 5, 18. Wolfson interprets these statements to mean the soul was as immaterial as its pattern "rather than substantive divinity."

[54] Wolfson, *Philo,* vol. 1, 390; *De Specialibus Legibus* III, 36, 207; *Quis Rerum Divinarum Heres* 48, 230, 234; cf. *De Opificio Mundi* 23. See also *Legum Allegoria* I, 13, 42; *De Decalogo* 25, 134; *Quod Deterius Potiori Insidiari Soleat* 24, 86–87, 90.

[55] Howard Eilberg-Schwartz, who explores the implications of interpreting the analogy between man and God with reference to the corporeal body of God, says there is "no statement anywhere in ancient Israelite literature that explicitly criticizes the notion of God having a body," and characterizes his work as resisting "spiritualizing and Hellenistic models that continue to inform modern understandings of monotheism" (Howard Eilberg-Schwartz, *God's Phallus and Other Problems for Men and Monotheism* [Boston: Beacon Press, 1994], 8–10). See *Interpreter's Dictionary of the Bible,* vol. 2, 682–85, and vol. 4, 433.

[56] David Tobin Asselin, "The Notion of Dominion in Genesis 1–3," *The Catholic Biblical Quarterly* 16, no. 3 (July 1954): 277 n. 5, 277–94.

rationality or free will. . . . A man's *nephesh* is a totality with a definite stamp . . . ultimately transmuted into a definite mode of activity. . . . Nor did [the Israelite] consider man's power of reason as a [faculty] of the *nephesh*. . . . There is simply no Hebrew equivalent to our 'think,' the arrangement of ideas systematically according to abstract categories." Thus "to 'investigate, remember, make present' are on a practical level: they are factors directing the whole *nephesh* towards an object. . . . To 'investigate wisdom' is . . . to determine the will to wise action. Knowledge is practical, experimental, dynamic."[57] This characterization of *nefesh* does not "constitute an essential difference between man and . . . inanimate creation, for in the Semitic personalized concept of nature, all creatures are endowed with a volitional dynamism." "Existence and activity are not distinct," and Godlikeness resides only in the particular activity of man, that of dominion over all living things. Godlikeness is functional, not substantive: "man does not rule over the animal kingdom because he is God's image: rather, he is God's image precisely because he rules over the animal kingdom, thus sharing God's universal dominion." Moreover, "the value or strength or content of a living thing, to an Israelite, could only be assessed by the value, strength, or content of what emanated from it; thus man's *nephesh* is evaluated in terms of his . . . words (more than mere sounds, they are perceptible embodiments of his *nephesh*)."[58] It is in the activity of speech, the power of naming the animals, that man's dominion over living things resides.

Tellingly, Asselin is embarrassed by such a functional, even corporeal, interpretation of *imago Dei*. Writing from a Catholic perspective, he explains, "[T]he Israelite did not enjoy the advantages of a language and culture based upon Hellenic philosophy and capable of distinguishing a faculty from its actuation. . . . His notion of God's image could not possibly be as refined as that of the Christian, nor could his thinking and experience rise above the practical, experimental, dynamic order of things in which the problems of life were met and answered. He knew no metaphysics on which to base thought-structures such as we are accustomed to." But Asselin excuses this inadequacy, saying we should not "be dismayed by the concrete, crude and inexact categories in which his thought was moulded, since the theological value of his assertions in no way depends on our systematic precisions about the soul, reason, will, etc. Our Blessed Lord Himself managed quite well without them."[59] That estimate is, of course, the dominant one in the West. It is onto-theology's version of metaphysics' privileging of "refined" subjec-

---

[57] Gerhard von Rad echoes Asselin's warning against spiritualized interpretations of *imago Dei*, saying, "[I]nterpretations . . . are to be rejected which proceed from an anthropology strange to the Old Testament and onesidedly limit God's image to man's spiritual nature, relating it to man's 'dignity,' his 'personality' or 'ability for moral decision,' etc." (Gerhard von Rad, *Genesis: A Commentary* [Philadelphia: Westminster Press, 1972], 58).

[58] Asselin, "Notion of Dominion," 281 n. 11, 283–84, 278 n. 5.

[59] Ibid., 281–82.

tivity. The spiritualizing of the Israelite conception of God and man—enabled, in good part, by Philo's syncretism—is apparent in the differences between biblical and Christian interpretations of *imago Dei*. Rather than a functional image of a dynamic God whose creative power is linguistic, the *imago Dei* of Christianity became, ultimately, substantive likeness. Indeed, because it was substantive, the relation between it and God was not merely one of likeness but of identity, though personalized in Jesus Christ. Paul called Christ the Spirit of God Incarnate,[60] and, thus, insofar as "Jesus is . . . Himself a Spirit (for 'God is a Spirit') . . . He is *the* Image of God, and not simply, like man, 'made *in*' it."[61]

Hans Jonas, who identifies the creation as the most influential Judaic conception in the West, calls the incarnation the most influential Christian, a mystery in a sense that creation is not, radically transforming the Hebrew conception of God.[62] Alone among the deities of the ancient Near East the Judaic God did not create through procreation but through fabrication, producing artifacts unlike the artisan. In generation, alternately, the likeness between begotten and begetter is assumed. The Christian conception of the incarnation retained the pagan assumption of likeness between God and the world contained in the notion of emanation, in which "a pervading homogeneity of being unites Man, Nature and God." *The Interpreter's Dictionary of the Bible* supports such a reading. Pointing out that the Septuagint translation of "image" suggests something more than "likeness"—rather, a "perfect reflection of the divine prototype"—it translates "likeness" as *homoiousis*.[63] In effect, Philo's notion of immanent *logos* had bridged the chasm between the pagan belief in the immanence of spirit and the biblical conception of God's radical transcendence. Though Philo did not call the immanent *logos* the soul or mind of the world, Wolfson says "in Philo's version of Plato," immanent Logos takes the place of universal soul, and "the incar-

---

[60] Paul, I Corinthians 15:47.

[61] Davidson, "Image of God," *Encyclopedia of Religion and Ethics,* 163. For Paul, insofar as Christ was God's substantive image, it was "only in relation with Christ that man can attain the likeness to God" (*Interpreter's Dictionary of the Bible,* vol. 2, 685). It was Paul and John who projected mystifying elements derived from Philo onto the historical life of Jesus, thus laying the ground for the trinitarian conception of God. Like Philo, John understood *logos* as immanent, and, like Paul, as "become flesh," and followed Paul in calling *logos* the only begotten Son of God (See Wolfson, *The Philosophy of the Church Fathers,* chap. 10). Thus "the *logos* of Philo . . . ceased to be created by God and became begotten of God." While John, like Jesus, used the designation "Son of God" metaphorically, the mystical interpretation of the incarnation became doctrine with the Council of Nicea's determination that *logos* was generated "by nature" rather than will (227–32). Though the Fathers distinguished their position from pagan anthropomorphizing religions and mythologies, they introduced a mystifying *homoiousis* between God and created world, with its promise of the possibility of knowledge, into a biblical tradition containing neither.

[62] Jonas, "Jewish and Christian Elements in Philosophy: Their Share in the Emergence of the Modern Mind," *Philosophical Essays,* 28.

[63] *Interpreter's Dictionary of the Bible,* "Image of God," vol. 2, 682–85.

nate Logos of Christianity is analogous to . . . [it]. In [Christianity], the Logos is in a man; in [Philo], the Logos is in the world."[64]

Philo's spiritualized cosmology and the consequent spiritualizing of anthropology provided the ontological *homoiousis* that could justify epistemic knowledge of made truths for a Christianized West. Jonas himself credits Philo's identification of *logos* and *davar* with the introduction of the epistemic concerns of the Greeks into theology, saying, "The problem of objectification, and with it that of reversing or partially unmaking it, was bequeathed to Western theology from its origin in the mating of the Biblical word with the Greek *logos*." He illustrates "[w]hich side of the double parentage would be dominant and which recessive . . . what happened to the Biblical word through [Philo] and his successors," with an allegory Philo tells based on the "etymology of the name 'Israel' . . . mean[ing] 'He who sees God.'" For Philo, "Jacob's acquiring this name . . . represent[s] the God-seeker's progress from the stage of hearing to that of seeing, made possible by the miraculous conversion of ears into eyes." Jonas believes the allegory reveals Philo's interpretation of the knowing of God in terms of the preeminence of vision—intellectual contemplation rather than audition—in Hellenic thought. The "seeing" of God's voice becomes primary "[b]ecause that which God speaks is not words but works, which the eye discriminates better than the ear. 'Works,' finished realities, are what God 'speaks,' that is, what he . . . puts before our eyes. And the finished or perfected is objectively present and can only be looked at; it presents itself in its *eidos*." Philo establishes the "ontological correlate" of vision for the knowing of God by insisting that God is "the highest being." For Jonas, Philo's tale is "a parable for that turn . . . which he himself and . . . Christian theology . . . underwent . . . from the original hearing of the call of the living, nonworldly God . . . to the theoretical will for vision of the supernatural, divine truths."[65]

In Philo the God of the Whirlwind became the Divine Architect of the *Timaeus*.[66] Yet, it is Philo's formulation of *verum-factum* as a principle of

---

[64] Wolfson, *The Philosophy of the Church Fathers*, 202–3, 365–66.

[65] Jonas, "Heidegger and Theology," *The Phenomenon of Life*, 235–39. The quotations are Philo, "De Decalogo," 47, and "De Abrahamo," 57, in the Greek edition of the Loeb Classical Library, ed. L. Cohn and P. Wendland (Cambridge: Harvard University Press). Boman also mentions this "Greek" shift from hearing to "seeing through the eyes of the soul" in Philo (Boman, *Hebrew Thought*, 201). See also Blumenberg, *Legitimacy of the Modern Age*, 284–88 and 24 n. 21.

[66] St. Jerome noted that Greek philosophers of Philo's time said of him, "Either Philo is speaking like Plato or Plato like Philo" (St. Jerome, *De vir. ill.* 11; quoted in Albrecht Dihle, *The Theory of Will in Classical Antiquity* [Berkeley: University of California Press, 1982], 90). David Satran says this perception led to "the (probably fruitless) debate whether [Philo] is primarily a Jewish exegete or a Hellenistic philosopher" ("Hellenism," *Contemporary Jewish Religious Thought*, 331–38). Antipathy to "foreign wisdom," which led the rabbinic tradition to ignore Hellenistic Judaism, accounted for the disappearance of Philo in Jewish thought until the sixteenth century (334).

cognitive construction that, for Blumenberg, points the way out of modernity's dilemma, since, for it, "truth," though artifactual, is a product of mind, and thus possessed by its maker *as theory*.[67] Blumenberg does not appreciate the extent to which the biblical view of order and the process that produces it is alien to the dualist, static conceptual structure of Greek cosmology. Philo's characterization of the eternal, unchanging, necessary, rational order of the cosmos as the contingent acts of an omnipotent will did not introduce Hebraic voluntarism into Greek metaphysics. Rather, in retaining Plato's metaphysics, it sacrificed the radically existential, linguistic nature of biblical creativity, a conception too "alien" to be accessible to a hellenized theological tradition.

Scripture and Its Precursors: The Postmodern Reading of the Hebraic Originary

> The speech of God are His actions. . . . [T]he writings of God are His creations and the word of God are His writings. . . . Behold, the book that God wrote is everything which exists.[68]
> —Rabbinic sayings, quoted by José Faur, "The Splitting of the *Logos*: Some Remarks on Vico and the Rabbinic Tradition"

> The necessity of commentary, like poetic necessity, is the very form of exiled speech. In the beginning is hermeneutics.
> —Jacques Derrida, "Edmond Jabès and the Question of the Book"

In the process traced from Philo's substitution of *logos* for *davar,* with all the mystifications that substitution entailed, God became Being and *imago Dei* spiritual substance. Eventually, the tradition's "thought about human beings" as a "transference to human beings of a thought . . . about God as Being" culminated in the Cartesian conception of man as subject of knowledge and action. In that historical development the radical alterity between Greek metaphysics and biblical worldview—the belief in a Creator-God whose creativity was linguistic and in man as *imago* of God functionally, by virtue of his possession of language—was lost.

That alterity was lost to the West, that is, fallen under the hegemony of a hellenized Christianity, but sustained in the Judaic. Though Judaism too came under the influence of Greek thought in the medieval period, it retained

---

[67] Philo had something Descartes lacked—the assurance that intelligible order, the knowledge of which was derivative, was cosmological. Still, Descartes's operational conception of knowledge, which promised mastery of nature, control over human well-being, even an infinitely progressive future, was not an undesirable alternative to that assurance.

[68] Rabbinic sayings. The reference for the first is *Midrash Tehillim* CVII, 3, ed. Salomon Buber (New York: Om Publishing, 1947), 462; the second, R. Tudah ha-Levi, *Kuzari* IV, 25; the third, R. Levi ben Gereshom, *Pirush 'al ha-Tora* (Venice, 5307/1547) fol. 113 b–c.

that alien notion of a reality constituted by the dynamic, effectual power of word inseparable from deed and thing. It did so particularly in the rabbinic tradition, "the most idiosyncratic element of Judaism," one commentator says, which "seemed esoteric and remained outside the cultural code of the West."[69] The rabbis believed the written Torah had been left intentionally incomplete and was meant to be accompanied and supplemented by an oral Torah that explained, elaborated, and interpreted the written: "[T]ext and its interpretation . . . [were] not seen as two separate entities, but as twin aspects of the same revelation."[70] The word, thus, was not only God's, as in the written Torah, but theirs as an oral tradition. Through their hermeneutic interaction with God—reading, interpreting, reinterpreting, and adding to the divine language—the rabbis kept alive belief in the effectual and constitutive power of language.

In the context of contemporary postmodern concerns a number of writers have turned to the rabbinic tradition to recover a linguistic worldview as ancient as the Greek. In *Golden Doves with Silver Dots* José Faur, for one, distinguishes the ontological or metaphysical from a linguistic view of the world. Faur traces the hostility between philosophy and rhetoric in the West to the fact that its conception of knowledge was founded on the Greek "splitting of the *logos*" between word and idea. For philosophy, language was merely the expression of universal or ideal categories of thought—an inherently flawed expression that corrupted pure ideality. That opposition did not occur in Judaic thought because for it God's *logos* (*dabar*, *'imra*) was a "dynamic, creative force. . . . The Universe was effected by His word. . . . [T]he speech of God is His performance. . . . *Memra* [the Aramaic version of the word] does not function according to some preestablished order: it *establishes* the order. More precisely, it is the actual manifestation of God."[71] Since creation "not only was realized through speech [but] actually *is* the speech of God," *logos* as *dabar* refers both to the "things" God created and the "words" He spoke.

One purpose of Faur's discussion, beside recovery of the linguistic nature of the Judaic worldview, is to characterize that linguistic nature as semiological. Drawing on the writings of Saussure and Benveniste, Faur says that for the Greeks, a thing *is*, whereas in the created world things, which are the

---

[69] José Faur, *Golden Doves with Silver Dots: Semiotics and Textuality in Rabbinic Tradition* (Bloomington: Indiana University Press, 1986), xi.

[70] Handelman, *Slayers of Moses,* 31. The rabbinic tradition dates from the Second Temple—4th century B.C.E.—to 6th century C.E. See chap. 2, 27–50, and Faur, *Golden Doves,* chap. 4, 84–113.

[71] Faur, *Golden Doves,* 23–24. See also José Faur, "The Splitting of the *Logos:* Some Remarks on Vico and the Rabbinic Tradition," *New Vico Studies,* vol. 3 (1985): 85–103. Though Faur uses the term "ontological" for the Greek tradition, and "semiological" for Judaic, I use the term "ontological" for the latter. There is, of course, no "ontology" as such outside Greek metaphysical assumptions, but the term enables me to distinguish the view positing the linguistic creation of a real world from epistemological efforts to ground knowledge of reality.

word of God, *signify*. Thus, whereas metaphysics subsumes the universe to the categories of ontology, for the Jews the world is a semiological system. Faur distinguishes the latter from the Aristotelian conception of world as material nature, which gave rise to mechanistic conceptions with the emergence of modern science. David Nieto, spiritual leader of the Sephardic community in London (roughly contemporary with Vico), criticized the scientific conception of nature not only because it was mechanistic, but also because it conceived nature as universal. There were particular natures, Nieto said, but no "universal nature"; rather, God himself "is nature." The identity of God and nature, which would have been pantheistic in a metaphysical system, was not for Nieto, for whom God was a providential agent who continuously repeated the creative process and whose creative acts were speech.[72] "Whereas Heidegger . . . conceived of the poet as a Maker, the Hebrews conceived of the Maker as a poet," Faur says.[73] God is "eminently literate: He has something to say, the whole creation is the speech or book of God. An ontological world, unreadable and value-free, posits a God who is fundamentally illiterate, and therefore unacceptable to the people of the book." "The speech of God are His actions . . . [and] the writings of God are His creations and the word of God are His writings." Thus what metaphysics characterized as nature was, for the Jews, a book. "Behold," R. Levi ben Gereshom said, "the book that God wrote is everything which exists."[74] The book is Israel's national symbol, the identification between it and the book absolute and total. Even "God is the consequence, not the cause, of the law [Tora]."[75]

In rejecting the "metaphysical" notion of the world as nature Nieto also rejected what followed from it, the conception of knowledge as objective, as value- and context-free. Belief in the possibility of knowledge could arise only within metaphysics: the world as book was not an object of knowledge but something to be read, and reading was not a literal process. While for metaphysics the *is* can only be re-presented, in a semiological system the "*transformation* of the original into a system of values" always involves iteration or repeatability, and no repetition is identical to the original.[76] There is no authoritative or final version of the book God writes, not even in the intention of its author. The text is "independent of the author; it uses the author,

---

[72] Faur, *Golden Doves*, 26–27.

[73] Ibid., xxi. "As a poet," Faur adds, "God must hide his own omnipresence." Poets are dissimulators (xxii).

[74] Faur, "The Splitting of the *Logos*," 91–93.

[75] José Faur, "Law and Hermeneutics in Rabbinic Jurisprudence: A Maimonidean Perspective," *Cardozo Law Review* 14, no. 6 (May 1993): 1661. The identification of Hebrews, writing, and book metonymically includes Desert: "In Hebrew thought, Book and Desert are contingent upon one another. . . . 'The word cannot dwell except in the silence of other words. To speak is, accordingly, to lean on a metaphor of the desert.' . . . Desert, [like Book] . . . is the national symbol of the Hebrews" (Faur, *Golden Doves*, 4–5; see also xx; 9). The quotation is Edmond Jabès, *Du Désert au Livre* (Paris: Pierre Belford, 1980), 101.

[76] Faur, *Golden Doves*, xvi.

rather than the other way around," a view corroborated in the Talmud and
by the rabbis in the saying that, when the people of the book accept the book,
"[t]he Tora is no longer in the heavens."[77]

In developing the radical differences between epistemic and interpretive
processes, Faur says in a semiological system truth (*'emet*) or meaning and
the articulation of meaning are not separable: meaning derives from the linguistic structure. The Greek distinction between the two led to the privileging of thought; speech was merely the means by which ideality was made
"present." The rejection by Plato and the philosophic tradition of writing,
which is iterable and in which ideality is absent, was a rejection of reading
and interpretation. *Derasha,* on the other hand, is an interactive process between reader/interpreter and divine speech, whether as the book of the world
or as written law.[78] Its function is not to discover meaning but to generate
it. Faur explicates this relation with reference to Saussure's distinction between signifier and signified. *Derasha* functions as signifier, the sound-im-
age of a word, and the signified is always "suspended or modified" in the
interpretive process. The object of commentary is to "raise the level of per-
plexity. . . . [It] bears no resemblance whatsoever to the original."[79]

Before Saussure introduced to modern linguistics the notion that meaning
is a "function of the differences and differentiations established by the linguistic system," it was, Faur continues, inherent in Hebrew semiology. It was
embedded in the root *byn,* from which came the preposition *"ben,"* or between. The "dreamt up" word ["differance"] that Derrida says he struggled
to find to designate "difference and articulation," had been formulated by
the Hebrews as *'ot,* meaning the sign or letter that articulates meaning. "Unlike a symbol, which is significant in itself, *'ot* as a letter is significant only
in syntagmatic opposition: according to the rabbis, a single letter does not
constitute writing."[80] Thus interpretation is not only textual, but contextual,
and, since every part is interrelated, the context is the semiological system.
The distinction between inner and outer, or assertion of a frame marking that
distinction, cannot be made; likewise, the Western notion of *parergon,* of
what is only "adjunct" or "supplement," cannot be invoked. For the Hebrews, the Scroll symbolizes the impossibility of distinguishing what is inside
and what outside a frame. It is scrolled inward, indicating it is "thoroughly
cross-referential and therefore self-referential." The Torah is read, reread,
and reinterpreted annually in a circular process affirmed in the holiday of

[77] Ibid., 15, 119. See Faur, "Law and Hermeneutics," 1674.
[78] There are, in fact, two Torahs. The relation between the written and oral Laws is the semiological one between golden doves and silver dots. The latter is the interpretation of the former
(xvii).
[79] Ibid., xviii–xix, 121.
[80] *'Ot* also means "absolutely unique" or "different," and as such, God is the ultimate *'ot,*
who functions "as the final difference that escapes articulation and identification" (Faur,
Golden Doves, xxiv–xxv).

Simhat Tora, when a new cycle of reading is begun on the day the old is completed.[81]

Unlike the metaphysical system privileging spatiality and, therefore, visual and simultaneous thinking, the interpretive, circular thinking of the Hebrews is successive and temporal. Meaning or truth that is successive is not perceived visually, but "at the auditory level." The Hebrew prayer that begins with the *Shema* is an injunction to Israel, not only to "hear," but to "understand and acknowledge." Emphasis on the auditory helps explain the absence of the inner/outer distinction for the Hebrews, particularly in understanding human personhood. As visual thinking concerns itself with the presence of ideality in a spatial world, "[h]earing functions as the nexus between human interiority and exteriority. . . . [T]hrough auditory speech, reflective experience is realized. Upon hearing oneself talk, the interiority/exteriority of the 'I' is simultaneously experienced."[82] This simultaneity helps account for the absence of the subject-object distinction for the Hebrews. As God is equated with his action, which is speech, human life—what the West considers subjective existence—is identified with speech. Faur draws on Benveniste's conception of person, in which "[t]he ground of subjectivity is linguistic. What enables man to conceive himself in terms of *I* is the act of speaking." The personal pronoun refers neither to concept nor to individual; its "function . . . is to transform language into speech." Language is the very ground for the category of person, since it "is the capacity of the speaker to posit himself as 'subject.' . . . '[S]ubjectivity,' whether it is placed in phenomenology or in psychology . . . is only the emergence in the being of a fundamental property of language. 'Ego' is he who *says* 'ego.'" In the light of the linguistic nature of "subjectivity" and personhood, even the biblical notion of man, which in Christianity is interpreted substantively as a spiritual, rational *imago* of divine nature, can be interpreted semiologically. In rabbinic literature the common term for nature is *matbea,* one meaning of which is "seal" or "stamp," which includes the "image of God" stamped on Adam's "soul." The human soul is thus "not conceived of in ontological terms, but rather as a semiological entity bearing the imprint of the supreme authority [analogous to the imprint of a coin]."[83]

Whether one agrees with Faur's semiological reading of the rabbinic tradition, his accomplishment is to make an alien worldview effaced by metaphysics more familiar to readers taught to think by the latter. The need to do so is evident in Blumenberg's effort to draw on that worldview to legitimize the transformation from epistemic to pragmatic conceptions of knowledge. Though Blumenberg claims to recover a theme "new to philosophy," his understanding of the biblical conception of "radical beginnings" is only

---

[81] Ibid., xxvi–viii, 28.

[82] Ibid., 32–33, 47–48. See also 29–32. For a discussion of vision, hearing, time, space, and cyclicity, see *Slayers of Moses,* 33–37.

[83] Ibid., 41–43, 80, 139–42.

a variant of onto-theological interpretations of the Bible. Even when medieval voluntarism and Nominalism valorized the arbitrary and omnipotent God of scripture, turning him into *Deus absconditus,* or when negative theology placed God beyond subjecthood and Being as an ineffable Nothing, the subjective nature of God and created beings was always presumed. By turning from substantive subjectivity and drawing on the linguistic turn in contemporary thought Faur makes accessible the "alien" notion of a Creator-God as "poet," of "radical beginnings" as linguistic, of language as infinitely iterable. He does what Blumenberg fails to do—he "denaturalizes" the ontological presumption of divine and human subjectivity and the belief in the possibility of knowledge, however delimited, that presumption grounds.

The view of the creative process as linguistic, and the created world as a book, subverts Blumenberg's effort to derive theoretic knowledge from the Hebrew Bible's conception of radical beginnings. Blumenberg never really discusses the biblical conception of originary making, characterizing it solely with reference to Hellenistic and patristic sources such as Philo and Irenaeus.[84] Distinguishing Philo's use of logic from Plato's, Faur, like Blumenberg, emphasizes its Judaic elements,[85] but does so to stress its semiological nature. Blumenberg takes no note of the linguistic nature of radical beginnings for the Hebrews. What is important for him are precisely the subjectivist, intellectual aspects of Philo's interpretation, which are more Greek; particularly important is the idea that, though the Sovereign Author is arbitrary and willful, his creativity is cognitive, his created truths accessible immediately to him and mediately to others *as theory.* And, tellingly, regardless of whether Philo's own understanding of *logos* was linguistic, in the syncretic process furthered by his writings the linguistic meanings of the term were subsumed to rational subjectivity. In relation to his influence on the West— and importance to Blumenberg—Philo had turned the poet-God of Genesis into the Divine Architect of the *Timaeus.*

As a Jewish scholar, Faur did not need to discover the constructive power of language, the radical sense in which the world was a book, in contemporary postmodern writings. But, being a Jewish scholar, he is more able than traditional scholars to "recognize the voices" of Saussure and Benveniste in the rabbinic tradition, and the voice of the rabbinic in them. This recognition of voices, which characterizes alchemical readings, allows me, in turn, to argue an affinity between the Hebraic conception of language and the hermeneutic, rather than with structualism or semiology. Such an interpre-

---

[84] Blumenberg, *Legitimacy of the Modern Age,* 305.
[85] Faur, *Golden Doves,* 24. Faur says, "Philo's preference for *logos* rather than for . . . 'soul' or 'mind' . . . clearly indicates that he wanted a term semantically equivalent to the biblical *dabar* and *'imra,*" which is semiological (24). If Philo, however, hoped to Hebraize the Greek *logos* by investing it with the meanings of *dabar* and *'imra,* he was not successful; the differences between the terms were too great.

tation is suggested by Paul Ricoeur in his criticism of Lévi-Strauss's "transpositions from the linguistic model to its ultimate generalizations" in *The Savage Mind.* The "example" Lévi-Strauss gives of that transposition is not "exemplary," Ricoeur claims, because his linguistic model is drawn from totemistic cultures. He refers to Gerhard von Rad's account of "Old Testament theology"—"exactly the inverse of that of totemism"—to distinguish between structural and hermeneutic comprehension. "What is decisive in understanding the core of meaning of the Old Testament? Not nomenclatures or classifications, but founding events. If we limit ourselves to the theology of the Hexateuch, the signifying content is a kerygma, the sign of the action of Jahweh, constituted by a complex of events. It is a *Heilgeschichte.* . . . The structural method does not exhaust their meaning, for their meaning is a reservoir of meaning ready to be used again in other structures. . . . Starting from a network of signifying events, it is the initial *surplus* of meaning which *motivates* tradition and interpretation."[86] Ricoeur's characterization of hermeneutic as the appropriate means of understanding a world made by "founding events" is as helpful as Faur's structural interpretation in challenging Blumenberg's appeal to biblical creativity to legitimate theoretic knowledge. The biblical conception, *whether structural/semiological or existential/hermeneutic,* cannot yield "knowledge," however pragmatic. A linguistically created world, either as system of signs or as founding events, must be interpreted, and interpretations are not possessed as theory. Neither do they "exhaust" signs or founding events, which, as "reservoirs of meanings," call out for continuous interpretation.[87]

A fuller interpretation of the Judaic worldview as hermeneutic is given by Susan A. Handelman, who traces the Hebraic understanding of language in contemporary literary theory. Like Faur she distinguishes rabbinic hermeneutic from Greek metaphysics. Whereas the latter's "science of signification" related phonic signifiers to ideal referents, "a 'silent ontology'," the rabbis believed "every verse, letter [of the Torah] . . . contains . . . a plurality of meanings and references. . . . [I]nterpretation is not essentially separate from the text itself . . . but . . . part of the continuous revelation of the text. . . . The text is a self-regenerating process." Creation and interpretation are thus continuous processes, the oral Torah as divine as the written. Handelman, too, emphasizes the intertextuality of interpretation, which assumes the "unity (and reversibility) of text."[88] There is no outside point of reference. Faur and Handelman differ, however, in their understanding of the

[86] Paul Ricoeur, "Structure and Hermeneutics," *The Conflict of Interpretations: Essays in Hermeneutics* (Evanston: Northwestern University Press, 1974), 45–48. Ricoeur quotes from *Theology of the Historical Traditions of Israel.*

[87] Blumenberg, who wants to make God's knowledge exclusive to him, does not consider that that "knowledge" may be radically different from theoretical or cognitive "knowing."

[88] Handelman, *Slayers of Moses,* 4–10, 39, 49, 63.

language of the book: where Faur reads through Saussure's semiology, Handelman reads through Derrida and his critique of structuralism.[89] Thus she distinguishes between the Greek view of language as sign, a "semiotic system, an abstract 'seeing' of the invisible," and Jewish hermeneutic.

Handelman characterizes Jewish hermeneutic as "displacement," a term that "constitutes the Jewish historic condition of Exile" and metonymically suggests the theme of nomadic wandering in the desert.[90] For hermeneutic, "word and thing are intimately interconnected; the[ir] relation . . . is not the relation of abstract to concrete, but rather the characterization of the inner specific reality of the thing. In place of *representation* is *grasped reality*." The alternative to Greek logocentrism and semiotics is not another semiotic, but the radically different logic of the rabbis that retains the *concreteness* of language "without the abstracting, idealizing movement of Western thought." Drawing on Roman Jakobson she characterizes the logic allowing for that "abstracting idealizing movement" as metaphoric, and the one in which a multiplicity of inferences are played out as metonymic. The issue between the two is the nature of predication: "metaphor . . . depends on a relation of resemblance where there is a transfer of one word or name or idea for another. Resemblance here passes over into substitution, election, identification, cancellation, and the differences underlying the transfer are effaced."[91] Metaphor is thus a substitutive identity within the context of an Aristotelian logic based on the relation between subject and predicate. Hebrew, on the other hand, "does not have any form of the verb 'to be' in the present tense. Predicative utterances are linguistically constructed through the juxtaposition of nominal forms in a free order." In metonymic logic the relation among words is a "contiguous, serial play of signifiers, through combination and contexture." While metaphoric relations collapse metonymic displacement, which is endless, rabbinic interpretation is "the succession of links on the chain of metonymic signification . . . where signified and signifier do not merge":[92] "resemblance never effaces difference, *as if* never becomes *is*, the literate is never canceled. . . . With the recognition of the *if*, the difference, the coexisting predicates retain their independence and do not cancel each

[89] Derrida criticizes Saussure and Benveniste for assuming subjectivity and privileging voice over writing, and stresses the complicity between speech and the metaphysics of presence. He levels a charge at Benveniste that hits Saussure and Faur as well, saying the notion of language as system would "never have been possible outside the history (and) of the concepts of . . . *episteme*" (Jacques Derrida, "The Supplement of Copula: Philosophy before Linguistics," *Margins of Philosophy,* trans. Alan Bass [Chicago: University of Chicago Press, 1982], 175–205, 180).

[90] Susan A. Handelman, "Jacques Derrida and the Heretic Hermeneutic," *Displacements: Derrida and After,* ed. Mark Krupnick (Bloomington: Indiana University Press, 1983), 98–129, 98–99. Elsewhere she distinguishes Jewish hermeneutic from the German tradition culminating in Gadamer.

[91] Handelman, *Slayers of Moses,* 62, 19, 55.

[92] Handelman, "Jacques Derrida and the Heretic Hermeneutic," 104 (see her reference, n. 14); 109–10.

other out, thus generating further interpretation. Rabbinic thinking presents us with a process, not a product."[93]

While "logos reifies metaphor in its reappropriation of presence and suppresses the fertility of language," metonymy, Handelman continues, "suffers the unending nature of desire and nonfulfillment, endlessly multiplying the chain of signifiers . . . a mode of displacement, from signifier to signifier, without any reference to a signified . . . the predominantly Jewish mode of displacing (and approaching) the Father." Moreover, since the rabbis were not concerned with the be-ing of nouns but with relations, and relations are between sensible and sensible rather than sensible and non-sensible, metonymy retains the concreteness of language lost in metaphor (and, I believe, in semiotic interpretations of rabbinic logic). "With the recognition that the metaphysical realm is at bottom metaphorical, and that there is no independent essence 'beyond' . . . language retains its *physis,* its concreteness, and is preserved. The claims of the letter are vindicated." Metaphor is, in effect, "a 'fundamental mode of what was for the Hebrews idol-worship.' The pagan gods were actually thought to be embodied in the forms that were metaphors of their powers, whereas the Jewish God is not in any of His appearances, which are only arbitrary creations. . . . Metaphor thus invites sacralization, whereas metonymy is connected with indeterminacy."[94]

Just as a logic of displacement differs from a logic of substitutive identity, so does acknowledgment of absence in metonymy differ from the elision of absence in metaphor's assertion of identity and presence. The Greeks feared absence, Handelman adds; in their ontology "absence is intolerable. In the reconciliation of the logos with itself, what is other must be returned to the same." Alternately, for the rabbis "*absence does not equal non-existence*"; it is the very condition of existence. Rabbinic hermeneutic "is a text whose writing is precisely this presence-as-separation."[95] It is this ancient form of hermeneutic, the belief that absence is the very condition of existence, on which Derrida draws to celebrate the radical play of language. "Absence, otherness, the 'trace,' all of Derrida's prime terms, are parts of a vocabulary that seeks to evade the trap of Being or Nonbeing of Greek philosophy. Derrida's reality is not Being, but Absence; not the One, but the Other; not Unity, but plurality, dissemination, writing, and difference. Reb Derissa . . . is the new High Priest of the religion of Absence."[96]

[93] Handelman, *Slayers of Moses,* 55–56.
[94] Ibid., 158–59, 20.
[95] Handelman, "Jacques Derrida and the Heretic Hermeneutic," 116–17. Handelman argues that these trends—a logic of displacement, an evasion of Greek Being for Writing and Absence—characterize the "heretic hermeneutic" of Freud, Bloom, Derrida, Lacan. While Derrida criticizes hermeneutic, what he rejects is the hermeneutic of recovery characteristic of the Protestant, not rabbinic, tradition.
[96] Ibid., 116. Similarly Geoffrey H. Hartman says, "Hebrew tradition holds that both the oral and the written law were given to Moses on Sinai. . . . The prohibition against images obliged a channeling into the written word of imaginal energies. Derrida in this is Hebrew rather

Handelman's claim of an alternate source for Derrida's hermeneutic—indeed, of an alternate tradition of hermeneutic—is as important as Faur's in uncovering the radically alien view of reality as a book, and in making the relation to that reality linguistic and interpretive rather than epistemic.[97] The difference between Hebrew and Greek/Christian worldviews is of great importance to Derrida. Indeed, he links his critique of philosophy's spiritualizing of language to the spiritualizing of God and God's relation to man—the effect of Greek logic on an emergent Christianity. In that process belief in the possibility of knowledge was affirmed within Christianity, and hermeneutic devalued.

Reb Derissa and the Originary Language of Exile

> Writing is the moment of the desert as the moment of Separation. . . . God no longer speaks to us; he has interrupted himself: we must take words upon ourselves. . . . The Jew [is he] who elects writing which elects the Jew. . . . [T]he situation of the Jew becomes exemplary of the situation of the poet, the man of speech and of writing.
>
> [T]he writer is at once everything and nothing. Like God.
> —Jacques Derrida, "Edmond Jabès and the Question of the Book"

In an essay on Emmanuel Levinas, Derrida says Levinas "make[s] the origin of language, meaning, and difference the relation to the infinitely other," and suggests what "is only a hypothesis for us . . . [that] one calls this experience of the infinitely other Judaism."[98] Drawing out the radical implications of Judaism as the Other of the tradition that systematizes language, knowledge, world, God, Derrida metonymically tropes the absence of *logos* as writing, and writing as Judaic.[99] In "Edmond Jabès and the Question of the Book" and "Ellipses" he contrasts the metaphysical tradition with an understanding of the world as the fragmentary, disjunctive, equivocal inaugural writing of a Jewish god. Like Canguilhem, Reb Rida, to whom Derrida appeals for that alternate view, knows that the idea "man has of his own poetic power" corresponds to his idea "about the creation of the world . . .

---

than Hellene: aniconic yet intensely graphic. It may be more than the accident of entering the philosophical tradition at a certain point in its history that made him choose as his polemical instrument the notion of ecriture" (Geoffrey H. Hartman, *Saving the Text: Literature, Derrida, Philosophy* [Baltimore: Johns Hopkins University Press, 1981], 17).

[97] Handelman goes on, for example, to relate Freud's "science" of interpretation, psychoanalysis, to this tradition.

[98] Derrida, "Violence and Metaphysics: An Essay on the Thought of Emmanuel Levinas," *Writing and Difference,* trans. Alan Bass (Chicago: University of Chicago Press, 1978), 79–153, 151–52.

[99] Derrida consciously situates his critique of Greek metaphysics, logocentrism, in a "Jewish" perspective.

[and] the radical origin of things." "There is the book of God," Reb Rida says, "in which God questions himself, and there is the book of man . . . proportionate to that of God."[100] Using the trope of the book to discuss "the problem of origins," Derrida distinguishes between the books of God and men in the Judaic tradition, and the Book of Nature in the metaphysical. He acknowledges that the West at times conceives of its God as an author, one of whose books is a revelation of his will toward humans; the other, the Book of Nature, manifests the orderly effects of his creative power. Yet even when writing appears valorized in the West, it remains, he claims, a metaphor for speech.[101] If the God of the tradition had actually authored a "book," it would not have been one in which he interrogated himself, since it would have contained no "open spaces" in which a question could emerge. Its logical structure would have reduced to "narration, philosophic discourse, or the order of reasons or deduction . . . the essential discontinuity and non-contemporaneousness" of language itself. Such a book would misconstrue language: it would fail to realize "[t]he other originally collaborates with meaning. . . . The caesura does not simply finish and fix meaning . . . but . . . make[s] meaning emerge." If the God of classical philosophers, who "neither interrupted nor interrogated himself, did not stifle himself," had written, he would have produced the "rectilinear" Leibnizian book. But, Derrida adds, "the God . . . whose actual infinity did not tolerate the question, precisely had no vital need for writing."[102]

If the God of the tradition has no need for writing, if the image of the world as book is merely a decorative figure projected onto a metaphysical order whose eidetic structure transcends language, the God of Edmond Jabès is nothing other than his language, the creator of a world that is only a book, its structure not logical but grammatical. Derrida shares Jabès's "unpenetrated certainty that Being is a Grammar; and that the world is in all its parts a cryptogram to be constituted or reconstituted through poetic inscription or deciphering, that the book is original, that everything *belongs to the book* before being and in order to come into the world. . . . 'The world exists because the book exists.' . . . To be is to-be-in-the-book even if Being is not the created nature often called the Book of God during the Middle Ages. 'If God

<hr/>

[100] Jacques Derrida, "Edmond Jabès and the Question of the Book," *Writing and Difference,* trans. Alan Bass (Chicago: University of Chicago Press, 1978), 64–78. I discuss this work in "Derrida, Vico, Genesis, and the Originary Power of Language," *The Eighteenth Century: Theory and Interpretation* 34, no. 1 (spring 1993): 65–84.

[101] Jacques Derrida, "The End of the Book and the Beginning of Writing," *Of Grammatology,* trans. Gayatri Chakravorty Spivak (Baltimore: Johns Hopkins University Press, 1984), 15. Another example is the writing of truth on the soul in the *Phaedrus.*

[102] Derrida, "Edmond Jabès," 71. Derrida generally uses "book" in a negative sense, to refer to a totality, and "text" for the writing that "could be opened only if the book was closed." In "Edmond Jabès" and "Ellipses," however, he uses "book" in a positive sense. See "Ellipses," *Writing and Difference,* 294–300.

is, it is because He is in the book.'"[103] Jabès's God is "in the book" because God himself is not an origin; rather, it is his writing that is *originary*. The distinction between onto-theological origin and originary language is Derrida's distinction between speech and writing, between the garden, where God as Presence speaks, and the desert of exile, where the lost immediacy of God's voice testifies to his absence. Only in absence, the silence of the desert, can human language originate—"Absence is the permission given to letters to spell themselves out and to signify"—and the language of absence is writing: "Writing is the moment of the desert as the moment of Separation. . . . God no longer speaks to us; he has interrupted himself: we must take words upon ourselves."[104]

Derrida's privileging of writing is just this insistence on the absence of a Divine Subject, a ground of truth, a center of meaning, an answer to all questions. Absence is the opening of the proportionate books of man, books of endless interrogation, endless interruption and displacement, in which men like Jabès attempt, "always in vain—to retake possession of his language (as if this were meaningful) by any means . . . and to claim responsibility for it against a Father of Logos." Derrida reinscribes the image of loss, the desert, with another, a "powerful and ancient root," the site of human—poetic—language and thus of literality and historicity; a root that is itself the origin of the Jew, "a race born of the book."[105] The Jew is he "who elects writing which elects the Jew, [a pure and founding] exchange responsible for truth's thorough suffusion with historicity," and "the situation of the Jew becomes exemplary of the situation of the poet, the man of speech and writing." For Derrida, the Jew/poet is the "Other" of the tradition in which the Presence of God or *logos* ennobles reflection and the rational soul, turning the latter into a Subject of knowledge. Derrida does not displace philosopher for poet but, rather, deconstructs the subject-position occupied by the philosopher, since in the movement of poetry and history "the book becomes a subject in itself and for itself." One of Jabès's characters asks, "*Do we formulate speech, or does it fashion us?*" and elsewhere Jabès answers, "Words choose the poet." The poet is "both bound to language and delivered from it . . . the *subject* of the book . . . [as] the book is indeed the subject of the poet. . . . [I]n its representation of itself the subject is shattered and opened. Writing is . . . made into an abyss, in its own representation." "[T]he writer," Derrida adds, "is at once everything and nothing. Like God."[106]

The language of poetry and history can never be a language of truth, an

---

[103] Derrida, "Edmond Jabès," 76–77. The quotations are from Edmond Jabès, *Le Livre des questions* (Paris: Gallimard, 1963), 32–33. Neither Jabès nor Derrida shrinks from the full import of textuality. The *Livre des questions* describes the "generation of God himself," Derrida says, and quotes Maister Eckhart: "God becomes God when creation says God."

[104] Derrida, "Edmond Jabès," 68, 72.

[105] Ibid., 73, 64–65. The quotation is "Edmond Jabès," 26.

[106] Ibid., 65, 69–70.

end to interruptions and questions, since it is always interpretive: "The necessity of commentary, like poetic necessity, is the very form of exiled speech. In the beginning is hermeneutics."[107] The need to answer every question with a question is due not to some accident *within* history, a fall from original grace, but, rather, to the "original opening of interpretation . . . a rupture within God as the origin of history." Writing is a "hermetic and secondary" language, "[o]ur writing, certainly, but already His, which starts with the stifling of his voice and the dissimulation of his Face." The site of "freedom," the "very opening of the Question," is a "negativity" at the heart of God, who "does not act in the simplest ways . . . is not truthful . . . is not sincere." Such a God "was unthinkable for the classical rationalists," though actually, Derrida adds, a dissimulating God, a God of "irony" and "ruses," was not wholly unthinkable.[108] Hegel had condemned Kant for believing in "a jealous, envious God, who hides and guards his *Da,*" a "Jewish" God.[109] Though Derrida does not mention it, Descartes too evoked such a God in his anxiety that an arbitrary deity, a *genius malignus,* created us "so that we are always deceived."[110] It was to meet the threat to knowledge posed by that Nominalist and biblical God that Descartes affirmed a ground of certainty in the thinking subject. Jabès's tradition does not offer him that alternative, which derived from the Hellenic privileging of *logos* and rational soul. In the absence of *logos* or subject the Jew has only the book, its language a "poem inscribed just beyond the phenomenology of the mind."[111]

The textualism of Jabès and Derrida is more radical, however, than merely a critique of Descartes. The question raised by the *Book of Questions* is, Derrida says, ontological before it is grammatical, or, rather, "the embedding of the ontological and grammatical within the *graphein.*" Though writing is a derivative language, there is *no lost original language* in which a subject, God or *logos,* is present. "Original, radical illegibility" is "the very possibility of the book."[112] What disappears in the repetition of writing is the "self-identity of the origin, the self-presence of so-called living speech. That is the center. The first book, the mythic book, the eve prior to all repetition, has lived

---

[107] Ibid., 67. Though poet and rabbi are both bound to an "exiled speech" that commits them to the "*shared* necessity of exegesis," that "interpretive imperative is interpreted differently by [each]. . . . [T]he poet does not simply receive his speech and his law from God," while the rabbi "has no need of a poet's intercession" (67; see also 311 n. 3).

[108] Ibid., 67–68.

[109] Derrida, *Glas,* trans. John P. Leavey Jr. and Richard Rand (Lincoln: University of Nebraska Press, 1986) 213–14. Derrida says Hegel dismisses Kant's claim that "we can know nothing of God" because Kant's God was "Jewish"—that is, a "jealous God" who hides his presence. For Hegel a good God does not dissemble.

[110] René Descartes, "Principles of Philosophy," *A Discourse on Method, Meditations on the First Philosophy, Principles of Philosophy,* trans. John Veitch (London: J. M. Dent, 1994), pt.1, v, 152.

[111] Derrida, "Edmond Jabès," 68.

[112] Ibid., 74, 77. This is not an irrationalism, Derrida says, since the eventual opposition of "rational" and "irrational" is itself "within the book."

on the deception that the center was sheltered from play: irreplaceable, withdrawn from metaphor and metonymy, a kind of *invariable first name* that could be invoked, but not repeated. The center of the first book should not have been repeatable in its own representation. Once it lends itself a single time to such a representation . . . once . . . written . . . it is the abyss, is the bottomlessness of infinite redoubling." Like Nietzsche Derrida does not shrink from this abyss but, rather, "affirm[s] the nonreferral to the center." "Why," he asks, "would one mourn for the center? Is not . . . the absence of play and difference, another name for death?" The center is the sign of the "unnameable bottomless well . . . the book attempted to fill, the void which reempties itself and marks itself with imprints." With books "proportionate to the book of God" the poet joyously "affirm[s] the abyss . . . inhabit[s] the labyrinth . . . write[s] the hole."[113]

In his writings Derrida continually returns to the Other who "received from God the power and the mission to name," and figures him as "Jew." "All those who deal or inhabit language as poets are Jews—but in a tropic sense."[114] Though the Jabès essay is Derrida's most extended elaboration of that trope, elsewhere he examines the means by which philosophy rejected concrete, inaugural language, turning it into a signifying system for an ideal world.[115] In "The Supplement of Copula" he attributes belief in that signifying character to the logical function the Greeks attributed to the verb "to be." The copula asserts the identity of subject and predicate. In Aristotle, Being, the nominal form of the copula, the most privileged of the "categories of thought," came to designate "the conceptual essence of a thing," taking on a transcategorical function. Derrida builds on Benveniste's claim that Aristotle's categories were not logical, conceptual, or ontological, but characteristics of the Greek language: the foundational assumptions of metaphysics were actually a function of the linguistic provincialism of the Greeks.[116] The move from sensible to intelligible that the copula effected was repeated early in the development of Christian theology in the spiritualizing of a text-based religion. With the substitution of *logos* for *davar* and the "literalizing of the metaphor" of the Son, the dynamic, concrete, eventful word of the biblical God became a substantive incarnation of Divine Spirit. For Paul the incarnation was the fulfillment *of* letter *as* Spirit, its transcendence enabling Christianity to displace the religion of the book with a spiritualized theology. "Paul is not only antinomian," Handelman says, "he is also antitextual." The very refusal of the Jews to turn from text to spirit, from sign to thing signified, constitutes their intransigence. For them the *"reification*

---

[113] Derrida, "Ellipses," 296–300. The theme of the abyss recurs in Derrida's writings.

[114] Derrida, "Shibboleth," *Midrash and Literature,* ed. Geoffrey H. Hartman and Sanford Burdick (New Haven: Yale University Press, 1986), 307–47, 340.

[115] If, indeed, philosophy ever had such a view of language.

[116] Derrida, "Supplement of Copula," *Margins of Philosophy,* 175–205, 196. And, Derrida reminds his readers, "as is known, ancient Semitic did not have a verb 'to be'" (201).

of signs" is idolatry or fetishism, "a desperate attempt to render *presence.*"[117]

In recovering the linguistic character of the Hebraic tradition Derrida problematizes the assumption of substantive subjectivity or spirituality in philosophy and onto-theology, tracing the process in which the copula reifies the metaphoric identification of subject and predicate, turning it into self-identical essence. He exemplifies that process in Hegel's conception of the realization of Spirit in the dialectical movement of history, the logical and ontological *Aufhebung* from concrete to abstract in language, law, morality, knowledge. For Hegel "[t]he concept relieves the sign that relieves the thing."[118] Characterized by love, the family is an early stage of the objectification of spirit, its most spiritualized form the Christian Holy Family. Hegel uses the spirituality of the Holy Family to mark the *Aufhebung* of the concreteness and literality of Judaism, and Derrida responds by deconstructing both Holy Family and Hegel's speculative philosophy, revealing the role the copula plays in mystifying the principle of identity on which spirituality depends. Only in the identification of Father and Son effected by the logical power of the copula is the Holy Family constituted, and only at that point of reification does the notion of God as Spirit emerge in history. "Spirit is neither the father nor the son but 'filiation,' " a product of the linguistic assertion "The Father *is* the Son."[119] And, only in the incarnation and the ritual iteration of mystical identity in the Last Supper are man and God, infinite and finite, one.[120] The relation of identity in which, for Hegel, the concreteness and literality of language "overflows itself" in the concept—and Spirit realizes itself in history—is for Derrida not logical, ontological, chronological, but linguistic.

Hegel is particularly scathing in his attack on the childishness of a religion and language incapable of family, love, abstraction, spirituality: "Why doesn't the Jew comprehend" when Jesus calls himself the son of God? Hegel asks, and Derrida answers: "On the contrary, he conceives what he utters. . . . That is his limit: he conceives. . . . Now the father-son relation is inconceivable." "Since this unity cannot be stated in the understanding's abstract language, it requires a kind of metaphoricity. . . . Through its semantic tenor, [the metaphor] stands, like life . . . beyond the dead concept, beyond the understanding's finite analysis, beyond the objectifying determination." Against this "ontological sense [of] the metaphors . . . of life" that the copula of metaphysics bequeathed to Christianity and speculative phi-

---

[117] Handelman, "Jacques Derrida and the Heretic Hermeneutic," 106–7. Similarly Faur says the *logos* of John is "unwritable" and "therefore antibook and antitext" ("Law and Hermeneutics," 1657).

[118] Derrida, *Glas,* 8. Derrida's critique focuses on Hegel's *Philosophy of Right.*

[119] Ibid., 30–31. He says in ancient near-eastern religions, including Judaism, god was referred to as "spirit," but it was no more than an empty name.

[120] Ibid., 31, 56.

losophy, Derrida questions "What do [the Jews] do when . . . the unity of essence (*Weseneinheit*) of father and son is presented to them?" and responds, "They cry out scandal." "When one is a Jew," he adds, mocking Hegel's own tone of derision, "when one does not comprehend life . . . only an accessory metaphor is seen there, a rhetorical auxiliary without its own proper truth. . . . The Jew . . . sees precisely a metaphor, only a metaphor, a finite image leaving the finite and infinite separate. . . . The Jewish tongue . . . speaks without yet knowing how to speak, without being able to develop fully the sperm of the *logos*."[121]

The Secularization of the Language of Exile

> What Heidegger calls the forgetting of Being is simply the forgetting of Writing. . . . When . . . [he] thinks he is thinking Greek (ur-Greek), he is thinking Hebrew.
> —Geoffrey H. Hartman, *Saving the Text: Literature, Derrida, Philosophy*

Derrida uses his thematizing of the Judaic to draw out the radical implications of the inability to go beyond language to the spiritual unity of infinite and finite. The assertion that God is Love, Life, Man, Son, Spirit is "accessory metaphor . . . a rhetorical auxiliary without its own proper truth." But for "Reb Derissa," the meaning of Judaism is that language itself is "accessory metaphor." The theme of the inseparability of the ontological and grammatical is not original with Jabès, but, he reminds us, with that very "tradition itself."[122] That language and ontology—that word, deed, thing, idea—are inseparable, that hermeneutic is "the very form of exiled speech," was "forgotten" by the West until remembered by Heidegger. But Heidegger himself forgets what Jabès and Derrida remind us: that commentary and poetry, not philosophy, have always been the language of the nomadic Jew/poet exiled in the silence of the desert. In speaking of Derrida's linking of writing and being, Geoffrey H. Hartman says of Heidegger's lapse: "What Heidegger calls the forgetting of Being is simply the forgetting of Writing; and . . . this forgetting goes together with a privileging of spoken speech. . . . In the light of this emphatic light everything else appears obscure; especially the Hebraic development of aniconic writing and self-effacing commentary—of *textuality*. When Heidegger, then, thinks he is thinking Greek (ur-Greek), he is thinking Hebrew."[123]

That Heidegger too forgets the role the originary power of language plays

---

[121] Ibid., 80–85, 73.

[122] Derrida, "Edmond Jabès," 74.

[123] Hartman, *Saving the Text*, xix. For comparisons of Heidegger and Derrida in relation to Greek and Hebraic perspectives, see John D. Caputo, *Demythologizing Heidegger* (Bloomington: Indiana University Press, 1993), especially 209–14; *The Prayers and Tears of Jacques Derrida: Religion without Religion* (Bloomington: Indiana University Press, 1997).

for the Hebrews in his effort to remember Being is a theme of Derrida's writings. The differences between Heidegger and Derrida are obscured, however, when the hermeneutic traditions on which each draws are not distinguished. Handelman corrects this by providing genealogies of the two traditions. Derrida's hermeneutic of displacement, she points out, is usually interpreted as an "extreme extension[] of a Nietzschean-Heideggerian tradition of 'de-construction.'" Nietzsche and Heidegger were, however, part of a nineteenth century German philosophic tradition that included Schleiermacher, Hegel, Feuerbach, Dilthey, and Gadamer and that was deeply rooted in Protestant biblical hermeneutic.[124] Freud has also been identified with that tradition but, Handelman argues, the hermeneutic culminating in Heidegger and Gadamer cannot explain Freud or Derrida, who are "extension[s] of the line of Jewish Rabbinic hermeneutics." When the Jews rejected Christianity's theological claims, Christianity rejected the Jewish tradition of interpretation—including the oral law handed down with written scripture—and reinterpreted the latter "in terms of the figures of Jesus." The effects "were to collapse and cancel the endless multiple meanings . . . [of] each word and letter of the Torah, and to make all the words subordinate to and embodied in the single word-become-flesh in a literal person . . . absolute signifier and signified together." The incarnation of the *logos* "celebrates not the exaltation of the word but its transformation from the linguistic order into the material realm, its conversion into the flesh." In distinguishing between old and "fulfilled" word, Christianity reduces the "Old" Testament to "mere" words, signs pointing to the true "word made flesh," a substantive spiritual reality. At that point "[t]he opposition between literal and metaphorical is instituted, and allegory becomes a predominant mode of interpretation."[125]

Handelman's distinction between Protestant and Judaic hermeneutic traditions supplements Derrida's critique of the complicity between philosophy and Christian onto-theology, and his use of the trope "Judaic" for those who do not share in it. For Derrida and Handelman, the priority of epistemology to which the subjectivism and spiritualism of the dominant tradition leads—apparent even when the tradition turns toward hermeneutic—obscures an alternate poetic understanding of the world and language. The differences between the two hermeneutics are apparent in differences between the conception of language Hans-Georg Gadamer identifies with the incarnation, and Walter Benjamin with Genesis. Both strive to recover the originary potency of language forgotten in the privileging of human subjectivity, a linguistic making convertible with a "knowing" no longer epistemic but hermeneutic, and both find the paradigm of that conception in divine language. But, while the theology of *verbum* to which Gadamer appeals betrays

---

[124] Handelman, *Slayers of Moses*, 130. The case could be made that Nietzsche is closer to "Jewish" hermeneutic.

[125] Ibid., 4, 32.

its origins in the subjectivism Heidegger considers the essence of humanism, Benjamin's more biblical conception of God and creative language does not distinguish "mentality" from language. Gadamer, a student of Heidegger's, was similarly heir to Protestant hermeneutic, and its inability to transcend subjectivity and to grasp the linguisticality of language is evident in his characterization of two conceptions of language he considers dominant in the West, *logos,* derived from Plato, and *verbum.*

For the tradition of *logos* truth was not a problem of language at all, Gadamer states, but of the proper method of thinking. Truth was pure "structure of intelligibility," the paradigm of which was number.[126] Denying the Platonic view that the word is mere sign unrelated to being, he insists "language and thinking about things are . . . bound together." He is unable, however, to formulate a conception of the unity of word, thought, and thing that transcends spiritualist onto-theology. This is evident in his characterization of the alternate conception, *verbum,* which "does more justice to the being of language and so prevented the forgetfulness of language in Western thought from being complete." He identifies *verbum* with the incarnation, which relates "thought" more closely to speech, while avoiding Greek dualism: in the incarnation *logos* is not embodied in flesh; it becomes flesh. Though medieval theology relied on the Prologue of John and applied "Greek ideas to its own theological task," Gadamer insists that it "acquired by this very means a dimension foreign to Greek thought": "if it is only in the Incarnation that speech is fully realized, then the logos is freed from its spirituality." In effect the doctrine of the incarnation introduced "the essence of history into Western thought, brought the phenomenon of language out of its immersion in the ideality of meaning and offered it to philosophic reflection: in contrast to the Greek logos, the word is pure event."

Gadamer admits the "human word," the external "act of uttering, of speaking the word out loud," is "utterly rejected in Christian dogmatics." What is important, however, is that the incarnation "situates the problem of language entirely within inner thought" as "mirror and image of the divine Word." The "miracle of language" revealed in the mysteries of the Trinity and the incarnation is that "the word that is true . . . has its being in its revealing." The question remains as to what that inner word *is,* "how is it a real word without sound," and, Gadamer speculates, "Are we not here using the unintelligible to explain the unintelligible?" He insists, however, that the inner word is "more than simply the Greek logos"; even if it is not "the event of utterance . . . [it] still has the ontological character of event . . . a characteristic belonging to the meaning itself . . . like a curse." Yet, despite his effort to grasp the immediacy, unity, eventfulness of the linguistic word, the inherent dualism of the Aristotelian and medieval positions from which

---

[126] Hans-Georg Gadamer, *Truth and Method,* trans. Joel Weinsheimer and Donald G. Marshall (New York: Crossroad, 1992), 405–28.

Gadamer starts prevents him from doing so. He says *logos* is not embedded in flesh, but becomes flesh, yet in "Christian dogmatics" "flesh" is a metaphor for man, who remains a dualistic being. Once one begins with the assumption that the agent of production, generation, or speech is spiritual or subjective, one cannot get beyond dualism, no matter how "immanently" one conceives subjectivity.[127] Gadamer asks whether his discussion of the inner word is not using the "unintelligible to explain the unintelligible." In using onto-theology to characterize hermeneutic he might more pointedly ask if he is not using the mystified to explain the unintelligible.

Benjamin, who similarly struggles with the relation between "mentality" and language (and retains not only the language of subjectivity but also that underlying current of pagan mysticism that ultimately influenced even Judaism) is more successful in grasping the eventfulness of language. Like Gadamer Benjamin distinguishes language from sign, but unlike him relates language to Genesis because, like Genesis, he presupposes "language as an ultimate reality, perceptible only in its manifestation."[128] Thus, in explaining "the proposition that the mental being of man is language" he identifies language with the "language in which creation took place. In the word creation took place, and God's linguistic being is the word."[129] The language of the word is "naming," and in naming "only language itself is communicated." Naming is the "rhythm by which the creation of nature . . . is accomplished. . . . Let there be—He made (created)—He named. . . . In this . . . the deep and clear relation of the creative act to language appears each time. With the creative omnipotence of language it begins, and at the end language as it were assimilates the created, names it. Language is therefore both creative and the finished creation; it is word and name."[130]

For Benjamin language, not subjectivity, constitutes whatever functional *homoiousis* exists between God, man, and nature, and name-giving constitutes man's Godlikeness. Benjamin accounts for that similitude by distinguishing between God's creation of man and his creation of nature. Whereas God created each part of nature with the word, he created man with the "mediation" of matter, into which he breathed his breath, "at once life and mind and language." In this way man is "invested with the *gift* of language and is elevated above nature." There is a "special relationship between man and

---

[127] The subjectivism of the conception of language inherent in the doctrine of the incarnation was already clear in Augustine, for whom "Christian eloquence" becomes, literally and figuratively, "a vessel of the Spirit bearing the Word to mankind." See Marcia L. Colish, *The Mirror of Language: A Study in the Medieval Theory of Knowledge* (Lincoln: University of Nebraska Press, 1983), 25–26, 50–55.

[128] Walter Benjamin, "On Language as Such and on the Language of Man," *Reflections: Essays, Aphorisms, Autobiographical Writings,* ed. Peter Demetz, trans. Edmund Jephcott (New York: Schocken Books, 1986), 314–32, 322. Benjamin adds that this language is "inexplicable and mystical," but gives a linguistic, rather than spiritual, meaning to "mystical." See note 127.

[129] Ibid., 323. Language communicates mental being, but "mental being communicates itself *in* language and not *through* language. Languages . . . have no speaker" (315–16).

[130] Ibid., 322–23.

language," because God did not "subject [man] to language, but in man God set language, which had served *Him* as medium of creation, free. God rested when he had left his creative power to itself in man." It is "*language as such* [which] is the mental being of man. . . . All nature, insofar as it communicates itself, communicates itself in language, and so finally in man. Hence he is the lord of nature and can give names to things."[131]

Benjamin draws out the implications of this conception of language for knowledge, saying, "Only through the linguistic being of things can [man] gain knowledge of them from within himself—in name. God's creation is completed when things receive their names from man." Naming thus yields knowledge, but "knowledge" is *never* independent of naming. "In receiving the unspoken nameless language of things and converting it by name into sounds" man translates "imperfect language into a more perfect one, and cannot but add something to it, namely knowledge." The "knowledge" convertible with originary naming is not the conceptual knowledge of the tradition, of course, since its model is the creative act in which "name is creative because it is word, and God's word is cognizant because it is name."[132] Man is "knower in the same language in which God is creator. God created . . . *the knower in the image of the creator*." Benjamin achieves that convergence of knowing and radically originary making, which neither Blumenberg's conceptual understanding of making, nor Gadamer's of *verbum* as event of "inner thought" without sound, attains. For Benjamin (as for Heidegger and Vico) the language that creates by naming is an event in-the-world, a language that *sounds*.[133] And, the "knowledge" that man "adds" to the "unspoken nameless language of things" by naming the world, *the only knowledge "convertible" with making,* is a hermeneutic closer to Nietzsche's more "rabbinic" hermeneutic of suspicion than to Gadamer's still too onto-theological version.

Verum-Factum *as the Principle of Poetic Ontology*

In discussing the Hebrew understanding of language and hermeneutic, neither Benjamin and Derrida nor Handelman refers explicitly to *verum-factum*. Faur does, however, claiming that for both the Hebrews and Vico

---

[131] Ibid., 321–23, 318–19.

[132] Ibid., 318–19, 325–26, 323. Benjamin distinguishes the relation between God's language and his knowledge from that of humans. Whereas God "made things knowable in their names," man "names things according to knowledge." It is the *former* relation that I claim Vico and postmodern writers attribute to humans.

[133] Ibid., 324. A language of names yielding knowledge is not the mystical conception in which "the word is simply the essence of the thing," Benjamin insists, since "the thing *in itself* has no word, being created from God's word and known in its name by a human word." Benjamin goes on to describe, in ways similar to Vico and Heidegger, the loss of creative language. Language becomes imitative, no longer a cognizing naming but "knowledge from outside," like the "knowledge of good and evil" after the fall. This is "the birth of the *human word*," the word as sign.

the principle of convergence expressed skepticism toward the tradition's belief in the possibility of knowledge, and valorized the artifactual over the natural.[134] But Faur believes that Vico ended the crisis of skepticism, brought to a head in the sixteenth and seventeenth centuries by Montaigne, Charron, and particularly Francisco Sánchez, by drawing out the implications of *verum-factum*.[135] Sánchez denied that knowledge of cognition was possible because it involved knowledge of the human soul and, since one could comprehend only what one had created, such knowledge was not possible.[136] Vico drew on *verum-factum* to refute skepticism in *Ancient Wisdom* but, as Jaime Balmes pointed out, in acknowledging that man could not know what he had not made, Vico "opened the widest door" to skepticism. However, in using only *Ancient Wisdom* in his criticism Balmes, Faur charges, failed to appreciate Vico's "brilliant strategy" in the *New Science,* that of using *verum-factum* to provide an epistemological ground for knowledge of the historical world, thus ending the crisis of skepticism.[137]

In *Golden Doves* Faur draws out the affinity between the *verum-factum* principle and the Hebraic semiological worldview. In that the latter "conceives of physical phenomena (and historical and personal events) . . . as speech and writing," it rejects "the rigid 'nature/history' opposition. . . . [I]t is man's interaction with the world that determines value and significance." As R. Aqiba argued, the "acts of man," the constructed, "were superior" to the given or natural. "This perception bears upon the 'nature/artificiality' issue," Faur claims. "Through man's active participation . . . the world is transformed and . . . nature becomes artificial and thus accessible to man." Faur relates this view to Vico's use of *verum-factum* in the *New Science,*[138] though he goes on to identify Vico's understanding of "accessibility" with that of Berlin, for whom the knowledge insured by *verum-factum* is an idealist knowing "from the inside." Yet Faur's own understanding of the rabbinic worldview as semiological, or Derrida's that "everything belongs to the book before being and in order to come into the world," or Benjamin's that "language as such is the mental being of man," rejects the dualism inherent in Berlin's idealist conception of knowing from the "inside." In the tradition to which Faur, Handelman, Derrida, and Benjamin appeal, *there is in effect no "real" other than what is made with language: the "real" is always arti-*

---

[134] Besides the article discussed here, see Faur, "The Splitting of the *Logos.*"

[135] Implications that Faur considers epistemological. Despite his appreciation for the affinity between Vico and Hebraic thought, he does not draw out the linguistic and hermeneutic implications of *verum-factum, focusing instead on the epistemic.* I discuss the writings of Donatella di Cesare, who does, in chap. 3, nn. 135, 136.

[136] Sánchez drew on Maimonides (José Faur, "Francisco Sánchez's Theory of Cognition and Vico's *verum-factum,*" *New Vico Studies,* vol. 5 [1987]: 131–46, 131–33). Sánchez's skepticism was related to his background as son of *conversos,* Iberian Jews forced to convert to Christianity. Faur's argument is a response to Croce, who, in defending Vico against Jaime Balmes, dismisses Sánchez's prior position as inconsequential.

[137] Ibid., 142–43.

[138] Faur, *Golden Doves,* xxii–xxiii. See "Splitting the *Logos,*" 98.

factual. Insofar as nature and the human world are linguistic they are not known "from the inside"; they are books to be read and interpreted.

Though Faur himself does not draw out the more radical sense in which, in the *New Science,* Vico's understanding of originary language takes him beyond a subjectivist conception of human nature and the epistemic concerns it supports, he is one of the few who see affinities between Vico and the Judaic notion that man's constructive linguistic "interaction with the world" determines value and significance. He provides, moreover, a Judaic account of linguistic interaction that presumes the embodied nature of humans. If one approaches Vico's understanding of being human and originary language from that embodied rather than subjectivist perspective, then the problem with which, in different ways, Croce, Löwith, Milbank, and others wrestle— how to achieve the convergence of making and knowing, given the traditional assumption that human activity is intentional—is more easily resolved. *Poiesis* can be identified with originary language unconditioned by subjectivity. The syncretic historical process that turned the poet-God of Genesis into a spiritual Being, and *davar*—the unity of word, deed, thing— into a spiritualized *Logos,* so elided such a *poiesis* from the tradition that not even Blumenberg, who overtly goes back to the Judaic conception of radical beginnings, much less Löwith and Milbank, can conceive it. The spiritualized conception of language that all share with Gadamer prevents them from grasping Vico's poetic insight, that the creative potency of first men, though "infinitely different" from that of a God who creates by knowing, was "divine" even so, the creativity of a poet-God inconceivable within onto-theology.

My purpose in this extended discussion of the rabbinic view of language is not to suggest a similarity between it and Vico's philosophy. They are in fact very different formulations. For Vico, what is brought together in metaphor is an ontological identity constituting the real of the human world, a reality delimiting the play of interpretation on the part of both poets and philosopher-historians, for whom social and historical institutions established by linguistic interpretations must satisfy needs and utilities. There is no metonymic displacement or endless play of signifiers when the survival of first men is at stake. Nor do I suggest a historical relation between Vico and the Judaic tradition.[139] What I am suggesting is that the latter provides a par-

---

[139] My argument is not historical but thematic, suggesting affinities among nontraditional understandings of humans which, as Blumenberg, Heidegger, Canguilhem remind us, inevitably become a comparison with God. Of Vico's knowledge of biblical or rabbinic Judaism, or of that tradition's influence on him, I make no claim. Faur, however, argues a historical relation on the basis of the affinity that Jewish thinkers felt for Vico's writings. He mentions Sephardic thinkers who knew of Vico's writings as early as 1731, when Vico sent a copy of the *New Science* to Joséph Attias. The Sephardim found in Vico an alternative to Enlightenment rational secularism, and applied "Viconian concepts to the interpretation of classical Hebrew texts and history" (José Faur, "Vico, Religious Humanism and the Sephardic Tradition," *Judaism* 105, vol. 27, no. 1 [winter 1978]: 63–71, 67). Faur speculates on the historical influence of Jews on Vico as

adigm of interpretive human interaction with the world in which meaning and value are constructed linguistically, not subjectively. Vico's understanding of the *poiesis* of first men and of the humans genetically descended from them has affinities with that paradigm. Indeed, the very historical existence of such a paradigm denaturalizes the humanist tradition's equation of human existence with subjectivity. It is in this *functional,* rather than historical, sense, that I argue in the following chapter that Vico's poetic conception of first men secularizes the originary linguistic activity of the Creator-God of Genesis.

---

well, mentioning Alonso de Cartagena, a fifteenth century Spanish *converso* and "founder" of religious humanism, Yehuda Abarbanal, Moshe Almosnino, and Menasseh ben Israel, an associate of Grotius. Faur also argues affinities between Vico's methods and the Sephardim, particularly their passion for law over nature as criterion of truth and ethics, their indifference to science, their privileging of rhetoric over logic.

3   The Strange
Verum-Factum *and the Secularization of Poetic Ontology*

[A]s God is nature's artificer, so man is the god of artifacts.
—Giambattista Vico, *On the Most Ancient Wisdom of the Italians*

In such fashion the first men of the gentile nations, children of nascent mankind, created things according to their own ideas. But this creation was infinitely different from that of God. For God, in his purest intelligence, knows things, and, by knowing them, creates them; but they, in their robust ignorance, did it by virtue of a wholly corporeal imagination. And because it was quite corporeal, they did it with marvelous sublimity; a sublimity such and so great that it excessively perturbed the very persons who by imagining did the creating, for which they were called 'poets,' which is Greek for 'creators'.
—Giambattista Vico, *The New Science*

ALCHEMICAL READINGS, Nancy S. Struever claims, make "room for vital changes in philosophic problematic" by focusing on "confrontational dislocative tendencies in the text." This chapter explores the "confrontational dislocative tendencies" of the *New Science,* and the vital change in philosophic problematic they enable—a way of historical being other than "being subject," a way obscured, Heidegger tells us, by the "fleeting cloud shadow . . . [of] truth as the certainty of subjectivity." Though Vico himself was fully aware of the "dislocative tendencies" of his insight into the poetic nature of first men—the "master key" of the *New Science*—the implications of identifying the genetic condition of humans as poetic, the sense in which that identification is "dislocative" of his entire intellectual tradition, has not been appreciated. Indeed, whether in the name of Platonism or Neoplatonism, of a Latin or Renaissance rhetorical tradition, of historicism, even of Catholic onto-theology, the tradition persistently claims him as its own. Vico himself, however, understood that dislocative tendencies are inevitably obscured by traditional readings; he understood that judging "distant and unknown things" by the "familiar and at hand" was a property of the human mind. The poetic nature of first men was just such a "distant and unknown thing," and he never let his readers forget he struggled twenty long years to grasp its strangeness. He did not realize that those to whom he sent his manuscript had not endured such a struggle, that they read only through the familiar conceit in which humans show up as subjective beings, an essential subjectivity which, if not fully present at the beginning of human development, is so at its *telos*. It is that conceit, Heidegger claims, first formulated in Plato's assertion of an intelligible reality known by a soul homogeneous with it, that constitutes humanism. Though Latin and Renaissance rhetors often wrote out of a different sensibility, privileging the constitutive role of language and valuing interpretation over the *episteme* of philosophy, their readers read them through their own more familiar humanist anthropological and epistemological assumptions. The "virus" of a reified human subjectivity was even interjected into an alien biblical tradition of embodied humans, turning it into the vehicle of a spiritualized anthropology.

The subjectism of that humanist tradition, woven from strands of Platonism, Neoplatonism, and onto-theology, was only coming into presence in Vico's lifetime. Vico senses the danger posed by its celebration of analytic rationality, which reduces the world to a "gorgeous mansion" in which humans do no more than "move the furniture around," though even he cannot foresee the success of the Cartesian worldview, the full outline of "modernity."[1] Yet, though he writes before the full realization of the philosophy of the subject, though he is the earliest and one of the most profound critics of the dangers it poses, in yet another irony of Western history his readers understand him wholly within its "frame," his "new science" merely a variant of the philosophy of the subject and of the hegemony of epistemology.

Though himself an heir to humanism, Vico escapes its hold by means of a pedagogy whose constructive value he understands very well. He ascribes his intellectual development as "philosopher-historian"—indeed, as civil being—to an autodidacticism displacing a pedagogy based on logic, algebra, and criticism, for the study of ancient languages, poetry, history, oratory, topics, plane geometry. Yet the very success of his self-education, which enables him to discover his master key, so estranges him from his contemporaries that the first edition of the *New Science* falls "on barren ground." Those to whom he sends it give "not the faintest sign that they have received it," confirming his belief "it has gone forth into a desert." Vico's sense of estrangement is not so much social or intellectual as existential. Nomads, Lyotard observes, "make the desert, no less then they are made by it," and the

[1] Giambattista Vico, *On the Study Methods of Our Time,* trans. Elio Gianturco (New York: Library of Liberal Arts, 1965), 21.

desert to which Vico refers in his letter to Father Giacco is not his scholarly Neapolitan world but one of his own making. As he struggles to understand the poetic genesis of first men, he can no longer maintain the familiar conceit that humans are, essentially, subjective beings, or its comforting promise of human knowledge adequate to objective reality. With the loss of that foundation his epistemic enterprise *must* change, whether he understands that or not. Once one begins to explore the limit between nature and culture, Derrida points out, one must concern oneself with the founding concepts of philosophy and philology, and that is to step outside those founding concepts. Whatever Vico intends by the phrase "new science," it can no longer be science in the epistemic sense comprehensible to traditional philosophy or philology, now brought into question by his master key.

Vico's existential sense of the abyssal condition of first men, nomadic wanderers in their "desert"—the forests, a world without order or one whose order is inaccessible—forces him to raise the question of the origins of human existence more radically than had his onto-theological tradition. He comes to understand that only if first men are by nature—that is, *genetically*—makers, only if their making is originary—that is, poetic—only if it takes place in linguistic and social behavior and the physical labor made possible by bodily skills, can they make a human place in the world, a clearing in the forest. Whether Vico himself understands the full implications of his belief that "The nature of institutions is nothing but their coming into being . . . at certain times and in certain guises," that "Things do not settle or endure out of their natural state," one implication is certainly that humans whose genetic nature is poetic can never be other than poets.[2] His master key has taken him beyond a *subjective* to a *new* humanism, a poetic ontology of embodied beings-in-the-world making order, meaning, and value out of their bodily skills; making, indeed, the artifactual reality of their human world. Though the convergence of *verum* and *factum* implicit in the *New Science* is misunderstood as the conceptual remaking of the epistemic truths of history, that convergence is *ontological*. The *vera* of history are *themselves facta*—true, real things of the world—yielding not conceptual "truths" but the hermeneutic self-understanding that "knowers" of made trues are their *makers*. While Vico's new, poetic humanism is not the new way of being-human called for by Heidegger—it is, for one, more anthropocentric than Heidegger envisions—it is an ontological hermeneutic of beings in-the-world too strange to be understood by his readers.

Those readers are not only contemporaries to whom Vico sends his manuscript, but also all whose consciousness has been formed by the pedagogic practices and intellectual structures of modernity. Whether they define themselves as Cartesians, they share a Cartesian mentality that objectifies and sets

---

[2] Giambattista Vico, *The New Science of Giambattista Vico,* trans. Thomas Goddard Bergin and Max Harold Fisch (Ithaca: Cornell University Press, 1988), 147, 134.

before the mind the world as picture: they think of themselves as epistemo-logical subjects. I intend to sharpen the "confrontational dislocative tenden-cies" in the *New Science* that make room for Vico's new, ontological, poetic, humanism. I do so through comparative studies of the *New Science* with other nomadic writings, whose strangeness marks them as alien to human-ist assumptions.

Some of those writings reflect a biblical sensibility in which embodied humans and their God exist in an abyss; in which originary language and physical labor, *whether* divine or human, make order, meaning, and value, bringing into being an artifactual world, no less real for being so. If the orig-inary language of the Hebrew God created the natural world, his silence forces his people to take up their own "originary" language, to make mean-ing by interpreting the fragments of "divine" language left to them. Ironi-cally, the onto-theological conception that the language of a spiritual God is itself spiritual mystifies the conception of originary language. In defiance of that misreading Derrida figures the alien of metaphysics as "Judaic," the Other that cannot be encompassed within the tradition of *logos*. Those who struggle to inscribe the "theme of the infinite exteriority of the other" within that tradition are Jewgreeks, condemned to use the language of metaphysics to do so. Jewgreeks are always in our midst, nomads who, unable to credit the vision of a world illumined by *logos*, wander in exile between a sense of the "infinitely other" and inherited conceptual and linguistic structures in which they inscribe that sense. Fear of the abyss haunts their writings: cloaked in skepticism, nominalism, existentialism, nomads are subdued, at times domesticated, by the spirit, or language, of system. So masked, they are not always recognizable. They exist either as curiosities within the tra-dition they contest or, like Vico, are appropriated as "precursors" by later movements.

The writers of a second set of texts, the postmodern, similarly assume that abyssal condition, the need to create order, meaning, and value in so im-poverished a state that the only means to do so is with originary language. I use the term "postmodern" here functionally rather than substantively, in the sense that Blumenberg relates occupants of recurring historical positions to one another by virtue of cosmic or acosmic functions. If the modern is not other than the position reoccupied by those sharing a benign cosmic vision of human existence, linked by no more than the belief that humans are sub-jective beings capable of knowledge, the postmodern is the position reoccu-pied by nomads unable to accept that vision. Without the authority of chronology or eidetic content, "modern" and "postmodern" are interpretive or aesthetic sites cutting across historical periods, metaphors for sensibilities meaningful only in agonistic relation. So total has been the hegemony of the cosmic vision that only radical critiques that position themselves as "post-modern" are able to bracket its naturalness, contextualize its historical and cultural origins, constitute a perspective identifying alternate ways of "inhabiting the labyrinth." In this functional sense it is not the use of post-modern texts to bring out dislocative tendencies in the *New Science* that is anachronistic, but the assumption of Vico's position within a modernity fully realized only with Kant and nineteenth century German idealism. I draw primarily on Nietzsche and Heidegger for the postmodern perspective.[3] While the substantive differences between Heidegger and Vico are great, perhaps more telling than the affinities, the two share an existential sense of human strangeness that functions to subvert traditional anthropology. By bringing out affinities between Vico's understanding of the linguistic setting up of historical worlds and Heidegger's hermeneutic ontology, I distinguish the new, poetic humanism emerging in Vico's last work from the humanism of his earlier writings.

That traditional humanism is particularly evident in *Ancient Wisdom,* the most metaphysical of Vico's writings. My discussion brings out the relation between it and the *New Science,* while emphasizing the ultimate rupture between them. Despite that rupture, which Vico stresses in describing his long struggle to get beyond familiar conceits, almost all interpretations of his last work take for granted its grounding in humanism's metaphysical assumptions, the unquestioned belief in a *homoiousis* between the intelligible object of knowledge—history—and subjective knower-makers. I supported that claim in chapter 1 with analyses of those interpretations, dwelling particularly on the transmission of metaphysical assumptions in medieval onto-theology. Those assumptions dominate *Ancient Wisdom,* particularly in Vico's use of the principle *verum et factum convertuntur.* Most interpretations discussed in chapter 1 assume a continuity between the idealist conception of making in *Ancient Wisdom* and the *New Science,* and none sees the challenge to traditional metaphysical assumptions posed by Vico's master key.

Since most interpreters assume Vico's *verum-factum* is epistemological, they concern themselves with the nature of the knowledge it legitimates. Yet, whatever Vico himself meant by knowledge or science in the *New Science,* it could not have been compatible with traditional views. Knowledge was traditionally of causes, and, since Vico identified the nature of a thing with its genesis, and genesis with *poiesis,* he identified the object of "knowledge"

[3] Portions of this chapter have been published in essay collections and journal articles. See "Creative Activity in Vico and the Secularization of Providence," *Studies in Eighteenth Century Culture,* vol. 9, ed. Roseann Runte (Madison: University of Wisconsin Press, 1979), 337–57; "A Genetic Interpretation of Divine Providence in Vico's *New Science,*" *Journal of the History of Philosophy* XX, no. 2 (April 1982): 151–69. For the relation between Vico and Derrida, see "Derrida, Vico, Genesis, and the Originary Power of Language," *The Eighteenth Century: Theory and Interpretation* 34, no. 1 (spring 1993): 65–84; for Vico and Nietzsche, see "The Secularization of Origins in Vico and Nietzsche," *The Personalist Forum* 10, no. 2 (fall 1994): 133–48; for Vico and Heidegger, see "Situating Vico Between Modern and Postmodern," *Historical Reflections/Reflexions Historiques* 22, no. 3 (fall 1996): 587–617, and "Embodying the Eye of Humanism: Giambattista Vico and the Eye of *Ingenium,*" *Sites of Vision: The Discursive Construction of Sight in the History of Philosophy,* ed. David Michael Levin (Cambridge: MIT Press, 1997), 167–96.

convergent with the "true" as the "made." But that identification did not characterize the made or making as subjective, the only claim that could insure the *homoiousis* necessary for an epistemic relation between making and "knowing." In the West an irreconcilable antithesis exists between claims of the primacy of subjectivity and of causality. Croce formulates the issue most sharply, though one could say of him what he says of Sánchez: he does not realize "his hand is resting on a treasure." Though he emphasizes the uniqueness of Vico's claim of a *convergence* of making and knowing, he too assumes a *homoiousis* between the object of knowledge and man as knower, not realizing that assertion is the metaphysical ground of scholasticism. Croce's conception of *verum-factum,* like scholasticism's, is a variant of the idealism endemic to philosophy. It is not too much to say that *all* epistemological positions are idealist. Nominalism's skepticism toward knowledge, on the other hand, derives from an insistence on the primacy of divine causal power that transcends God's intellect (though not, of course, his subjectivity), thus denying that *homoiousis.* Causality can never be elevated to equivalence with intellectual subjectivity without compromising the possibility of knowledge. This is the point of Mackie's critique of maker's knowledge.

Vico scholars such as Löwith and Milbank, who stress with Croce the convergence of making and knowing in Vico's principle, try to strengthen causal potency by relating it to the model of divine creativity in Genesis. They are not successful because they reduce the biblical model to the traditional conception of creation as a subjectively conditioned, intentional act productive of intelligible artifacts. Neither realizes that the causal principle in the Hebrew Bible is language unconditioned by thought and incapable of providing a logical or ontological ground of knowledge. The Hebrews never made epistemic claims, understanding that if creation were a function of originary language, the artifacts produced would be "texts" accessible only to interpretation. Balmes (and Mackie, by implication) are quite right that the view that "intelligibility is only possible through causality" leads to skepticism. It did so for the biblical tradition, it did so for Nominalism, and both Cusa and Vico were all too aware of that danger. But while Cusa insures the possibility of "knowledge"—delimited as self-knowledge—by retaining a Neoplatonic conception of divine and human making, Vico ultimately embraces the causal principle of Genesis, language, though he may not have realized that the new science he builds on it is not epistemic but hermeneutic.

Interpreters of Vico are unaware of the threat to the epistemic nature of *verum-factum* posed by the equivalence of causality to knowing, since they assume that making, including divine making, is conditioned by subjectivity. In chapter 2 I discussed efforts that attempt to elevate the causal potency of *verum-factum* by identifying it with the conception of divine creativity in the Hebrew Bible. Despite his effort, Blumenberg does not realize that his conception of the unity of knowing and making presumes the primacy of subjectivity and the subjective *homoiousis* between knower and made disallowed by the radical skepticism he tries to overcome. For him, as for Cusa, Descartes, and the moderns who use *verum-factum* to legitimate the construction of theory—Bacon, Galileo, Locke, Hobbes—"the locus of man's originary potency . . . is . . . intellect." Though Blumenberg believes that his functional historiography keeps him from the eidetic assumptions of more traditional secularization interpretations, in appropriating the power of the Hebrew God he makes what Heidegger calls the "ultimate error": he understands man's "ek-sistent essence as if it were the secularized transference to human beings of a thought that Christian theology expresses about God."

Blumenberg's discussion of *verum-factum* is important, however, because more than any other commentator he draws out and sharpens the profoundly skeptical implications of *verum-factum*, ultimately subverting his own effort to ground modernity's pragmatic epistemology on it. He finds those skeptical implications explicit in Cusa and Nietzsche. Cusa, he charges, never gets beyond the self-referentiality implicit in *verum-factum*. Blumenberg believes that Bruno, Descartes, and the moderns do so, without realizing that self-referentiality is *inherent* to the principle; that the knowledge the maker recovers can never be other than the hermeneutic understanding by the "knower" that she is maker of the known. Nietzsche goes beyond even the delimitation of knowledge to self-knowledge to deny the possibility of knowledge at all. By imputing "the least possible binding force" to reality, Nietzsche embraces the "absoluteness of art" and identifies creativity wholly with originary metaphoric language. Against the moderns' epistemic notion of humans as knowers, Nietzsche turns to an ontological view of humans as creators of their world. By acknowledging the absence of any "pregiveness" to the world, even of human subjectivity, Nietzsche comes closer than any "modern" to the radically originary creativity of the biblical God who is poet rather than architect.

The discussion of the biblical conception of ontological creativity in chapter 2 draws on postmodern writers who recover its radical nature by approaching it outside the conceits of philosophy or onto-theology. As quotations from Blumenberg, Heidegger, and Canguilhem in chapter 2 emphasize, human self-image in the West is inevitably based on an analogy with God, and varies with the image of God. If the unity of word, act, thing in *davar* expresses the biblical conception of the ontologically creative language of a poet-God, Philo's transformation of *davar* into *logos* injects the "virus" of subjectivity into the biblical tradition. Though the turn from linguistic creativity to a theology of incarnation provides the Christianized West with the metaphysical base the Greeks believed necessary for knowledge, what is lost is the originary power only language offers; indeed, what is lost is the primacy of causality over the metaphysical principles of identity and *homoiousis*. Nowhere are the differences between those alternatives more apparent than in epistemological and ontological interpretations of *verum-factum*. In the Vico literature those who claim *verum-factum* as an epistemological principle secularizing the divine unity of knowing and making understand that unity on the model of the incarnation. For Löwith and Milbank the incarnation seems to provide that more unified conception of spirit and body Vico embraces, and Milbank even argues that the medieval theme of *verbum mentis* brings out the priority of language in divine making. From a more Hebraic perspective such as Derrida's, the incarnation is the very symbol of that mystifying spiritualization of divine language that destroys its originary power.

Neither Faur nor Handelman uses the term "ontology" in relation to *verum-factum,* or, indeed, in relation to the Hebraic notion of the created world as Book (though Derrida does). Strictly speaking, ontology is not possible outside the foundational assumptions of metaphysics. Thus, I take liberties in calling *verum-factum "ontological,"* insofar as it secularizes a divine linguistic creativity productive of a real, albeit artifactual, world. I compound the impropriety by applying the term "poetic ontology" to the new linguistic humanism I attribute to Vico and consider a secularization of the Hebraic, doing so to sharpen the distinction between it and the epistemic humanism of Hellenism. Certainly the principle formulated in *Ancient Wisdom* is the traditional epistemological version Vico derives from scholasticism and attributes to ancient wisdom. By the *New Science,* however, Vico grasps a poetic conception of humans and human making that precludes an epistemic conception of the convertibility of making and knowing—even, I argue, for men of the third age. His insight into the embodied nature of humans who exist in a world of material necessity and produce true things—the artifacts of a real, concrete world, including its abstract language and conceptual truths—and who do so with language and with social practices, does not provide the homogeneity between knower and known that grounds epistemology. His is an ontological determination of humans as makers rather than as epistemic subjects. Like Nietzsche, Vico embraces the absoluteness of art; for both men reality is artifactual (as is the world created by God). Moreover, though humans of the third age forget they create their reality—including their truths, their very subjective nature—Vico, like Cusa, understands that knowing is never other than "self-knowing," a reflexive hermeneutic "knowing" that knowers and their trues are *facta* of human making.

On the Most Ancient Wisdom of the Italians
and the God of Neoplatonism

The concern with origins that places Vico in the existential position of the Jewgreek is already present in *Ancient Wisdom*. The obscurity of that work—impenetrable even to its reviewers, who say of one of its main theses, "[I]t envelops the whole treatise in a darkness that is almost palpable"—suggests the nomadic writer struggling to inscribe an alien understanding of the human condition within the linguistic and conceptual constraints of his tradition.[4] He is, to be sure, continuing the critique begun in *On the Study Methods of Our Time* against the dominant intellectual current of his age and its preeminent philosopher, René Descartes.[5] The palpable darkness of *Ancient Wisdom* is due not merely to Vico's resistance to modern philosophy, however, but also to the direction that resistance is beginning to take. In opposition to Descartes, Vico puts forward an epistemology and a metaphysics—the wisdom of the ancients he claims to uncover in the early languages of the Italians. Though the etymological method he uses to uncover that ancient wisdom is part of the humanist trappings of *Ancient Wisdom,* the conception of human nature and knowledge Vico claims to find with it points the way to a new humanism that brings into question the old.

Vico is strikingly prescient in foreseeing the dangers to which Cartesian philosophy leads, dangers inherent in the hegemony of a human subjectivity that objectifies and systematizes the world. Writing in terms almost as existential and apocalyptic as Heidegger's, he likens modern physicists to "certain individuals who have inherited from their parents a gorgeous mansion," so completely and luxuriously appointed they can do nothing except "move the furniture around . . . add some ornaments and bring things up to date."[6] He is equally caustic about the effects of applying geometric method to practical life, quoting Terence's quip that those who do so do "no more than spend [their] labor on going mad rationally." The rationalization of social practice was akin to "driv[ing] a straight furrow through the vicissitudes of life as if whim, rashness, opportunity, and luck did not dominate the human condition."[7]

As prescient as he is, however, Vico cannot foresee the *telos* of modern philosophy in the critical self-reflection of Kantian philosophy and its identification of humans as subjects of abstract knowledge. With the advantage of hindsight Heidegger makes explicit what it means to live in a "gorgeous mansion," though his metaphor for sterility is an enframed picture. The modern age is, in effect, the age of the world picture, meaning not merely that man has a mental "copy" of the world, but also that philosophic and

[4] Giambattista Vico, *On the Most Ancient Wisdom of the Italians: Unearthed from the Origins of the Latin Language,* trans. L. M. Palmer (Ithaca: Cornell University Press, 1988), 139.
[5] By the time Vico wrote *Study Methods* in 1709, his early interest in Descartes had ended and he had taken up arms against the new philosophy, appealing both to Greek philosophy, which he believed probabilistic, and to a rhetorical tradition that cultivated prudence (*Study Methods,* 18, 33–34). He preferred Platonic philosophy to Stoicism and Epicureanism because of its rejection of materialism and its social ethics (*New Science,* 499). Rejecting the "pernicious pedagogy" of his age, which taught method and criticism, thereby impoverishing the skills of common sense and eloquence, he emphasized the rhetorical art of discovery, which strengthened perception, memory, and imagination, and "topics," the source of common sense, the "criterion of practical judgment . . . [and] eloquence" (*Study Methods,* 13–15). See also the lecture included in the *Autobiography* warning against the study of algebra and the premature exercise of criticism (124–25).
[6] Vico, *Study Methods,* 21.
[7] Vico, *Ancient Wisdom,* 98–99. The Terence quote is *Eunuchus,* 62–63.

scientific method prescriptively sets before him a "structured image that is
the creature of man's producing which represents and sets before," and man
becomes the being who "gives the measure and draws up the guidelines for
everything that is. . . . Man brings into play his unlimited power for the calculating, planning and molding of all things." This "objectiveness of representing, and truth . . . as the certainty of representing first showed up in the
metaphysics of Descartes," in which "the very essence of man itself changes
in that man becomes subject." With this determination "[t]here begins that
way of being human . . . given over to measuring and executing, for the purpose of gaining mastery over that which is as a whole." What begins in this
"doctrine of man" is, in effect, humanism as "a moral-aesthetic anthropology," "that philosophical interpretation of man which explains and evaluates whatever is, in its entirety, from the standpoint of man and in relation
to man." From this "acme," subjectivism establishes itself in "the planetary
imperialism of technologically organized man."[8] Unlike Vico, Heidegger
finds this metaphysical anthropocentrism destined in Plato's reduction of Being to "thinking as *ratio*." The nihilism Nietzsche claimed the *telos* of the entire tradition had its beginnings in Greek humanism.

Though Heidegger acknowledges that "[m]an cannot, of himself, abandon
this destining of his modern essence or abolish it by fiat," he believes that
"[b]eing subject as humanity has not always been the sole possibility belonging to the essence of historical man." Yet, "such is the darkening which
that truth as the certainty of subjectivity . . . lays over a disclosing event
[*Ereignis*] that it remains denied to subjectivity itself to experience."[9]
Though Heidegger's own way out of traditional humanism is as problematic
as the subjectivist anthropocentrism it means to replace, his critique raises
provocative questions concerning humanism that contextualize the discussion of Vico in this chapter. The first is whether humanism, insofar as it is
anthropocentric, is as inevitably dualist and subjectivist—and, therefore, ni-
hilist—as Heidegger believes, devaluing what it values insofar as "what is
valued is admitted only as an object for man's estimation."[10] Is what is "valued" *necessarily* "objectified and devalued" when man does the estimating?
It is for Heidegger, because it is the mental act of a subject who enframes by
setting "whatever is, itself, in place before oneself just in the way that it
stands with it." The question persists, however—can there be a humanism
that, though anthropocentric, is not subjectivist? Certainly Vico, whose early
works are preoccupied not only with nurturing humane social existence, but
also with the epistemic goal of grounding certain knowledge, began his in-

[8] Martin Heidegger, "The Age of the World Picture," *The Question Concerning Technology
and Other Essays,* trans. William Lovitt (New York: Harper Torchbooks, 1977), 115–54, 128–
35, 152.
[9] Ibid., 153.
[10] Martin Heidegger, "Letter on Humanism," *Basic Writings,* ed. David Farrell Krell (San
Francisco: Harper, 1993), 213–65, 251.

tellectual life as a traditional humanist, and, in retaining belief in the value of communal existence and in the ability of humans to create their social world, resolutely retains an anthropocentric perspective. Yet, while doing so, Vico enriches and transforms his understanding of what it means to be human, taking his anthropology beyond subjectivism and epistemic concerns. He grasps the poetic nature of humans and envisions a *poiesis* that, while assuming the centrality of human activity, conceives it as ontologically constructive of linguistic and social practices, the very being of humans in-the-world. The following discussion traces Vico's path from the early humanist assumptions that "destine" an epistemic relation *to* the world, to a "poetic" conception of being human *in* the world. As such, it is another way of answering the question Jean Beaufret set to Heidegger: "*Comment redonner un sense au mot 'Humanisme'?*"

The endeavors of *Ancient Wisdom* that put Vico on the path to the poetic insights of the *New Science* include the formulation of an epistemology undermining the Cartesian, and a metaphysics—palpably obscurer—accounting for the origins or causes of extension and motion in matter, and power or force—and, therefore, spirit, mind, will, and prudence—in humans. Though Vico believes he finds these positions in an original wisdom hidden in the language of the ancients, the obscurity of *Ancient Wisdom* arises from the inadequacy of his methods. Vico's perplexed reviewers are aware of that inadequacy and unwittingly provide him with the key to his own master key, saying, "[H]e should not have tried to trace [the most ancient philosophy of the Italians] in the origin and meanings of Latin words . . . [but] by unearthing and disinterring . . . the oldest monuments of ancient Etruria," that is, its laws, religious rites, and philosophies.[11] Vico initially resists that suggestion but, referring to his controversy with the reviewers in his *Autobiography* fifteen years later, acknowledges "the dissatisfaction with grammatical etymologies which Vico had begun to feel was an indication of the source whence later, in his most recent works, he was to recover the origins of languages . . . [and] principles of poetry different from those . . . hitherto accepted."[12] The difference between *Ancient Wisdom* and the *New Science* is, in effect, the difference between the traditional methods with which he pursues *original* wisdom, and his later confrontation with the existential question of the *originary*—the more radical question, to paraphrase Heidegger, "Why is there human rather than bestial existence?"[13] Why, that is, are there religions, laws, customs, languages *at all*? Vico already begins to answer

---

[11] Vico, *Ancient Wisdom,* 149.

[12] Vico, *The Autobiography of Giambattista Vico,* trans. Max Harold Fisch and Thomas Goddard Bergin (Ithaca: Great Seal Books, 1963), 153.

[13] Martin Heidegger, *An Introduction to Metaphysics,* trans. Ralph Manheim (New Haven: Yale University Press, 1987), 1. Heidegger's question, repeated throughout the work, is "Why are there essents rather than nothing?" "Essent" is the translator's rendering of *Das Seiende,* meaning "existents, things that are" (ix).

these more originary questions with the positions his reviewers find most obscure—metaphysical points and *conatus*—though he does so in the language
and conceptual apparatus of traditional metaphysics. Neither they nor Vico
realizes the extent to which he is moving beyond foundational assumptions,
not only of Cartesian metaphysics, but also of metaphysics itself, to the question of the originary that recurs, in more radical form, in the *New Science*.

The first question Vico tries to resolve by returning to the wisdom of the
ancients is the nature of knowledge. Since that question becomes for him a
function of the creative potency of the knower, he develops it in the context
of a theory of divine causal agency and the relation of divine to human
agency. In etymologies of *verum* (the "true"), *factum* ("what is made"), *intelligere* ("to read perfectly," "to have plain knowledge," "to understand"),
cogitare ("to think," "to gather"), *ratio* ("reckoning," human "endow-
ment"), *legere* ("to read") he uncovers what he claims is an ancient understanding of the true. From the notion of combining or gathering which these
words contain ("reading" as a combining of the written elements of a word,
"understanding" as a "combining of all parts of an object from which its
most perfect idea may be expressed"), Vico assumes "'The true is precisely
what is made' (*Verum esse ipsum factum*)."[14] Since "[t]o prove something
from causes is to effect it," he concludes that "demonstration is the same as
construction."[15] In this "gather[ing] of the elements of the truth that it contemplates," the mind makes the truths it knows, though Vico qualifies this
making. "The physicist cannot truly define things [and] . . . assign to each
its own nature and thus truly make it, for that is God's right." What man defines are "the names themselves, and on the model of God [*ad Dei instar*] he
creates . . . as if from nothing" the point and line—"feign[ing] . . . the elements of words from which ideas are stimulated." Not only do humans create mere fictions; their fictions are linguistic.[16]

In establishing the convertibility of true and made *thing*, Vico looks to divine making as the model of convergence, since the first *vero* "is in God, because God is the first Maker," and "He is the Maker of all *things*." The first
vero is infinite and complete, containing "all the elements of *things*, both external and internal," and knowing consists in putting "the elements of
things" together. Here Vico makes several distinctions concerning God's
knowing, the first between the ancient conception of knowledge and truth
and one "reconciled with our own religion," a distinction made necessary
because the ancients believed the world eternal while for Christianity the
world was created in time out of nothing. Thus he distinguishes between created and uncreated, "begotten," truth, identifying the latter with "the Word"
of scripture containing "the ideas of all things—as well as the elements of all

---

[14] Vico, *Ancient Wisdom*, 45–47.
[15] Ibid., 64–65. By "cause," Vico means "giving order to the matter or the chaotic elements
of a *thing*, and composing its scattered parts into a whole" (64–65).
[16] Ibid., 51.

ideas."[17] This is the distinction between creation *ad extra* and *ad intra* over which Löwith and Milbank disagree, the latter presuming the trinitarian conception of creation, the former, the biblical conception of God as craftsman.[18] Vico also distinguishes between divine and human knowing. On one level they are the same, since "[j]ust as divine truth is what God sets in order and creates in the act of knowing it, so human truth is what man puts together and makes in the act of knowing it." Thus human science, like God's knowledge, is of the "genus or mode by which a thing is made; and by this very knowledge the mind makes the thing, because in knowing it puts together the elements of that thing." The difference between them is that God's knowing, *intelligentia,* "reads all the elements of things whether inner or outer, because He contains . . . them" and gathers them all, while human discursive thought is *cogitatio,* which knows only the "outside edges of things."[19] Though man cannot know nature because he does not contain the elements that constitute it, he "turns this fault of his mind to good use and creates two things," the point and the unit, abstract fictive elements that constitute mathematical science. "For when the mind gathers the elements of the truth that it contemplates, it cannot do so except by making the truths it knows." With this delimited conception of human knowledge, Vico rejects Descartes's claim to ground certain knowledge on the *cogito:* Descartes cannot know the human mind because he cannot make it.[20]

Though Vico cannot give an account of divine nature, since humans do not make that "true thing" either, an image emerges from his characterization of God's knowing and causal agency. In the context of his etymological "discovery" of the convertibility of the true and made, he characterizes God as Maker. Thus, though *verum-factum* is generally identified as an epistemological principle and functions as such in *Ancient Wisdom,* even there it asserts the *unity* of knowing and making and, as such, is an ontological principle identifying God as a Maker creating *real things* that are true—that is, intelligible. As the translator points out, the literal meaning of *verum esse ipsum factum* is "the true is the thing made [or done] itself." Unfortunately, *verum* is usually translated in the Vico literature as "truth," rather than as "true thing," suggesting concepts or propositions and obscuring its ontological meaning. Fisch notes the problem of translation, saying "I depart from English usage in the direction of Vico's Latin. English permits us to speak . . . of the . . . true . . . but not of the trues. . . . But Vico's *verum* means the true, not the truth, and its plural *vera* means not the truths but the trues

---

[17] Ibid., 46–47. Emphasis added. I italicize the word "thing" to emphasize the ontological nature of divine making (see ibid., 109). The closest Vico comes to describing the elements gathered is an obscure discussion of genera, or metaphysical forms (58–59).

[18] Vico makes a similar distinction in the *Autobiography* in relation to human making, but there it is Platonic, not theological (*Autobiography,* 127).

[19] Vico, *Ancient Wisdom,* 45–47. The reviewers take issue with Vico's etymologies (see ibid., 147).

[20] Ibid., 50–51, see also 65. See Vico's critique of Descartes, 52–56.

of intelligibles; that is, *the things, other than sentences or propositions,* that are true in the transcendental sense of intelligible."[21] Similarly, the *"vero"* of the Italian texts, usually translated as "truth," can be rendered "true." To heighten awareness of the ontological rather than conceptual nature of *verum,* wherever the Italian texts of *Ancient Wisdom* or the *New Science* use *vero* in relation to the made, I insert the word "true" in brackets for the word "truth" given in English translations.[22] As the "true" that God makes is a *thing,* so, I argue, the trues that humans make are the *things* of their real, historical world. Even more, I argue that for the God whose making is a model for Vico's poets, and for humans, true *things* are inseparable from the words and deeds of the creative act.

That Vico wants to strengthen that divine ontological potency limited by the Neoplatonic and scholastic emphasis on divine intellect becomes increasingly clear in *Ancient Wisdom.* Some argue that Vico does so by adopting the Nominalist conception of a voluntarist God. Yet, though he says, "God makes even the smallest things by infinite power," the God in *Ancient Wisdom* is not the willful deity of Nominalism, but the Neoplatonic deity of scholasticism, "the purest infinite mind." For Vico, as for Cusa, it is God's intellect that creates: "God generates divine [trues] by exercising His intellect and makes a created [true]. . . . [A]ll those things that are, are 'the thoughts of God.'" Vico consciously moves away from the intellectualism of the Neoplatonic God, however, with a greater emphasis on causality in the notion of gathering. In defining "cause" as "that which contains in itself the elements of the thing it produces and disposes them, and thus . . . forms and

[21] Max H. Fisch, "Vico and Pragmatism," in *Giambattista Vico: An International Symposium,* ed. Giorgio Tagliacozzo and Hayden V. White (Baltimore: Johns Hopkins University Press, 1969), 401–24, 407–8. Emphasis added. Pompa uses "true" for the singular *verum* or *vero,* but "truths" for the plural, "for purely stylistic reasons," since both mean "that which is true" not as proposition, but as "the thing which is true" (*Vico: Selected Writings,* ed. and trans. Leon Pompa [Cambridge: Cambridge University Press, 1982], xvi). While I agree that Vico's *verum* means "true," in the *New Science* it does so, not, as Fisch says, as a transcendental, but as "true thing"; that is, not as an intelligible object of epistemology but as an ontologically real *thing.* Fisch's and Pompa's problem is not ultimately one of translation but of interpretation—neither gets beyond the modern conceit that subjectivizes "trues" as products of cognition. Similarly, James C. Morrison misses the ontological significance of *verum-factum.* Pointing out that in *Ancient Wisdom* "*[v]erum* is *factum* is not a doctrine about the nature of truth but about the true," he concludes that *verum* and *factum* are substantively "one and the same entity" (582), and criticizes Croce for calling Vico's philosophy *"gnoseologia,"* since "Vico himself did not view 'theory of knowledge' as a distinct philosophical discipline. Beginning in this way . . . creates the false impression that for [Vico] the central problem was the nature of knowledge . . . [rather than, as Vico says] the unity of the true and the certain" (586 n. 31). Yet Morrison does not draw out the ontological implications of this convergence, but presents an idealist interpretation of Vico's epistemology derived from onto-theological notions of God. "[T]o know is to make the object known in and through the act of knowing it" (583). (James C. Morrison, "Vico's Principle of *Verum* is *Factum* and the Problem of Historicism," *Journal of the History of Ideas* 34, no. 4 [October–December 1978], 579–95.)

[22] The term "true" is always the appropriate one in relation to God's creations, and in the *New Science* it is the appropriate term for the human creation of an ontologically real social world. What is made conceptually in *Ancient Wisdom*—geometry, metaphysics—are "truths."

comprehends the mode of them, and by comprehending it sends forth the effect," he criticizes "philosophers [who] having fallen into a great many mistakes . . . [hold] that God works like a demiurge and that the things He creates cause other things." Rather, "the unique cause is the one that needs nothing else to produce its effect, being that which contains in itself the elements of the thing it produces."[23] Despite this emphasis—his effort to grasp an *unmediated* conception of divine causal agency—Vico cannot yet get beyond the intellectual deity of *Ancient Wisdom*. Nor, since God's ontological and epistemological gathering is the activity of His subjective nature, can he get beyond the conception that human creativity analogous to it is conceptual.[24]

Though Vico still thinks within the context of subjectivist assumptions, he is moving toward a more radical question: What if human making is as ontological as divine making? He finds in ancient wisdom a conception of origins closer to the "primitive" model of the making of the craftsman. To make that creation *ad extra* more compatible "with our own religion" he brings it together with creation *ad intra*. His intent is to strengthen the creative potency of the God of "our own religion," but he cannot do so as long as he retains a spiritualized conception of it. He is fairly successful in establishing an analogy between divine and human making in *Ancient Wisdom,* because there the analogy is limited to the epistemological process of knowing the fictive concepts humans make themselves. Like the Nominalists, he has given up knowledge of the true things created by God and is not yet concerned with the human making and knowing of the trues of the real human world.[25] In the *New Science,* however, he claims more than that humans know the con-

[23] Vico, *Ancient Wisdom,* 109–10. See also 128, 94, 124.

[24] If Vico's view of knowledge has any affinity with voluntarism, it is with the latter's emphasis on the contingency of God's conceptual subjectivity. In *Ancient Wisdom* Vico is still interested in grounding knowledge, and only the subjectivity of creators and knowers insures even delimited versions of knowledge. Eckhard Kessler traces the influence of the notion of the contingency of God's subjectivity from the thirteenth century voluntarist John Duns Scotus to Vico's "conceptual subjectivism" (Eckhard Kessler, "Vico's Attempt Towards a Humanistic Foundation of Science," *Vico: Past and Present,* ed. Giorgio Tagliacozzo [Atlantic Highlands: Humanities Press, 1981], vol. 1, 73–88). Kessler says Scotus rejected the assumption of *homoiousis* grounding medieval Aristotelian science's belief in a correspondence between logical and ontological necessity, attributed the contingency of the world to God's voluntarism, and retained science as contingent knowledge, "relating it to its efficient cause, a free creative power." Scotus's argument was drawn out in different directions; to the Terminists, who limited science to mental processes cut off from reality, and Renaissance humanists, who attributed creativity to human subjectivity and made knowledge a function of it rather than the object. Kessler traces the humanist strand through Petrarch and Salutati to Vico, who legitimates a contingent science—first mathematics, then history—of "conceptual subjectivism." Kessler may be correct in relating Vico's construction of mathematical science to Scotus's conceptual voluntarism, but that relation cannot explain the more radically originary ontological making that becomes central in the *New Science.*

[25] With his etymologies, Vico says, he discovered an ancient maxim: "[M]an works in the world of abstractions in the same way that God works in the real world" (156; see also 168–69).

ceptual truths of the history they make—he claims that what humans "know" are the true things of the historical world, and that humans do so because they are the makers of those trues. The "conceptual subjectivism" of Scotus and Renaissance humanism cannot account for this ontological making. The pressing problem in the Vichian literature is to understand how Vico achieves an equivalence of knowing and *ontological* making, and the only model of divine convergence that does not subsume making to knowing is the *ad extra* creativity of Genesis. In that model God creates true things in a creative act unconditioned by subjectivity—the only kind of creating, Mackie points out, that allows for maker's knowing.[26]

Vico's concern with origins in *Ancient Wisdom* leads him not only to a causal theory of knowledge, but also to the metaphysical causes of extension and motion in matter, and of power or force and, therefore, spirit and mind, in humans. Though humans cannot know these causes, they have the conceptual ability to create fictive mathematical and metaphysical accounts of them. They turn "the vice of our mind . . . its extremely narrow compass, in that it . . . does not contain what it affects to know," to good use, creating two fictions with abstractions—"the point that can be drawn and the unit that can be multiplied." In this way man creates "a kind of world of shapes and numbers . . . [and] knows infinite truths within himself."[27] These abstractions are constructions in several senses. They are paradigms of the truths humans can make, supplying "proof from causes . . . because the human mind contains the elements of the truths that it can order and compose . . . so that demonstration is the same as construction, and the true is the same as the made."[28] Further, as fictions created by mind, they are the elements the mind gathers to make the fictive physics and metaphysics with which it accounts for God's creation of the material world.

In Vico's own process of making, his etymologies constitute another "element." From his discovery that "For the Latins point [*punctum*] and momentum [*momentum*] were synonymous"—an indivisible thing that moves—he surmises that ancient Zenonians derived a metaphysical point from the geometric. While geometers consider the definition of the point purely nominal, Zenonians considered it "the definition of a real thing," since it is "the image of what the human mind is capable of thinking in regard to the indivisible power of extension and motion."[29] For Vico the meta-

---

[26] John Milbank undermines his claim that Vico "subverts the Platonic Paradigm" by appealing to subjective intention, saying, "Despite Vico's proposal of the priority of the made, it remains the case that the maker must always have a vague anticipation of what he is to make" (*The Religious Dimension in the Thought of Giambattista Vico* [Lewiston: The Edwin Mellen Press, 1991], pt. 1, 142).

[27] Vico, *Ancient Wisdom*, 50–52.

[28] Ibid., 65. Palmer says some commentators consider *Ancient Wisdom* internally inconsistent, moving from a "constructive epistemology to an ontology of Neoplatonic forms and to a metaphysics of Zenonian points" (24–28).

[29] See Vico's account, 69–71.

physical point Zenonians considered real is a fictional element gathered into a fictional metaphysics resolving questions of beginnings—the physical and metaphysical questions concerning God's creation of the world. The specific problem it resolves is how God, himself a Being not extended and at rest— "the purest, infinite mind"—creates from elements He gathers within himself a material world of extended bodies and motion. The metaphysical point is the mediating link between God and the natural world, a link not itself physically extended, but having the power of extension. The point possesses *conatus,* the metaphysical power of motion that is the link between a God at rest and a physical world in motion. Like the metaphysical point Vico finds reference to this fictive *conatus* in his etymologies, in which *conatus* or force (*vis*) and power (*potestas*) are synonymous with the *essentia* of the Schoolmen. "Because God makes even the smallest things by infinite power . . . the essence of things is power. . . . The unextended [being] makes extended ones, and arouses conatus, composes motions, and while at rest, it moves everything." As extended bodies and motion are the subject of physics, so the *power* of extension (metaphysical points) and the *power* of motion (*conatus*) belong to metaphysics. Together they explain beginnings, since, "at the very beginning, things begin to exist out of their own nothingness" through them. "Nature is motion. . . . The works of nature are brought into being by conatus and brought to perfection by motion. In sum, the genesis of things presupposes motion, motion presupposes conatus, and conatus presupposes God."[30]

As central as *conatus* is to Vico's conception of the natural world in *Ancient Wisdom,* it is as ambiguous and controversial as is the notion of providence in the *New Science*—appropriately so, since the two notions serve a similar function. Together they account for the natural and human worlds in immanent, holistic terms—*conatus* for the vitalistic phenomenon of motion, life, thought, mind, soul, and spirit in matter and material bodies; providence for the intelligibility and social nature of historical process.[31] That Vico desires to put forward an immanent, holistic conception of both natural and historical worlds is not generally accepted in the literature, since most interpretations hold that for Vico order is the product of subjective intention, supplied, primarily, by a transcendent providence. Ironically, even those who credit Vico with a philosophy of immanence can characterize it only reductively, turning Vico into either an idealist or a mechanistic materialist. For Croce, "The theory of metaphysical points, in which God appears as the great geometrician . . . is as it were a symbol of the necessity of interpreting

[30] Ibid., 109–10 (see *Autobiography,* 151–52); 75; 79. Vico argues that *conatus* should not be considered physics but metaphysics. See 82 for his "Heraclitean" description of nature as constant motion and change.

[31] I argue that in the *New Science* Vico secularizes providence as human creativity. The God of *Ancient Wisdom* is transcendent, since Vico is discussing God's creation of the world, but Vico uses the metaphysics of *conatus* to provide a fictive account of how God creates.

nature in idealistic language. We find here and there a theologian Vico, an agnostic Vico . . . but look where we will among his works, we shall never find a materialistic Vico."[32] Alternately Bedani, arguing a deterministic interpretation of *conatus,* says in the seventeenth century the term described "the link-force or 'virtue' existing between rest and motion . . . which enables animate objects to translate the apparently immaterial impulses of the world of sense, feeling or thought into activity at the level of the body as physical or mechanical action."[33]

Croce's certainty that Vico could never be a materialist stems from Vico's repeated rejection of the mechanistic conception of nature and Croce's own inability to conceive of a physical world that avoids mechanism without being idealist—a third position I call naturalism rather than materialism. Croce's difficulty stems from the fact that the traditional distinction between matter and spirit or subjectivity assumes that both are *substances,* a metaphysical distinction overcome only by reducing one substance to the other. The problem does not arise if one begins with the assumption of a physical world that is not substance, but *inherently* dynamic and vital—a monist assumption no more metaphysical than materialism, idealism, or dualism. That Vico is doing so in *Ancient Wisdom* is suggested by his use of *conatus* to provide a naturalist rather than materialist conception of humans. For him *conatus* as the power of motion is ubiquitous in a physical world not composed of separate substances. The material body "moved by a motion common to all bodies" is air, the pressure of air being "God's perceptible hand, by which all things are moved," causing the motion by which water rises in a siphon, fire burns, plants grow, animals frolic. In relation to the human organism, Vico appeals once again to etymology to show that the Latins called air *anima,* meaning soul, distinguishing it from *animus,* spirit. "Thus, we may surmise that the ancient philosophers of Italy defined soul and spirit by reference to the motion of air. And truly air is the vehicle of life." Air moves blood (as *spiritus vitales,* vital spirits), nerves (as *spiritus animales,* animal spirits), and heart, the "seat and abode of the spirit"; "the mind," in turn, "depends on the spirit." The Latins attributed immortality to spirit rather than soul, since the motion of souls is tied to the corruptible body while the motion of *animus* is free and "yearns for . . . immortality." This last argument is "obscure," Vico's reviewers charge, because Vico's attribution of immortality to *animus* is functional, based as it is on freedom of choice rather than the substantive terms of the rest of the discussion.[34]

---

[32] Benedetto Croce, *The Philosophy of Giambattista Vico,* trans. R. G. Collingwood (London: Howard Latimer, 1913), 142.

[33] Gino Bedani, *Vico Revisited: Orthodoxy, Naturalism and Science in the Scienza Nuova* (Oxford: Berg, 1989), 267. Even "[t]he Cartesian dichotomy between immaterial mind and mechanical body was thus resolved . . . in terms of this intermediary force," Bedani adds.

[34] Vico, *Ancient Wisdom,* 83–89. Vico refers to the Christian fathers, who distinguished man from beast with freedom of choice, to support the "dogma" that man was created with an immortal spirit. In effect Vico's argument for immortality rests on authority, not philosophy. In

Indeed, the whole discussion of *anima* and *animus* is obscure, and Vico's critics are quick to note their misgivings. They question Vico's claim that the ancient Italian conception of spirit was "largely uniform" with Christian beliefs in immortality and free will, the latter the distinction between man and beast. They ask, "[I]f spirit is nothing but air moving in the nerves, and if air is body, and every body is corruptible, how can we ever conclude that the spirit is not corrupt but immortal?" And, "if heart, arteries, blood, nervous system, juice and animal spirits are . . . in beasts," they too possess spirit as well as soul, "[s]o where is the difference between men and animals?" And again, if nerves—and therefore heart, arteries, blood—receive motion from animal spirits, how could the motions of spirit be voluntary and derive from free will?[35] The sharp-eyed reviewers have detected the tenor of Vico's entire discussion of *conatus*—an ultimate denial of any dualism between a physical body and nonphysical substance.[36]

Vico supports his distinction between *animus* and *anima*—between spirit, which is free, immortal, and supported by Christian dogma, and soul, animated by *conatus* and tied to, ultimately finite with, the body—by associating spirit with mind and soul and body with "faculties." Though the mind has a more elevated status through its association with spirit, it is passive, deriving thoughts and ideas from God. "*Facultas,*" on the other hand, "signifies an unhindered and ready disposition for making (*facere*). Hence, faculty is the ability to turn power into action. The soul is power, sight an activity, and the sense of sight a faculty." Since the senses are faculties, Vico disagrees with scholasticism that sensations are in things: "[W]e make the color of things by seeing, flavor by tasting, sound by hearing, and heat and cold by touching." Thus he emphasizes human making rather than a passive receptivity to the world, though locating making in bodily senses rather than in subjectivity. By the *New Science* Vico attributes all human making, including the developmental making of abstract thought and knowledge, to the senses. He finds support in the ancient Italian philosophers for the view that

the *Autobiography* Vico also identifies *anima* as air, the "principle which gives the universe motion and life." He traces a causal process from *animus,* ether, whose mind (*mens*) was Jove, which comes to men from Jove. Spirit, in turn, acts on soul, insinuating air, thus motion and life, into the blood. Vico gives another string of etymological associations reinforcing the physicality of animate life. Since the word *coelum* means both "chisel" and "great body of the air," he conjectures that Egyptians thought "the instrument with which nature makes everything was the wedge," signified by the pyramid. Similarly, he says the Latins called *ingenium* nature, "whose principal property is sharpness; thus intimating that nature forms and deforms every form with the chisel of air" (148–49).

[35] Ibid., 142–43.

[36] Palmer translates *animus* and *anima* as spirit and soul "[f]or stylistic reasons," and follows Fisch's translation, "rather than the obvious alternatives 'the principle of life' and 'the principle of feeling.'" Those "obvious alternatives" bring out even more strongly the naturalistic tenor of Vico's discussion (85 n. 1). As Palmer says, "[J]ust as conatus explains the origin and conservation of the physical world, so . . . the principle of life—what Vico calls air—explains the origin and development of thinking" (32). Badaloni, she says, calls Vico's position an "obvious naturalism."

there is "no sect of gentile philosophy that recognized that the human mind was free from all corporeity. Hence they thought every work of the mind was sense," though he distinguishes this truth from those of revealed religion: "But our religion teaches that the mind is quite incorporeal."[37] Already in *Study Methods* and *Ancient Wisdom,* Vico emphasizes the role of imagination in human thinking. Sense perceptions are stored in memory, and memory "signifie[s] the faculty that fashions images," imagination. *Ingenium,* which the Latins considered "one and the same" with *natura,* is that part of imagination connecting "disparate and diverse things." But unlike the radically originary nature of that activity in the *New Science,* in these earlier writings its role is limited to pedagogic practices and rhetorical and logical argumentation. *Ingenium,* for example, originally meant "acute" from its application in geometry, and because "an acute wit penetrates more quickly and unites diverse things," *ingenium* is an art of discovery, a synthetic means of "finding something new" in which "we do not just discover the truth, but make it."[38]

As Vico presents the metaphysical views in *Ancient Wisdom* as the wisdom of the ancients, he also claims to find in it an epistemological principle equating true and made. Thus, though Zenonians believed in the reality of their metaphysics, Vico understands the geometric point as only a "paradigm, or likeness, of the metaphysical power that sustains and contains extended matter. . . . Hence, we can reason about the essence of body only on this model and not otherwise, because we have no other science, save mathematics, that proceeds on the model of divine science."[39] Though he believes that the theory of metaphysical points is a construct, he defends it passionately against his reviewers, who consider it fanciful and obscure. Even if his

[37] In the *Autobiography* Vico similarly distinguishes between "eternal truths . . . not of our making" and the rest, in which "we feel a liberty by thinking them to make all the things that are dependent on the body . . . and contain them all within ourselves," and identifies "thinking" with bodily skills. For eternal truths we "conceive as principle . . . an eternal idea," as Plato had done. But *verum-factum* denies to humans "eternal truths . . . not of our making" (127). By the *New Science,* Vico realizes that "lofty truths" develop genetically from the language and social practices of the poets, that "[t]he order of ideas must follow the order of [*cose,* things]" (*New Science,* 238). Fisch translates *cose* as "institutions," obscuring the concrete reality of what first men create. See *New Science,* xliii–xliv for his justification of the term. I insert the word "thing" (and where appropriate "word" or practices) in brackets for "institutions," but warn against understanding "thing" substantively. To avoid that connotation for what is created with the word (*davar*) Handelman uses the term "reality," in a nonmetaphysical sense (Susan A. Handelman, *Slayers of Moses: The Emergence of Rabbinic Interpretation in Modern Literary Theory* [Albany: State University of New York Press, 1982], 32).

[38] Vico, *Ancient Wisdom,* 95–97, 104. See *Study Methods,* 24. Palmer translates *ingenium* as mother wit, because it was the customary term in the period for mental activity (See 96 n. 5). I agree with Michael Mooney that "wit," associated with aesthetic and literary usage, has a narrower meaning than *ingenium* comes to have for Vico; that is, as mind, human nature, the human capacity for making (Michael Mooney, *Vico in the Tradition of Rhetoric* [Princeton: Princeton University Press, 1985], 135 n. 84.) Unless quoting directly from Palmer, I use "ingenuity."

[39] Vico, *Ancient Wisdom,* 125.

etymologies do not prove the antiquity of metaphysical points and *conatus,* he says, he believes in the truths he himself makes by gathering those etymologies with the conceptual elements of geometric truths. Vico's readers may wonder why, in the context of his rhetorical concerns, he struggles so hard and apparently so unsuccessfully to provide arguments for constructed metaphysical theories that envelop his treatise "in a darkness . . . almost palpable," why the futility of doing so is not apparent even in this early work.

The answer lies in the agonistic nature of *Ancient Wisdom,* Vico's intent to counter the Cartesian view of beginnings with his own. Vico's reviewers cannot understand him because he and they tell their stories within radically different paradigms. The Cartesian, Vico charges, errs in its conception of extension and motion. The dualism between *res cogitans* and *res extensa,* missing the vitalistic, holistic, metaphysical origin of the physical world, shores up a materialist conception of nature. Like Epicurus, Descartes takes atoms as the basic elements of matter. By adhering to Aristotle and Epicurus rather than Zeno, Descartes, failing to see there is a thing not extended but capable of extension, "assumes that matter has been created and goes on to divide it."[40] By discovering that the ancients attributed the power to maintain extended matter and to sustain motion in an individual substance, Vico "reclaims for Italian philosophers the points of Zeno and purges them from the evil representation given them by Aristotle . . . [and] Descartes." The metaphysical point and its *conatus* is a paradigm of "indivisible substance which is nothing but an indefinite power and an effort of the universe to produce and sustain all . . . particular things," a substance bridging the dualism not only between God and extended matter, but also between *res cogitans* and *res extensa,* accounting not only for extension and motion, but also for the power of life, thought, mind, soul.[41] As Fisch says, with the hypothesis of metaphysical points "we escape dualism by taking the substance of bodies to be incorporeal, the causes of motion to be motionless; and thus, instead of taking the physical world as brute fact, we *explain* its existence."[42]

Regardless, the hypothetical nature of Vico's metaphysics and his intent to avoid both Cartesian dualism and Epicurean materialism escape Vico's reviewers, and they accuse him of materialism. By the *New Science* Vico will have found a way to avoid both by filling a lacuna in Epicurean-Lucretian philosophy—its too prosaic empirical/conventional theory of language. With his insight into the poetic nature of humans, he will account for the way embodied beings, solely with bodily skills, produce a language not reducible to physical processes or tied indexically to the natural world, a language incapable of providing knowledge but wonderfully able to *create* a world that did not exist in nature. With it, he attains the goal he failed to

[40] Ibid., 76.
[41] See Palmer, 13.
[42] Fisch, "Vico and Pragmatism," 410.

reach in *Ancient Wisdom*—a naturalistic anthropology closer to Epicurus than Descartes, which, while withholding knowledge adequate to God's created world, grants a more divine gift, the ability to create human meaning out of nothing.

Just as the agonistic character of *Ancient Wisdom* manifests itself in Vico's challenge to Descartes's anthropological, physical, and metaphysical dualism, so too it is apparent in his challenge to Descartes's epistemology. Descartes does not go beyond extension and motion to the metaphysical cause of the physical world, Vico charges, because he does not go beyond the "certainty" of "clear and distinct" ideas or the *cogito* to the *causes* of certain knowledge. The Venetian critics repeat Descartes's error: they puzzle over and turn from Vico's "obscure" geometric proofs—his paradigm of made truths—and appeal to their own subjective certainty, to the greater clarity and distinctness of their ideas of extension and motion. Vico replies, "[T]o know clearly and distinctly is a fault of the human understanding and not its virtue."[43] Descartes's ideas are "evident" only because they stop at physics and never get to the metaphysical cause of the physical world—never discover there is in metaphysics a thing not extended yet capable of extension, not moved but arousing motion.

But, Vico is quick to acknowledge, man *cannot* know those metaphysical causes: they concern "powers and the infinite," while physics knows only "forms and determined things." The human mind cannot understand the limitless and formless, since "'*Può andarle racccogliendo, ma non già raccoglierle tutte*,' (One can keep on picking things up, but never get them all together)." The mind cannot know what it cannot gather. A more telling criticism is that Descartes justifies his physics with the criteria of clarity and distinctness, and those criteria with subjective certainty. But, Vico stresses, awareness of one's thinking is merely consciousness, not knowledge, since consciousness "is not conscious of the causes of thought," and "[t]o know (*scire*) is to be cognizant (*nosse*) of the causes out of which a thing is born."[44] Descartes does not reach causes because he stops at his subjective mind, paradoxically doubting everything but the certainty of subjective essence foundational to epistemology itself. This is where Vico's search for origins engages Descartes's foundationalism. If Descartes had searched for causes deeply enough, he would have realized that the metaphysical cause of extension and motion could not be known, nor could the cause of his own mind. And, reaching those epistemic limits, he would have realized that, though humans *cannot* know the infinite, they *can* construct a paradigm of it in geometry. He would have gone beyond Aristotle and Epicurus to Zeno, and with a constructed geometric point hypothesized a metaphysical point and from it a hypothetical physics and metaphysics. He would have gone beyond the *cogito*

[43] Vico, *Ancient Wisdom*, 132.
[44] Ibid., 76–77, 54–56. See also 130.

to a causal theory of knowledge, the assertion of an originary power enabling humans to construct a meaningful world not given to them, as Vico had done.

Though in the next section I emphasize the degree to which Vico goes beyond the conception of origins in *Ancient Wisdom* to a more alien story disjunctive of the philosophic and rhetorical traditions on which that work draws, I am mindful of the later Vico's insistence on the genetic nature of all ideas. Despite its strangeness, the *poiesis* of the *New Science* did indeed have its genesis in the questions asked and solutions feigned in the earlier work. Like Descartes, Vico searches for certain knowledge, but unlike him, looks for the *cause* of certainty the *cogito* cannot supply. He finds it not in physics or in metaphysics, but in theology's principle that the true converts with the made, and in the conception of God's making as gathering. Though one may question whether Vico believes in the truths he attributes to ancient wisdom, they provide the core of the new, uncanny humanism of the *New Science*.[45] Like *Ancient Wisdom*, Vico's last work is preoccupied with origins, locates origins in "divine" creativity, and understands human agency as analogous to divine. In both works Vico strives to maximize divine potency, free it from constraints imposed by a Neoplatonic model in which making is mimetic of *a priori* order, and identify it as an ontological act productive of true things in the world.

Vico is successful in *Ancient Wisdom* only in relation to God's making of the physical world. Though he retains a Neoplatonic conception of God, he rejects the notion that divine making is conditioned by logical or conceptual priorities and insists it is wholly convergent with knowing. God remains a subjective deity, however, and Vico tries to minimize the role of thought in the creative process by going beyond even Nominalist or voluntarist theology to the God of an ancient religion. He cannot know how that deity creates, given the limits of *verum-factum,* but his desire to strengthen causal potency is clear from his feigning of that process. To deny or at least to limit any subjective mediation of that potency, he describes it as a gathering of elements rather than as mimetic reproduction. Absent is any distinction between ideal or conceptual reality and material thingness (even Fisch misses Vico's rejection of the Neoplatonic model). Ignorant of Neoplatonic, Christian, or trinitarian theology, the ancients defined God as Maker, making as *ad extra,* and the made as at once material artifact and real world. Indeed, in the creative process Milbank disdains as that of a craftsman, *there is no real other than material artifact.*

---

[45] I resolve this hermeneutic problem for myself by assuming that Vico's intent in going back to the ancients is to put forward a metaphysics closer to his own than the Cartesian. In response to the reviewers' doubts as to whether the doctrine of metaphysical points is Zeno's, Vico says, "[I]f in the end you don't want to accept this statement as Zeno's, I am sorry, but I must give it as my own. But I will offer it to you anyway, alone and not supported by great authorities" (168–69).

Though the God of the ancients did not create the world but merely ordered it, the conception of creation *ad extra* is as close as Vico comes in his early writings to the logically or conceptually unconditioned *creatio ex nihilo* of Genesis, given his retention of a subjective deity and of gathering as an intellectual constructive process.[46] But Vico's very success in enhancing God's potency limits his ability to establish an analogy between it and human creativity. Certainly, just as God makes and knows, so too man makes and knows: on the same model [*ad Dei instar*] on which God founds the true world "man feigns for himself and . . . is in a way the God" of nominal metaphysical points that underlie extension in the physical world. But a fundamental difference exists between divine and human knowing and making. Since God is the maker of all things, his is a "completed truth . . . represent[ing] . . . all the elements of things, both external and internal, since He contains them."[47] His gathering produces the true—that is, real—material things intelligible to their maker, a perfect unity of ontology and epistemology. Man's making, "confined to the outside edges of things" and limited to elements contained only in his mind, produces only conceptual truths; it is merely epistemological.

This is the problem Vico wrestles with—and solves—in the *New Science*. His need to attribute to humans the maximum of *ontological* construction unconditioned by rational or even subjective intention becomes clear to him in the intellectual effort of the next twenty years. It is not Vico's conception of God that changes in that period, but his understanding of the existential condition of first makers, the extremity of their need, the radical nature of the "divine creativity" that can fabricate what they need.[48] He gives up constructing the inadequate epistemological truths of a fictive metaphysics and raises the more radical existential question of the Godlike ontological origin, not of the human sciences, but of the human world itself. His commentators do not take seriously enough the existential nature of the problem that so radically distinguishes the *New Science* from *Ancient Wisdom*. When Vico attributes divinity to his poets, they conjure the Neoplatonic model, if only in assuming that divine making derives from God's subjective nature. As his poetic insight deepens, so too does his naturalistic understanding of humans, and subjectivist formulations of human Godlikeness, which Löwith and Milbank retain, become unacceptable. He strengthens the analogy between man

[46] The inability to appreciate the subjectively unconditioned nature of the biblical act of creation runs through the Vico literature as well. In saying, "There are no externals to the objects of geometry. They are inside the mind. Geometrical thought is an analogue to creation ex nihilo, the mode of divine creation," Verene is thinking not of creation *ex nihilo* in Genesis but of the Neoplatonic version of creation (Donald Phillip Verene, *Vico's Science of Imagination* [Ithaca: Cornell University Press, 1981], 49).

[47] Vico, *Ancient Wisdom*, 73, 46.

[48] I have no reason to think the God in whom Vico believed through faith was other than the Neoplatonic God of medieval theology. But that God was neither object of philosophic knowledge nor model of poetic creativity.

and God by making man, like God, a poet—a creator—but insists man is so in a way "infinitely different from that of God. For God, in his purest intelligence, knows things, and, by knowing them, creates them; but they, in their robust ignorance, did it by virtue of a wholly corporeal imagination . . . for which they were called 'poets,' which is Greek for 'creators.'" [49] What is the nature of a corporeal, imaginative creativity "infinitely different" from that of a Neoplatonic God? Vico goes beyond naturalistic explanations of social life such as innate human sociality, or Epicurus's and Lucretius's notion of evolutionary development, to ask a question they had not asked: if human existence is not innate but made by corporeal beings, what *activity* can produce it? His difficulty in grasping his master key is just this problem of understanding the nature of *poiesis* immanent in human bodies, "mindless," yet sufficiently originary to resolve the most existential of problems: how a human way of being comes to be where none had existed.

It takes Vico twenty years to understand *poiesis,* to realize that what is creative about the first men is an originary metaphoric language capable of bringing into existence what is not given in nature, of so informing the physical labor and social practices of its creators that linguistic fictions become the true things of a real human world. This is a conception of human Godlikeness and creativity Vico has not previously articulated.[50] But whether he intends it or not, his assertion of human ownership of an originary language secularizes an ontological potency that had belonged solely to the God of Genesis. With the appropriation of originary language, Vico goes beyond mere analogy between humans and God to reoccupy, on behalf of humans, the position left vacant by the insufficiency of a theological maximum. And, he does so in a more radical sense than his modernist contemporaries. His poets do not merely reproduce pre-given reality; they make the real *ex nihilo.*

The New Science *as Divine* Poiesis

The Grossi Bestioni. Vico identifies the subject of the *New Science* as "the origins of [things], religious and secular, in the gentile world," and calls

---

[49] Vico, *New Science,* 376. Vico does not refer specifically to *verum-factum* in the *New Science,* but for veiled references to it see 331, 349.

[50] Even in *Ancient Wisdom,* however, Vico anticipates this conception of the omnipotence of divine language. Saying Moses expresses "divine omnipotence in the phrase *dixit et facta sunt* (He spoke and they were made)," he draws out the relation between God's speech and fabrication: "For the Latins *dictum* (said) was the same as *certum* (fixed, certain). . . . Moreover, *fatum* (spoken, i.e., fate) is the same as *dictum;* and *factum* (made) and *verum* (true) are interchangeable with *verbum* (word). And when the Latins themselves wanted to express agreement that something could be quickly done, they said *dictum factum* (no sooner said than done). And they called the final outcome of both deed and word *casum* (fall, chance, case). . . . Thus, the deeds of God are His words, and the outcomes of things are the lot (*casus*) of the words that He speaks" (106–7). Elsewhere Vico says, "[W]ith His creative act He speaks. So that the works of God are His words, which were called 'fates'" (127).

the work a "science" because it "explain[s] the particular ways in which [things] come into being; that is to say, their nature, the explanation of which is the distinguishing mark of science." With such explanations "we reach those first beginnings beyond which it is vain curiosity to demand others earlier; and this is the defining character of [first] principles."[51] Since "first beginnings" account for the "way in which this first human thinking arose in the gentile world," Vico describes the hardship of that discovery, in which "we encountered exasperating difficulties which have cost us the research of a good twenty years. [We had] to descend from these human and refined natures of ours to those quite wild and savage natures, which we cannot at all imagine and can comprehend only with great effort." Elsewhere he is more specific, saying, "We find that the principle of these origins both of languages and of letters lies in the fact that the first gentile peoples, by a demonstrated necessity of nature, were poets who spoke in poetic characters. This discovery, which is the master key of this Science, has cost us the persistent research of almost all our literary life, because with our civilized natures we [moderns] cannot at all imagine and can understand only by great toil the poetic nature of these first men." The first men were "poets," creating "things according to their . . . wholly corporeal imagination. And because it was quite corporeal, they did it with marvelous sublimity; a sublimity such and so great that it excessively perturbed the very persons who by imagining did the creating, for which they were called 'poets,' which is Greek for 'creators.'"[52]

Vico's insistence on the difficulty of understanding his master key is, in effect, a warning to his readers of its strangeness, which he attributes to the vast difference between civilized men and the gentile fathers: "[T]he nature of our civilized minds is so detached from the senses, even in the vulgar, by abstractions . . . and so refined by the art of writing, and . . . spiritualized by the use of numbers, because even the vulgar know how to count and reckon, that it is naturally beyond our power to form the vast image of . . . 'Sympathetic Nature' . . . [or] enter into the vast imagination of those first men, whose minds were not in the least abstract, refined, or spiritualized, because they were entirely immersed in the senses, buffeted by the passions, buried in the body. That is why . . . we can scarcely understand, still less imagine, how those first men thought who founded gentile humanity."[53] The "stupid, insensate, and horrible beasts" he invokes are closer to the first men described by Epicurus, Lucretius, and Nietzsche than to Western accounts of primitives or rustics—the latter all too human.

Vico explains the prehuman condition of the beasts by distinguishing between the chosen people and gentiles, and places his myth of the origins of the latter in the context of biblical and pagan stories of the flood. He specu-

[51] Vico, *New Science*, 346. See also 314: "Doctrines must take their beginning from that of the matters of which they treat."
[52] Vico, *New Science*, 338, 34, 376.
[53] Ibid., 378.

lates that after the flood, the races of Ham, Japheth, and Shem "repudiated the religion of their father, Noah, and fled into the forests." Wandering for one hundred to two hundred years without religion to hold them "by marriage in a society of families," they lost social customs and became bestial and savage, solitaires copulating indiscriminately with "wild, indocile and shy" women and abandoning their children.[54] In this condition they lost language, the ability to reason or think, even their human bodies. Drawing on mythic accounts of primeval giants roaming the earth, Vico speculates that the beasts, who must have lived in their own filth, absorbing nitrous salts from their feces, became giants. Sons of the earth (autochthones) such as the cyclops, entirely immersed in the senses, buffeted by the passions,[55] these prehuman, wholly embodied, "stupid, insensate and horrible beasts" provide Vico with the *tabula rasa* on which he writes his own narrative of originary events, a naturalistic myth in response to a now more radically existential question of origins.

Despite Vico's effort to communicate to readers the momentous nature of his insight into a poetic way of being, despite his naturalistic revision of the biblical story, his master key has been too strange to understand. The conceit that philosophers and philologians share, that humans are inherently subjective beings, prevents them from imagining even protohumans without the consciousness so essential to their own human existence. Even rhetors who insist on the unity of language, mind, and society cannot imagine an embodied primordial existence wholly without subjectivity, and reduce Vico's master key to the inherited wisdom of the rhetorical tradition. A tradition that conceives no greater form of "ingenuity" than the "perception of similarities" cannot comprehend the need for a radically originary creative act.[56] Vico's frequently expressed analogies between first men and children, his characterization of the age of gods as the childhood of the race, similarly mute the strangeness of his master key.[57] Yet Vico's first men differ radically from children; even in the first *New Science* he is quite explicit about this. In distinguishing them from "children . . . born into nations in which speech already exists," he concludes, "[W]e can scarcely understand and are totally unable to imagine either how the first men or the impious races must have thought, *in that state in which they had yet to hear a human word,* of the

---

[54] For Vico's account of early gentile history, see ibid., 13, 62, 169, 192, 301, 373, 380, 369–70, 376, 524.

[55] Ibid., 61, 338, 369–73, 378. At the National Endowments for the Humanities Summer Institute on Vico at Emory University in 1993, Gustavo Costa pointed out that, though Vico sided with the moderns in astronomy, his medicine and chemistry were "archaic," his theory of nitrous salts drawn from alchemy.

[56] Rhetoric's conception of development assumes more is given than does an originary conception—social existence and the presence of language, for example. Development is *padeia* or *Bildung.* Vico, however, asks *why* there is a human world *at all,* and assumes an originary event to answer that existential question.

[57] Vico, *New Science,* 186–87, 206, 211–12, 215–16, 231, 375–76, 412.

coarseness with which they must have given form to their thoughts and the disorderly way in which they must have connected them. . . . *[W]e are unable to draw a single comparison, not only with our own . . . illiterate rustics but with the most barbaric inhabitants of the polar regions and of the African and American deserts,* whose customs . . . are so extravagant by [the standards of] our own civilized natures as to excite horror in us. For such people are at least born among languages . . . and they must have some ability to reckon and to reason."[58]

Vico's myth of origins is similarly reduced to the familiar with the identification of gentiles as postlapsarian men, cut off from truth and morally and spiritually bereft but human nonetheless. This interpretation is central to Mark Lilla's *G. B. Vico: The Making of an Anti-Modern.* Lilla distinguishes Vico from the moderns and rejects epistemological interpretations of *verum-factum,* as I do, but goes on to deny that the principle attributes any causal agency to man, since "to extend the *verum-factum* . . . to man himself opens the possibility not only that man can obtain knowledge, but also that he is, in some sense, like God."[59] For Lilla history in the *New Science* is providential, an interpretation he justifies with the metaphysical and theological assumptions of Vico's earliest writings, which he believes remain constant to his last. Throughout his writings, Lilla argues, Vico's goal remains the same—to combat philosophic skepticism: first, the epistemological skepticism he rejects in his earlier works, then the skeptical assumptions of modern political and moral theories he takes on in writings after *De uno.* Thus Vico turns from modern thought to an inherently conservative view of order and authority based on irrational social institutions such as religion, custom, the *sensus communis,* and embraces so providential a view of history that Lilla is hard put to account for the free will he believes Vico desires for the sake of a corrective *practica.*[60]

[58] Giambattista Vico, "The First New Science," *Vico: Selected Writings,* 42. Emphasis added. By age seven, Vico says for contrast, children born into nations in which speech exists have large vocabularies, so "when any vulgar idea is awakened in them, they skim quickly" through it. Similarly, they learn to count better than "children of less civilized nations." He also refers to the bestial "wanderings" of the "sons of Noah" in the last version of the *New Science,* saying, "[I]f these lost races had persisted in humanity as the people of God did, they would . . . have remained in Asia . . . since it is not a natural custom to abandon one's native land through caprice" (299–301).

The passage from the first *New Science* illustrates another difficulty in grasping the radical nature of first men: Vico's frequent use of subjectivist language or references to mind when describing them. He may not have realized that the more he grasped their poetic nature, the less appropriate that language became. Pompa distinguishes two meanings of "mind"—a broader "cognitive capacity," and a narrower sense in which it is synonymous with "understanding." Pompa considers the latter a "specific mode of cognition," while I believe in the context of Vico's poetic philosophy, that all "mental" activity, including "understanding," is a "sense-making" taking place in the inherently interpretive practices of poetic language.

[59] Mark Lilla, *G. B. Vico: The Making of an Anti-Modern* (Cambridge: Harvard University Press, 1993), 29–30.

[60] Lilla distinguishes his providential interpretation from more orthodox versions, claiming Vico "naturalizes" religion (144–45, 224–34). Lilla's "naturalized" interpretation of Vico's

Though Lilla and I both emphasize the almost apocalyptic nature of history in the *New Science,* we differ in our understanding of the existential human condition that makes degeneration and *ricorsi* inevitable.[61] His is an extreme example of familiar misreadings of Vico's master key, the reduction of its strangeness to traditional conceits. He acknowledges that Vico shares many of the skeptics' "more realistic" assumptions about human nature: that man is fearful, needy, ignorant, "driven by will and desire, [that] politics [is] governed artificially by custom and authority." He claims, however, that Vico opposes the metaphysical and anthropological bases of skepticism—its rejection of providence, its materialism, individualism, denial of innate sociability, natural justice, right[62]—because for Vico "[m]an is not a beast; he is a divinely created being who originally shared his faculties with God, and who is now a carrier of His *conatus*. Only skeptics like Hobbes and Spinoza," from whom Vico "clearly" wants to distinguish himself, "find *conatus* in our animalistic bodies, lowering us to the level of beasts." Though Vico owes much to Epicurus, for Vico "there is nothing necessary or natural about man's bestialization." Modern Epicureans "confused man's post-diluvian decline with his essential nature. . . . [S]ince the Flood . . . [man] has lived entirely through his body," but this is not his *natural* condition. What redeems man is *conatus,* which Lilla interprets, on analogy with the incarnation, as substantive. As the incarnation was a "singular act of divine accommodation to human sin," so with *conatus* God offers "a more continuous accommodation to our remaining weaknesses, one which brings man back to common sense, to religion, family, custom, and authority."[63]

Denying the bestial nature of first men, Lilla identifies them as fallen, the poverty of their nature the epistemological, moral, spiritual effects of disobedience to God. Thus he denies anything radically strange or unfamiliar about them, denies they are creators who possess an originary language, denies, in effect, the significance Vico attributes to his twenty-year struggle to grasp their nature and the master key to which it led, since he believes he finds them already described in the Orations.[64] The vast difference between

---

providence is, however, resolutely spiritual and transcendent, and, of the *storia ideale eterna,* resolutely idealist. In the context of his idealism, Lilla reduces philology to philosophy, claiming philology merely confirms the truth of God's ideal pattern, and devalues language as a "linguistic corollary" to ideal history, saying merely that for Vico "developments [of mind] . . . left traces in . . . languages (135–37)."

[61] Lilla, *G. B. Vico,* 225.

[62] Ibid., 59, 61–66. Lilla means by modern skeptics "Epicureans" such as Hobbes and Machiavelli, "Stoics" such as Spinoza, "Pyrrhonists" such as Bayle. For an interpretation arguing Vico's relation to the atheism and materialism of skeptics, see Frederick Vaughan, *The Political Philosophy of Giambattista Vico: An Introduction to La Scienza Nuova* (The Hague: Martinus Nijhoff, 1972).

[63] Lilla, *G. B. Vico,* 100, 169. See also 36–44, 75–76, 155–57, 168, 207.

[64] Ibid., 15–23. Lilla says in the first Oration Vico described the effects of the fall, and in the second, the *stultus,* the fool, as exemplar of man's fallen state—ignorant of and disobedient to eternal law, at war with himself, driven by passion. Without Lilla's gloss on Vico's text, a reader turning from the originality of the *New Science* to the second Oration, delivered in support of

those Vico called *stulti* in that early work—beings who, though childlike, ignorant, foolish, spiritually lost, are still human, possessing language and social customs—and his *bestioni* disappears, and with it, the existential nature of Vico's concern with origins. Lilla is right that Vico, unlike the skeptics, believes that a human world is not possible without piety and religion, a sense of shame, a *sensus communis,* without authority or principles of justice and right. But those social elements of the human world are not present in the *grossi bestioni:* if they exist at all they must be made. For Lilla the claim that "the world has been made by men sounds like Hobbes, Machiavelli, Hegel and Marx," because the only conception he has of human agency derives from humanism and liberalism, which assume a degree of reason and freedom Vico denies to humans. Lilla thus misses the nontraditional, nonhumanist conception of human *poiesis* in the *New Science.* So far is Vico from any humanist conception of "freedom" that by the last *New Science* he does not even hold out the possibility of the corrective *practica* Lilla tries to salvage; the abyssal *ricorsi* Vico warns of is inevitable, the mark of the tragic nature of man, the finitude of human artifacts.

I can think of nothing in the humanist philosophic tradition comparable to Vico's account of his twenty-year struggle to free himself from familiar conceits, to enter into "the vast imagination" of embodied beings and to grasp the radical differences between them and "even the most vulgar" among us. (It is of course a theme familiar to literature.) This may account for Lilla's turn to such traditional examples as the fallen, the *stulti,* to understand Vico's *grossi bestioni.* If he had read more alchemically, he might have found in non-humanist writings such as Nietzsche's and Heidegger's comparable struggles that avoid materialism, yet think human existence out from under the "fleeting cloud shadow of subjectivity." Heidegger goes beyond familiar definitions of man to what he calls *"to deinotaton,* the strangest of the strange." The strange is "the basic trait of the human essence," a condition "surpass[ing] the limit of the familiar" and "disclosed only to poetic insight," "cast[ing] us out of . . . the customary, familiar, secure . . . [and] prevent[ing] us from making ourselves at home." As *to deinotaton,* we are "homeless," and "make ourselves being at home" only within historical worlds. Like Vico, Heidegger asks the most existential of questions—Why is there a human world rather than none?—and, like him, claims that in language and social practices occasioned by language "artworks" show up, setting into place historical worlds.[65] It is the affinities between these two accounts of the historical "working" of artworks that I explore.

---

a humanist conception of education, would consider its depiction of moral and spiritual warfare a fairly typical example of Christian humanism, written, perhaps, by Erasmus.

[65] Heidegger, *Introduction to Metaphysics,* 149–51. Heidegger's existential question is "Why are there essents rather than nothing?" which I paraphrase.

Unlike Vico, Epicurus, Lucretius, and Nietzsche, however, Heidegger does not speculate about a time *before* a historical world, to imagine the way animals without history become human. And, while for Epicurus and Lucretius that process is a natural, organic evolution, only Nietzsche, like Vico, identifies his embodied beasts as artists who construct their human existence, and do so with a creativity irreducible to physical processes. Akin to Vico's insight "into the vast imagination" of embodied beings Nietzsche imagines the "dreadful heaviness" that falls on sea animals "compelled to become land animals or perish." "Incredibly uncouth, coarse, external, narrow, straightforward, and altogether *unsymbolical* in meaning to a degree that we can scarcely conceive," they are "most involuntary, unconscious artists—wherever they appear, something new soon arises, a ruling structure that *lives*."[66]

For Nietzsche, as for Vico, the creative activity of "unconscious artists," while grounded in bodily skills, is a function of linguistic and social practices, though Vico's account of the relation between bodily skills and creativity is even more primordial than Nietzsche's. Nietzsche does not explain the ability of his "beasts of prey" to use language or to establish social relationships. Rather, he identifies existence itself with a metaphysical will to power ceaselessly striving to enhance life by creating new forms, while Vico struggles to describe a primordial creativity bringing into existence not only language and social practices, but also a power or force accounting for the genetic development of human life. Nietzsche calls the linguistic, social process that ultimately constructs human existence a "learning to remember," "breeding" an "animal with the *right to make promises*," who can "ordain the future in advance . . . think causally . . . decide . . . what is the goal and what the means. . . . become *calculable, regular, necessary*." The most foundational social practice, debt [*Schulden*], is a "contractual relation between creditor and debtor" that grants the creditor the right to inflict pain on the debtor as a sign of his promise, and through the mnemotechnics of pain there emerges "the budding sense of exchange, contract, guilt, right, obligation . . . together with the custom of comparing, measuring, and calculating power against power. . . . Setting prices, determining values, contriving equivalencies, exchanging—these preoccupied the earliest thinking of man to so great an extent that in a certain sense they constitute thinking *as such*." As these practices repress instinctual life, consciousness—man's "weakest and most fallible organ"—develops. "Thus it was that man first developed what was later called his 'soul'. The entire inner world, originally as thin as if it were stretched between two membranes, expanded and extended itself, acquired depth, breadth, and height, in the same measure as outward discharge was inhibited."[67] Even the contemplative life of priests

---

[66] Friedrich Nietzsche, *On the Genealogy of Morals,* trans. Walter Kaufmann and R. J. Hollingdale (New York: Vintage Books, 1989), II.16.84; I.6.31–32.

[67] Ibid., I.6.31–32; I.2–3.25–27; II.1.57–58; II.2.59; II.16–18.84–87.

and philosophers is nothing other than the ascetic practices of this constructed subjectivity.

For Nietzsche, the phenomenon of language is similarly derived from "unconscious" bodily processes fueled by the will to power. "What is a word?" he asks. "The portrayal of nerve stimuli in sounds." The relation of sound to external cause is nothing other than a series of metaphoric displacements—"nerve stimulus into an image," image "reshaped into a sound." Similarly every general concept is but another metaphoric "overleaping of spheres," the fit of a word to multiple dissimilar experiences, and truth itself nothing other than "a mobile army of metaphors, metonyms, anthropomorphisms . . . without sensory impact," "collective lies" that man fabricates "out of his own self." The world can be understood only "as a human-like thing," the illusions of an *"artistically creative* subject"[68] constituting the beliefs and values of subjective existence.

If Nietzsche takes for granted the ability of prehuman animals governed by a will to power to use language and to establish debtor-creditor relations—the means of constructing subjective existence—Vico thinks more primordially the poverty of his first men. Given their "minimum of ontological predisposition," Vico must assert a "maximum of constructive potentiality" on their behalf. Though Lilla denies that for Vico humans are "in some sense, like God," Vico explicitly attributes "divine creativity" to them, and in doing so avoids not only materialism but also subjectivism. In describing Vico's response to mechanistic-egoistic political theorists such as Hobbes, Malebranche, and Spinoza, Amos Funkenstein is more nuanced than Lilla, who believes that Vico attributes innate sociality to humans. Though Vico, like the materialists, rejects natural law theories and a natural social instinct and considers society artifactual, Funkenstein argues that he does not consider social institutions mere conventions. For Vico, "'Natural law' is . . . founded neither on social instincts nor on a computation of enlightened interests. It is rather the very immanent, regular, 'ideal' process through which civilization emerges time and again as man's acquired collective 'second nature.'" Though Vico radicalizes the antithesis between nature and convention, making man's very humanity an artifact, he has more significantly "reinterpreted nature to stand for the very *process* through which man acquires a *second,* social nature," a process accomplished through the "mediatory" function of imagination Lilla discounts. History is not the product of mechanistic-deterministic forces but of man's "spontaneous creativity."[69]

[68] Friedrich Nietzsche, "On Truth and Lying in an Extra-Moral Sense," *Friedrich Nietzsche on Rhetoric and Language,* ed. and trans. by Sander L. Gilman, Carole Blair, and David J. Parent (New York: Oxford University Press, 1989), 246–57, 246–52.

[69] Amos Funkenstein, "Natural Science and Social Theory: Hobbes, Spinoza, and Vico," *Giambattista Vico's Science of Humanity,* ed. Giorgio Tagliacozzo and Donald Phillip Verene (Baltimore: Johns Hopkins University Press, 1976), 187–212, 203; *Theology and the Scientific Imagination from the Middle Ages to the Seventeenth Century* (Princeton: Princeton University Press, 1986), 179, 280–83.

Funkenstein's interpretation of imagination stands out because, being functional rather than substantive, it more successfully avoids the dangers Lilla fears—reductive materialism, and idealist-humanist anthropologies reifying the subject of historical making. Certainly in the *New Science*, as in the *Autobiography* and *Ancient Wisdom*, sensation, memory, imagination remain skills of the body: "In that [original] human indigence, the peoples, who were almost all body and almost no reflection, must have been all vivid sensation in perceiving particulars, strong imagination in apprehending and enlarging them, sharp wit in referring them to their imaginative genera, and robust memory in retaining them. It is true that these faculties appertain to the mind, but they have their roots in the body and draw their strength from it."[70] But, though it retains corporeal "roots," the function of imagination has been reconceived. In *Ancient Wisdom* Vico called it "the eye of *ingegno*," analogous to judgment, "the eye of intellect" grounding an art of discovery for humanist pedagogy.[71] In the *New Science* Vico attributes "inventive" seeing not to a subjective but to a corporeal eye. No longer a conceptual process of *discovery, ingenium* is *originary,* creating two things not given in nature—images, constituting the metaphysics of the poets, their "forms of being," and the significations of those forms, fixing their identity and turning them into "true things" of the human world. These images and significations constitute poetic wisdom, which "must have begun with a metaphysics not rational and abstract . . . but felt and imagined as that of these first men must have been, who, without power of ratiocination, were all robust sense and vigorous imagination. This metaphysics was their poetry, a faculty born with them (*for they were furnished by nature with these senses and imaginations*)."[72]

"Their poetry was at first divine," Vico continues, because "they imagined the causes of the things they felt and wondered at to be gods." Indeed, since it is axiomatic that "[w]herever a people has grown savage in arms so that human laws have no longer any place among it, the only powerful means of reducing it is religion," the first image created must be some "confused idea of divinity" capable of reducing their savagery. *Ingenium* makes that "confused idea" out of the kaleidoscope of fleeting, disparate sensations bombarding the *giganti* in the forests, though not before its eye is opened by one particularly traumatic sensation, auditory rather than visual, the sound of thunder.[73] Several hundred years after the flood, "the sky fearfully rolled

---

[70] Vico, *New Science,* 819. Indeed, these faculties "appertain to mind" by creating it. See also 699.

[71] Vico, *Ancient Wisdom,* 104. The translation has "mother wit," but I retain the *ingegno* of the Italian version (*Opere,* 303). Elsewhere I distinguish Vico from the traditional privileging of intellectual vision, emphasizing the significance of hearing in the *New Science*. See Luft, "Embodying the Eye of Humanism: Giambattista Vico and the Eye of *Ingenium*."

[72] Vico, *New Science,* 699, 375; see also 779. Emphasis added.

[73] I interpret the Jove event as a "metaphoric seeing," which includes the sound of thunder, and stress hearing over visual "seeing." Similarly, John Schaeffer says the Jove "metaphor is both

with thunder and flashed with lightning. . . . Thereupon a few giants . . . were frightened and astonished by the great effect whose cause they did not know."[74] Raising their bodily eyes they saw for the first time with the eye of *ingenium*, a "seeing" more ontologically eventful than can be explained by such conceits of subjective invention as the perception of similarities.[75] Not even Nietzsche's account of the metaphoric nature of perception explains it. For Vico, ontologically eventful seeing is a violent conjoining of sensations that do not belong together, a violent projection of those sensations, felt in animate bodies, on an inanimate world, a violent fixing of dissimilar sensations into a metaphoric unity by such other "dissimilarities" as mute and articulate languages.[76]

And, indeed, Vico vividly re-creates that violent, eventful conjoining of dissimilar visual, auditory, felt sensations and signifying gestures. The thunder that occasioned fear in the giants, incarnate in the shaking of their great bodies and the "shouting and grumbling" that "expressed their very violent passions," led them to project their bodily sensations onto a stormy sky, enabling them to see what did not exist in nature or reason. They saw—that is *imaged*—the sky as the animate body of a god: "[B]ecause . . . the nature of the human mind leads it to attribute its own nature to the effect," the *giganti* "pictured the sky to themselves as a great animated body . . . who meant to tell them something by the hiss of his bolts and the clap of his thunder." "In this fashion the first theological poets created the first divine fable, the greatest they ever created: that of Jove, king and father of men and gods, in the act of hurling the lightning bolt; an image so popular, disturbing, and instructive that its creators themselves believed in it, and feared, revered, and worshipped it in frightful religions." With that act, one of *abyssal poverty* rather than *human awareness,* however childlike, foolish, or fallen, "man . . . makes himself the rule of the universe . . . [and] made of himself an entire

---

auditory and visual. . . . But orality is primary in that it is sound that identifies the sky as alive, and it is sound that provides the opportunity for interpretation. The giants . . . respond to the immediacy of sound with bodily fear, which in turn provokes the metaphoric leap," and "In Vico's account, language begins, not with men speaking, but . . . listening" (John D. Schaeffer, *Sensus Communis: Vico, Rhetoric, and the Limits of Relativism* [Durham: Duke University Press, 1990], 91, 87). Alternately, Marcel Danesi argues that for Vico the "first form of consciousness . . . was 'visual'" (Marcel Danesi, *Vico, Metaphor, and the Origin of Language* [Bloomington: Indiana University Press, 1993], 84–89). Gianfranco Cantelli similarly emphasizes visual over acoustic stimuli.

[74] Vico, *New Science,* 377.

[75] "Children excel in imitation," Vico says, and gestures, facial expressions, shaking, pointing, running, elicited by thunder and the sight of the sky, were imitations of its turbulence (Ibid., 215). Despite this "imitative" behavior, the bodily sensations of the beasts were not at all "like" the sky, and the act of bringing them together was originary, not mimetic.

[76] "When men are ignorant of the natural causes producing things, and cannot even explain them by analogy with similar things, they attribute their own nature to them," Vico says, and takes as axiomatic that "Because of the indefinite nature of the human mind, wherever it is lost in ignorance man makes himself the measure of all things" (Ibid., 180, 120; see also 181, 220, 236).

world. So that, as rational metaphysics teaches that man becomes all things by understanding them . . . this imaginative metaphysics shows that man becomes all things by *not* understanding them . . . and perhaps the latter proposition is truer than the former, for when man understands he extends his mind and takes in the things, but when he does not understand he makes the things out of himself and becomes them by transforming himself into them."[77]

The act Vico describes is not only devoid of epistemic significance, but is also unconditioned by the subjectivity that grounds the possibility of knowledge *at all*. For Vico, as for Nietzsche and Heidegger, beings—prehuman *or* human—are *in-the-world,* and *being-in-the-world* is a *hermeneutic activity constitutive of historical existence.* Nietzsche and Vico differ from Heidegger in making humans the source of that ontological hermeneutic, but only Vico, without recourse to Nietzsche's metaphysical will to power, asks how beasts, *solely with bodily skills,* can perform the interpretive activity that makes them human. The originary act he narrates accounts not only for the language and foundational social customs of first men, but also for the presence of *conatus,* the functional equivalent of Nietzsche's metaphysical will to power, and of fear, which Nietzsche assumes "natural" to his first men. My argument here is twofold. First, that for Vico, *conatus,* as a phenomenon of the *human* rather than *material* world,[78] *is not presupposed by but is brought into existence in the primordial act,* and second, *as such,* is neither a material nor a spiritual substance, but a function wholly of choices the beasts *must* make—given the limits imposed by brute necessity on their choices—to satisfy the needs and utilities of *human* life, and of the practices in-the-world that realize their choices.[79] Thus, in identifying *conatus* as the "movement of the will" with which *giganti* curb "the impulse of the bodily motion of lust," Vico identifies the "free choice" to curb lust as *nothing other than* such practices as "forcibly seizing their women . . . dragging them into their caves . . . keeping them there as perpetual lifelong companions"; or, in choosing to check "their bestial habit of wandering wild," as acquiring "the contrary custom of remaining . . . settled in their fields."[80]

---

[77] Ibid., 377, 379, 405.

[78] Vico distinguishes "moral" *conatus* from mechanistic theories: "But to impute conatus to bodies is as much as to impute to them freedom to regulate their motions, whereas all bodies are by nature necessary agents. And what the theorists of mechanics call powers, forces, conatus, are insensible motions of bodies" [340].

[79] A functional interpretation of *conatus* is akin to Funkenstein's functional interpretation of imagination. It is also compatible with Joseph Mali's view that, against prevailing interpretations of *conatus,* which were "psycho-physical," mechanistic, and deterministic, for Vico "seemingly natural conative emotions are, in fact, historical" and "culturally conditioned." *Conatus* is "the ability of human beings to invent and set up conventional norms over against their natural impulses." (Joseph Mali, *The Rehabilitation of Myth* [Cambridge: Cambridge University Press, 1992], 120–22.)

[80] Ibid., 340, 1098, 504. *Conatus* does not, of course, make men "free" in the humanist sense of enabling rationally determined choices, including the choice to control the appetites. The

This functional view rejects *substantive* interpretations of *conatus*—materialist ones reducing it to physical processes, for example, or those, like Lilla's, in which it is a spiritual link between transcendent providence and humans. True, Vico seems to distinguish the action of will and its "free" choices from the body in ways that suggest anthropological dualism. *Conatus,* he says, holds "in check the motions impressed on the mind by the body. . . . This control over the motion of their bodies is certainly an effect of the freedom of human choice, and thus of free will, which is the home and seat of all the virtues." Thus it "does not come from the body, whence comes concupiscence," but, rather, "from the mind," and because it comes "from the mind" it is "properly human."[81] Yet, I argue, for Vico mind *itself* is an artifact constructed by social and linguistic practices. Mental or spiritual activity is no more substantively distinct from the body than is *conatus* or "free will." This functional *conatus* is consistent with the metaphysical version in *Ancient Wisdom,* since, except for the qualification that God is the ultimate cause of the world, both account for motion, life, thought, mind, soul, in immanent, monistic, naturalistic terms. In *Ancient Wisdom,* fictive metaphysical points and *conatus* enabled Vico to maximize causal agency in the world without resorting to Descartes's dualistic metaphysics or Epicurus's reductive materialism.[82] In the *New Science,* he is no longer concerned to account for motion in the world, but for human life, and does so with a process both "divine," because creative, and a function of human agency. No longer a fictive metaphysical property of matter, much less Nietzsche's overtly metaphysical will to power logically preceding human existence, *conatus* is inseparable from *practices* that the beasts *must* "freely" perform to satisfy human needs and utilities in the face of natural necessity.

Conatus is not only functional but also artifactual, since brought into existence in the same eventful act and moment as Jove. Vico says as much: though he says fear "arouses" *conatus,*[83] he claims it is the image of Jove

---

choices of *grossi bestioni* are always limited by natural necessity, and, such is their abyssal bestiality, their options in satisfying "human needs and utilities" are severely conscriped. Man is not free, for example, to establish social existence on any but religious grounds; nothing short of terror caused by the frightful image they create can force them to "choose" to control lust. (See Vico's attack on Bayle, 334, 1110.) What Vico means by freedom is, ultimately, the ability of bodily skills—perception, memory, imagination—to respond to natural necessity and to satisfy human "needs and utilities" by creating a world not given in nature, and, thus, free "from" nature. These choices constitute the *sensus communis,* itself another determinant of "free" choices.

[81] Vico, *New Science.*

[82] Certainly *conatus* derived from God insofar as God was creator of the world, and was, therefore, a mediating link between divine potency and extended, motile matter, but it was so wholly as an *immanent source* not only of motion, but also of life, thought, mind, and soul. Thus it functioned for Vico as immanent link between *res cogitans* and *res extensa.*

[83] Vico, *New Science,* 689. Since the ambiguity of the word "arouse" allows for both materialist and transcendent interpretations, it can certainly tolerate a constructivist interpretation. I take Milbank's statement "Human beings . . . are a true *source* of *conatus* like God, and unlike other creatures, because they inaugurate language" as making a similar point.

that creates fear—that is, a *human,* not animal, fear, the fear of divinity. Certainly fear and *conatus* are "natural" in that both are immanent in or produced by the body; neither, however, is *given* in nature. Vico stresses the artifactual nature of the process set in motion by the creation of human fear. The means that providence "ordain[s]" to "found the nations" is piety, he says, without which no human society can exist, since "poetic morality began with piety." Piety, in turn, "sprang from religion, which properly is fear of divinity." In children "piety is instilled . . . by the fear of some divinity," while in their bestial state *giganti* are "quite without that fear of gods, fathers and teachers which chills and benumbs even the most exuberant in childhood."[84] Vico concludes, "[I]t was fear which created gods in the world; not fear awakened in men by other men, but *fear awakened in men by themselves.*"[85] The *grossi bestioni* are so far from being children or *stulti* that they acquire human fear only in the imaginative process of "acquir[ing] a second, social nature." The extreme poverty of Vico's first men contrasts even with Nietzsche's, for whom it is not the gods they create that create fear, but a fear *natural to them* that creates gods. The notion of god grows, Nietzsche says, when primitives transfer to tribal ancestors the sense of obligation instilled by the creditor/debtor relation. "In the end the ancestor must necessarily be transfigured into a god. Perhaps this is even the origin of gods, an origin . . . out of fear!"[86] Vico's insight into the inadequacy of the first men made such a proto-euhemerist position impossible.

For Vico, the act of making human mindfulness begins in the corporeal skills of making a thing—that is, in the making of an image signified and fixed with the language of naming that originates with it, and the practices inseparable from image and name. That act is not only creative, a *poiesis,* but also ontologically significant, modifying the behavior of creators who, believing and worshiping their *factum,* bring into existence a human world not given in nature. Only with such a "divine" creative language the "stones of Deucalion and Pyrrha . . . the rocks of Amphion . . . the men who sprang from the furrows of Cadmus or the hard oak of Vergil . . . the frogs of Epicurus . . . the cicadas of Hobbes . . . the simpletons of Grotius . . . the giants called 'Big Feet' . . . the cyclopes of Homer . . . began to think humanly."[87] The ontological nature of Vico's poetic conception of language is missed, however, when read through familiar rhetorical and philosophical conceits about the nature of language. So powerful are these familiar conceits—particularly of a subjective *homoiousis* between knowers in the third age and

---

[84] Ibid., 369, 503, 1097–98. Vico's use of "piety" has the "ancient sense" Heidegger also invokes in calling piety "obedient, or submissive . . . to what thinking has to think about," that is, to what shows up "in the clearing" (Martin Heidegger, *On the Way to Language,* trans. Peter D. Hertz [San Francisco: Harper, 1982], 72).

[85] Ibid., 382. Emphasis added. See also 14, 178, 191, 1112.

[86] Nietzsche, *Genealogy,* II.19.88–89.

[87] Vico, *New Science,* 338.

poetic language—that they undermine interpretations that expressly attempt to capture the radical nature of Vico's conception of language, even (though none uses this language) the ontological potency of *poiesis*. In the following section I discuss three commentaries that go far in doing so. Ultimately, however, those of Donald Phillip Verene and Gianfranco Cantelli undermine their radical insights. Though both have a strong sense of the corporeality of first men, neither overcomes misconceptions derived from the conceit of subjectivity—Verene, because he desires to ground historical knowledge on the imaginative nature of the poets, an effort that assumes a subjective *homoiousis* between meditators and first men, Cantelli, because his very effort to avoid presuming subjectivity prevents him from appreciating the metaphoric character of originary poetic making. The third interpretation, by Donatella Di Cesare, though only suggestive of a fully developed conception of poetic language, supports my interpretation of the affinity between Vico's *poiesis* and the Hebraic.

The Divine Originary Power of Human Language. For his part, Verene seems to attribute to Vico an ontological question, saying in the *New Science* Vico asks not "how the mind functions in relation to the object to produce knowledge . . . [but] how the mind comes to have something before it at all." Vico answers by attributing to "mind" a "power to rise beyond immediacy." "Immediacy is the state of pure flux" in which particular sensations cancel out prior ones, "each moment is new . . . there is no place, no *topos* for thought." "Nothingness" comes to an end only when "mind" makes that place "through its power to produce an identity." "A [single] sensation is apprehended as the being of other sensations," becoming a "permanent reference point of the flux of sensations which now have their being in it" and through which meaning can be grasped. *Fantasia* makes that fixed point by forming "an image or metaphor" with mute and articulate signs. The metaphor "brings forth the *is* as the given of human mentality. . . . [T]he primary act of intelligibility takes place."[88] Verene's sense of the originary nature of metaphor is evident in his insistence that the "poetic mind" does not form *universali fantastici* from analogy or the perception of similarities, but "through . . . immediate identities between elements." No two sensations are alike in the flux, no particular sensation like a universal. Rather, in the poetic metaphor "the *is* itself is made. . . . [A] universality is achieved through the particular. An identity is made." Memory is the power to return to the moment fixed by imaginative universals: "Once they can repeatedly grasp thunder and fear as Jove, the first men have made sensation into a kind

[88] Verene, *Science of Imagination,* 80–83. Yet even Verene, who has done so much to focus attention on imaginative universals, does not draw out the radically nontraditional implications of the notion.

of thought. . . . The process of 'finding again' . . . is accomplished through the imaginative universal's power of identity."[89]

Verene has an acute sense of the bodily nature of the beasts and the unity of bodily sensation, mute and articulate language, thought and meaning. Describing the ontological significance of the creation of Jove, the first *is* of the human world, he says, "Vico asks us to imagine a beginning point of human experience in which all was body and bodily motion, in which meaning was an action between bodies, and in which human thought was nothing more than the bodily act of sensation. . . . Sensation is the act . . . through which the *mind initiates for itself* what is to be known or thought. . . . There is true speech only at the level of sense." Bodily gestures constitute meaning: "The meaning of Jove's signs is initially nothing more than the trembling of the bodies of the *giganti* and the motion of their flight in fear into their caves. . . . Here there is also no grasp of mind or self as separate from body. . . . To mean something is to do it. If fear is meant it takes the form of actual flight." Memory is nothing more than the repetition of bodily gestures: "Jove as the fear felt by the first men is imitated by them; they shake their bodies like the sky-body of Jove himself. . . . This primordial power [of "re-presentation"] . . . is slowly transformed into the world of human symbols, into the medium of language and cultural institutions in which all sensation is modified and given shape."[90]

Verene's effort to grasp the unity of language, body, thought is undermined, however, by his retention of the tradition's conceit that mind, consciousness, or thought is the site of meaning and knowledge. Ultimately, he either presumes as prior or reifies as subsequent to the originary event some form of subjectivity, a birthright that, in the third age, insures epistemic knowledge of origins. The "symbolic" nature of the first language, for example, "allows [Vico] to show that the first men . . . did not think the same as modern men, but . . . did in fact *think*."[91] Similarly, though the *universale fantastico* is a sensory and linguistic *topos,* with it "something *is for the mind*. . . . [It] is an understanding of how the *is* itself comes into consciousness." Though he says, "For Vico the body is a metaphor of the mind," in the context of Vico's master key and Verene's own sometimes strong awareness of the embodied nature of thought, "mind" can only be a metaphor for the linguistic and social making accomplished by bodies.[92]

---

[89] Ibid., 76, 82–83, 104.

[90] Ibid., 85–87, 104–5. Emphasis added. See also 104–5.

[91] Ibid., 74. Verene makes reference to a "type of linguistic symbolism" that anticipates "contemporary semiotic science." However, see Ernesto Grassi's pointed warning against invoking the idealist logic of symbolic forms, as Cassirer does. For Grassi, "the logic of imagination must be put into the closest possible connection with work as the humanization of nature" (Ernesto Grassi, "The Priority of Common Sense and Imagination: Vico's Philosophical Relevance Today," *Social Research* 43, no. 3 [autumn 1976]: 553–80, 570).

[92] Ibid., 173–74. Emphasis added. See also 93.

Subjectivism even undermines Verene's sense of the constitutive power of language. Though he identifies that power with the rhetorical invention of topics, inventiveness remains a power of mind (however much buried in the body)—"the *universale fantastico* as a conception of both topic and metaphor is a conception of *how the mind brings forth its own being.*" Verene cannot let speech or topics carry the weight of human meaning: "[T]here is no contrast between what is sensed . . . thought . . . signified," he claims, without questioning what the term "thought" adds to "sensing" and "signifying." Revelatory of the hold subjectivism has on him is his deviation from the rhetorical insights of two scholars he cites as important to his interpretation, Ernesto Grassi, who enabled him to understand the significance of rhetoric for Vico, and Andrea Battistini, whose work on imaginative universals is important for his theory of metaphor.[93] Verene says he goes beyond them in claiming that, for Vico, the metaphoric nature of language became "a principle of mythic mentality, one which has implications for the philosophic conception of metaphor as the basis of thought." He understands Vico's theory of "metaphor in a broader sense than it has in the four-fold scheme of the tropes, seeing it as the first principle of mind," "the first of the operations of mind in the act of knowing." He does not realize that his "broader" interpretation gives metaphor the subjective core that constitutes a *homoiousis* between it and conceptual thinking. What had been Grassi's and Battistini's emphasis on the rhetorical notion that metaphoric language is sense-making *in its own right* becomes a "conception of the imaginative universal *as the basis of epistemological theory,*" "*the principle of knowledge itself.*"[94] Despite his insistence on its ontological significance, Verene reduces Vico's question, "how the mind comes to have something before it at all," to "a completely new epistemological question."[95]

That "new epistemology" begins with divination, the poetic art with which first men "read" the *topoi* they project onto the natural world. "Divination, the ability to read real words," develops from the "initial bodily gesture," and is matched in the third age by "recollective *fantasia,*" Verene's "general term for the Vichian manner of thinking," the very "form of Vico's science." As the basis of philosophic thought, recollection is the form of memory grounding "reflective thought on the image rather than . . . concept." Because it "contains in itself elements that reflect *in a one-to-one fashion* the elements in the memory structure of original or mythic *fantasia* . . . recollective *fantasia* [is] the form of thought whereby Vico reaches a knowledge of the first humans." Though this strong epistemic claim seems counter to Vico's own statement that "we cannot at all imagine and can comprehend

[93] Ibid., 171, 174. Emphasis added. See also 87, 11, 78–79.
[94] Ibid., 77–80. Emphasis added. See Verene's distinction between his, Battistini's, and White's accounts of Vico's rhetorical theory of tropes (160).
[95] Ibid., 80–81. Emphasis added. Poetic wisdom contains "a theory of knowledge not to be found elsewhere in Western philosophy" (69).

only with great effort" poetic nature, Verene claims Vico is referring only to the "*immaginare*" and "*intendere*" of rational men who approach an object from the outside. In its poetic sense "*[f]antasia* is the power to know from the inside, to grasp the object in its inner nature." This knowing "from inside" accounts for the convertibility of *verum* and *factum*. Recovery of the true through recollective *fantasia* is not mere formulation of conceptual truths, but a return to the origin of human thought "in such a way as to remake the human world as something true for us."[96] Vico's new science is, thus, performative, its "proof . . . found through the reader making it for himself . . . a true or necessary narration wherein the reader *correctly orders events*. . . . Since the human is the maker of the world . . . he can be the certain knower of this world. His account . . . will be a *vera narratio,* or true speech . . . like the natural speech through which the mind originally gives form to the world."[97] The *New Science* is that recollected *vera narratio;* it is "metaphysical truth . . . *generated out of the mind* itself . . . as images that actually contain the providential structure of reality." This remaking of the truths of the poetic image is the convergence of *verum* and *factum* constituting knowledge. "If Vico is not claiming this . . . significant penetration into the thought of the first men, then he is claiming very little when he speaks of the twenty years required to discover the principle of . . . *universale fantastico.*"[98]

Verene distinguishes his conception of recollective epistemology grounded on *fantasia* from Pompa's position that for Vico knowledge is self-conscious reflection.[99] He is so concerned to distinguish his imagistic conception of Vico's epistemology from Pompa's conceptual one that he does not realize how much more they have in common. For both, the possibility of any form of epistemology is based on a subjective *homoiousis* between philosopher-historians and theological poets; for both, the bridge between the *vera narratio* of philosopher-historian and poet is *thought. Fantasia* is the power to know "from the inside," which Verene identifies with what Vico calls "meditation." He who "meditates" his science, Vico says, narrates to himself this "ideal eternal history" so far as he himself makes it for himself. For Verene, to meditate "is to think continually and closely," thus "recall[ing] the true narration of the myth." Though he adds meditation "has the aim of a . . . true narration that remakes the world in language," for him that narrative is not a *linguistic* construction but the recovery of the "divine structure of the world," the ideal eternal history.[100] Though Verene believes that recollective

[96] Ibid., 85–87, 99–101. Emphasis added. Verene refers to Vico's paragraphs 338, 378, 700.
[97] Ibid., 156. Emphasis added. Verene refers to Vico's paragraphs 349 and 401.
[98] Ibid., 124–25, 101. Emphasis added. The "master image" of recollective imagination is the *storia ideale eterna,* an image of the ideal truth of the providential structure of history.
[99] Acknowledging that what Pompa means by reflection and he by recollection is "quite close," Verene insists they differ significantly because Pompa does not ground reflection in the origin of human mentality, "the activity of *fantasia* . . . the original exercise of [mind's] powers" (154–55; 155 n. 72).

imagination transcends the alternatives of *Geist* and *Leben* in German idealism, it merely repeats the idealist gesture of *Verstehen* in Berlin and in German historicism. Like Pompa, he remains within the idealism of epistemic
philosophy. Ironically, the knowledge Verene grounds on the *homoiousis* between meditating philosopher-historians and *fantasia* is more total than any
epistemology based on concepts. "To recollect is to order things in terms of
their origin, to obtain a *totalization* of all the fragments of the activity of the
human spirit through a progressive ordering of things between the origin
point, once found, and the form of the present mentality from which the ordering takes place." "This process," Verene continues, "cannot be fully typ-
ified by the notion of *reflection* . . . a logical term . . . [but by] a sense of
self-identity that extends through time from the origin to the present. We
must reperceive with our memory what this first world is like before it can
become an object of reflection."[101]

The knowledge derived from *fantasia* is narration, to be sure, and Vico's
science "a literary science," but for Verene "narration" is wholly *representational*: "The *New Science* is a representation *by the mind to the mind*
of the way in which humanity has all elements in common with itself . . .
[so] that the bond between the particular and the universal is expressed and
all . . . understood through causes. . . . [R]hetoric . . . is a *science* of narration which can comprehend the particulars of the human world in terms
of *necessity*. Narration must tell us the story of the . . . *necessary sequence
of the ideal eternal history*." "Understood in this sense," Verene adds,
"rhetoric is an activity in which the mind constructs a knowledge of itself."[102] In attempting to capture the basis of Vico's epistemology in *fantasia* rather than in concepts, Verene sets his sights too low; he is content
to distinguish Vico from traditional epistemology, while the consequence
of Vico's twenty-year effort was to go *beyond* epistemology to *poiesis*.
Vico's discovery of the embodied nature of first men, of the genetic relation
between them and all humankind, of the poetic nature of language and its
creation of human meaning eliminate the possibility of that subjective *homoiousis* that metaphysics believes necessary for knowledge. Whatever
Vico's new science is—and it is certainly *vera narratio*—it cannot be so in
an *epistemic* sense.[103]

I discuss Verene's epistemic interpretation of "meditation and narration"
at length because it illustrates the problem of capturing the ontologically
originary power of language while retaining the conceit of human subjectivity. Gianfranco Cantelli makes a similar attempt. He is more successful in

---

[100] Donald Phillip Verene, "Imaginative Universals and Narrative Truth," *New Vico Studies*, vol. 6 (1988): 1–19. The paragraph referred to is 349.

[101] Verene, *Science of Imagination*, 154–55. Emphasis added.

[102] Ibid., 165. Emphasis added.

[103] I argue that a "knowing" of meaning created with language is hermeneutic understanding.

retaining the corporeality of first men and the inseparability of poetic language from human behavior—physical, ritualistic, social—though he does so only by making an absolute distinction between mute and articulate languages. Believing articulation expresses subjective intent, he insists that only vulgar language is articulate, that the poetic is wholly mute. Correspondingly, he distinguishes between imaging and vocalizing, emphasizing the primacy of visual perception for first men and acoustic for men of the last age. Though he gives a compelling account of the bodily nature of poetic language, his inability to imagine articulation without subjectivity compromises two central aspects of Vico's *poiesis;* the metaphoric nature of poetic language, and the genetic relation between the poetic men and languages of the first two ages and of the third. I discuss him at this point to illustrate, from the perspective of a non-subjectivist language such as the Hebraic, the conceited nature of the belief that articulate language, and thus the men who speak it, are *necessarily* subjective, a conceit Vico himself overcomes in understanding the genesis of human existence from the poetic language of corporeal beasts.

Vico, Cantelli argues, goes back to the "divine language" of Egyptian hieroglyphics to find the natural origins of language among men conceptualized in Epicurean terms. Hieroglyphics is a "'natural language' par excellence, that is, a language in nature expressing and revealing divinity,"[104] and human language "is born as a response" to it.[105] Nature is a book the first readers read with their bodily senses and an imagination awakened by terror, believing they read the linguistic signs of a deity who "wished to make manifest his own will." The experience of the sky as the language of Jove is the birth of meaning, "beast-man's first thought."[106] Cantelli nicely depicts the poetic responses of first men to a natural world they experience as a semiotic system. With its gesture the object in the sky "shows its meaning," and the poets respond with the mute hieroglyphic writing of their bodies, gestures referring not to the object in the sky *but to its gesture.* "Between the divine language and the originary language spoken by man *there is, therefore, a substantial homogeneity;* an indissoluble nexus unites the object of which one wants to speak and the sign."[107]

Human and divine language are homogenous, the former mimetic of the latter—a bodily reproduction achieved through the sensation of sight. For Cantelli a strong, seemingly essential, relation exists between the divine gesture in nature, the mute hieroglyphic response of beastly bodies, the imagistic character of poetic language—the fables—and vision. Hieroglyphics,

---

[104] Gianfranco Cantelli, "Reflections on the Vichian Thesis That the Original Language of Humanity Was a Language Spoken by the Gods," *New Vico Studies,* vol. 11 (1993): 1–12.

[105] Gianfranco Cantelli, *Mente corpo linguaggio: Saggio sull'interpretazione vichiana del mito* (Firenze: Sansoni Editore, 1986), 93. Translations are by Jeff Gburek and me.

[106] Cantelli, "Reflections on the Vichian Thesis," 9.

[107] Cantelli, *Mente corpo linguaggio,* 94. Emphasis added.

fables, myths "'speak[ ] to the eyes' and not to the ears."[108] Poetic characters are "nothing but 'pictures', reproductions of images . . . presented to the fantasy through the organ of sight," because an object "in its concrete spatial dimension can only be individuated and recognized through sight."[109] Such a natural, immediate "proportion" does not exist between sound and "bodies gathered by the sense of sight. . . . [S]ound does not reproduce the language of gods." This sharp distinction between visual and acoustic sensations forces an almost absolute antithesis between divine language, mute and imagistic, and vulgar, which, emerging with the plebeians and characterizing the age of men, is articulate, conventional, utilitarian, and concerned primarily with communication. Cantelli makes this distinction so sharply he has trouble accounting for what he considers the "apparent inconsistency" of Vico's characterization of three ages and three languages as both successive and contemporaneous.[110]

More seriously, Cantelli's distinction between poetic and articulate languages undermines the poetic nature of Vico's philosophy. First, it denies the genetic relation between poets and poetic language and humans who speak a vulgar language, thus establishing a nonpoetic origin for the men and languages of the third age. Just as "anti-Vichian," the sharp distinction between visual and auditory sensations compromises the metaphoric nature of poetic imaging.[111] Cantelli believes the bodily nature of the poets necessitates the extreme distinction between mute and articulate languages, visual and auditory sensations, since for him the emission of sound is tied to and expresses "sentiments and passions . . . housed in the soul of man." Voices "are the natural manifestation of all that is subjective in human experience."[112] "Through the mute signs man takes possession of nature, constitutes their

---

[108] Cantelli, "Reflections on the Vichian Thesis," 2–3.

[109] Cantelli, *Mente corpo linguaggio*, 104.

[110] Ibid., 96–97, 99. See also 105. Cantelli refers to par. 446. Cantelli's distinction between divine and articulate languages and identification of the latter with the plebeians is so complete that Gustavo Costa criticizes it as a "sociological" approach reducing differences in language to an opposition between lords and slaves, and making plebeians the sole progenitors of men. Cantelli forgets, Costa continues, that Vico himself did not believe in the superiority of the heroes but only that the heroes believed in it (Gustavo Costa, review of Gianfranco Cantelli, *Mente corpo linguaggio: Saggio sull'interpretazione vichiana del mito*, New Vico Studies, vol. 5 [1987]: 169–72). Cantelli considers Vico's account of language inconsistent because Vico attributes different languages and letters to each age while claiming languages and ages originated together. References to the *New Science* are 429, 446–48. See also 428–32. For references to vulgar language, see 439, 446, 931, 935–96.

[111] Though Cantelli says man does not see images in nature but signs, he sometimes writes as if an immediate correspondence exists between sight and image, rather than as if sight is one sensation among others—acoustic, kinesthetic, and so on—which *ingenium* brings together into a poetic (that is, metaphoric and interpretive) image not accessible to any one faculty. For example, in discussing sight he says, "Images represent in all naturalness that which is perceived as external," and an image "presents itself immediately as external" (*Mente corpo linguaggio*, 96).

[112] Cantelli, *Mente corpo linguaggio*, 96. See also 96–106.

meaning, reducing nature to his own needs and designs. With acoustic signs (poetic locution) man reveals to himself his own passions and sentiments that accompany this conquest and reduction." Articulation, moreover, expresses intentionality, and a language of intention is abstract, conventional, and referential. Cantelli acknowledges that Vico does not "propose explicitly a theory of vocal expressions as manifestations of sentiments," but believes it follows from Vico's view that voice is a sign of an experience "whose meaning is already established and reproduced in a visual image." But Cantelli's belief that "images" are wholly visual ignores the role that sound plays in fixing the image of Jove. More fundamentally, the distinctions between outer and inner, perception and thought are so "familiar" he can not get beyond them. If, however, one accepts Vico's claim that *ingenium* is a skill of the body *entire,* if one takes seriously his warning of the difficulty in understanding the poetic-metaphoric nature of bodily "seeing," then the claim that *pa* vocalizes a fear experienced in a body unconditioned by subjectivity, that the Jove "image" is a metaphor made up of acoustic as well as visual sensations, is not so "strange."[113]

Indeed, Vico himself refers both to the vulgar articulate language characteristic of the third age, and the poetic articulation that corresponds to mute language, saying, "[A]t the same time that the divine character of Jove took shape, articulate language began to develop." Poetic articulation begins with the sound uttered by the beasts in their terror at the sight of the being imaged in the sky, the onomatopoeic *papa*.[114] Unlike vulgar articulation, the poetic is originary, since the disparate sensations forced together in the metaphor Jove include not only the *sight* of a turbulent sky and bodily sensations of terror, but also the *sound* of thunder and the articulation *papa*. Articulation fixes the image with the power of a name, the metaphoric name of that imaged body. "'Name' and 'nature,'" Vico says, "meant the same thing."[115] Vico makes clear the poetic power of articulation from the etymology of another word originating "from the interjection of fear," the sound *paian,* from *pai,* aroused by the serpent Python. From it he derives the emergence of song or heroic verse, the oldest form of which was the prophesizing of oracles and sybils. The singing of laws, then history, follows the singing of prophesies; thus, "if the peoples were established by laws, and if

[113] Ibid., 105–8. The Vico passage is 448. Cantelli himself says though exclamation is an "integral part of and constitutes" primal experience, it is experienced "with an emotionally stirred and disturbed soul" (113–14).
[114] Vico, *New Science*, 429, 446–48. See also 428–32, 454. For references to vulgar language, see 439, 446, 931, 935–96.
[115] Ibid., 494. Fables were not "in accord with the nature of the things . . . dealt with," since they differed from "the sacred language invented by Adam, to whom God granted divine onomathesia, the giving of names to things according to the nature of each." Rather, poetic language was a "fantastic speech making use of physical substances endowed with life and most of them imagined to be divine" (401).

among all these peoples the laws were given in verse, and if the first [things, practices] of these peoples were likewise preserved in verse, it necessarily follows that all the first peoples were poets."[116] It is not clear why Cantelli believes so strongly in the correlation between voice and subjectivity that he does not credit references to poetic articulation, but that inability undermines his understanding not only of poetic metaphor, but also of the men of the third age and their genetic relation to the first.[117]

Another argument that undermines Cantelli's conception of the originary power of poetic language is his distinction between the materiality of "divine signs"—a sky that shakes, gestures, and shouts in the voice of thunder—and a subjective or spiritual presence behind that sensory language. It was significant for the development of human existence, he explains, that first men experienced as a "primary and original datum [what] does not conform to the perception of that which is sensory, but is rather the thought or the image of a divinity which . . . can never be given in . . . the senses." Sensory data had to be experienced as a sign not meaningful in itself, but, rather, as signaling the presence of a spiritual being behind the sign: "The sky is not Jove, it is only a portion of him . . . the 'body' of Jove . . . the 'medium' through which Jove manifests himself. . . . If Jove had not manifested himself . . . then [man] would never have arrived at a 'thought,' an 'idea.'" Thus man "interpret[s] the universe as the word spoken or written by a Speaking-Being who, with his speaking, wished to say something to man."[118] The strong case Cantelli makes that the *homoiousis* between corporeal beings and nature is constituted by language is thus undermined by this subjectivist claim that "behind the visible and sensible appearance of phenomena—visible to eyes, perceptible to ears—constituting their meaning, namely their divine nature, is the same consciousness internal to man . . . his own lived interiority."[119]

Because Cantelli interprets divine signs in the sky as a manifestation of spiritual being, he attributes to the *New Science* a spiritual theology at odds with the Epicureanism he also finds in it. He admits that, unlike hermeticism, Epicureanism is compatible with Vico's denial that hieroglyphics reveal eso-

---

[116] Ibid., 449, 470. See also 461–71, 228–33.

[117] Cantelli does not refer to Derrida, though his position supports Derrida's view that philosophy privileges phonetic language, considering speech the articulation of thought. Derrida's critique is directed, however, against a tradition that explicitly identifies speech as expressive of subjectivity, while Vico's account of poetic language, mute *or* articulate, presumes the bodily nature of first men.

[118] Cantelli, "Reflections on the Vichian Thesis," 7–10. See also Gianfranco Cantelli, "Myth and Language in Vico," *Giambattista Vico's Science of Humanity*, ed. Giorgio Tagliacozzo and Donald Phillip Verene (Baltimore: Johns Hopkins University Press, 1976), 47–63, 51. Interestingly, Cantelli here switches from the emphasis on nature as hieroglyphic sign of a god to the notion that god speaks the world, that he is a Speaking-Being; that is, that speech is merely the expression of a subjective agent.

[119] See Cantelli, *Mente corpo linguaggio*, 113–15.

teric doctrine,[120] but insists Vico's model "for representing the genesis of the original language continues to be . . . Neoplatonic" because "[t]he Epi-curean-Lucretian element, though abundantly present, is . . . totally insuffi-cient in explaining the complexity of the elements which come together to constitute [Vico's] philosophy of language." The only way to explain that philosophy is through a fusion of "Epicurean naturalism and hermetic sacrality."[121] Cantelli derives from that fusion "an even more radical posi-tion" than the contemporary one that claims "without language no thought would be possible. Speech . . . [is] the condition of thought." Vico's more radical position is that "not only the first thought is born with the first word, but also that with the first word and the first thought is also born the first object of which man would have had conscious experience and to which he would have referred." This "extreme conception . . . embraced and set forth with total awareness only by Vico" is a "simple consequence of the concep-tion of Neoplatonic and hermetic origin," that man experiences language not as a tool but as "immersed in a significant reality which . . . communicated that which a god . . . intended to tell him," an experience that is the "com-ing of self-consciousness."[122]

Cantelli rightly characterizes Vico's position as the radical one in which word, thought, thing emerge together, but wrongly understands it as Neo-platonic-hermetic. The immanent spiritualism of that tradition is antithetic to Vico's understanding of that unity. Moreover, it undermines Cantelli's own notion of a "substantial homogeneity" between mute gestures of beasts and a natural world perceived as divine hieroglyph. Given the monistic nat-uralism that runs from Vico's early Epicureanism to the immanent function-ing of *conatus* in *Ancient Wisdom* and of *poiesis* in the *New Science,* the distinction between a divine language *in* nature and a spiritual presence *be-hind* it cannot be made. Though in appreciating the unity of word, thought, and thing, Cantelli, like Verene, comes close to grasping the ontological con-structiveness of poetic language, he too undermines its *originary* power. For him, human creativity is ultimately merely a *mimetic* response to the sight of a semiosis in nature spoken by a Speaking-Being.[123]

The notion of "divinity" in the *New Science,* I argue, is more compatible

---

[120] Indeed, Cantelli says Vico's philosophy of language and history of humanity is closer to the Cartesian, the "philosophic position of greatest contrast to . . . Neoplatonic and hermetic thought" ("Reflections on the Vichian Thesis," 4).

[121] Cantelli, "Reflections on the Vichian Thesis," 5.

[122] Ibid., 10–11. But even this insight into the ontological significance of language is muted by Cantelli's subjectivism. He says, for example, "Mute actions of the body . . . and their im-ages are not signs . . . [but] the content which . . . will be instead the objects to which our ar-ticulated language will refer." Calling this Vico's "hypothesis of an originary mute language," he adds that it has to do with the "natural connections to the ideas the primitive mind can form of bodies" (*Mente corpo linguaggio,* 91). Also, hieroglyphic and mythic images "signified men-tal images which were the fruits of primitive man's fantasy that . . . attributed reality to that which was not given in sensory experience—divinity" ("Reflections on the Vichian Thesis," 7).

[123] Cantelli, "Myth and Language in Vico," 47–49. The Vico quote is 34.

with Vico's monistic naturalism. The "divine" is not, *substantively,* a spiritual presence in nature, but, rather, a predicate—the unity of knowing and making—that traditionally belonged solely to God. When attributed to humans, the predicate is a *functional* secularization of divinity. "[H]istory cannot be more certain," Vico says, "than when he who creates the things also narrates them"; thus the "divine" proofs of the new science give humans a "divine pleasure, since in God knowledge and creation are one and the same thing."[124] Just as the conception of God that humans create is always a projection of their sense of self—a principle Vico understands as well as Canguilhem—so too the attributes of divinity they appropriate for themselves reveal their self-image. Vico avoids the "ultimate error" against which Heidegger warns, of explaining human "ek-sistent essence" as a "secularized transference to human being, of a thought that Christian theology expresses about God." Both Neoplatonism and onto-theology make that error in conceiving humans, like God, as spiritual or subjective substance, an analogy emanating from the conceit of scholars.[125] Rather, Vico's understanding of the divine unity of knowing and making functionally approximates the creative potency of a Creator-God. The only conception of "divine creativity" compatible with Vico's naturalism—and, therefore, the only one that can be possessed by corporeal beings—is linguistic. Thus, in claiming that "the first men of the gentile nations . . . created things according to their own ideas," he adds, "[b]ut this creation was infinitely different from that of God. For God, in his purest intelligence, knows things, and, by knowing them, creates them; but they, in their robust ignorance, did it by virtue of a wholly corporeal imagination . . . for which they were called 'poets,' which is Greek for 'creators.'"[126]

The first *factum* that theological poets made with corporeal imagination was the god they created in their own image by projecting their bodily sensations onto the sky. Though that image was as physical as its creators, it was "divine," since in its physical "gestures" and thundering "voice" the beasts saw and heard the *language* that created their human existence.[127] The god

[124] Vico, *New Science,* 349.

[125] While secularization theorists such as Löwith and Milbank do not assume that the secularized essence of God is rational, they do assume it is subjective.

[126] Vico, *New Science,* 376.

[127] Thus the god that poets imaged in the sky could not have been, as Cantelli believes, a spiritual presence—a Neoplatonic deity—*behind* language manifest in nature, but only, like them, a corporeal being whose language was embodied. Moreover, "since things do not settle or endure out of their natural state," the gods of later ages must also be divine in a functional sense, because of their creative language. Spiritual or intellectual conceptions of God can come only from revelation. The question of God's embodiment was left unanswered in ancient Israelite literature, as Howard Eilberg-Schwartz and others note. One commentator describes the Israelite God in a way suggestive of the image the beasts created out of their bodies: God's "principle manifestation beyond sheer presentness is through language that is declaratively gestural and physical and sometimes through gestures that are unspeakably raw and direct. The speaking God is a paradigmatic and primary Hebrew adventure" (Arthur Cohen, "Life Amid the Par-

they "saw" was, in effect, a poetic image of the divine *poiesis* they possessed in their own bodily skills of sensation, memory, and *ingenium*. If there is a divine paradigm of that *poiesis*—a causal agency identified not with mind, soul, or spirit but language—Vico would have found it not in his onto-theological tradition but in Genesis. Whether he was influenced by such a paradigm I do not know—I do not claim historical influence or relation between Judaic notions and the *New Science*, but, rather, an affinity between the ontological creativity Vico attributes to the language of embodied beings and calls divine, and the ontologically creative language of a poet-God. Certainly one of the most overt clues of that affinity has not been appreciated. When Vico refers to the "poetic logic" by which "poetic metaphysics" signifies bodies imagined by theological poets "to be for the most part divine substances," he gives an etymology of *logos,* whose "first and proper meaning was *fabula,* fable," and in Italian, "*favella,* speech." Since "speech was born in mute times . . . *logos* means both word and idea." He continues: "Thus the first language in the first mute times . . . must have begun with signs, whether gestures or physical objects, which had natural relations to the ideas. For this reason *logos,* or word, meant also deed to the Hebrews and thing to the Greeks." Myth was thus defined as "*vera narratio,* or true speech," though not as "a language in accord with the nature of the things it dealt with," as was Adam's, but as "a fantastic speech making use of physical substances endowed with life and . . . imagined to be divine."[128] This identification of *logos* with *davar* has not been sufficiently appreciated. Battistini is surprised, for example, that Voss, in giving a different philological proof "of the synonymy of *verum* and *factum*" than Vico's ancient Italians, reconciles it "with the ancient Hebrews." Rejecting the traditional etymons of *verus* Voss settles on the Greek ἐρεῖν, "to speak," which he confirms with reference to the Hebrews "because in Hebrew *davar* is not only 'word' or 'speech' which is its particular concept [or meaning] but also denotes 'thing' or 'deed.'"[129] Battistini does not draw out the significance of this "surprising" source of Vico's equation of *verum* and *factum*. Like other commentators, he may assume that the meanings of *davar* and *logos* are synonymous, since the traditional understanding of *logos* effaces the Hebraic view that *davar* is not an expression of thought or a sign in a signifying system, but, rather, an ontological event *in-the-world* existentially inseparable from "deed" and "thing."

Commentators who interpret Vico's philosophy as secularizing theological notions do not appreciate the significance of Vico's identification of *logos* with *davar,* much less the importance of distinguishing among different

---

adigms, or the Absence of a Jewish Critique of Culture," *Journal of the American Academy of Religion* 14, no. 3 [fall 1986], 514).

[128] Ibid., 401–2.

[129] Battistini, Andrea, "*Vico e l'etymologia miopoetica,*" *Lingua e Stile,* vol. 9 (1974): 31–66. Pamela Vaughn translated the Latin.

conceptions of God the one secularized in the *New Science*. For Western thinkers "God" is always spirit. Similarly, those interpreting *verum-factum* as secularizing a divine attribute do not understand the need to assert a maximum of causation to retain the ontological potency of making and to avoid its subordination to knowing. Those who do, such as Löwith, Milbank, Blumenberg, and, to some extent, Fisch, go to the biblical God as paradigm of causal agency, but undermine that move by identifying that deity with the trinitarian model. Even Milbank, Cantelli, and Gadamer, who identify divine causality with language, cannot conceive of language other than as expression of inner subjectivity.[130] Judaic interpreters, on the other hand, do not assume that God's language or deeds manifest subjective intellect or intention. Nor, in considering the relation of man to God as *imago,* do they conceive the *homoiousis* between them *substantively* as rationality or even subjectivity. For them, Godlikeness is *functional,* the possession of a language at once word, idea, deed, thing.[131]

There are no sustained interpretations of affinities between the *New Science* and Judaic or rabbinic conceptions of divinity, certainly none suggest-

[130] Frederick R. Marcus's article, "Vico and the Hebrews," *New Vico Studies,* vol. 13 (1995): 14–32, exemplifies interpretations from a non-Hebraic perspective, as do the other works to which he refers. In a recent book Milbank elaborates on his interpretation of Vico by exploring the metaphoric, poetic, creative nature of Hebrew, but does so from the point of view of such eighteenth century "Christian apologists as Warburton, Berkeley, Löwith, Vico, Hamann and Herder," who aimed to undermine the materialist view of culture with a conception of its poetic origins. Milbank claims Vico went beyond Hamann and Herder in stressing the "*double origin* of language, Hebraic and 'pagan',' " and adds, "No commentator on Vico has yet grasped the real implications of this," that for Vico even the Hebrews had a poetic language and culture (*The Word Made Strange: Theology, Language, Culture* [Oxford: Blackwell Publishers, 1997], 107). Yet, though Milbank argues that Vico and the other "apologists" believed man "an *original* creator" of the human world who "participates in some measure in creation *ex nihilo*" (79), he does not interpret their linguistic creativity as a secularized version of divine. Vico, indeed, searched for a "transcendental constraint for cultural activity" emerging from "cultural objects themselves." Drawing on his conception of *factum* as the *verbum* of God, Milbank claims Vico found that transcendental constraint in the *verum-factum* principle, thereby promoting the "made, cultural object . . . to the status of a divine transcendental . . . and this is equivalent to saying that God in his creation *ad intra* in the *Logos* 'incorporates' within himself the creation *ad extra,* including human history," a position, he believes, "nearly identical" to Cusa and Hamann (79–80). This interpretation is part of Milbank's overall intent to deny such "nonsensical" claims as Mark C. Taylor's that the postmodern obsession with language is a " 'secondariness' consequent upon the 'death of God' " (106). Milbank argues that eighteenth century Christian writers overcame the "ontology of substance" to move toward a view of "reality as constituted by signs" (85). Thus the "turn to the subject" more poetic than the "foundationalist" one of the moderns was initiated *within a Christian theological context* (35 n. 38), and "radical linguisticality . . . secretly promoted" by a Christian semiosis (84–85; see also 97, 110–12). Milbank does not appreciate the "radical linguisticality" of the Hebrews themselves, which enabled them to hold a view of divine and human creativity that never assumed the substantive onto-theology he tries so hard to overcome. Nor does he appreciate the radical sense in which Vico secularized that linguisticality.

[131] "[I]n man," Benjamin points out, "God set language, which had served *Him* as medium of creation, free. God rested when he had left his creative power to itself in man" (Walter Benjamin, *Reflections: Essays, Aphorisms, Autobiographical Writings,* ed. Peter Demetz, trans. Edmund Jephcott [New York: Schocken Books, 1986], 321–23).

ing a secularization of the Hebraic conception of the ontological potency of originary language. To my knowledge only two discussions incorporate a Hebraic perspective at all. One is the relation Faur draws between Vico's use of *verum-factum* and the skeptical role the principle plays for Hebraic thinkers such as Sánchez. Yet even Faur believes that Vico ultimately uses the principle to reject skepticism and to justify knowledge (albeit delimited) of the historical world. Though Faur does not draw out the more radical implications of the Hebraic conception of language to reinterpret the *New Science,* he does bring out the central issue in the relation between Vico and it. In describing Hebraic semiology, which "conceives of physical phenomena (and historical and personal events) as significant indexes that are to be interpreted and decoded as speech and writing," he says, "[T]he Hebrews reject the rigid 'nature/history' opposition . . . [and] the absolute autonomy of nature" and stress the human "interaction with the world" that transforms it. The "acts of man," the constructed, are superior to the given or natural.[132] Faur associates this view with Vico's *verum-factum* and, despite accepting Berlin's historicist epistemological interpretation of the principle, is clear that in the Hebraic view to which he likens Vico the worlds of nature and human existence, including "subjectivity" and "knowledge," are made with language. Both worlds are texts, and texts are not known epistemically or "from the inside," but are read and interpreted. For the rabbis, God writes the "book of nature": for Vico, the texts humans can read are those written with their own metaphoric language—the one projected onto the sky and divined by theological poets, and the social-historical world made by that act and divined by philosopher-historians of a later age.[133]

Faur suggests an affinity between the *New Science* and the rabbis' semiological conception of nature. Cantelli might more satisfactorily have used it than hermetic semiology to supplement the illiteracy of Epicurean naturalism. I do not pursue that line, since the conception of divine language I believe the *New Science* attributes to humans is not semiotic but hermeneutic. In distinguishing between the former, which he calls structural, and the latter, Ricoeur says the "core of meaning of the Old Testament" is made up of "founding events" whose "signifying content is a kerygma, the sign of the action of Jahweh, constituted by a complex of events . . . a *Heilgeschichte* [sacred history]." Structuralism cannot "exhaust their meaning," which "is a reservoir . . . the initial *surplus* of meaning which," in a

---

[132] José Faur, *Golden Doves with Silver Dots: Semiotics and Textuality in Rabbinic Tradition* (Bloomington: Indiana University Press, 1986), xxii–xxiii. See also "The Splitting of the *Logos:* Some Remarks on Vico and the Rabbinic Tradition," *New Vico Studies,* vol. 3 (1985): 85–103.

[133] For Vico, the world is "text" in a sense closer to Hebraic—or Derridean—meanings than to traditional conceptions of the Book of Nature. While the book is logocentric and yields knowledge, texts are written in originary language and must be interpreted.

network of signifying events, "*motivates* tradition and interpretation."[134] As in *Heilgeschichte,* so too in *Menschengeschichte* [human history]—"founding events" originating in language must be interpreted, not known. This hermeneutic, semantic character of language is brought out in the second discussion using a Hebraic perspective to interpret *verum-factum.* In an article in *Bollettino Del Centro Di Studi Vichiani,* Donatella Di Cesare takes issue with interpretations stressing its transcendental nature, and emphasizes the "linguistic, and consequently pragmatic, element" "form[ing] the core of the *verum-factum* principle." She calls that principle "*praxis*" in the sense that I use *poiesis,* since it "produce[s] its own objects" with language, the "mediating term between *verum* and *factum.*"[135] The centrality of language in the *New Science* has not been unanimously recognized, she acknowledges, or, where recognized, fully credited as an attempt to refound philosophy.[136] In two sections of her article reproduced in *New Vico Studies* she traces the history of Vico's *verum-factum* from *Study Methods* to the *New Science,* showing Vico's increasing emphasis on language and awareness that language characterizes "human nature . . . in its sensible and imaginative reality . . . becom[ing] the very model on which the convertibility of *verum* and *factum . . .* is based." By *De constantia,* Vico derives from *verum-factum* not only the position that the first language was poetic but also a corresponding emphasis on making over knowing.[137]

In the sections of the article not reproduced in *New Vico Studies,* Di Cesare develops the pragmatic hermeneutic character of poetic language. She criticizes interpretations identifying Vico's philosophy as precursor of the nineteenth century historicist hermeneutic tradition, such as Gadamer's and Betti's. Not sensitive enough to the originality of its hermeneutic character, they deny the "central axis around which it is constituted . . . a new way of understanding language."[138] That "new way" is nothing less than a "subversion (*capovolgimento*) of the linguistic perspective" dominant in all in-

[134] Paul Ricoeur, "Structure and Hermeneutics," *The Conflict of Interpretations: Essays in Hermeneutics* (Evanston: Northwestern University Press, 1974), 45–48.

[135] Donatella Di Cesare, "*Verum, Factum,* and Language," *New Vico Studies,* vol. 13 (1995): 1–13. Parts 3 and 5 of the *Bollettino* article appear in *New Vico Studies.*

[136] Donatella Di Cesare, "*Parola, logos, dabar: Linguaggio e verità nella filosofia di Vico,*" *Bollettino Del Centro Di Studi Vichiani* (Naples: Bibliopolis, 1992–93), vols. 22–23, 251–87, 256. Translations by Jeff Gburek and me.

[137] Di Cesare, "*Verum, Factum,* and Language," 2, 7. *De constantia* was written in 1721, four years before the first version of the *New Science, Scienza Nuova in forma negativa.*

[138] Di Cesare, "*Parola, lògos, dabar,*" 251–53. See section 1, 251–56, for the distinction between Vico and nineteenth century hermeneutic and historicist developments, and 2, 256–60, for Vico's relation to traditional rhetoric. Gadamer, she points out, draws only on *Study Methods,* not on the *New Science,* thus emphasizing Vico's relation to traditional rhetoric and missing Vico's "entirely new understanding of language . . . decisively beyond the borders of traditional rhetoric by assuming a hermeneutic orientation." Gadamer fails to appreciate "that link between rhetoric and hermeneutic that Gadamer himself wants to valorize," and perpetuates the link between Dilthey and Vico (253–54). Betti also reduces Vico to historicist themes (255).

terpretations of Vico, the rhetorical, by which she means an "instrumental" conception of language experiencing truths outside language. Vico comes to understand that language contains its own truth, a "primary human experience of the real" recognizable in its "semanticity." Language is at once "constitutive" and "interpretive" of the civilized world. Thus, the necessity to study the genesis of language "extends itself to all things," because the study of language is itself a study of beginnings. The understanding that language is not the *vehicle* of human culture but its *form* "separates Vico from the Italian humanistic tradition," to which he is otherwise indebted. "It is via the word that man emerges in civility." For this reason religion and law—for Vico "the very conditions of civility"—"are of necessity poetic. . . . [T]his rooting of religion and law in language unfolds itself with an eye not so much towards the intersubjective dimension, but rather toward the poetic dimension, through which language seems to reveal itself to be the first form and model of every human doing/making."[139]

Di Cesare expands on this distinction between the poetic/metaphoric and rhetorical character of *universali fantastici* in the last two sections of the *Bollettino* article. Man cannot *make* "sense" of causal relations in nature until he *gives* "sense" to them, she says, which he does by investing events with purpose, thereby humanizing them. By means of poetic language, he makes himself the source of meaning. The poetic trope is a "phenomenological predication that actualizes itself in the dynamics of making sentences," an act based on sensory experience, thus "spring[ing] from an immediate rapport with reality."[140] "The affirmation of the primacy of sense understood as an unrepeatable semantic act is proof of Vico's interest in speech and its pragmatic values, having as its effect the emergence of the civilized world." A philosophy based on sense, on the individual, on the historicity and semanticity of language is philology, its chosen method of study hermeneutic, which "interpret[s] the creative linguistic act in which the *factum* and the *verum* convert themselves and by which force the course of history unfolds." Hermeneutic brings to light "originary metaphoric sense. . . . *This discovery with which the originary metaphoric sense comes to be reanimated is no less creative* than that first formative act of *fare* because, restoring a sense which it apparently no longer has, it reveals itself as a labor in all respects similar to the 'sublime labor' of poetry."[141]

Di Cesare goes far in her brief discussion in identifying Vico's philosophy as poetic and hermeneutic. We differ in that though she stresses the creativity of hermeneutic, for her it is primarily what Ricoeur calls a hermeneutic of recovery—that is, a method of historical study—rather than, as I argue,

---

[139] Ibid., 257–60. Di Cesare refers here to *Diritto Universale* XIII, 20.

[140] Ibid., 282. See also 280–83. I differ with Di Cesare's view that Vico's poetic tropes are inductions from similar traits. Her discussion is drawn almost wholly from *Istitutiones oratoriae*.

[141] Ibid., 284–87. Emphasis added.

an ontologically creative sense-making of the men of the third age. Further, though she continually notes the analogy Vico makes between divine and human creativity, she does not call the human a secularization of the divine. She does, however, emphasize the linguistic nature of creativity, pointing out that in *Ancient Wisdom,* Vico characterizes both divine and human knowing as *legere,* a gathering akin to reading, thus anticipating the importance of language in later writings. Even where man creates mathematics, like God, by combining, he does so with language, since "mathematicians merely define names, given that naming already amounts to creating."[142] Language "feigns" a world. And, though in *Ancient Wisdom* the word comes into being properly only in God, by the *De constantia* Vico increasingly takes a positive view of human creativity, coming to believe that the first men were poets who grasped things with their senses and "combined them in a way reflecting divine creativity," thus humanizing a natural world divinely created. "Man's self-creation is a linguistic creativity, on the model of God's."

Despite this observation—and this is the biggest difference between us— Di Cesare believes that Vico maintains the distinction between human and divine creating. She refers to 349, in which he says that, unlike the poets, God creates by knowing, and says though Vico adds that human creative naming takes on "a reality greater" than mathematics, he continues to use the word "*fictio*" (feigning) to describe it.[143] Though what humans create is true, though poetic truth can "body forth a world," it is *fictio* because it is limited to the truth of words, while the truth of things "is the exclusive property of God."[144] Despite Di Cesare's insistence on the poetic, hermeneutic nature of Vico's philosophy, she does not make the more radical claim that poetic creating is ontological, productive not only of the proper and true, but also of a concretely real human world. Nor, though noting the distinction between the linguistic creativity of corporeal poets and a spirit-god who creates by knowing, does she make a connection between human linguistic creativity and that of the poet-God of Genesis.

Even so, Di Cesare has an acute sense of the affinity between Vico's conception of poetic language and the "vision of language" in the Bible. She and Faur are almost alone in discussing that affinity and bringing out the significance of Vico's reference to *davar.* Part 4 of the *Bollettino* article is devoted to an account of Vico's relation, historically and conceptually, to the He-

---

[142] Ibid., 264–66; "*Verum, Factum,* and Language," 4–6.

[143] Ibid., 276–79; "*Verum, Factum,* and Language," 8–11. The English translation in *New Vico Studies* is incorrect. Following endnote 17 the translation says, "Vico argues that in its basic sense *fingere* means *facere;* the derivation of *fingo* from *facio* thus opens a new perspective," but Di Cesare credits Salutati, not Vico, with the connection between *fingere* and *facio* that creates "a new perspective" (*"Parola, logos, dabar,"* 278).

[144] And, though she says, "The poetic truth of the word is thus man's primary, unique truth," she assumes that "[t]he rational stage, the high noon of knowledge, can develop beyond the auroral poetic stage" (11).

brews and that biblical "vision."[145] Though she discusses Vico's influence on the Jews of his day, she is more interested in the influence of the Hebraic tradition on him, and particularly the "biblical vision" of language on the formulation of *verum-factum,* a topic "so neglected in Vico studies." She cites Vico's reference to *davar* as "passed over in silence" in the literature, adding that though one often speaks of Vico's relation to the "Christian Platonic metaphysic of the *Logos* . . . one should understand the *Logos,* or *Verbum,* not so much in the Greek sense but rather—as Löwith has intuited—in the biblical sense." The true key to creation in the Bible is *davar,* a word important not only for its semantic content but also for its pragmatic value, a function of the "peculiar orality of the ancient Hebrew world." As "distinguished from and counterposed to *Logos,*" which was eventually reduced to its logico-linguistic value as a discursive manifestation of rational, abstract thought, *davar* means deed united with word and thought, inseparable from the effect produced in reality. For this reason the great concern that runs through Western philosophy, "the truth-value of the word and its conformity to the thing," has no ground for the Hebrews, to whom "truth reveals itself . . . in conformity with action."[146]

In the light of this relation between word and deed, Di Cesare says it is "troubling" and "difficult to believe" that neither the historical nor thematic relation between the Hebraic tradition and Vico's *verum-factum* "has been taken into consideration." Since in *Ancient Wisdom* Vico gives divine creation as the model of the convertibility of true and made, one is "compelled to suppose that Vico moved from the first chapters of Genesis and in a kind of commentary on them developed the principle of *verum-factum,*" a move incomprehensible except that Vico recognizes in language itself "the condition of that convertibility." In Genesis, after all, "language is presupposed as the ultimate reality which can only be considered within its unfolding," and acts of creation "are characterized by the immediate . . . nexus of speaking and doing."[147]

Di Cesare goes on to say that with his breath, God "entrusted his creative

[145] Di Cesare notes that in the *Autobiography* Vico recounts sending five copies of *Scienza nuova Prima* to Signore Giuseppe Athias, "most learned amongst the Jews of this age in the science of the sacred language." Athias, head rabbi of the Jewish community in Livorno from 1733, was received by the scholarly community in Naples, including Vico and Dorio, in 1725; shortly after, Vico sent him samples of his manuscript. Di Cesare says that though at the time Vico reports living as a stranger in his own country, virtually unknown, "Athias was among the few to display a reverent esteem for him, having intuited perhaps better than any other the geniality of Vico's doctrine." In the face of Enlightenment rationalism and universalism, which was *"non di rado esplicitamente anti-ebraiche* ("not infrequently anti-Semitic")," Jewish scholars, particularly the Sephardic, recognized Vico's "cultural pluralism" as an alternative, a rapport of which only Faur among Vico commentators has taken note. See 267–70 for the influence of Vico's ideas on Talmudic hermeneutic, particularly in Livorno.

[146] *"Parola, logos, dabar,"* 272–74. Also see p. 265 n. 45. This meaning of *davar* is found everywhere in the Jewish tradition, she says, but associates its relation to action with intentionality, which my more postmodern interpretation of it rejects.

[147] Ibid., 272–74

power" to man. "God did not create him with the word, did not subject him to language, but had allowed this precise medium of his creativity to flow in him freely. Not himself named, man becomes the giver of names."[148] However, retaining the distinction from *Ancient Wisdom* between the "truth of words" and the "truth of things," she does not attribute to Vico a conception of human *poiesis,* which, like the creative potency of the Hebraic God, is ontologically creative of a real world of *things.* Even so, De Cesare's entire discussion, particularly her emphasis on the significance of *davar* for Vico, leads to a denial of that distinction between words and things, whether God's or man's. That distinction derives, after all, from classical philosophers (who were themselves reacting against the Sophist's more pragmatic conception of language), as does the distinction between "proper" and fictive languages, or, indeed, between "essential" reality and various kinds of "fictive" worlds. If Vico's conception of the poetic word is, like *davar,* a unity of word, idea, deed, thing, then what is created with the poetic word *is the world of things, a world at one and the same time artifactual and real.*

Though Di Cesare does not draw out these more radical implications, her understanding of the semantic, pragmatic, hermeneutic nature of the poetic word—qualities it shares with *davar*—goes beyond both Verene and Cantelli in capturing Vico's conception of divine *poiesis.* The strength of Cantelli's view is his emphasis on the corporeal nature of first men. In this he is even more successful than Verene, whose concern with grounding the recovery of historical knowledge on recollective *fantasia* presupposes a subjective *homoiousis* between meditating knower and imaginative object of knowledge. Though Di Cesare does not discuss the corporeality of first men, or see Vico's conception of poetic language as rejecting subjectivity—she even refers to his notion of the "subject"—the affinity she perceives between his conception of language and one that is a unity of idea, word, deed renders subjectivity superfluous. And, she herself makes the association between the "pragmatic" value of *davar* and the "peculiar orality of the ancient word," for which, as Faur points out, hearing "functions as a nexus between human interiority and exteriority . . . [t]hrough auditory experience."

In claiming that Vico retains the distinction between words and things, Di Cesare points out that though he associates the meaning of *davar* as "deed" with the Hebrews, he relates its meaning as "thing" to the Greeks. But the character of "thing" important for Vico, enabling him to relate it to "deed," is actually more Hebraic than Greek. As Handelman points out, *davar* means "thing" not in the Greek sense of substance but as "essential reality."[149] And so it is with Vico: the fantastic poetic word he associates with *davar* is for

[148] Ibid., 274-75.
[149] Susan Handelman, "Jacques Derrida and the Heretic Hermeneutic," *Displacements: Derrida and After,* ed. Mark Krupnick (Bloomington: Indiana University Press, 1983), 103. Once again, Fisch and Bergin's translation of *cose* as "institutions" rather than "things" obscures the concrete reality of what is created.

him an ontologically effective word inseparable from the deeds and things that constitute essential reality, the concrete social "things" that make up the human world. Though Di Cesare does not draw out the radical implications of the relation between Vico's thought and the Hebraic, she, more than any other commentator, grasps the affinity between the poetic conception of language on which Vico's hermeneutic rests, and the unity of idea, word, deed in the biblical "vision" of poetic language.

Heidegger, Grassi, and the Poetic Understanding of Logos, Davar, *Gathering.* Of theorists most taken with the ontological power of language who challenge philosophy's distinction between word, thing, deed—for example, Nietzsche, Heidegger, Gadamer, Foucault, Derrida—only the last explores the affinities between an ontologically potent language and the Judaic tradition. All, however, share the belief characteristic of Judaism that language is ontologically originary, that a linguistically constituted reality is not an object to be known epistemically, but a text to be interpreted, that hermeneutic is not the activity of subjects but of beings-in-the-world. Ironically, though in later works Heidegger associates the eventfulness of poetic language with Greek and German, his understanding of eventfulness is closer to the view Vico associates with *davar*. One is reminded of Hartman's comment that when Heidegger thinks he is thinking Greek, he is thinking Hebrew. In his critique of traditional humanism and call for a more primordial thinking of human beginnings, Heidegger says "Being subject as humanity has not always been the sole possibility belonging to the essence of historical man," and charges that "such is the darkening which that truth as the certainty of subjectivity . . . lays over a disclosing event [*Ereignis*] that it remains denied to subjectivity itself to experience."[150] The beginning that Vico attributes to poetic language is just such a "disclosing event . . . denied to subjectivity itself to experience." In this section I discuss affinities between Vico and Heidegger, making no claim of historic or eidetic relationship, believing, with Borges, that historical meaning emerges in reading. By questioning human existence outside the conceits of humanism and modernism—so familiar they are not recognized as such—Nietzsche's and Heidegger's writings enable me to read the *New Science* more open to its strangeness. The Hebraic tradition, as alien as it is to the content of these texts, is a touchstone for these readings, since for it disclosing events always take place in language, outside the "darkening" imposed by the truth or certainty of subjectivity.

For Vico, as for Heidegger, disclosing events are existential happenings setting up finite historical worlds, and for both, worlds come to presence in the words, deeds, and true things—artworks all—of beings-in-the-world. For Vico presencing originates in inventive imagination and runs a course from bestial existence through three social ages, culminating in the dissolution of that finite art-work, the historical world. Though for Heidegger his-

---

[150] Heidegger, "The Age of the World Picture," 153.

torical worlds that disclosing events set up do not run the genetic course Vico describes, they too are finite, ending in the rigidification of practices that originary events set into place. Both men create myths accounting for the existential happening of disclosing events, and though a difference between them emerges here, that difference is only apparent, not real. Though Vico's myth emphasizes human agency and Heidegger's rejects anthropocentrism for the "unconcealment" of Being, each myth serves to establish the *unintended* nature of disclosing events.

For Heidegger, "the fundamental position of the Western spirit, against which our central attack is directed" is the "distinction between being and thinking" begun with Plato. That distinction can be overcome only by recovering a more "primordial" thinking. While Vico finds in ancient myths accounts of *grossi bestioni* whose inability to distinguish between self and world forces a dependence on "primordial" imaginative sense-making, Heidegger finds in Sophocles and pre-Socratic fragments a time when man was "*deinotaton,* the strange . . . the violent one," caught between an abyssal earth and the historicity of Being, and the emergence, from that conflict, of *Dasein,* the historical *essent.* For Heraclitus, Parmenides, and the pre-Socratics, being and thinking (*physis* and *logos*) were thought together. Being discloses itself as *physis,* a "self-blossoming emergence . . . which manifests itself in such unfolding and perseveres and endures in it," and in which a thing "introduces itself to us, places itself before . . . us and as such stands before us . . . and . . . is present, that is, in the Greek sense, *is.*" The "truth" of *physis* is *aletheia,* the "unconcealment of being."[151]

In belonging to *physis, logos* did not originally mean thought, understanding, reason, discourse or the speech of subjective beings. Tracing *logos* to its etymological root in *legein,* Heidegger recovers its primordial meaning as gathering, collecting, bringing together, a "relating of one thing to another." As the "steady gathering of the intrinsic togetherness of the essent, that is, being . . . *logos* has the character of permeating power, of *physis.*" When *physis* and *logos* are "thought together . . . being-human is *logos.* . . . Standing and active in *logos,* which is ingathering, man is the gatherer." "[L]ogos as gathering becomes the ground of being-human. . . . To be a man means to *take* gathering *upon oneself,* to undertake a gathering apprehension of the being of the essent . . . so to *administer* unconcealment."[152] The understanding of *logos* as gathering comes to an end when Plato distinguishes *physis* from *logos,* fixing what shows up for human subjectivity as

---

[151] Heidegger, *Introduction to Metaphysics,* 117. See 116–28, 149–50, 14, 180–81, 102.

[152] Ibid., 130–40, 171–72, 174. As distinct from the representational thinking of moderns the primal thinking of pre-Socratics was *noein,* a term Parmenides used in the sense of "apprehension." Apprehension is not "subjective perception," but what "comes upon man as the one who . . . opens himself to what presences," "a process in which man first enters into history as a being . . . [or a] happening that has man." Parmenides "says nothing about man, or man as subject," but rather the opposite: "being dominates and appears."

eidos. The fixing of being as *eidos* distinguishes the *essence* of a thing from its *existence,* and, as idea comes to the fore—"the domination of thinking as *ratio* . . . over the *being* of the essent"—actual beings are devalued as "mere appearance." Accordingly, the truth of *physis* as emerging being reduces to "*homoiousis* and *mimesis,*" to "correctness of vision, to apprehension as representation," while *logos* as gathering, an event of unconcealment, a saying that takes place in language, becomes language as "statement." What had been unconcealment (*aletheia*) for the pre-Socratics becomes truth as "correctness of the logos," the saying of "something about something."[153]

In *Ancient Wisdom* Vico also uses etymology to identify God's thinking and creating as gathering. *Cogitare* is to think and to gather, and causation is the "giving of order to the matter or the chaotic elements of a thing" by "composing its scattered parts into a whole." Since the God of that earlier work is Neoplatonic, Vico emphasizes the cognitive nature of gathering, though gathering is also linguistic, since *intelligere* is to read perfectly, to combine the written elements of a word. Though not characterized explicitly as such in the *New Science,* the causal agency Vico attributes to humans in that later work—and continues to call "divine"—retains the two positions with which he strengthened divine agency in *Ancient Wisdom:* creation as a gathering of elements on the model of reading, and the fabrication of things in the world *ad extra.* In the context of Vico's master key, gathering or reading becomes a poetic—that is, creative—activity identified with linguistic and social practices. Regardless of historical accuracy, the etymologies Vico and Heidegger feign function to transform the traditional static, subjectivist understanding of *logos* into an ontologically potent and meaningful gathering, the unity of word, deed, thing Vico associates with *davar.*[154]

For both Vico and Heidegger, gathering, the unconcealment of being, takes place only in an existential "open" or clearing. "Wherever a present being encounters another present being or even only lingers near it . . . there openness already rules. . . . Only this openness grants to the movement of speculative thinking the passage through what it thinks." Associating the German "*Lichtung*" with "the older . . . *Waldung* [foresting] and *Feldung* [fielding]," Heidegger says, "The forest clearing [or opening] is experienced in contrast to dense forest. . . . To lighten something means to make it light,

[153] Ibid., 178, 185–86. See also 120. Thinking now took place wholly within the categories of Aristotelian logic. What showed up in the philosophies of Plato and Aristotle was *eidos* and *energia,* in the Middle Ages the createdness of things, for Kant the "transcendental making possible of the objectivity of objects," for Hegel and Marx the "dialectical mediation of the movement of the Absolute Spirit and the historical process of production," for Nietzsche the "will to power positing values," and at the historical end of philosophy, science and the dominance of technology and cybernetics.

[154] Faur distinguishes Philo's *logos* from the Greek because the latter is static; it "'gathers,' it synthesizes and organizes according to a pre-established order." Philo's *logos,* closer to Aramaic *Memsis,* is not determined by but establishes order, the active, dynamic spirit of God (*Golden Doves,* 24). What Heidegger means by "gathering" is closer to the Aramaic than Greek.

free and open, e.g., to make the forest free of trees at one place. . . . The clearing is the open region for everything that becomes present and absent. . . . All philosophical thinking that explicitly or inexplicitly follows the call 'to the matter itself' is . . . already admitted to the free space of the clearing."[155] Presciently, the disclosing event that fixes the first human place happens, for Vico, in forests, or rather, in clearings that make "the forest free of trees in one place." The event is an *Ursprung* in Heidegger's sense of the term, a founding leap setting up a historical world distinct from the abyssal forest, distinguishing humans from gods and animals, world from earth.

Moreover, in Vico's myth of origin, as in Heidegger's, unconcealment is "not simply given; it is achieved by work [in the Greek sense of *ergon*, the creation that discloses the truth . . . of something that is present]: the work of the word in poetry, the work of stone in temple and statue, the work of the word in thought, the work of the *polis* as the historical place in which all this is grounded and preserved." The working of artworks transports us out of the realm of the ordinary: "Art lets truth originate . . . in a founding leap." If the artwork founding the social world for Vico is the image of Jove, for Heidegger one that does so is the Greek temple. Though the temple housing the figure of a god is holy, it is not the god that makes it holy, since it is by means of the temple that "the god is present in the temple." The temple-work "fits together and at the same time gathers around itself the unity of those paths and relations in which birth and death, disaster and blessing, victory and disgrace, endurance and decline acquire the shape of destiny for human being. . . . [I]t first gives to things their look and to men their outlook on themselves. . . . [I]t is the world of this historical people." The world thus set up "is never an object that stands before us and can be seen. World is the ever-nonobjective to which we are subject as long as the paths of birth and death, blessing and curse keep us transported into Being. . . . In a world's worlding is gathered that spaciousness out of which the protective grace of the gods is granted or withheld." Artworks granting the unconcealment of historical worlds, whether Greek temple, crucified god, powerhouse on the Rhine—or image of Jove—also set forth the earth. As the site of conflict between world and earth, "*[t]he work lets the earth be an earth*": resting on rock, the temple "holds its ground against the storm raging above it and so first makes the storm itself manifest . . . first brings to light the light of the day, the breadth of the sky, the darkness of the night . . . the invisible space of air."[156]

---

[155] Martin Heidegger, "The End of Philosophy and the Task of Thinking," *Basic Writings*, ed. David Farrell Krell (San Francisco: Harper, 1993), 427–49, 441–43. But, Heidegger adds, "philosophy knows nothing of the clearing." See also Ernesto Grassi, *Vico and Humanism: Essays on Vico, Heidegger, and Rhetoric*, Emory Vico Studies, vol. 3 (New York: Peter Lang, 1990), 97–98, 160–66.

[156] Martin Heidegger, "Origin of a Work of Art," *Poetry, Language, Thought*, trans. Albert Hofstadter (New York: Harper & Row, 1971), 15–87.

Heidegger calls all originating art in which man becomes a historical be-ing "poetry,"[157] and, "[s]ince language is the happening in which for man beings first disclose themselves to him each time as beings poesy—or poetry in the narrower sense—is the most original form of poetry in the essential sense."[158] The emergence of language, and the power of language to origi-nate historical worlds, is itself due to its essential form *as* poetry. "The ori-gin of language is in essence mysterious. And this means that language can only have arisen from the overpowering, the strange and terrible, through man's departure into being. . . . Language is the primordial poetry in which a people speaks being."[159] Language, "understood rightly," is the house of Being. It "alone brings what is, as something that is, into the Open for the first time. . . . [B]y naming beings . . . [it] first brings beings to word and to appearance. . . . Such saying is a projecting of the clearing, in which an-nouncement is made of what it is that beings come into the Open *as*. . . . Pro-jective saying is poetry: the saying of world."[160] Heidegger quotes Stefan George: "Where word breaks off no thing may be." "Thing" is anything that *is,* even the gods: "Only where the word for the thing has been found is the thing a thing. . . . [N]o thing *is* where the word, that is, the name, is lack-ing." "[T]he relation between thing and word is among the earliest matters to which Western thinking gives voice and word, and does so in the form of the relation between being and saying. This relation . . . announces itself in a single word . . . *logos.* It speaks simultaneously as the name for Being and for Saying."[161]

Despite differences among Heidegger's, Vico's, Nietzsche's, Benjamin's, and Derrida's formulations, one finds in all an almost inarticulate effort to capture a shared sense of the existential relation between poetic word, nam-ing, and the coming into being of things. Unlike Vico and Nietzsche, Hei-degger does not argue the nonsubjective nature of an ontologically potent human language, since he already situates his writings outside the meta-physical distinction between material and subjective substance, body and soul or mind. As *logos* is for him *legein,* an eventful gathering at one and the same time word and thing, so too Vico's Jove is *logos,* and in Heidegger's dual senses—as gathering, and as language. What "gathers" are "disparate and diverse" sensations, fixed by a name into an image visible neither to bod-ily nor to intellectual vision, then projected back onto the world. Just as for Heidegger "[s]aying" is a listening "to the grant,"[162] so too for Vico the sen-sation that first opens the "eye of *ingenium*" is thunder, "heard" existen-

---

[157] Heidegger, *Introduction to Metaphysics,* 144.

[158] Heidegger, "Origin of a Work of Art," 74.

[159] Heidegger, *Introduction to Metaphysics,* 171–72. Heidegger distinguishes the violence and eventful immediacy of originary language from everyday language.

[160] Heidegger, "Origin of a Work of Art," 73–74.

[161] Heidegger, "The Nature of Language," *On the Way to Language,* trans. Peter D. Hertz (New York: Harper & Row, 1982), 61–62, 80.

[162] Ibid., 75–76.

tially: a receptive listening to being. And, if the image of Jove was more real to the *giganti* than the forests in which they wandered, it was made so in the mute and articulate languages that originated with it. Vico knows as profoundly as any Western thinker—except perhaps those whose primordial "thinking" produced the book of Genesis—that "language alone brings what is, as something that is, into the Open for the first time." For him, as for Nietzsche, Benjamin, Heidegger, Derrida—though each in his own idiosyncratic way—language is an event *in-the-world,* as the *logos* of metaphysics and *verbum* of onto-theology are not. Only Vico and Derrida, however, perceive the relation between *logos* as eventful gathering of word and being, and the ontological power of *davar,* the gathering of word, deed, thing.

The most significant difference between Vico and Heidegger is Vico's identification of the first men as godlike creators of their historical world, an anthropocentrism Heidegger overtly rejects for the "call of Being." For Heidegger, creativity is not the "self-sovereign subject's performance of genius," but "free bestowal": "It is not the *N. N. fecit* that is to be made known. Rather, the simple *'factum est'* is to be held forth into the Open by the work: namely this, that unconcealedness of what is has happened here, and that as this happening it happens here for the first time; or, that such a work *is* at all rather than is not."[163] It is not incidental that the one commentator to interpret Vico in terms of Heidegger's existentialism is Heidegger's former student Ernesto Grassi, and that, though countering Heidegger's assessment that humanism is always subjectivist and identifying Vico as a humanist, he feels he must deny that Vico's humanism is anthropocentric: "Vico's concern is not just a mere anthropological capacity, for which Heidegger attacks Humanism. . . . [W]e are far removed from the interpretation of poetry found in German Idealism."[164] Neither Heidegger nor, surprisingly, Grassi conceives of an anthropocentrism that does not presume the subjectivity tainting philosophic humanism, or one in which beings-in-the-world make themselves human with linguistic and social practices. Yet that more naturalistic, embodied notion of human agency is implicit in Grassi's interpretation of Vico and, I argue, characterizes the beastly poets who secularize the originary language of a Creator-God.

Grassi's interest in Heidegger stemmed from their mutual rejection of German idealism. Ironically, his scholarly interests lay with Latin and Renaissance humanism, while Heidegger's aim in recovering Greek thought always included a "polemically formulated rejection of Latin thought."[165] Though

---

[163] Heidegger, "Origin of a Work of Art," 76, 65.

[164] Ernesto Grassi, *Heidegger and the Question of Renaissance Humanism: Four Studies* (Binghamton: Center for Medieval and Early Renaissance Studies, 1983), 39.

[165] See Grassi's personal account of his relationship to Heidegger and Heidegger's philosophy in Ernesto Grassi, *Rhetoric as Philosophy: The Humanist Tradition* (University Park: The Pennsylvania State University Press, 1980), 1–8.

it was Grassi who first published Heidegger's "Letter on Humanism," his writings are devoted to rejecting Heidegger's charge that humanism "forgets" Being. That criticism was appropriate to the metaphysical, rationalist humanism deriving from Plato, but Heidegger, Grassi charges, remained ignorant of the humanism rooted in pre-Socratic philosophy. Though periodically "interrupted" by the recurring influence of Platonism and Neoplatonism, humanism in its various forms—the Latin tradition of Cicero and Quintilian, or the Renaissance humanism culminating in Vico—retained the pre-Socratic openness to Being that Heidegger struggled to recover. Challenging views that reduce humanism's concern with language to grammar or rhetoric, or identify its philosophy as either Neoplatonic or "the rediscovery of man and his immanent values," Grassi claims "one of the central problems of Humanism . . . is not man, but the question of the original context, the horizon or 'openness' in which man and his world appear."[166]

For Grassi as for Heidegger, the question of originary openness distinguishes pre-Socratics from the metaphysical tradition begun with Plato's fixing of what shows up in the clearing as *eidos*. The concern with the clearing and with presencing was forgotten until Renaissance humanists once again took as a starting point the problem of originary openness and the unhiddenness of Being. Like Heidegger, they too believed that the violence of the poetic, metaphoric word opens "a path to the clearing," that *logos* is originary, that Being and the word—saying—are one. Distinguishing between the temporalization of the biological being, defined by "'directive' signs" or coding, a *Zoosemiotic,* and the temporalization of the historical being, which is not given but found, Grassi says that only the word wrenches man from his situation as a biological being caught in the world of natural necessity, and enables him to emerge as historical being, *Dasein,* the realization of ingenious imaginative capacities that "humanize" reality and set up man's specific form of "being-in-the-world."[167] Grassi finds these "Heideggerian formulations" in Dante, Bruni, Boccaccio, Pontano, Mussato, and Salutati, until, with Landino, Neoplatonic metaphysics comes to the fore and humanism once again forgets Being.[168]

Humanism forgets Being, that is, until Vico's twenty-year struggle brings him back to the clearing: "It is Vico, with his theory of the topical, ingenious and imaginative form of thought, who truly makes clear to us what the philosophical meaning of the Humanist tradition is." For Grassi, the essence of Vico's thought is not understood "by those who limit themselves to uncovering the function of the imaginative universals as a substitution for rational

---

[166] Grassi, *Heidegger and the Question of Renaissance Humanism,* 17. Grassi began to study Vico in 1975, under the stimulus of Giorgio Tagliacozzo. See Domenico Pietropaolo, "Grassi, Vico, and the Defense of the Humanist Tradition," *New Vico Studies,* vol. 10 (1992): 1–10.

[167] Grassi, *Vico and Humanism,* 125–32. See also 149–51, 160–66.

[168] Grassi, *Heidegger and the Question of Renaissance Humanism,* 93–94. See also 17–26, 51–64, and *Vico and Humanism,* 100–107.

concepts. . . . [It] emerges by recognizing—which is rarely done—that the problem of Vico is the *realm within which man appears in his concrete and total realization.*" Vico "hit upon a completely new way of confronting traditional metaphysics. . . . [F]or Vico *the problem of the true is subordinate to the problem of the appearance of human reality. The bursting forth of Being in human historicity from time to time,* always in new forms, realizes itself originally in the poetic, imaginative word (*parola fantastica*) in function of which the world appears in its human significance. Vico's problem is that of what opens the realm of human sociality," a problem resolved with the "metaphorical, mythic word" and the notion of the clearing within which things show up.[169] Vico's account of the *bestioni* describes the move from man's original biological condition to the emergence of *Dasein* within a historical world: the fear that wrenches them from their biological situation forces them to look for a different "code," the myths and archetypes made with the poetic word. "In the word we have the specifically human attempt to overcome the isolation of vital objects from the subject. . . . In language is realized the unity of subject and object . . . in their historical reality."

Grassi, as much influenced by Marx as by Heidegger, enriches his existential interpretation of Vico by bringing the three together. All share the same "point of departure . . . the negation of traditional metaphysics," but "Vico and Heidegger pose their problem much more radically" than Marx, who "criticizes and refutes Hegel's metaphysical dialectical thought, but . . . stops within the scheme of traditional thought." For Marx "[t]he theory of work as the mediation of nature always presupposes as its initial point of departure the reality of beings (i.e., nature, man, and sociality)," thus forgetting the presencing, temporality, and finitude of Being. Alternately, the question Vico, Heidegger, and the pre-Socratics ask is "In what original realm does the significance of work, sociality, and the historicity of man appear?" The priority of this question of "the appearance of human reality" over "the problem of the true" is undermined, however, by epistemological interpretations of Vico. In questioning the identification of Vico with modernity's epistemological project—no less epistemological if imaginative recollection is substituted for rational reflection—Grassi insists that with the formulation of the *parola fantastica,* Vico grasps the originary nature of beginnings. Vico's "work is a real phenomenology, a description of how human reality 'appears' . . . step by step." "Heidegger is the only thinker who could have shed some light on Vico. Unfortunately, blinded by the traditional interpretation of Humanism as essentially a form of Platonism and Neoplatonism, Heidegger took an anti-Humanist position without ever knowing or reading Humanist authors, in particular Vico."[170]

---

[169] Grassi, *Vico and Humanism,* 134, 166. Emphasis added. See also 170, where Grassi again contrasts the "poetic word" with "theories of knowledge," specifically referring to Cassirer's misguided epistemic concerns. See also "The Priority of Common Sense and Imagination" (570).

[170] Ibid., 157, 159, 180–81. See also 110–11, 160.

Though sketchy, Grassi's discussions of the relation between clearing and poetic word and the transformation from the human biological situation to the realization of historicity underscore the naturalistic dimension of Vico's poetic understanding of onto-genesis. However far beyond the original biological condition of humans the human world develops, *it must always satisfy natural needs,* and doing so requires the concrete involvement of humans—their social practices and labor—in the world, an emphasis far removed from either German idealism or mystical interpretations of Heidegger.[171] Grassi's discussion brings together the various themes I pursue: a monistic conception of nature running from *Ancient Wisdom* to the *New Science,* a naturalism that, though tying human activity to the satisfaction of needs and utilities, is neither reductive nor mechanistic, but, in Funkenstein's words, reinterprets nature to "stand for the very process through which man acquires a second, social nature," and the imaginative, interpretive character of that process—"divine" because originary, and originary through the power of the poetic word, inseparable from the deeds and things of beings-in-the-world. Such a naturalistic-imaginative process comprises an ontological hermeneutic in which the work-being of artworks, showing up in eventful unities of words, deeds, and things, sets into place historical worlds. My conception of that process differs from Heidegger's and Grassi's, since neither could conceive of an anthropocentrism that does not assume human subjectivity, while I identify humans as creators of artworks and claim that, for Vico, the gathering of word, deed, thing is a human *poiesis* as much "denied to subjectivity to experience" as Heidegger's "disclosing events." In the following section I retell Vico's account of that process, bringing out the ontological nature of the making of true things that not only secularizes the creativity of the God of Genesis but also humanizes the "granting" of Heidegger's Being.

The "Settling" and "Enduring" of Poetic Things. If the master key of the *New Science,* that the first men of the human world were poets, is Vico's final response to the question of origins raised in *Ancient Wisdom,* by the *New Science* that question had taken on the existential import of Heidegger's query "Why are there essents rather than nothing?" Like Heidegger, Vico finds the answer in disclosing events of language, and, like Heidegger, understands that "[t]he strangest of all beings *is* what he is *because* he harbors such a beginning in which everything all at once burst from superabundance into the overpowering and strove to master it."[172] But whereas for Heidegger meaning resides in an "event" that "presences" only as long as palpable in the social practices of a historical world, for Vico the poetic event originates a patterned and recurrent process unfolding genetically through three ages. Vico's insight into the poetic origins of the human world had brought with it the genetic axioms he took as corollaries: "The nature of [things—*cose*] is nothing but their coming into being (*nascimento*) at certain times and

---

[171] Ibid., 124–36. See particularly 133.
[172] Heidegger, *Introduction to Metaphysics,* 155.

in certain guises" and "Things do not settle or endure out of their natural state."[173] In this section I discuss that "natural state" in which "settled" and "enduring" things originate, and argue that, since men of the first age come into being as poets, whose only skill is a language incapable of representing the world, but marvelously productive of things not present in it, *the men of the third are "nothing but" poets,* their creativity a function of their language, including the abstract language they make with their poetic language, and with which they construct not only their abstract sciences but also their own artifactual subjective existence. Though the fixed nature of Vico's ontologically constructive genetic process seemingly belies the temporality and finitude of Heidegger's historical worlds, the poetic logic that structures it does not derive from a metaphysical conception of being or *logos,* but from Vico's insight into the human condition—a condition as temporal and finite as for Heidegger, as abyssal and tragic as for Nietzsche.

Vico takes as axiomatic that "Wherever a people has grown savage in arms so that human laws have no longer any place among it, the only powerful means of reducing it is religion."[174] Thus the historical process begins with the gathering of perceptions that creates the image of Jove, fixed into an ontological unity with the poetic word *pa.* Vico calls that which gathers *factum,* a made thing, which is also *certum,* a certain of the historical world, and *verum,* since it is a true thing (though not, of course, understood as such in the first two ages.) The image fixed by *pa* is the artwork Jove, whose showing up first distinguishes humans "from gods and animals, world from earth," and gathers "the unity of those paths and relations in which birth and death, disaster and blessing, victory and disgrace, endurance and decline, acquire the shape of destiny." That image is ontologically inseparable from deeds and things in-the-world. Thus when Vico refers to religion he specifies the religion of the auspices, emphasizing that by religion he means not subjective "belief" in the divinity of the image that shows up, but the social rituals and artifacts that gather with that image.[175] The lower half of the frontispiece that begins the *New Science,* the *Dipintura,* a hieroglyph of the artworks whose working sets up the human world, depicts those artworks that set into place the practices of religion: the altar, "because among all peoples the civil world began with religion," when "each nation began to take auspices"; the *lituus,* the staff with which the augurs took auguries and observed the auspices, and thus a hieroglyph of the art of divination "from which . . . the first divine [things, *cose*] took their origin"; and fire and water, present in sacrifices during the interpretation of the auguries.[176]

[173] Vico, *New Science,* 147, 134. But Heidegger too acknowledges the "destining" of later events. Thus Plato's fatal fixing of *eidos* sets the world on the way to becoming picture ("The Age of the World Picture," 131, 143–44).
[174] Vico, *New Science,* 177.
[175] Vico enumerates them in detail. See ibid., 504–18.
[176] Ibid., 8–10. The frontispiece was drawn by Domenico Antonio Vaccaro "under the direction of Vico," and engraved by Antonio Baldi.

The creation of Jove arouses fear in the creators, and with fear *conatus,* the movement of the will that curbs the impulses of the body, giving rise to piety. Once again, piety is not a spiritual or psychological phenomenon, but the practices of public morality associated with observation of the auspices. The extent to which "public morality" is *nothing other* than those practices is obscured, however, by Vico's references to "mind" as that which curbs bodily impulses, such as "lust."[177] But *conatus* and "mind" are themselves *functional* terms for behavioral changes created in the social customs that originate with the practice of the auspices. Vico is explicit about the relation of those behavioral changes, particularly those associated with marriage and burial, to the eventual emergence of subjective existence, saying, "[T]he virtue of the spirit [which] began . . . to show itself" through *conatus* was "one of the great benefits conferred on the human race by heaven . . . through the religion of the auspices." The practices of marriage and burial are depicted hieroglyphically in the *Dipintura* through the artworks in which they show up—the torch, "lit from the fire on the alter," and the cinerary urn.[178]

With those practices the first men live settled lives, leading to the cultivation of the fields, depicted by a plough. Vico finds the history of physical labor in the myths of Hercules, Bellerophon, and Cadmus, beginning with the burning of the forests, the discovery of grain—the "golden apples" of ancient myths, "roasted among the thorns and briers"—and its cultivation.[179] With a fanciful etymology Vico relates the mythic figure of the cyclops, giants with one eye in the middle of the forehead, to that history, claiming that Homer's reference was a corruption of the "true heroic phrase that 'every giant had his *lucus*'," a word meaning both "clearing" and "eye." The term originally meant *orbes terrarum,* the lands the poets cleared and cultivated, which were always circular. Thus "[e]very clearing was called a *lucus,* in the sense of an eye." In associating physical labor with a clearing in the forest, Vico brings together two later senses—those of Marx and of Heidegger—in which a clearing is the setting up of the human world.[180] Cities come to presence in those clearings, becoming asylums for the giants who had not chained themselves to the earth with the practice of the auspices. Crafts too show up, the arts being "'real' poems [made not of words but of things]." From the distinction between the fathers and their *clienteles* commonwealths arise, "guarding the confines and the [things, *cose*]" that unite the private interests of family monarchies.[181]

---

[177] Ibid., 1098, 340, 504.

[178] Ibid., 504, 11–13. See also 505–18, 333, 529. From the rituals of "religion, or divine terror" associated with burial, the belief in immortality arises.

[179] Ibid., 539, 544, 546, 549. See also 387, 503.

[180] Ibid., 564. The Heideggerian, Marxist associations coexist with Vico's own emphasis on "piety" in setting up the social world: "the boundaries of the fields were fixed and maintained" with the ritual practices of "a frightful religion," and the first walls built and consecrated with "bloody ceremonies" (550). See also 777.

[181] Ibid., 553, 217, 629. Vico uses the term "form" to refer to "mind" in this and other passages, calling "those who labor in the trades and crafts" the body of the commonwealth and

Idealist readings of the *New Science* obscure the extent to which the origin and genetic development of this history consist of nothing other than words, deeds, things—the social practices and artifacts of beings-in-the-world. Grassi counters idealist interpretations—he specifically mentions Cassirer's—by stressing the significance of work in this process. Vico's basic problem, he claims, is to determine "the structure of human historicity," and insists "the determining force of the humanization of nature is always work." Work is not "the result of a generalized, abstract 'creative' act," but always takes place in a "concrete context": "[T]he logic of imagination must be put into the closest possible connection with work as the humanization of nature, otherwise imagination and its products would have to be defined as 'unreal' activities diverting from historical reality."[182] Grassi says the "ingenious faculty" "radiates human spirituality," but insists the term "spiritual" does not substantively distinguish "mind" from "body," spirit from matter. These distinctions are purely structural; while animals complete the work of satisfying organic needs with innate schemata, humans must seek new schemata. Since the "fulfillment of needs leads to . . . new kinds of needs . . . new forms of work . . . new forms of society . . . human society never 'is,' it is always 'becoming.'" Grassi believes that this account of work is compatible with Marx, but says Marx does not go beyond it, and uses the term "spirituality" to characterize that "beyond." For Vico work originates "from a 'lack' of innate schemata that leads to the necessity to *search* for schemata." This need for "spirituality"—an imaginative faculty that creates schemata—is actually a function of "deficiency," a mark of the unspiritual, "abyssal" material world.[183]

The genetic development of history, governed by choices that, though "freely" made, *must* satisfy determinate human needs, runs its course in the ages of gods, heroes, and men (which, though distinct, can exist simultaneously). As the last age degenerates into decadence, men fall back into bar-

---

the mind "form"; that is, he generally uses the term "mind" or "mental" functionally, rather than substantively. The artworks setting into place the civil world are depicted in hieroglyphs of fasces, sword, purse, balance, the caduceus of Mercury.

[182] Grassi, "The Priority of Common Sense and Imagination," 573–74, 570. Grassi exemplifies the dynamic relation between imaginative activity, need, and the necessity to satisfy need, with the labors of Hercules. Work is never a mechanical alteration of nature, an "inexplicable act of violence," but is preceded by an "interpretation of nature," by "establishing relationships (similitudes) between what man needs . . . [e.g., to quench thirst] and what his senses report to him in each specific concrete situation in nature," leading to "appropriate action. This is the meaning of work." The establishment of relationships occurs through ingenuity and imagination (564–65).

[183] Ibid., 566, 577–80. Only "lack" constitutes "freedom," since man is not bound to what is absent in nature. Grassi identifies free, "spiritual" work with art and the moral regulation of the passions. In this sense it is "underivable" from material work: only imagination enables man to create a world that satisfies "spiritual needs." Max Horkheimer and Walter Benjamin also draw on Vico to go beyond Marx's failure to appreciate the role of mythology in man's response to material necessity. See Joseph Mali, "Vico, Benjamin, and other German Mythologists," *Clio* 26, n. 4 (summer 1997): 427–49.

barism and a *ricorso* of the pattern. Vico characterizes the historical process in various ways—the nature of peoples is "first crude, then severe, then benign, then delicate, finally dissolute"; or, the development of social [things] proceeds through forests, huts, villages, cities, academies—but it is always communal, a function of shared linguistic and social practices that constitute a *sensus communis* within which individual choices always realize social ends. Vico is equally clear that the historical process is ontological, creating the very humanity of the beasts: "[T]he founders of gentile humanity by means of their natural theology (or metaphysics) imagined the gods . . . by . . . logic . . . invented languages; by morals, created heroes; by economics, founded families, and by politics, cities; by their physics, established the beginnings of things as all divine; by the particular physics of man, in a *certain sense created themselves.*" Vico characterizes the creative process as both *educare,* "the education of the . . . body," which reduces giant bodies to human size, and *educere,* the "heroic education of the spirit," which "bring[s] forth in a certain way the form of the human soul . . . completely submerged in the huge bodies of the giants": "[T]he founders of gentile humanity in a certain sense generated and produced in themselves the proper human form in its two aspects. . . . [B]y means of frightful religions and terrible paternal powers and sacred ablutions they brought forth from their giant bodies the form of our just corporature, and . . . by discipline of their household economy they brought forth from their bestial minds the form of our human mind."[184]

Just as the form of the human body was lost when descendants of Ham, Japeth, and Seth, living in filth, absorbed the nitrate salts in their feces, it is regained with *educare,* the *practice* of cleanliness. *Educere,* too, originates in practices derived from *bodily* skills, those of perception, memory, and imagination, which create the image of Jove, "the terror of [which] . . . humbled not only their bodies but their minds."[185] Though Vico continually refers to minds or souls as if they were substances, his entire discussion of *educere* describes the presencing of social and linguistic *practices,* since only in practices does an artifactual subjective existence gather. Thus he stresses that everything the human "mind" understands comes "from the senses," and "from something it senses, it gathers something which does not fall under the senses," gathering being "the proper meaning of the Latin verb *intelligere,*" the process that leads from sensory to subjective, conceptual existence.[186] Vico calls the process of *educere* a history of "ideas," troping it as a tree from whose branches grow such social "constructs" as poetic logic, morals, economics, physics, cosmography, astronomy, chronology, geography. With these "sciences" the poets imagined their gods, invented languages, created

[184] Vico, *New Science,* 141, 242, 239, 367, 520. See also 524, 692.

[185] Ibid., 371, 502. See also 14, 334, 516.

[186] Ibid., 363. Vico attributes to the corporeal bodies of beasts the same skills identified as corporeal in the *Autobiography* and *Ancient Wisdom,* perception, memory, imagination [819].

heroes, founded families and cities, fashioned the cosmos, measured time.[187] The abstractions emerging from these poetic forms of sense-making would be later reified by men of the third age as real substances, essences, or forms, the "objective referents" of philosophic or scientific knowledge. Citing, for example, the poetic use of "the verb *contemplari* for observing the parts of the sky whence the auguries came," Vico says "contemplation" is the "observation" "of the heavens with the bodily eyes" that takes place in the "science of auguries," from which came the "first *theoremata* and *mathemata,* things divine or sublime to contemplate," "eventuat[ing]" in turn in "metaphysical and mathematical abstractions."[188] This process of gathering, traced in the *New Science* and proceeding, as it does, from poetic metaphysics to metaphysical abstractions, differs from the gathering of mathematicians in *Ancient Wisdom* in that it is not a subjective making *ad intra*. Since "[t]he order of ideas" follows "the order of [things, *cose*]," the process is an *ad extra* making of social *things,* such as the auguries. Vico never lets his readers forget the relation between the development of mind and the performance of social practices, insisting it is "by the progress of customs and deeds . . . the human race must have marched."[189]

There is another fundamental aspect of *educere* that accounts for the *ad extra* "bringing forth" of soul or mind, that is, subjective existence. Vico calls the poetic wisdom that follows the creation of the first poetic thing—the religion of the auspices—divination, the reading of signs in the sky, which the poets believed to be "real words, and . . . nature . . . the language of Jove." He also says of vulgar astronomy: "[T]he first peoples wrote in the skies the history of their gods and their heroes."[190] In this way he makes explicit what is implicit in his history of ideas, his belief that the practices that constitute the sciences and human wisdom—indeed, conceptualization itself—are linguistic. His history of "ideas" is, in effect, a *history of linguistic practices, always inseparable from customs and physical labor,* which he traces from concrete to abstract formulations. Thus, he tells us, from concrete images—poetic signs written in the sky—prose speech emerges, a function of the contraction of the parts of poetic speech to a single word. Correspondingly, hieroglyphs and heroic letters become vulgar letters. With vulgar genera, "the minds of the peoples grew quicker and developed powers of abstraction, and the way was prepared for the coming of the philosophers, who formed intelligible genera."[191]

[187] Ibid., 367. In tracing that development Vico reminds us of the material basis of poetic wisdom, as, for example, that chronology begins with the practice of farmers who "counted their years by their harvests of grain."

[188] Ibid., 391. See also 710–40. Beyond the wisdom of natural theology is Christian theology, the science of divine things (365–66).

[189] Ibid., 238, 739. This is the relation that idealist interpretations, such as Lilla's, reverse (Lilla, *The Making of an Anti-Modern,* 135–37.)

[190] Vico, *New Science,* 379, 729. For references to divination, see 342, 379–81.

[191] Ibid., 460. Vico gives as example the concrete particulars of the poetic phrase "the blood boils in my heart," which formed the word *ira.* He refers to a "mental language common to all

Because the linguistic process Vico traces takes place primarily in the practice of jurisprudence, Vico criticizes philosophers who interpret divination as "natural theology," saying it should be studied as civil theology. "[T]he intellect was brought into play in the great assemblies" of the commonwealth, since in the understanding of law—or rather in the intention [*jus*] expressed in the law, which was the agreement of the citizens as to "an idea of a common rational utility"—universals were formed. The Athenians understood "intention" as "spiritual in nature" because it had to do with rights not attached to corporeal things, and, thus, indivisible and eternal. Observing that the "enactment of laws" involved an "agreement in an idea of an equal utility common to all," Socrates "began to adumbrate intelligible genera or abstract universals by induction," while Plato, "reflecting that in such public assemblies the minds of particular men, each passionately bent on his private utility, are brought together in a dispassionate idea of common utility . . . raised himself to the meditation of the highest intelligible ideas of created minds, ideas which are distinct from these created minds and can reside only in God."[192] Though Vico characterizes the development from the practices of divination to jurisprudence and philosophy as the "bringing forth" of the "form of the human soul" or the "quickening of minds" enabling "the meditation of the highest intelligible ideas," his account makes clear that what he means by "souls," "minds," "intelligible ideas"—or "God," for that matter—*can only be the concepts created by the abstract language produced in public assemblies and reified as "spiritual substance."* Man is "properly only mind, body, and speech," he says, and "speech stands . . . midway between mind and body"; that is, midway between the mute language of the body and the silent abstractions of conceptual language and mathematics.[193]

In exemplifying the development of "abstract thought," in which "[w]ords are carried over from bodies . . . to signify the [words and practices] of the mind and spirit," then reified—a process analogous to Nietzsche's understanding of the creation of concepts and essences—Vico traces the emergence of the metaphysical conception of human nature from poetic physics—that is, from the images the poets had of their corporeal nature.[194] When the poets "contemplat[ed] . . . the nature of man," they "understood so little of in-

---

nations, which uniformly grasps the substance of things feasible," but this referent is one of the propositions giving "the foundations of the certain" and refers to "various articulate languages living and dead" (161–63). The term "mental," like the term "ideal," seems to mean "common." Thus he says the "mental dictionary" assigning origins "to all the diverse articulate languages" issues from "underlying agreements which . . . obtain among them." (145). See also 35, 445, 542, and *The First New Science*, 387. Vico surmises that, because of its "extreme abstractness," a number system developed last, after abstract language (642).

[192] Vico, *New Science*, 1038, 1040–41. Vico gives a subtle account of how abstract notions of "indivisible" and "eternal" are created in consideration of rights. Plato, he notes, intrudes "his doctrine of mind or intelligences: that Jove was the mind of ether, Vulcan of fire, and the like" onto the "many and various divinities" created by the poets (691).

[193] Ibid., 1045.

[194] Ibid., 237.

telligent substances . . . they did not understand the human mind itself insofar as, by dint of reflection, it opposes the senses." Thus what rational metaphysics would call "being," theological poets "understood . . . quite grossly in the sense of eating," and, Vico surmises, this must have been the first meaning of the abstract verb "*sum.*" Likewise, the poets "apprehended substance, that which stands beneath and sustains, as residing in the heels because a man stands on the base of his feet," an apprehension poetically imaged in the myth of Achilles. The poetic understanding of such abstract things as souls and spirits was similarly rooted in bodily experiences. The soul, the agent of motion the poets "thought . . . the vehicle of life" and "placed" in the air (also called *anima*), had its "subject" in veins and blood. Spirit (*animus*), the vehicle of sensation (and for Vico the agent of conation), which the poets placed in the ether, was located in "nerves and neural substance." Vico concludes, "[I]n a crude fashion [the poets] apprehended the lofty truth that ideas come to man from God, which later the natural theology of the metaphysicians proved by invincible reasoning against the Epicureans who would have it that they spring from the body."[195]

Despite this disclaimer, the truths of the "natural theology of the metaphysicians" and the eternal truths of Plato (with which Vico identifies his own philosophy), including the "doctrine of mind or intelligence," *are exactly the kinds of "lofty truths" verum-factum denies to humans.*[196] There can be no *"subjective" or "mental" life without abstract language:* "*thinking*" is a *linguistic practice,* and *philosophy* is nothing other than the *social practice derived from abstract language,* a practice developed in enacting laws in public assemblies.[197] It is no wonder that Vico concludes that, since "knowledge of . . . divine things" proceeds from diviners to lawgivers such as the Seven Sages, then to those who "wisely ordered and governed commonwealths," and only later to philosophers as metaphysics or natural theology, the "principles of metaphysics, logic, and morals issued from the market place of Athens."[198]

---

[195] Ibid., 696. See also 692–702.

[196] In *Ancient Wisdom* and the *Autobiography* Vico distinguished between ideas made by corporeal beings, which "spring from the body," and abstract, eternal ideas, including Plato's "doctrine of mind or intelligence" or the ideas of "being" or "substance" of "rational metaphysics." To avoid Aristotle's materialism Vico derives from Plato the notion of "ideal eternal law . . . observed in a universal city after the idea or design of providence" (*Autobiography*, 127, 121–22), which becomes the *storia ideale eterna* of the *New Science*. Though this and similar passages lend support to idealist interpretations of Vico, in the context of his delimitation of human truths to the made, Platonic "truths" are unknowable. What Vico wanted from Platonic philosophy, against the Aristotelian, was the notion of "mind" as causal principle, and as immanent in the world. H. P. Adams says Vico confused the Neo-Platonic notion of emanation "with the conception of God as immanent" (*The Life and Writings of Giambattista Vico* [London: George Allen & Unwin, 1935], 32).

[197] Vico could as easily have said, as Nietzsche did, that thinking is "a philosophic way of speaking without speaking aloud."

[198] Vico, *New Science,* 365, 1043. See also 342. Moreover, Vico insists that the function of philosophy is to take the place of religion in prompting virtue and inhibiting vice. He reproves

Not coincidentally, the poetic physics of the *New Science* corresponds to the account Vico gives in *Ancient Wisdom* of notions the ancient Italians had of their nature. In both works human ideas are corporeal in origin, but only in the later is Vico able to explain *how* a spiritualized conception of human nature derives from concrete images made with bodily skills. He had come to understand how natural philosophy "recapitulates" *educere,* the linguistic process of bringing forth "the form of the human soul" from giant bodies; that is, how it brings forth "forms from matter" with abstract language. The ideas of rational metaphysics—being, soul, spirit, mind, intelligent substance—are no other than "refine[ments]," "spiritualiz[ations]," "abstraction[s]" of concrete metaphors by means of the "art of writing . . . [and] any practice of counting or reckoning."[199] Only Epicureans retain a corporeal image of humans, and only in a vulgarized version, since they understand neither the linguistic nor the social nature of the process by which corporeal beings "bring forth" subjective existence. Vico's poetic physics is, ultimately, his own resolution of the conflict he himself feels between the "lofty spiritual truths of the metaphysicians" and Epicurean anthropology.[200] Both are fictive theoretical constructions made by philosophers, but neither metaphysicians nor Epicureans understand the linguistic nature of their constructs.

Philosophy reaches its high point with the practice of eloquence during the heroic age, but, with the degeneration of commonwealths, skepticism and "false eloquence" arise, undermining the *sensus communis* and leading to that decadence in which men, preoccupied with private interests, live "like wild beasts in a deep solitude of spirit and will." Turning cities back into

---

Polybius for saying if there were philosophers in the world there would be no need of religion, claiming that without the practice of the auspices there would be neither commonwealths, philosophy, science, nor virtue. Ironically, though Vico traces philosophy to the Greeks and characterizes his as Platonic philosophy as the meditation of the highest intelligible ideas, the philosophic practice he most values as nurturing virtue and inhibiting vice is the "robust and most prudent eloquence" of the Roman rhetorical tradition.

[199] Ibid., 520, 699. Lilla also discusses this passage, but to a different end. Vico, he says, historicizes "the pretensions of philosophy" to reveal that philosophic "truth is nothing but a historical by-product of religious certainty." "Only science," which reveals that truth, "seems, miraculously, to escape history's grasp, and the only freedom Vico's science offered was . . . conserving religious wisdom." Lilla does not realize Vico is describing the process by which *both* religion *and* science are constructed poetically (Lilla, *G. B. Vico,* 229–33).

[200] Vico even says the first men "understood generation in such a way that we do not know if later scholars have been able to find a better" (*New Science,* 697). In commenting on Michael Mooney's book at a session of the American Society for Eighteenth Century Studies, Gustavo Costa, referring to the influence on Vico of Thomas Willis's *The Anatome of the Brain,* for whom "[i]magination is a certain undulation or wavering of the animal Spirits" in the blood (7), "detects" Willis's "ideas" in Vico's discussion of blood, *anima,* and *animus* in "Poetic Physics" (3), adding, "We should never forget that imagination is viewed by Vico in biological terms." Vico was aware that "ancient thought was rather similar to the materialist philosophy held by the libertines and the followers of experimental science, such as Willis," and "transposed Willis' physiological data into the early intellectual history of mankind" (4). One could argue, from Costa's observation, that Vico "projected" onto his anthropology of first men a naturalism supported by the science of his day.

forests, they fall into a "barbarism of reflection" more savage than the "barbarism of sense," ending the first *corso* of human existence.[201] Vico does not say much about the men of the third age, but most interpretations do not capture the linguistically constructed nature of their subjective existence. It is generally assumed that for Vico, as for Descartes, humans are subjective beings *substantively,* and, thus, capable of epistemic knowledge, differing only in that for Vico subjectivity develops genetically from poetic origins and knowledge is delimited to what humans themselves make. But Vico's critique of Descartes, mounted on epistemological grounds in his early works, becomes radically ontological in the context of his poetic insights. *Educere,* understood as a *constructive* rather than organic or evolutionary process, *cannot* produce "mind" or "soul" in the substantive sense of Cartesian anthropology. With an imaginative language derived from corporeal skills, poets can make only words, deeds, and things, and, as that language becomes more abstract, rational, and cognitive, the deeds and things inseparable from abstract words constitute a subjective, rational way of being-in-the-world—an artifactual human way of being so familiar it is taken as natural.[202]

Though I characterize *educere* as an "ontological" process, I am aware that, strictly speaking, there is no "ontology" outside a metaphysics of identity. I use the term to emphasize that though the things of the human world, including human subjectivity, are made, they are no less real for being so. They are also true, made so in language. Thus, language is *always* poetic, *whether concrete or abstract.* The fictive reality of the human world is produced in an *interpretive* process in which words, deeds, and things poetically transform the natural world, making it useful for human "needs and utilities." In the context of Vico's master key, "ontology" has become a historical process, a hermeneutic in which the man who "does not understand . . . makes the things out of himself and becomes them by transforming himself into them." It may be "impossible that bodies should be minds," but it is just such a "credible impossibility" the poets make when they image the "thundering sky [as] Jove," and with that image the "credible impossibility" of human minds in corporeal bodies.[203]

That spiritual substances such as "soul" or "mind" or abstractions such as "rights" or "intelligible genera"—or even subjective existence itself—are fabrications of an ontologically constructive hermeneutic process is too

---

[201] Vico, *New Science,* 1101–6. Vico's belief that Greek philosophy nurtured eloquence may have been influenced by his view that the Academics were concerned with practical common sense, against the pre-Socratic focus on natural philosophy (*Study Methods,* 36–37). In *Ancient Wisdom* he similarly praises philosophy for making men "openminded, quick, magnanimous, imaginative, and prudent."

[202] Vico, *New Science,* 367.

[203] Ibid., 405, 383. Pompa and McMullin quote the latter passage to distinguish Vico's "scientific" conception of truth from poetic fantasies, which they consider "impossibilities." They are governed by the traditional distinction between the real and made, which Vico's philosophy challenges.

strange to be understood by moderns. It takes Vico twenty years to grasp the poetic nature of *educere,* a struggle his modern readers do not undertake. Even stranger are the genetic axioms derived from his master key; that is, that the "nature of [things, *cose*] is nothing but their coming into being . . . at certain times and in certain guises," that things "do not settle or endure out of their natural state."[204] These axioms are as true of such made *things* as the human mind, or knowledge, as of any other made thing. Even in the third age, humans are never *other than poets,* the sciences that constitute their "knowledge" never *other than fabricated,* their "knowing" never *other than hermeneutic understanding.* To be sure, the making of men who have made themselves a subjective way of being differs from the making of first men. Taking place in abstract languages and the social practices appropriate to them, this human making is conceptual. Vico identifies several kinds of conceptual creativity characteristic of the third age, the most important being the pedagogical practices by which beasts who have made themselves into social beings socialize their children. Though Vico's conception of the constructive power of pedagogy became more radical with his poetic insights, he had already found such claims in the rhetorical tradition. And, even in his earliest writings, he had distinguished between two kinds of pedagogical practices, each productive of a distinct way of being human and of a distinct way of doing philosophy. Too early an emphasis on the skills of criticism and judgment, he insisted, leads to uncivil ways of being in the world and produces Cartesian thinkers, while the arts of topics and oratory nurture that prudential wisdom so essential for social existence, and produce philosopher-historians.[205]

Besides the constructive processes of pedagogy, the dominant form of conceptual creativity in the third age is the making of rational truths and systems of knowledge with the abstract languages created in the marketplaces and "great assemblies" of the heroic. As he had with pedagogy, even before the poetic insights of the *New Science* Vico had realized that human knowledge was fabricated with language. Indeed, in *Ancient Wisdom* the mathematician not only creates by naming, he does so on the model of divine gathering, a linguistic making *ad extra.* Yet even in the *New Science* Vico

---

[204] Ibid., 147, 134.

[205] That pedagogy enables men to make more humane ways of being is dramatically exemplified in Vico's account of his own self-making, in which he resists Cartesian philosophy and makes himself into not only a social being but also a philosopher-historian. He explains that ability with a myth akin to the fall of humanity into bestial isolation, and the need of the gentiles to create their human existence. His own isolation was due to his fall when he was seven—literally, from a ladder—which rendered him unconscious, gave him a melancholy and irritable temperament "such as belongs to men of ingenuity and depth," and kept him from formal schooling, forcing him to become an autodidact. That event was reinforced by his nine-year absence from Naples during the rise of Cartesian thought and his idiosyncratic study of languages, poetry, history, and jurisprudence. While analytic pedagogy produced "arid and dry" humans who create rational philosophies, Vico's autodidacticism fit him for civil life, enabling him to discover his master key (*Autobiography,* 111–26).

does not always draw out the implications of his understanding that all conceptual knowing is a linguistic making. He is clear that mathematics, natural law theories, rational philosophies, and sciences of nature are fictive, but writes as if the "lofty spiritual truths of Platonic metaphysicians" are somehow exceptions.[206] But for Vico, "lofty spiritual truths," as well as the rational ideas and systems his contemporaries believed to be eternal truths they did not create, could only be linguistic constructs, narratives written in an abstract language genetically derived from a poetic one, forms of knowing that "forget" the poetic origin and genetic process that produce them.

Certainly Vico considers his philosophy a new "science."[207] But science is a "knowledge of causes," and in the *New Science* causes have become poetic, and "knowers" only those who understand their "truths" as made. Vico's autodidacticism had protected him from the amnesia of the moderns, enabling him to make a way of "knowing" that recovers poetic origins, to understand that *all* ways of knowing are genetically related to originary poetic wisdom, divination, the "science" of reading the divine language in the sky. He describes the "divining" of new scientists by saying, "[H]e who meditates this Science narrates to himself this ideal eternal history so far as he himself makes it for himself," and, since "this world of nations has certainly been made by men," it "cannot be more certain than when he who creates the things also narrates them." He thus establishes a relation between a meditator who meditates, narrates, and makes for himself the ideal eternal history, and "he who creates the things," which I take to be the original creators of the things of the historical world. Verene interprets this meditation, narration, and making as "recollective *fantasia*," in which the mind recovers the imagistic origins of conceptual thought and "reflect[s] in a *one to one fashion* the elements in the memory structure of original or mythic *fantasia* . . . the form of thought whereby Vico reaches a knowledge of the first humans . . . from the inside."[208] Making thus *remakes* the original process, producing a *vera narratio* of recollective imagination.[209] Verene supports this interpretation with the rhetorical notion of *topoi*, the "places" or images that

---

[206] From the Middle Ages a debate was carried on between constructivist and realist views of scientific theory, with the realism of Kepler and Galileo carrying the day. Though Vico assumed the constructed nature of geometric truths, he could just as well have considered physics a constructed science. For a Kuhnian interpretation of Vico's conception of science, see Raymond D. Pruitt, "The Sciences, The Humanities, and the Illusion of Progress: A Comment on Kuhn's *Structure of Scientific Revolutions* and Berlin's *Divorce Between the Sciences and Humanities*," *Perspectives in Biological Medicine* 25, no. 1 (autumn 1981).

[207] See Vico, *New Science*, 346.

[208] Verene, *Science of Imagination*, 99–101. Emphasis added. Vico himself, however, points out that understanding is neither memory nor imagination "since understanding . . . has nothing to go on where facts are not supplied by the senses" (738, 662). Moreover, Verene can only assume a relation between the understanding of new scientists and the sensory images of poets by assuming a subjective *homoiousis* between them.

[209] Ibid., 156.

constitute memory for the rhetor, a kind of "inner writing."[210] When "meditated by the individual, that 'inner writing'" comprises "a direct narration of the . . . causes of the human world." Yet, though Verene calls the *New Science* a literary "science of narration . . . that presents in language the inner . . . life of humanity,"[211] it is so for him not as a *linguistic* construction, but as an *epistemic* recovery of "inner writing," itself the "divine structure of the world," the ideal eternal history.[212] Rhetoric is merely handmaid to epistemology, and meditation and narration activities of mind.

If such a subjective mnemotechnic is not possible in a poetic science about the linguistic making of embodied beings, as I argue, what can it mean to "meditate," "narrate," and "make" an ideal eternal history?[213] Insofar as original poetic wisdom, the divining of the hidden in the divine language written in the sky, was an interpretive activity inseparable from words, deeds, things in the world, it was creative, transforming corporeal beings in the very act of interpretation. So too, the meditation and narration of philosopher-historians, as hermeneutic activities, are creative, producing meaning in words, deeds, and things in the world.[214] Ironically, the view that language is constructive and "knowledge" is interpretation is held today not by Vichians but by postmodern writers, whose skepticism toward epistemology's foundational assumptions leads them to believe that all human sense-making is hermeneutical.[215] Vico's "new scientific" hermeneutic differs from originary poetic hermeneutic, of course, since philosopher-historians, unlike the first poets, understand that their *verum* is *factum*. Though that hermeneutical "knowing" is not epistemic, as a "knowing" of causes it is *scienza* nonetheless, the self-referential "knowing" of "knowers" that they themselves are makers of what they know. Vico had come to the same understanding of *verum-factum* as Cusa, that it renders impossible the satisfaction

---

[210] Though Verene draws on Grassi's rhetorical interpretation of language, Grassi himself rethought rhetorical speech in terms of Heidegger's more radical conception of language as "showing."

[211] Verene, *Science of Imagination,* 188–91, 165.

[212] Verene, "Imaginative Universals and Narrative Truth," 14, 17.

[213] Indeed, if the genetic origin of abstract thought is poetic language, then the conception of memory as a subjective or introspective process, as, for example, in Augustine, must be rejected. If, as Nietzsche and Foucault believe, history is genealogy, so too is memory.

[214] Heidegger himself uses the term "meditative" to describe a hermeneutic occurring in the world: "The meditative man is to experience the untrembling heart of unconcealment . . . the place of stillness that gathers in itself what first grants unconcealment . . . the possible presencing of presence itself" ("The End of Philosophy and the Task of Thinking," 444–45; see also *The Question Concerning Technology,* 18–19).

[215] Vico's hermeneutic differs from German idealism's hermeneutic of recovery, which presupposed a subjective *homoiousis* between hermeneut and object. Hilliard Aronovitch, arguing that for Vico knowing is hermeneutic, similarly denies it is *Verstehen* ("Vico and *Verstehen*," *Vico: Past and Present,* ed. Giorgio Tagliacozzo [Atlantic Highlands: Humanities Press, 1981], vol. 1, 216–26). We differ in that I claim that not only historical understanding but *original* making are ontologically constructive hermeneutics.

of theoretic curiosity, that the "basic form of cognitive acts" is a "self-en-
closed game" in which "[h]uman being itself alone is the goal of the creative
process founded on it. Man does not go beyond himself when he is creator:
rather . . . he comes to himself."[216] Only when philological study enables
philosopher-historians to divine the *certum* of history as *factum* can they
grasp the reflexive *verum* that original creators could not "know":[217] the
"truth," or, rather, hermeneutic understanding, that all true things are made,
that she who understands that "truth" is, as the genetic descendant of original creators, herself its creator.[218]

As poetic divination generated true things rather than "truths," so too the
hermeneutic "meditation" of philosopher-historians produces true things,
not "truths."[219] What for the moderns is a subjectively grounded epistemic
recovery of the past is, in Vico's "new science," the creation of literary nar-

[216] Hans Blumenberg, *The Legitimacy of the Modern Age,* trans. Robert M. Wallace (Cambridge: MIT Press, 1986), 526, 533, 535–36. Quotations are to Cusa, *Compendium* VIII, VI;
De ludo globi II; *De coniecturis* I, 13. Cusa, however, like Philo, can retain some form of epistemology because he assumes that God and man are subjective beings. Philo claims that man
derives knowledge of astronomy mediately from God, a knowledge that includes man's understanding of his dependence on God as the source of truth; Cusa, that man knows mathematics
because, as *imago Dei,* he creates it. Philo's position is possible because his conception of God
is modeled on the Timaean Architect; Cusa's, because his is Neoplatonic.

[217] Verene claims that though in the first book of *Universal Law* Vico says, "[C]ertum est
pars veri," he denies that relation in the *New Science* and distinguishes between *certo* and *vero*
(*Science of Imagination,* 56). I argue that, when causes became poetic, *certum* is inherently *factum.* Indeed, if philologists and philosophers derive genetically from poets, if abstract language
and subjective practices are constructed, the relation between philology and philosophy must
be rethought; neither can be epistemic disciplines in the traditional sense. Though Vico distinguishes between consciousness of the certain and knowledge of the true (138–40), the distinction can only be between different characterizations of conceptual fabrication. Since the certain
and true are gatherings of words, philology and philosophy must be interpretive forms of reading, differing in that philosophic reading understands readers as creators or "gatherers" of the
words they read.

[218] Hermeneutic reflexivity is not self-reflection, which is cognitive. Verene distinguishes his
position from Pompa's emphasis on "reflection," while acknowledging that the two are "quite
close" (*Science of Imagination,* 155 n. 72). Pompa supports his argument with paragraph 80 in
the first *New Science.* Vico says, "[S]olely by the force of our understanding, we have entered
the nature of the first men" (*Selected Writings,* 120), which for Pompa means that the historian
can know the *causes* of the historical processes that produced him. But in 80 Vico also says,
"[T]he things which we have here conceived must be identical with the innermost substance of
our soul," and Pompa's interpretation of "reflection" assumes that the subjective "soul" of the
historian is identical with the subjective soul of poets. But if the soul is a product of corporeal
skills of perception, memory, imagination, what is recovered cannot be so as "reflection."
Verene's and Pompa's positions are variations on the theme of epistemic cognition, while
hermeneutic reflexivity is a relation through which "knowers" understand that what they
"know" is a linguistic construct they have created.

[219] Vico's use of the term "meditation" is itself textual, not subjective. In referring to the
copying of books before the invention of printing, he says, "[T]here is no better exercise than
this; we meditate on the text and write without haste or interruption. . . . By copying, we gain,
not a perfunctory knowledge, but an intimate familiarity with the original, and we are, so to
speak, transformed into the author's very self" (*Study Methods,* 73). Alternately in *Ancient Wisdom* he associates "meditation" with Descartes, whom he calls the "Great Meditator" (53) and
a meditator of innate ideas (162).

ratives about originary poetic creativity.[220] As the first men made true things with language, so Vico as philosopher-historian genetically related to those poets makes a narrative about human creativity, as certain and true as any *factum* of the human world. The *New Science* is, thus, a *poetic* science, and it is so in three senses. First, like all human things, it is a *factum* made with language. But, in a sense that no original *factum* can be, a poetic science is also a *science* of *poiesis,* since *as a science* it meditates on the certains [*certa*] of the historical world, understands that they are made things [*facta*], and understands the *verum* convertible with all made things—that all human trues are made. And, in a third sense, as the hermeneutic understanding of a "knower" that she is a creator, a poetic science is *itself* a poetic *way of "knowing."* As such, the *New Science* is as "fictive" as the human world is "artifactual." But, just as there is no "real" human world other than an artifactual one, so there are no "true" narratives, however abstract or methodic, that are not fictive. In the context of a master key revealing the linguistic construction of human meaning, the distinction between real and made, fictive and true, can no longer be made.

There is, of course, no subjective *homoiousis* between philosopher-historians and first men grounding their hermeneutic understanding that their *verum* is poetic *factum*. There is, however, a "homogeneity" based on performance. In his narrative Vico himself performatively enacts his understanding that he is genetically related to the first men who created meaning with language; that his narrative is a poetic *factum;* that he differs from his poetic ancestors in "knowing" that he creates his trues. Further, he tells us he is a creator by distinguishing his science from geometry in that it creates for itself the world of nations "*but with a reality greater by just so much as the [things] having to do with human affairs are more real than points, lines, surfaces, and figures are.*"[221] Even more, he distinguishes his new science from the rational texts of scientists and philosophers who have forgotten the

[220] Vico himself makes clear the genetic relation between meditative "thought"—the *vera narratio* of the philosopher-historian—and language—mute speech, the *vera narratio* of the poets—in his etymology of *logos.* Though philosophy defines *logos* as thought or reason, its "first and proper meaning was *fabula,* fable, carried over into Italian as *favella,* speech," which in Greek is "*mythos,* myth, whence comes the Latin *mutus,* mute." Vico surmises that "speech was born in mute times as mental language"—by which he means bodily gestures and acts— "whence *logos* means both word and idea." "It was fitting," he adds, "that the matter should be so ordered by divine providence in religious times, for it is an eternal property of religions that they attach more importance to meditation"—that is, mute language—"than to speech." "Thus the first language . . . must have begun with signs, whether gestures or physical objects. . . . Similarly, *mythos* came to be defined for us as *vera narratio,* or true speech" (401). And, similarly, the *logos* of philosophy genetically derived from *mythos* can never be *logos* as *ratio,* but must itself be the *vera narratio* or true mute speech of the philosopher, his own narratives.

[221] Vico, *New Science,* 349. Emphasis added. The unity of knowing and creating was immanent in the social world as well. Beyond narrative making, the "knowing" of philosopher-historians strengthens the skills of imagination and eloquence, making possible the prudential practices on which human society depends.

poetic origins of their texts, by creating it in his own metaphoric language. He calls his first men *giganti* and *grossi bestioni,* the pattern of history *storia ideale eterna,* history itself a *corso,* then *ricorso.* Vico's metaphors are ironic, to be sure, because he not only creates them but also knows them to be creations.[222] They remind his readers that Vico knows that his narrative does not correspond "in a one to one fashion" to images in the imaginative "minds" of original makers, or to actual events, or to an ideal pattern, but is his own true *factum.* They remind his readers that the only way of "knowing" that escapes the barbarism of reflection is one that remembers its poetic origin. How ironic that Vico's readers find the *New Science* obscure precisely because of the metaphors that tell them they cannot read the *New Science* epistemically, but as a narrative.[223]

[222] Vico identifies irony with the age of reflection (408). Though it is "fashioned of falsehood" because, since man can distinguish between figurative and literal speech, he is capable of lying, it is also essential for the self-reflexive hermeneutic of historical study.

[223] Hayden White, who does appreciate the metaphoric nature of the *New Science,* finds in it a "strict analogy between the dynamics of metaphorical transformations in language and the transformations of both consciousness and society" ("The Tropics of History: The Deep Structure of the *New Science," Science of Humanity,* ed. Giorgio Tagliacozzo and Donald Phillip Verene [Baltimore: Johns Hopkins University Press, 1976], 65–85, 76; see also 72–78). Though White says Vico appeals to consciousness as "constituting the world," he identifies "consciousness" as "the active and creative force" of language, saying, "The most significant difference between the first edition of the *New Science* (1725) and the last edition (1744) was the expansion of . . . the *creative* aspects of language. In the first edition, Vico does little more than assert that language is the clue to the understanding of primitive man's construction of a world in which he can feel at home"; in the last, his "insights into language and consciousness . . . break down the opposition of truth to fable." "Truth and fable are no more *opposed* than science and poetry," White continues, and suggests a third kind of knowledge between the literally true and the fabulous—the fictive—which transforms "the notion of the fabulous into a generic concept, generally descriptive of consciousness, of which the literally true and the poetic are species. If we admit the use of the notion of the fictive as a way of designating the general nature of human consciousness, we can then regard the true and the fabulous as simply *different* ways of signifying the relationship of human consciousness to the world . . . in different *degrees* of certitude and comprehension" ("The Irrational and the Problem of Historical Knowledge in the Enlightenment," *Tropics of Discourse: Essays in Cultural Criticism* [Baltimore: Johns Hopkins University Press, 1985], 135–49, 143–45). Irrationality and rationality themselves become no other than stages of a process directed by a pre-rational factor, speech. White limits the notion of the fictive to Vico's epistemological and psychological views, however, insisting Vico retains a distinction between an "aesthetic apprehension of reality" and a scientific or philosophic view. White himself is not primarily interested in the poetic language of Vico's age of gods but in the tropological character of language determining historical development and structuring the constructed historical narratives of the third age, rendering them poetic rather than epistemic: "The root metaphor of Vico's conception of history, then, is to be found in the theory of linguistic transformation that he used as a model of both consciousness's relation to its objects and the dynamics of consciousness's transformations in time" (84). In general White's view of constructive language is more structural, mine more hermeneutic.

Robert P. Crease is another commentator who emphasizes the narrative nature of the *New Science,* identifying its subject as an always "indefinite" human nature. Vico's injunction to narrate to oneself the ideal eternal history is an injunction to make a story by which humans are "known." "To apprehend human nature, one must know, not an essence or definition, but a story. The narrative provided by the *New Science* is therefore the essential vehicle by which human nature comes to be recognized by human beings: narrative for Vico is the means—the *only* means—of human self-recognition. . . . The actualization of self achieved through the narration

Vico reinforces the most radical implication of his master key—that humans are *always* creators—with the two most important metaphors he creates in the *New Science*. The first is divine providence. He calls the *New Science* a rational civil theology of divine providence because it is a "history of the [things] by which, without human discernment or counsel, and often against the designs of men, providence has ordered this great city of the human race." Providence functions in the *New Science* to insure the realization of social goals from private, egocentric choices. This notion—analogous to the modern notion of the "heterogeneity of ends"—enables Vico to distinguish the *New Science* from the philosophies of Stoics, Epicureans, and natural philosophers, all of whom are ignorant of the "providential" realization of social ends.[224] When the ironic metaphor "providence" is understood as a *transcendent* being, humans are understood as "divine" merely in the sense of remaking, epistemologically, the *storia ideale eterna,* the providential structure of history. This is the sense in which Verene calls the *storia ideale eterna* the "master universal" of the *New Science*. Though this onto-theological interpretation of providence is dominant in the literature, it does not, I believe, capture the radical sense in which the *New Science* is a "science of the divine and a divine science."[225] What Vico calls "providential"—the realization of social goals—can only be the effects that necessarily follow from the creation of the true things of the social world. While those true things—the artworks that set that world into place—emerge from *unintended* individual choices, they *must* satisfy beastly needs and utilities, and can *only* do so within the limits of natural necessity. This is why Vico specifies that the age of gods, "which everywhere . . . begin[s] in religion . . . correspond[s] to certain first necessities or utilities" that can be satisfied only by specific social customs.[226] Marveling at the "simplicity" and "naturalness" with which providence, against chance and fate, realizes social ends from unintended, individual choices, he equates "simplicity" and "naturalness" with the reduction of the "immense number of civil effects to four causes, the four elements of the civil world . . . religion, marriage, asylum and the first agrarian

---

. . . is not described but *produced*." I agree, but add that narration does not merely produce "self-recognition" or "self-presentation," but has the ontological function of *making* the narrator a *creator* of a narrative about the creative nature of humans (Robert P. Crease, "Narrative, the *Scienza Nuova*, and the Barbarism of Reflection," *Studies in Eighteenth-Century Culture*, vol. 24 [1994]: 107–19, 113–15). Crease himself goes on to undermine the constructive implications of his interpretation by calling "self-apprehension" an "epistemological triumph," adding that Vico "appears to fulfill the Cartesian model of knowledge."

[224] Vico, *New Science*, 342, 385.

[225] Verene considers the *storia ideale eterna,* the "master trope" of the *New Science*, an "inner writing" or providential structure recollected by the philosopher-historian (*Science of Imagination*, 156, 108, 116–22). Thus narrative making is not merely "an analogue of divine activity, but the true story of the presence of the divine as providence in human institutions" (56). Humans are "God-like in our making of its knowledge. God makes by knowing" (156).

[226] Vico, *New Science*, 734. For example, "in order to have a prospect of the open sky whence came the auspices," the beasts inevitably set fire to the forests (539).

law," meaning the social practices and physical labor inseparable from these elements.[227] Whatever Vico's theological beliefs, in the context of his new science providence works wholly through natural, immanent means.[228]

Even more revealing of the poetic nature of the new science than Vico's use of the metaphor "providence" is his explanation of why providence is called "divine." "*Divinari,*" he says, to divine, means to understand "what is hidden *from* men—the future—or what is hidden *in* them, their consciousness."[229] In this way Vico associates "divine providence" *functionally* with the interpretive practice of "divining," the reading of what is "hidden *in* [human] consciousness"—that is, the choices humans make that unintentionally lead to the social ends hidden *from* them in "the future."[230] Choices are hidden in "consciousness" because the "consciousness" by which men make their choices *is none other than the linguistic and social practices that constitute the sensus communis*. Thus, for example, in "divining" the mute language they projected onto the sky, the poets imaged it as Jove, unintentionally making the world meaningful by creating mind in nature and, in the process, setting into place their social world.[231] The divining that Vico urges philosopher-historians to practice—the divining of mind in the "economy of civil [things]"—is "divine" in the sense that poetic divining is not, since it is a reflexive form of the divining or gathering that the poets practiced unknowingly. In divining the civil "things" created by poetic language, the philosopher-historian similarly creates "mind"—that is, creates human meaning out of the *facta* of the past in a historical narrative—but knows he is doing so. He tells his readers so performatively: as the poets called the mind they created in nature "Jove," Vico as philosopher-historian ironically calls the one he creates in his historical narrative "divine providence."[232]

[227] Ibid., 630. See also 561, 557, 586, 981–98. Vico exemplifies the "simplicity" and "naturalness" with which providence works by recounting how the first men found the "perennial springs" that insured the cultivation of fields. They followed the eagles whom they believed sacred to Jove, to perform the auspices (287).

[228] Vico was a devout Catholic, but Catholicism allowed for the separation of faith and philosophy, and the relation between knowing and making precluded philosophic knowing of a transcendent Being.

[229] For a more complete discussion of the relation of providence to the notion of the "heterogeneity of ends," see Luft, "Creative Activity in Vico and the Secularization of Providence," *Studies in Eighteenth Century Culture.*

[230] Vico, *New Science,* 342. See also 365, 379, 381. In 343–54 Vico gives a "divine argument" for the "naturalness," orderliness, and social function of human [practices], since divine providence unfolds "its [practices] by means as easy as the natural customs of men." Mali similarly interprets divination as "foresight," akin to the prophesies of the Hebrew prophets (*Rehabilitation,* 107). Mali gives an interesting discussion of providence and divination, mediating between natural-human and theological interpretations (93–107).

[231] My likening divination to the hermeneutic of the rabbis may seem incompatible with Vico's claim that the Hebrews themselves were prevented from divination (167, 365). But the Hebrews were prohibited from divining the language that primitives projected onto nature. They, of course, had no need to do so, since they had the Torah.

[232] Vico, *New Science,* 342. Though my secularized interpretation of providence differs from Grassi's, I believe it is compatible, since the "naturalism" of Grassi's understanding of humanism is apparent in his discussion of providence. Grassi acknowledges that for Vico "history is

The term "divination" expresses Vico's belief that the "choices" with which the poets realize social goals are not consciously intended but are interpretive responses to natural necessity that satisfy "needs and utilities"; that divining is a skill immanent in those choices. That such a "providential" skill is not a *transcendent* but *functional* divinity "hidden in men" may be a "metaphysical assumption" on Vico's part, but it is no more metaphysical than the assumption of a transcendent providence. In effect, Vico has gone beyond metaphysics in the *New Science,* and the image of providence is, rather, a poetic way of accounting for the showing up of artworks that set up meaningful historical worlds, without appeal to purposeful agency, divine or human. For this reason "divine providence" is one of the two "master tropes" in the *New Science* that I find more significant than the *storia ideale eterna* that Verene identifies as such, an ironic trope of the originary trope "Jove," both of which poetically image the "mind" or "order" that poets and philosopher-historians alike "divine" in nature and history. In creating an ironic metaphor of the poetic trope, Vico tells his readers he "knows" that "mind" is the "divining" activity of humans themselves, that the "divine" is neither the *factum* "Jove" nor the *factum* "providence," but, functionally, the ingenious divining of poets and philosopher-historians alike. Thus, an even more "masterful" trope of the *New Science* than providence is that of the gentile fathers as poets, "creators" who create poetic universals. The *New Science* is a "divine science" in that it is a science of beings who are godlike in creating real things, and who create even as God creates, with language and the work of their hands. More important, it is a divine science in that the trues that the philosopher-historian knows are, like those of God's, convertible with his making, that *what* he knows is that *he is their creator.* In grasping the sense in which humans secularize divine creativity, Vico could have said with more truth what he said in *Ancient Wisdom,* that, as "God is the artificer of nature, [so] man is the God of artifacts."[233]

---

not created by men as such, but . . . determined by a superior order," that order is "the priority of poetry as the determining factor in man's historical world," and that "it is in poetry where our search should begin to find Divine Providence." "All of Vico's philosophy," he continues, "aims to prove how eternal civil history establishes an order through the theory of genius, fantasy, and the metaphysical word, a *natural providence. . . .* The necessity from which history springs forth is, in its originarity, *natural* and *abysmal.*" Grassi acknowledges that Vico says that in their natural state men desire "something superior to nature to save them," but adds, "[T]he only order that appeared was the inexorable continuity of history within which man arose, lived, and perished." The historical actor "can maintain not that 'I think therefore I am' but 'I die therefore I am.'" That is the "tragic character of existence" that Vico, and before him "Sophocles and Heraklitos," expresses. From the importance that divine providence plays in the *New Science,* Grassi concludes that the "anthropological perspective is absent from Vico's thought. Men are persons not by themselves but only in relation to whether they abide or not by [a superior] order. The *New Science* identifies this order in Divine Providence, and in this sense Vico's work reveals his religious intention," that of overcoming Stoic fate and Epicurean chance by showing that history answers the natural needs of men as a species (Grassi, *Vico and Humanism,* 193–98; emphasis added).

[233] Vico, *Ancient Wisdom,* 97. There is, of course, a distinction between moderns who create with the abstract, technical language of philosophy and science, and those who create his-

Ultimately, the difference between identifying the master trope of the *New Science* as the *storia ideale eterna* or as the poet-fathers of the race *depends on one's understanding of the nature of convergence*—that is, depends on whether one understands making as a function of knowing, or as equivalent with it.[234] One cannot appreciate the ontological power of the divine creativity that Vico attributes to humans in the context of traditional conceits about the nature of creativity—the Neoplatonic conceit that creativity is intellectual and mimetic, for example, or rhetoric's notion that "inventiveness" is the perception of similarities. Even Vico, who, in his early writings, identified perception, memory, and imagination as skills of the body, was unable to get beyond subjective conceptions of creativity until the last edition of the *New Science,* when he grasped its linguistic nature. He was forced to his "new science of *poiesis*" by insights it took him twenty years to understand—the radical incapacity of the first men, their need for a "maximum of constructive potentiality" in the face of a "minimum of ontological predisposition." Neither in rhetoric nor in his onto-theological tradition could Vico find such an abyssal sense of the human condition, or a recourse radical enough to alleviate it.[235]

That Vico found such a recourse in the ontological creativity of language is further obscured by the fact that there are not one but three distinct conceptions of creativity in the *New Science:* that of God, of poets, and of philosopher-historians genetically related to them. While Vico identifies the conception of God's creativity with a God who "in his purest intelligence, knows things, and, by knowing them, creates them," he distinguishes the creativity of the first men from that version, since they "created things according to their own ideas. But this creation was infinitely different from that of God . . . [because] they, in their robust ignorance, did it by virtue of a wholly corporeal imagination. And because it was quite corporeal, they did it with marvelous sublimity; a sublimity such and so great that it excessively perturbed the very persons who by imagining did the creating, for which they were called 'poets,' which is Greek for 'creators.'" The God whose creativ-

---

torical narratives with a language they understand as metaphoric. The latter retain the memory of man's poetic origins and understand the finitude of his constructs; the former, forgetting those origins and "enframed" by their constructs, fall into barbarism.

[234] Mali is closer to the mark in calling the *storia ideale eterna* a "conscious 'myth', a modern historical one . . . but one which, like the ancient myths . . . was true for his maker—a 'true narration' of the modern historian of civilization." He too emphasizes the relation between first men and historians, since both "equally participate in the same narrative process of making history insofar as they both make and remake its constitutive narrative myth for themselves . . . a fictive pattern." Indeed, "pagan mythological divinations . . . sacred Biblical prophecies . . . Vico's Science" and those the reader narrates to himself are all "true narratives." Mali, however, ultimately makes narration mimetic of an "ideal and eternal account of history" (Mali, *Rehabiliation,* 132–35; see also 71, 209). I consider narratives *linguistic constructs,* just as the trues of history are.

[235] Not even the fallen were as bereft of humanity as the *giganti.* Vico could, of course, have found such an abyssal sense in the nihilism of skeptics, but like Nietzsche his ultimate solution— a poetic anthropology—overcomes nihilism through creativity.

ity Vico distinguishes from that of his poets is the intellectual deity of Neo-platonism, while the creativity of the poets, a function of a corporeal imag-ination derived from bodily skills of perception, memory, and *ingenium,* manifests itself in a concrete, metaphoric, ontologically eventful language. That is why the poets, too impoverished to create as the mathematicians of *Ancient Wisdom* did, could create a world of nations "with a reality greater by just so much as the [things] having to do with human affairs are more real than points, lines, surfaces, and figures are."[236] The theological paradigm of a deity who brings into existence *ad extra* a concretely real human world where none had existed, and who does so with originary language and the labor of his hands, is not the intellectual Architect of the *Timaeus* but a poet-God. That Vico's distinction between two conceptions of divine creativity *is a distinction between two conceptions of God* has not been apparent to read-ers whose understanding of Genesis is filtered through an onto-theological tradition.

Besides the creativity of a Neoplatonic god and of poets who secularize the linguistic creativity of the God of Genesis, there is a third creative process in the *New Science,* that of men of the third age. *All* men of the third age are poets; they *must* be so, since, genetically, they derive from poets and heroes who, with an originary language, created their subjective ways of being-in-the-world. And, since "things do not settle or endure out of their natural state," the abstract languages they created with their poetic language, and with which they made their subjective existence, *are themselves poetic.* With those abstract languages, the men of the third age continue to create. First, they make their pedagogic practices and ways of knowing. Those who are made "subjects" by an education stressing analytic and critical skills use their abstract languages to produce sciences, philosophies, ideologies, conceptual truths they reify and project onto the world. Unable to remember or to re-cover the poetic origins of their languages, never understanding that they cre-ate their "truths," these "rational subjects" create, but their creativity is not "divine." The creativity of philosopher-historians is so, however, because their humanist pedagogical practices enable them to divine the reflexive "truth" that their "trues" are narratives, the *facta* of their own linguistic making. That divine convergence of *verum* and *factum,* does not, of course, yield epistemic knowledge, since the metaphysical ground of epistemology, a subjective *homoiousis* between knower and object of knowledge, does not exist. The "knowing" of philosopher-historians—that is, their knowing that they make their own historical and narrative trues—is a "divinatory"—that is, interpretive—process that takes place *in language.* That the men of the third age, and their "knowing," are themselves poetic, is not appreciated, however, because of the modern conceit that men of the third age, unlike those of the first, are not creators, but knowers of an objective reality. But

[236] Vico, *New Science,* 376, 349.

he who meditates or divines the *facta* of the past and creates his own narrative trues understands that they too are *facta;* that, as the descendent of the
first men, he is, like them, a divine creator who creates meaning with language. Attaining that hermeneutic understanding, Vico narrates it performatively, creating an ironic narrative in his own metaphoric language. The
certainty that the *New Science* yields derives from the fact that "he who creates the things also narrates them," and the divine pleasure Vico experiences
"in his mortal body" is palpable when he adds, "And this very fact is an argument, O reader, that these proofs are of a kind divine and should give thee
a divine pleasure, since in God knowledge and creation are one and the same
thing."[237]

Vico's grasp of a linguistic and concrete creativity unconditioned by subjectivity forces him to accept the ontological and skeptical implications of
verum-factum that Blumenberg tries desperately to exorcise. Awareness of
the original poverty of the human condition, of the need for a *poiesis* unconditioned by knowing in an abyssal world, forces him to embrace the
absoluteness of art in as existential a sense as Blumenberg attributes to Nietzsche, and, with Cusa, to accept the epistemic limits of that creativity, the
reflexive "knowing" that "human being alone is the goal of the creative
process." While there are vast differences between Vico's and Nietzsche's
conceptions of human existence, language, and creativity, both are unflinch-
ing in accepting the tragic consequences of their insights—that humans are
never other than creators, their reality never other than artifactual and finite,
their "truths" never other than fictive.

The Uncanny Poetic Humanism of the New Science

The sense of original human incapacity that Vico and Nietzsche share recurs, for Blumenberg, as an epochal phenomenon in the dialectical struggle
between belief in cosmic order and acosmic challenges to it. The modern
age's response to that latter crisis—an existential assertion, formulated in the
verum-factum principle, of an absolute foundation of knowledge in human
reason—appropriates a "maximum of constructive potentiality" in the face
of a "minimum of ontological predisposition." Though Blumenberg models
that "maximum" on the Hebraic conception of divine omnipotence, his interpretation retains a remnant of the belief in cosmic order that his own ac-

---

[237] Ibid., 349, 345. Gustavo Costa rejects Bedani's argument that the phrase "modification
of the mind of him who meditates it" refers to first men, not the historian, and sides with Pompa
that the "meditation" of the historian can take place only insofar as a developmental relation
exists between first "minds" and the mind of the historian. That relation establishes the *homoiousis* between knower and object necessary for knowledge, and Bedani's naturalism leads
him to reject such an idealist relation, assumed by Berlin and Verene as well as Pompa. Costa
is right that Vico believes there is *some* relation between the first men and historian allowing
for "meditation" and "narration," but, I argue, it is a poetic, performative relation rather than
subjective.

count of the challenges to it renders illusory, the belief in human subjectivity. It is that remnant against which Vico and Nietzsche, alone among the moderns, take aim. Insisting on the illusory nature of that belief and the nihilism to which it leads, both accept the tragic implications of creation in the abyss.

Writing at the end of the modern age, Heidegger confirms Vico's judgment, at its beginning, of the nihilistic tendencies of theoretic knowledge and the reduction of theory to technique. He too finds a "saving power" in a new way of being-human in the world. Reminding us that "[b]eing subject as humanity has not always been the sole possibility belonging to the essence of historical man," he warns that "truth as the certainty of subjectivity" conceals those disclosing events that reveal a different way of being human. Heidegger calls that "certainty of subjectivity" "humanist" because it is anthropocentric. From the perspective of subjectivity the world shows up only as humans say it must, thus "devaluing" what subjectivity values as "only an object for man's estimation."[238] Heidegger struggles to describe that new way of being human in-the-world, and, from "Letter on Humanism," his efforts are fueled by his critique of humanism.

I share Grassi's belief in the affinity between Heidegger and Vico. It is an affinity that characterizes nomadic writers who, unable to accept on faith the foundational assumptions of the West, confront the more abyssal problem of beginnings. For most—Sophists, Latin and Renaissance humanists, Vico, Nietzsche, postmodern writers—the power of language is the source of that order, meaning, and value of a historical world not given in nature. Grassi himself works as hard to naturalize Vico's "divine" poetic language as he does to avoid the mystification in Heidegger's notion of Being, and draws out the affinities of each with Marx. He does so with Vico by suggesting a naturalistic base between human needs and the poetic perception of the world. In pointing out that "[a]lready in classical Greek thought Pythagoras set forth the proposition that the similar can be grasped only through something similar [*similia similibus comprehendere*]," he suggests a *similitudo* that can take the place of the subjective *homoiousis* that grounds epistemology for the tradition. "The questions that urge themselves upon human beings arise only from the 'humanization of nature'," he says, and asks, "[H]ow does this 'humanization of nature' take place if not through *ratio*?" He answers, "[N]ature possesses a meaning only in regard to human needs. This presupposes that we discover a relation, a *similitudo*, between what the senses reveal to us and our needs." Since "[i]nsight into relationships basically is not possible through a process of inference but rather only . . . [through] invention and discovery [*inventio*]," similitude, he concludes, is *poetically made*.[239]

[238] Heidegger, "Letter on Humanism," 251.
[239] Grassi, *Rhetoric as Philosophy*, 5–7.

Grassi is right to give his version of *homoiousis* both a Marxist and a po-etic character, since man's mediation with the world is through both work and "inventiveness." This naturalistic relation between human needs and what our senses "reveal" to us constitutes the *similitudo* between humans and the worlds they make in the poetic humanism I put forward. The genetic process emerging from imaginative words inseparable from deeds and things and satisfying human needs—what Funkenstein calls Vico's reinterpretation of nature, in which man acquires his second, social nature—I call an onto-logical hermeneutic. The ubiquity of natural needs and the success of those social *things* that satisfy them—the *certa* of history—insures, for Vico, the uniformity and iterability of genetic development. Without Vico's more Marxist acquiescence to natural necessity, Nietzsche and Heidegger are not able to assert "uniformity" or "iterability," and, in different ways, disdain those qualities. But unlike Marx, Vico, Nietzsche, and Heidegger believe that *human* needs cannot be met *solely* by material processes. What humanizes the world for them are "artworks," the true, though fictive, unities of words, deeds, things—languages, religions, social practices, as well as tilled fields, walled cities, and temples—all of which set up historical worlds. Grassi, who identifies the *similitudo* between needs and what our senses reveal to us as *inventio* and calls the ontological hermeneutic that emerges "humanist," de-clines to call that process anthropocentric. For him, as for Heidegger, the relation between "anthropocentrism" and subjectivity is a necessary one: neither could get beyond the idealist meaning of the term. I began this book by questioning that assumption, and asking whether an anthropocentric hu-manism is *necessarily* subjectivist and nihilistic, whether it *necessarily* leads to an epistemic, demiurgic relation between humans and nature, whether valuing from a human perspective *necessarily* objectifies an object for a sub-ject. Because Heidegger believes this is the case, he escapes the "cloud shadow" of "truth as the certainty of subjectivity" only by turning to the presencing of Being in the pre-Socratics. One can, however, get out from un-der that "cloud shadow" along paths that do not return to the pre-Socratics or even remain within Hellenic thought.

In this book I have done so by returning to a more alien understanding of beginnings. The anthropology of modernity and German idealism that Hei-degger and Grassi reject culminates in Hegel's and Marx's deification of man as an earthly god. Blumenberg is right that, in reacting to skepticism, the moderns secularized the maximum causal agency imaged in Genesis, though he does not understand the subjectively unconditioned, linguistic nature of that agency. While the archetype of the modern Subject is the intellectual Ar-chitect of Neoplatonism, only Vico and Nietzsche attribute divine agency to an ontologically creative language. And, when Vico and Nietzsche take pos-session of that originary language, they do so from an anthropocentric posi-tion—from that valuing from a human perspective that sets up historical worlds.[240] Heidegger condemns such valuing because he believes from it the world shows up only as humans say it must. For Vico and Nietzsche there is no question but that worlds show up as humans say they must—there is no other source of order or value in the world but human valuing—but those who value are not *subjects* but wholly embodied, historically situated *beings-in-the-world*.[241] Nietzsche, it is true, emphasizes the *individual* quantum of power that makes the social world inherently agonistic and turns rhetoric into a weapon of social conflict. But, for Vico, a "humane" social world is one that values communal existence and mediates conflict by "eloquence," the rhetorical practice of social beings. Similarly, for Vico, as for Heidegger, social beings are open to what gathers, to the divining poetic word that sets up historical worlds. His poets and heroes, "providentially" transforming the natural world into the human with their divining languages and social practices, are the functional equivalence of Heidegger's eventful happenings in the clearing. Such an uncanny *poetic* anthropology of embodied beings-in-the-world is closer to what one commentator calls the "poetic materialism" of the Hebrew Bible, and another, in a different context, a "postmodern humanism."[242] As such, it is another way of answering the question Jean Beaufret set to Heidegger: "*Comment redonner un sense au mot 'Humanisme'?*"

In the introduction to this book I claimed that my interpretation was informed by the reading of two sorts of texts—the Hebrew scripture and rab-

[240] In interpreting Hobbes in the context of Maimonides and negative theology, Aryeh Botwinick provides a secularization argument of Nietzsche. Power is "a surrogate for God," he argues, and Nietzsche's "death of God" "usurps the role of God." "Nietzsche deciphers man after . . . [a] monotheistic conception of God," and understands God in terms of negative theology, thus "totally purg[ing]" the "literal content" of God's nature. Nietzsche's conception of man's essence, like God's, is associated with power that is "disclosed only through action" (186–87). This interpretation is part of Nietzsche's project "toward the abolition of interiority." Botwinick also relates Nietzsche to Judaism, saying Nietzsche's secularization of Augustine's effort to close the gap between willing and doing with power ultimately turns against Augustine and Christianity and, in sublimating rather than eradicating passion and will, becomes "an embrace in a key metaphysical sense of Judaism" (194) (Aryeh Botwinick, *Skepticism, Belief, and the Modern: Maimonides to Nietzsche* [Ithaca: Cornell University Press, 1997]).

[241] For Heidegger, however, "Being" shows up only in a historical world, in the conflict between "earth" and "world." Heidegger did not, as did Vico, go back to the primal beginnings of human ways of being.

[242] The first is Claude Tresmontant, *A Study of Hebrew Thought*, trans. Michael Francis Gibson (New York: Desclee Co., 1960), 47; the second, Gary Shapiro, review of *Heidegger and the Question of Renaissance Humanism*, by Ernesto Grassi, *Philosophy and Literature* 10, no. 1 (April 1986): 106–8. Shapiro is not referring to Vico here, but to Grassi, Derrida, Rorty, Hoy, whose views are "informed by an attempt to draw on the poetic resources of language for philosophical illumination and sensitive to the radically historical character of human existence" while retaining some humanistic virtues (107). Unlike many contemporary postmodern writers, Vico holds the ungrounded and unquestioned humanist metaphysical assumption that social life is more valuable than the bestial or solitary, a belief no less—but certainly no more—metaphysical than that humans are essentially subjective beings and knowers rather than actors or makers.

binic texts enacting the hermeneutic practices appropriate to the originary language of a Creator-God, and postmodern texts, particularly those that find affinities in the Judaic tradition. To what extent is a postmodern interpretation of the Judaic, and a reading of Vico in relation to either set of texts, "legitimate"? Certainly such an interpretation asserts neither historical nor eidetic relationships among them. It is, rather, a hermeneutic reading such as Borges describes in "Kafka and his Precursors." The rabbinic tradition is not Vico's "precursor," nor is it—or Vico—"precursor" of the postmodern. But a reading of both sets of texts transforms the reading of Vico. In both, in different senses, the human condition, the very *being* of humans, is set into place in ways radically alien to traditional humanism. The postmodern challenge to the modern—that is, the challenge of the most current version of an acosmic perspective to the most current version of the cosmic—shares with all acosmic views rejection of beliefs that cosmic views take on faith—belief in some form of unchanging, absolute, intelligible source or ground of order. In different degrees, acosmic writers find themselves in the same existential situation—nomads wandering in the desert outside the Garden. It is not that order, meaning, and value do not exist for them; it is rather that, insofar as they do, they are contingent, and dependent on unintended events or acts of power, whether divine or human. Those who find themselves in such a situation—Sophists, ancient Israelites, Nominalists, the more radical writers within the rhetorical tradition, postmodern writers—all appeal to the same constructive power. No matter how abyssal the world, how finite human effort, how tragic human fate, the only means of creating a human way of being-in-the-world is the power of language.

Though Derrida calls hermeneutic "the very form of exiled speech," he still distinguishes between two "interpretations of interpretation." "In the beginning is hermeneutics, but the *shared* necessity of exegesis, the interpretive imperative, is interpreted differently by the rabbi and the poet. . . . The original opening of interpretation essentially signifies that there will always be rabbis and poets. And two interpretations of interpretation." Derrida's distinction is between rabbis, for whom there are limits to interpretation, and poets, who embrace the abyssal lack of a center and for whom interpretation is an infinitely iterable play.[243] Vico is of course ultimately more rabbi than poet; there is no play of interpretation either for *bestioni* or philosopher-historians. The limits of divining are determined by needs and utilities the diviners must satisfy to exist; Nietzsche, more poet than rabbi, asserts the absoluteness of art above the value even of survival. For Vico the limit imposed by the need to insure social existence—a need that is for him an ungrounded act of faith—is so fundamental it not only determines the course

---

[243] Jacques Derrida, "Edmond Jabès and the Question of the Book," *Writing and Difference*, trans. Alan Bass (Chicago: University of Chicago Press, 1978), 64–78. Derrida's distinction accounts for the differences between what Ricoeur calls the hermeneutic of recovery and the hermeneutic of suspicion.

that history must follow, but, when inevitable degeneration occurs, it determines its *ricorsi* as well. But, despite his belief in the value of social existence and the regularity of genetic development, Vico goes further than the moderns in giving up the "familiar" conceits of humanism, in asking the questions that could not be answered—nor even asked—within his philosophic, rhetorical, or theological traditions. In his effort to understand the immanent causes of the human world, he discovers the master key that takes him beyond a concern with the formative processes *within* history, to the *setting up* of the historical world itself; to a timeless moment *before* historical time, when sentient beings took possession of a divine creative language.

Index

Leben, 41, 152
Legitimacy (Blumenberg), 69, 74–75
Leibniz, Gottfried, 20, 98
Levi ben Gereshom, 90
Levinas, Emmanuel, 97
Lévi-Strauss, Claude, 94
Lichtung, 169
Lilla, Mark, 138–40, 139–40n64, 142, 143
Locke, John, 62, 117
logos: davar and, 79–82, 87, 101, 109,
117, 159–60, 164–67; Derrida on, 97–
103; as Divine Word, 32–37, 37n52;
etymology of, 159, 189n220; Faur on,
88–94, 169n154; Handelman on, 94–
97; immanent, 86–87; and Judaism,
114; poetic understanding of, 167–75;
of Stoics, 82n44
Löwith, Karl: and causal potency, 116; on
God as Artisan, 35, 123; and incarnation, 118; and *logos,* 165; and man-God
analogy, 134; and *verum-factum,* 31–32,
33, 109; on Vico's providence, 31n40;
and voluntarism, 28
Lucretius, 52, 135, 136, 157
Lyotard, Jean-François, 112–13

Machiavelli, Nicolo, 21, 52
machine, world as, 20–22, 142
Mackie, J. L., 116
Maimonides, 108n136
maker's knowledge, 35, 73, 116
making, divine/human, 122–35
making/knowing, unity of: for God, 26,
123; for man, 19
Malebranche, Nicolas, 142
Mali, Joseph, 145n79, 192n230, 194n234
Marcus, Frederick R., 160n130
Marx, Karl: and clearing, 177, 177n180;
Grassi and, 174; Habermas and, 39; as
idealist, 46n83; materialist conception
of man, 25, 25n25; Verene and, 43–44
n78; Vico and, 5–7, 197–98; and work,
178, 178n183
master key, Vico's, 13, 76; Blumenberg's
misunderstanding of, 75; discovery of, x,
201; as existential, 175; and mechanistic
model of human construction, 23–24;
metaphor and, 149; and poetic ontology,
184–85; and *scienza,* 2–3; significance
of, 111–12, 113, 191; and subjective
grounding of *homoiousis,* 63; as uncanny, 136, 137–38, 185; and *verum-
factum,* 25
materialism, 50n100, 128, 131, 139, 143,
146; in Aristotle, 182n196
mathematics, 27; as constructed science,
29, 186n206; and gathering, 180; and
human knowledge, 71, 71n19, 188

n216; language and, 164, 185–86; as
rational model, 20n11; *scienza* vs., 189–
90; and subjectivity, 22; truth of, 32
McMullin, Ernan, 44–45, 47, 49n94
meditation, 1, 151–52, 186–88, 188n219,
189n220
memory, 130, 141–42, 148–52, 179, 187,
187n213
Memra, 89
Menasseh ben Israel, 109–10n139
Menschengeschichte, 161
Merquior, J. G., 5n8
Mersenne, Marin, 21, 62
metaphysical points, theory of, 38, 122,
126–35
metaphysics, Greek: assumptions grounded
in, xi; and eloquence, 184n201; and human creativity, 16–18; and incarnation,
117; Judaism and, 88–89; Nietzsche
and, 120; and origins of *verum-factum,*
26–28
metonym/metonymic displacement, 55
n116, 95–97, 101, 109
Milbank, John: and causal potency, 116;
and creative process, 133; on language,
34n45, 36–37, 160n130; on *logos,* 37
n52; and man-God analogy, 134; on Platonic paradigm of truth, 33n43, 126
n26; and trinitarian conception of creation, 123; and *verum-factum,* 32–35,
109; and *verbum mentis,* 118; and voluntarism, 28, 31
mimesis, 133, 144n75, 153, 157, 169; creativity as, 194; narration as, 194n234
modernism/modernists: and absolute
beginnings, 66–67; amnesia of, 186;
Nietzsche and, 73–76, 75n29; and secularization, 8; subjectivity and, xii, 20,
68–69; *verum-factum* and *homo faber*
and, 16–24; Vico and, 4–7, 111–18; on
Vico and rhetorical tradition, 49–61
Mondolfo, Rodolfo, 26–28
Montaigne, Michel de, 21
Mooney, Michael, 39, 53; and the conceit
of scholars, 54–55; incremental approach of, ixn1; and *ingenium,* 130n38;
on Vico and rhetorical tradition, 49–52
More, Thomas, 21
Morrison, James C., 124n21
myth: and clearing, 177; and development
of abstract thought, 182; of first men,
135–48; history as, 41; ideal history as,
194n234; origin of, 69n13; as *vera narratio,* 189n220

narration, 137; imagination and, 151–53,
186–87; irony of, 44; *New Science* as,
189–90, 190–91n223